Pinnacle Studio 19 Plus
and Ultimate Revealed

Jeff Naylor

Pinnacle Studio 19 Plus and Ultimate Revealed

ISBN number 978-0956486691

Published by
Dtvpro Publishing
34 Hillside Gardens
Berkhamsted
Herts, HP4 2LF

Copyright 2015 by Jeff Naylor

First Edition published October 2015

POD file version for this printing: 1_0_4

Software used: Pinnacle Studio 19 Ultimate build 19.0.2.251 and 19.1.0.282

For downloads, updates and support please visit

www.dtvpro.co.uk

Introduction

Pinnacle Studio 19 is a powerful program. It is not based on the classic line of Pinnacle Studio which ended in version 15, but on Avid Studio – a program developed to be a replacement for Avid Liquid, itself a fully-fledged broadcast application. The major enhancements for version 19 are the implementation of project bins, which allows a new project based way of using the Library, and a Multi-camera feature, but there are a number of other changes that make the program both more powerful and easier to use.

I want you to use this book as an alternative to wading through the manual, and it is often based on examples so that you can practice *Learning by Doing* wherever possible. If you are completely new to video editing, or at least Pinnacle Studio 19, then I'd encourage you to start at the very beginning.

I hear of people who work for months on their first editing project. They learn as they go, perhaps doing things the long way round at times, but getting great pleasure from it as they do so. Unfortunately, a few of those find themselves up a cul-de-sac. By making some short projects with me before embarking on your masterpiece, I hope you will avoid the dead ends.

I want this book to show you how to edit video, for which Studio is a means to an end. The pleasure should come from creating movies.

You can still use this book as a reference. I've included what I hope you will find a comprehensive index and the chapter descriptions will also help you navigate your way around.

What you need to use this book

The first five chapters require nothing more than a suitable computer and a copy of Pinnacle Studio 19 Plus or Ultimate. If you have graduated from earlier books in the series you will also have the large file you need to complete almost the entire book - the remaining files are all small and should not be too difficult to download. Please go to the appendix for details of what you need to download. The files can be sent to you on a disc if you don't have a fast Internet connection.

As I hope the title makes clear, editing with the basic version of Pinnacle Studio 18 isn't catered for, mainly because its features are so simple I don't think many people will need a book before they reach the limit of its power.

About this edition

This book was printed shortly after Studio 19's release at which time the program was still awaiting a patch to sort out a number of issues. I've tried to reflect this in the text, describing both the current and what I understand will be the final behaviour but if you are finding differences in the way things appear to function in your version of Studio please refer to the website where I will post any information that affects the book.

About the Author.

Jeff Naylor has worked in broadcast television since leaving school. In the 1980s he also developed an interest in personal computing which led to the publishing of several programs and books.

He began using Pinnacle hardware and software in the late 1990s as a means to making showreels for his directing work.

He has been determined to find constructive solutions to his editing problems since recovering from a Spinal Tap moment in 1999 when the computer very nearly went out of the window.

Author's acknowledgments

I would like to thank the regular members of the Pinnacle forum for their help and putting up with me, Pinnacle staffers Jon RT for permission to reproduce the Pinnacle Studio screenshots and Nick Glusovich for listening and acting on feedback regarding the program.

In particular I owe a great deal to John and Linda Bagnall for their really useful input.

My final thanks go to Fiona for correcting the many typos in the first draft and to my Mother for constantly asking how I was getting on with the book.

Thanks Mum.

By the same author:

Pinnacle Studio 15 Revealed

Pinnacle Studio 16 Plus and Ultimate Revealed

Videomaking - The Grammar Revealed

Pinnacle Studio 17 Plus and Ultimate Revealed

Magix Movie Edit Pro 2014 Revealed

Pinnacle Studio 18 Plus and Ultimate Revealed

Magix Movie Edit Pro 2015 Revealed

Contents

Some Basic Principles   1

How a Video Editing program differs from other types of data manipulation   1
Exporting and previewing   6
Proxy and Preview files   8
Why "non-linear"?   9
Storing and replaying moving pictures   9
Scanning   10
Still pictures as digital files   12
Video as digital files   13
Interframe compression   14
Bitrates   15
MP4, H.264 and beyond   16
Containing file types   16

Introducing Studio and Simple Timeline Editing   19

Getting Started   19
The File menu   20
The Help Menu   22
The Main Control Bar tabs   23
The Movie Editor Layout   23
Introducing Project Bins   25
Creating a new Project Bin   26
Adding media to a Bin   26
Using the Import Media dialogue   27
The Compact Library   27
Using the Player Window   29
The Timeline area   34
A Brief Introduction to Background Rendering   36
Setting up a Project   37
The Timeline Toolbar   38
Performing the first edit   40
Introducing Smart Editing   42
The Magnet   44
Time to tell the story   45

Arranging the tracks   46
Introducing Quick Trimming   48
Editing Terminology   52
Using Quick trim to loosen an edit   53
Video Grammar   55
Using Drag and Drop   58
Using Markers   59
Using Cut and Paste   60
The Storyboard Feature   61
Duration adjustment   64
Using the Source Preview window   66

Audio and Multi-track editing   73

Listening to the audio   73
Master Volume   74
The Audio Mixer   75
Volume Keyframing   77
Subtle Keyframe adjustments   81
Detaching the audio   82
Video and Audio Track Monitoring   84
Copying Clips on the Timeline   86
A new Smart mode feature   86
Automatically filling a gap   89
Automatically replacing a clip   91
Using Track Monitoring   92
A quick trip to the Library   94
Multi-track clip splitting   96
Overtrimming   97
Trimming Gaps   98
Multi-track deletion   99
Using the Track Locks   100
The Navigator   101
Clip selection and detached audio   102
Multiple clip selection   102
Selecting everything to the right   103
Moving clips in a multi-track project   104

Dragging from the Album or Player 105
Grouping 106
Closing Gaps 107
Adding Scorefitter Music 109
A note about SmartSounds 112
Simple Exporting 112

Using the Library 117

The two Library sizes 117
Media Assets 118
Project Bins vs. Watchfolders 119
How to see all your Library Media 120
Using Project Bins 121
Managing Project Bins 121
Avoiding Project Bins 122
Quick Import into a Project Bin 122
Quick Import into Library Media 123
Alternatives to Quick Import 124
Displaying assets other than media 124
Features of the Main Library 124
Browsing with Tabs 125
Using the Asset Tree Window 126
Asset Tree tools 127
The Browser Window Toolbar 128
The Group by tool 128
The Sort by tool 129
Sorting by date - a problem with video 129
More Filter tools 130
3D filter 130
Tags 130
Ratings 133
The Search Box 135
Combining filters 136
The Library Toolbar 136
Thumbnail view display options 138
Details View options 139

Thumbnail size slider   139
The Browser View Window selection and sorting   139
Using the Browser Window   141
Browser Functions   141
Browser items Context menu   144
Favourites   145
Collections   146
Subcollections   148
Sub-Subcollections, anyone?   149
Re-arranging collections   150
Special Collections   151
The Compact Library   152
Missing Media   152
Strategies for using the Library   153
Refreshing your Library   155
Protecting your the Library   155
Revealing Hidden Files and Folders   156
Backup   156
Restore   157
Importing a Library from an earlier version   157

Importing and Linking   159
Browsing   159
When not to use Quick Import or Browsing   160
Importer terminology   161
Opening the Importer   161
Import From and Tree view   161
Mode   162
Import to (in link mode)   164
Linking an asset to the Library   164
Recent Import Collection - a warning!   166
Copy Mode   166
Import to (in copy mode)   166
Metadata   167
Filenames   167
The Copy process   168

Copying from other devices 168
Displaying old thumbnails when importing camera files 169
Sorting by date issue with video files 170
A strategy for camera files 170
Scan for Assets 171
Import from optical media 172
DV and HDV 173
Failed to get video from device? 174
DV Capture settings 174
HDV Capture 176
Dropped Frames 176
Hard disc data rates – a capture bottleneck? 176
Analogue capture 179
An analogue video primer 179
Interlacing, frame rates and digital compression. 181
Capture hardware 181
A neat Analogue Capture alternative 182
A brief word about connections 183
Adjusting the input 183
Mode selection 184
More Analogue Capture issues. 185
What Capture setting should I use? 187
Webcam Capture 187
Stopmotion and Snapshot 188
Screen Capture 188
Watchfolders 190
Control Panel Import settings 192
Import problems 192
Cineform 193

Export 195

The Export Window 195
Export to File 196
What's a Codec? 198
The Player Window in File Export 198
Timeline Export callipers 199

Destination   199
Render Speed   200
MPEG-2   202
Windows 8/10 and MPEG-2   203
MPEG-2 Quality   203
MP4 files   206
H.264 files   206
Encoding H.264 options   206
Smart Rendering   208
Smart and H.264   209
A list of formats   209
Playing Back Files   211
Export to Disc   212
NTSC vs PAL   214
Disc Export Window   214
Disc Settings   215
The Creation choices   217
Advanced Settings   218
Pre-rendering to file   220
Using MyDVD Files   221
Examining the image   221
The VLC Player   222
Exploring a DVD Image   222
Burn Image   223
Bad Media?   225
Other burning issues   225
DVD player issues   226
Audio options   230
Burning multiple copies   230
Burn Disc   231
Using Imgburn   231
Labels - a warning   233
AVCHD Discs   233
AVCHD 2 Cards   234
Blu-ray Discs   235
Output to Cloud   236

YouTube upload   236
Other Cloud services   238
Output to Device   238
MyDVD   239

Smart Edit, Insert, Overwrite and Trimming   241

Smart Mode   241
Insert mode   241
Overwrite Mode   243
Smart Mode Drag and Drop   245
A new Smart mode feature   247
Smart Mode, Drag and Drop and Gaps   249
Gaps and dragging from the Library or Source viewer   249
Smart Mode Deletion   250
Trimming   253
Smart Mode Quick Trimming   253
Overtrimming   255
Advanced Trimming   256
Trim mode activation settings   258
Adjusting Trim points accurately   258
Trimming with the Player Windows   259
Setting, Removing, Changing or Adding trim points   259
Trimming with the Trim Editor   260
Two Trim Points   263
Adjusting the Placement   264
Adjusting the Content   265
Setting Trim Mode and Shift   266
Multi-track trimming   266
Overwrite and Advanced Trimming   269
Advanced Trimming and Transitions   269
Multi-track Trimming and keeping sync   271

Advanced Editing Features   275

Using Scenes   277
Refining Scene Detection   279

Creating Library Clips   282
Customising Library clips   284
Corrections   285
Adjusting settings accurately   290
Using the Stabilizer   293
Correcting Photos   294
Audio Corrections   296
Storyboarding the Movie   300
Speed   309
Snapshot   313
Transitions   314
Adding Transitions with the mouse   315
Replacing Transitions   318
Transition Context menu   319
Transitions and the Clip context menu   321
Transitions and the Storyboard   322
Adding multiple transitions   322
Adding transitions from the Library   323
Dynamic Length   324
Send To Timeline   325
The Effects Editor and transitions   325
Corrections in the Effects Editor   330
Effects in the Effects Editor   330
Keyframing effects   335
Using the Surround/Stereo Panner   340

The Title Editor   27

Safe Areas   348
Titles on the timeline   349
Titles and the Library   350
Text Settings   351
Looks   352
The Colour Selection box   353
Face, Edge or Shadow?   355
Motions   356
Alignment grid   358

Shapes   358
Order and Grouping   360
Background Settings and using other assets   362
Adding assets as layers   363
Arrows and Special Characters   364
Effects and Keyframing on Titles   366
Crawlers and Rollers   368
Creating long credit rollers   370
Stereoscopic text effects   371

Working with Photos   373

Using Markers with Music   378
Introducing Pan and Zoom   379
Pan and Zoom effect indicator   381
Using animation   381
Low Pass   384
Multiple Moves   384
Holding a still frame   386
Adding transitions to photos   388
Matching frames   389
Converting project formats   392

More Advanced Tools   395

Subprojects   395
Subprojects and Preview rendering   396
Adding Subprojects to the timeline   396
Subprojects as clips   400
Editing Subprojects   401
Refreshing the render files   403
A trimmed subproject retains its trims   403
Latency and subprojects   403
Using Trim mode for accuracy   404
When Subprojects don't work well   405
Extracting clips from Subprojects   406
Montage   408

SmartMovie   412
3D editing and monitoring   416
The Voice Over Tool   420
Audio Ducking   423
Add your Ducking first   427
Remove Ducking – Beware!   427
Voiceover quality   428
Quick Rotate   428

Multi-Camera Editing   431

Multi-Camera Workflow   432
Stage 1 – Source Selection   432
Stage Two – The Multi-Camera Editor   433
Syncing up the tracks   435
Audio Selection   435
Editing tools   436
The Main Preview screen   436
The Source Manager   437
Waveform Display   438
The Timescale and Timeline views   438
Track Headers   439
Importing a source using Right-click   440
Source Track operations   440
Selecting output   441
Target track operations   442
Target track context options   442
Stage Three – Multi-Camera in the Main Editor   442
The Three Camera Demo   443
Syncing up the sources   445
Sending Sources to the output tracks   447
Using the previews to select sources   449
Live Cutting   449
Adjusting the edits within the Multi-Camera Editor   451
Adding transitions   451
Removing transitions in the Multi-Camera editor   452
Transition duration   453

Opening and ending transitions 453
Putting the project into a normal movie 454
Editing as a sub-movie 454
Using Proxy Files 455

Keeping Movies in Sync 459

Smart Drag and Drop 459
The Initial Workflow 460
Reordering your story 461
A solution using Overwrite 464
Making Gaps 464
Using Overwrite 465
Closing the gaps 465
Detached Audio and Selection 466
Grouping 467
Deleting 467
Protecting tracks by locking when Deleting 468
Intelligent Deletion 469
Intelligent Insertion 469
Trimming a shot to make it shorter 470
Trimming a shot to make it longer 470
Using multiple Trim points 472
Transitions 476
Subprojects 477

Disc projects and Menus 479

Opening the Disc Editor 480
Creating a Menu 482
The Menu Editor 483
Defining Buttons 486
Setting Links 487
Unlinked Chapters 490
The Disc Simulator 491
Return to Menu markers 493
Intro Video 493

More Menu creation rules   494
More than one menu   497
Thumbnail buttons   499
Motion menus   504
Automatic Chapters and Links   506
AVCHD and Blu-ray discs   508

Understanding Studio   511

Hardware requirements   511
Installing Studio   513
Your serial number   513
The Install Manager   515
Re-installing – what are the risks?   515
Registering   516
Troubleshooting installations   516
The Reset function   516
Complete Manual Reset   517
Graphic card issues   518
Registration and activation   518
Regenerating activation keys   519
Restore Purchase   519
The Control Panel   520
Watchfolders   520
Audio devices   520
Event Log   520
The Export and Preview Panel   520
Preview Optimisation   522
Preprocessing for Export   525
Third party Codecs   525
Hardware Acceleration   525
Import   526
Keyboard   527
Project settings   528
Storage Locations   529
Project management and project packages   531
A few Frequently Asked Questions   532

Where's the patch?   532
Studio doesn't run unless you reboot   533
Wacky render issues   533
Why are the Render bars red?   534
Running out of memory   534
Converting and transcoding video files   534
Where can I get support for Pinnacle Studio?   535
Studio 19.5?   535

Appendix 1 - The files you need   537

Appendix 2 - Studio versions   538

Some Basic Principles

Video editing programs work somewhat differently to other programs that you might use on a computer, and understanding how they operate can save a lot of confusion. In addition, having a clear concept of how video is stored as a digital file will help you to troubleshoot issues you may have when working with the many different types of files that abound today. If your knowledge in this area is a bit sketchy, I'd urge you to read this chapter before diving into the rest of the book. Even if you think you have a good grasp of the principles there may be some valuable nuggets of information, so please come back to this chapter when your impatience to start editing has subsided!

How a Video Editing program differs from other types of data manipulation

When you work with a word processing program, you will often create a document from scratch. OK, you might start with a template of some sort; the layout of the page could be pre-defined, there may even be some text already present – your name and address and the date might be part of a letterhead template. However, the original content of the letter is typed into that document by the user and the file that is used to store the document contains the actual letters of text stored in a digital format. Even if you have copied the text from somewhere else and pasted it into your document, the text is added to the document file.

If you open a partially written document file in a word processor, add or delete a few words and then save the document again, you have made a permanent change to the document. If you don't want to change the original document you can perform a "Save As" operation on the edited document file and give it a new name, but if you just allow the program to overwrite the original document, any bits of text that have been removed are lost forever. (In reality, modern sophisticated programs may offer ways to recover the data, but you cannot rely on this.)

Other programs operate on "data" that isn't created by the user within the confines of the program. Consider a photo editing program. You have taken a photo with your camera which has stored the picture as a digitally encoded file. You transfer that picture file to the hard drive of your computer. It's most likely in a format called "Jpeg" but could be in one of dozens of other formats. As long as your computer's operating system knows how to decode the file it can display the picture for you. When you open the picture file in a photo editing program that also understands the Jpeg format, that program can not only display the picture, but allows you to edit it. You can crop it, alter the exposure or modify the picture in many other ways, depending on the sophistication of the program. However, when you have made the changes, you need to resave the file. Although the program will probably warn you of what you are about to do, if you save the modified picture with the same name, in the same format, you will destroy the original file. You may be able to recover the original picture (it might still be in the camera memory), but then again, you might not.

Photo Editing Process

The above process is called "destructive" editing. It's quite easy to avoid destroying the original picture file by careful use of "Save As" and alternative file names, but when you are manipulating a picture file, you are manipulating the data from that original picture.

Let's consider a more sophisticated use of an editing program, where you are using it to create a new object – for the sake of this example let's assume you have taken a picture of a child's birthday party and you want to produce a Thank You card with some text superimposed. You start a new, untitled picture and set the size to something suitable for printing. Now you **import** the picture from the file already saved on your computer. You find the picture is the wrong size and shape, so you shrink and crop it to fit the card, and then add some text using a tool in the editing program. You have made a new object, and you save the whole thing to a new file with a name that bears no relation to that of the photo that is part of the card. Even the file format will be different – if you use Photoshop, for example, the default file type will be .PSD, and not a Jpeg.

When you are working on the Thank You card, the editing program contains data relating to the picture, but once you save and reload the card from the publishing file, only the shrunken and cropped picture data is available to the program. If you delete the original, full size, picture file from your computer you can still load the publishing file containing the card and that will hold some, but not all, of the picture data.

Publishing program process

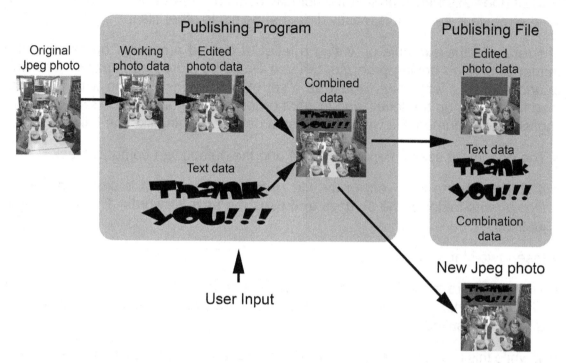

This more sophisticated way of working is still potentially "destructive" editing if you overwrite the original Jpeg. More importantly, it is potentially destructive in another way.

Let's assume someone else wants to print out the card. You can just give them the Publishing file and if they have the same program as you, they can do so - they don't need the original Jpeg. But what if that person wants to change your cropping because you have cut their child out of the frame? With only the Publishing file there is nothing that they can do about your editing because the part of the photo with their child in is not stored in the file you gave them.

This model is one which, in my experience, some people believe applies to non-linear video editing programs. It's an understandable assumption, but not normally how a video editing program works.

Video data takes up far more storage space than text or even pictures, so it makes sense to leave the video data on the hard drive and not try to embed it in the file that defines the edited version of the movie. The Movie project file that you save during, and at the end, of an editing session won't contain any video; neither is it likely to contain any pictures or music. There may be some raw data such as titles, but this will depend on the program.

So what does this Movie project file actually contain? Apart from information about how the movie is set up, it is mostly data that points to other files.

Let's return to the example of writing a letter. If a word processor operated in the manner of a video editing program, the text would be stored as separate files and the document file for a letter would be a set of instructions defining which parts of those files make up the letter, and in what order they are arranged. Translated into "English" the document file would be a set of data something like the following:

- The document uses a page size of A4 and the default text colour is black.

- It starts with the first word of the file *Home address* which is stored in the *My Documents* folder of the *C: drive* and uses the next 21 words. This text is right justified.

- Insert two blank lines

- The next word is the fifth word from the file *Letter to John* which is stored in the *My Documents/Letters* folder of the *C: drive* and uses the next 300 words. This text is left justified.

Now, while this is an unnecessary complication for a word processing program, there are a few advantages. The files *My address* and *Letter to John* can be huge, but the document file can be small. The files *My address* and *Letter to John* are also in no danger of being overwritten and can be kept in any accessible location as long as they can be read by the program.

What if you want someone else to read your letter though? If they don't have the same editing program as you, then it's no good sending them the document file. Even if they do have the same program, they will still need access to the text files referenced in the document file. So what you need to do is **Export** the letter. You might print it out, or you might make a new file that any computer can read – a simple text file or perhaps a PDF file. In the case of the text file, it would only contain the bits of the text specified by the document file – for example, it won't contain the first four words of the *Letter to John* file because they are only contained in the original text file. The export started at the fifth word.

Now let us take the above model and apply it to a video editing program so you can begin to see the advantages. None of the large assets – video, audio and picture files – that you use in the creation of a movie project need to be embedded in the file defining the movie. What is more, the computer only needs to bring the portions of the assets that it needs to display at any one time into the computer's fast RAM memory, leaving them stored on the hard disc. As long as it can access the assets quickly enough to show the movie in real time they can stay in their original locations.

Our Movie project file might translate into something like this:

- This movie has a resolution of 1920 by 1080 pixels and a frame rate of 25 frames a second.

- It begins at 00:00:00:00 (0 hours, 0 minutes, 0 seconds and 0 frames)

Non-Linear editing process

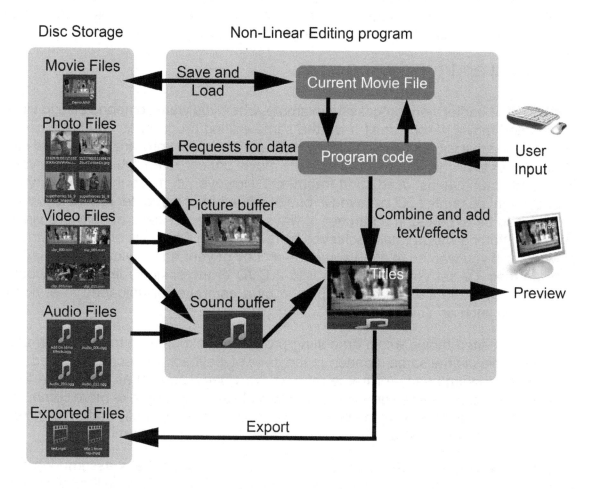

- At this point display the text "My Spanish Holiday" in Arial font, yellow 48 point centre justified over a black background.

- At 00:00:05:00 (5 seconds) fade out the text over a duration of 00:00:00:12 (12 frames – nearly half a second)

- At 00:00:6:00 (6 seconds) play the video from the file *28_6_13_01.AVI* stored in the folder *Holiday Videos/Spain 2013* on the D: drive, starting at 00:00:28:05 (28 seconds 5 frames in) for a duration of 00:01:15:00 (1 minute 15 seconds). During this shot, apply the video effect "Auto Colour Correction".

If you use a media playing program such as iTunes or Windows Media Player, where a playlist points to music files rather than containing them, the above concept will be familiar to you. An editing program is just more selective and can choose sections of a video or audio files rather than the whole file.

Exporting and previewing

Just as in the earlier word processing example, when you want someone else to view your edited movie, if they don't have the same editing program as you have used, you will need to export the movie. If they did have the same software, they would still need access to all the files referenced in the movie project, even if the files were very large and you have just used short fragments. However, in much the same way as a letter might be printed out or saved in one of a number of computer readable forms, movies can be exported in a number of ways. In the earlier days of software video editing, exporting was normally achieved by re-recording the movie onto a videotape. Nowadays if you wanted to send someone a copy of your edited video to be played through their TV set you would burn it to a DVD or increasingly likely, you would create a new video file that can be played by a computer or uploaded to a video sharing site such as YouTube.

Playing an edited movie within an editing program or exporting it to a file both use the source files in the same manner. In the case of playback to a screen, it needs to happen at the same pace (or frame rate) as the video was shot at. For export to a file it has to re-encode the video data into a new file and this may take more computer power than simply displaying the pictures. However, it doesn't really matter if it takes 30 seconds or 2 minutes to export a movie with a duration of one minute.

Real time preview may be affected by other factors though. Let's assume we are happy with our "My Spanish Holiday" movie and want to preview it from the beginning. With the cursor at the start of the movie, when we press the play control, the program generates the title specified, then after 5 seconds it fades it out over half a second.

Another half a second of a blank screen is sent out before the program begins playing the first video file from the hard disc, starting at the point specified.

One factor that may stop you being able to watch the edited movie in real time is the manner in which the source video is stored on the hard disc. If the data is in a very raw state it will be stored as a large file and even the latest computers will struggle to read that amount of data from the hard disc in the time it needs to achieve real-time playback. To avoid that problem almost all video files have their data compressed in some way so that they can be read faster than required. However, some types of compression are so complex that the video information cannot be decoded by the computer's processor quickly enough – depending on the power of the computer and the sophistication of the editing software.

Compression and playback

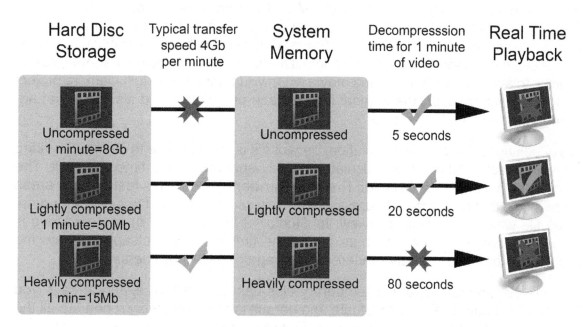

Therefore, if a video file is too lightly or heavily compressed it can overwhelm the capabilities of a computer to play it back smoothly. It is more likely that you will be trying to work with files that are heavily compressed than files that are simply too big, so CPU power may prevail, but not everyone can afford a very fast machine.

However, in addition to being able to fetch and decode the video data quickly enough, there may be other things that will hinder real-time preview. In the Movie project file I described earlier, you will notice that I specified an effect, "Auto Colour Correction" to be added to the shot starting at 6 seconds. The video editing program needs to calculate and apply this effect to the video data after fetching it from the hard disc but before outputting it to the screen. We will have a problem here if the effect takes a long time to calculate and apply to the video data. If it takes more than one second to add the effect to one second's worth of video we can't play back the video in real time – it is going to slow down and appear jerky.

Proxy and Preview files

What's the solution to the playback problem then? We have to be able to preview our video projects in real time in order to make any creative decisions or if we want to "print" them back to a tape. Two strategies are used to achieve this.

One approach is called **Proxy Editing**. Pinnacle Studio implemented the use of Proxy files in version 19 in order to make the Multi-Camera feature work smoothly. With proxy editing activated, any file you import has a shadow file (a proxy) generated. This file uses a medium compression format that will play back smoothly for preview purposes, and is used in place of the original file when you want to preview the project. In order to avoid degradation to the movie when you transfer the Multi-Camera project back to the main editor, the original files replace proxy files, and it's these that are used to produce the final movie.

Proxy editing isn't a complete solution, because it is still possible to overload a video clip with effects that can't be calculated quickly enough for real time playback. The more selective approach is called **Preview Rendering**. With this feature, any areas of the movie that aren't going to preview smoothly can be exported to a new temporary video file which is used for preview. In Studio 19 the progress of this rendering is shown with yellow and green bars above the timeline. They disappear once the section has been completely rendered. See page 522 for more details.

In some circumstances, these temporary files can be used for export to save you time at that stage. In Pinnacle Studio, the default is to use preview rendering all the time but you don't need it to work on the whole timeline - we will see how preview rendering can be used selectively later in the book.

So, if you have added some pretty complex effects and transitions to some parts of your movie, these may need to be preview-rendered. If there are some clips using a highly complex compression scheme that your computer struggles to play back in real time, these can be preview rendered as well. Perhaps whole sections of the movie don't need this treatment, though, saving you the time it takes to re-encode everything.

Why "non-linear"?

You may have noticed me bandying about the term "non-linear" without really explaining it.

Before the advent of Video, movie editing was non-linear. Film is little more than a series of individual photos on a strip of celluloid. Making a movie from a bunch of film clips allows you to build it up in sections and rearrange it with ease. Changing the finished product was easy too – you could cut bits of film out of the movie and repair the gap, or split the reel at a certain point and splice in a new section. So, the process isn't Linear, in a straight direction – you need not start at the beginning and work methodically to the end.

However, video used to be only recorded on tape, with the movie starting at the beginning of the tape and ending at the end. To edit your movie you copied across the bits you needed from a playback machine to a record machine in the order that you wanted them to appear. If you then decided to change your mind and swap two parts of the movie around, you had to go back to the point where your changes began and remake the whole movie from that point on. (OK, if you are familiar with audio tape recorders you might ask why video tape couldn't be spliced in the same way. It could, but it was an extremely delicate operation that didn't always work, and risked destroying the recording).

Once it became possible to store video data on a hard disc rather than a tape, non-linear Video editing became a practical proposition. What's more, because a Movie project file is nothing more than a complex playlist, you don't even need to move the video data around in the computer memory or on the hard disc – you just change the playlist. So in many respects it's faster and more flexible than film editing.

Storing and replaying moving pictures

Those digital files on your hard disc are nothing like a strip of celluloid with a series of still pictures on them, but the underlying principle of recording and playing back moving pictures is the same. We won't concern ourselves with how a strip of film is created, but through the wonders of lenses, light-proof housings, opening and closing shutters and chemical reactions, it consists of a series of semi-transparent images, each one taken a very short time after the other. If these images are projected onto a screen by shining a light through them in rapid succession, the human eye and brain isn't aware that they are individual pictures and any movement that occurs in the subject matter appears as natural movement. Each one of the images is called a frame.

A series of frames

The frame is the fundamental unit in film, television and video. The number of frames shown each second varies, unfortunately. Conventional feature films record and display 24 frames a second. The television system created in the USA (NTSC) uses 30 frames a second (actually, slightly less – 29.97 frames a second for technical reasons) and the European (PAL) system uses 25 frames a second. There are historical reasons for these incompatibilities, (and some other video standards as well). The basic principle, though, is that if you can show still pictures quickly enough, one after the other, the brain is tricked into thinking they are watching continuous action.

Scanning

There is a further complication with video. I really need to mention it now rather than glossing over the issue, but if this section confuses you, come back to it when you need to understand the difference between progressive and interlaced video.

Historically, a video picture was recorded by scanning a thin line across an image projected by the camera lens onto the face of a "Camera Tube". The scanning started top left and "read" the values across to the right of the picture, then moved down the image and scanned another line. Because of technical limitations, a better picture resulted if the first pass scanned half the image, then a second pass went back and scanned the gaps between the first set of lines. So, in a Top Field First (TFF) scanning system the first pass, called a **field**, scanned lines 1,3,5 and so on, and the second pass scanned a field consisting of lines 2,4,6 and so on.. The two fields were also played back like this, so instead of there being 30 (or 25) frames per second, there were 60 (or 50) fields per second. Just to make matters more complex, some types of cameras scan lines 2, 4, 6…. and then return to 1, 3, 5… thereby using a Bottom Field First scanning system.

These scanning schemes are called **Interlacing** and many TV broadcasts are still stuck with them today. They hark back to the days of not just camera tubes but also vacuum tube displays (CRTs – Cathode Ray Tubes). The alternative scanning scheme is called **Progressive** because the scanning progresses through the number sequentially – 1, 2, 3, 4, 5, 6… and so on.

Interlacing example with a low resolution format

Full Resolution

40x30 resolution

Lines   Top Field   Bottom Field   Lines

1 →   ← 2
3 →   ← 4
5 →   ← 6

Bottom field extrapolated to a full frame
has only 15 lines of vertical resolution

Most readers of this book will be watching video on solid state displays – the flat panel display of a Plasma, LCD or LED TV, or a computer, tablet or phone screen. These are natively progressive devices that don't need interlaced signals, but it is often best to let them convert the signals themselves rather than doing it beforehand. Converting interlaced video to progressive doesn't automatically make it "better" and if not done carefully can make it look considerably worse.

Problems start to occur when you try to show two fields at the same time, but a part of the scanned image has moved between scanning the first and second field. In the worst case, you might have to drop a whole field of information, resulting in half the vertical resolution of the scanned image. The illustration on the previous page shows this with a low resolution picture - 40x30 pixels - to make the example clearer. (It's not far off the resolution of very early mechanical scanning systems, though!)

To keep things simple, let's forget about interlaced video for the rest of this chapter.

Still pictures as digital files

When you print out a photograph taken with a digital camera, it is nothing more than series of coloured dots that blend into each other. The quality of the picture is a function of how accurate the colour of the dots is, and how many there are to the square centimetre or inch. The same is true when you display the digital photo on a TV or computer screen, except that the screen has a fixed number of dots – or **Pixels** (picture elements) – to the square centimetre or inch. If we enlarge our view of the photo, we can see the individual pixels that the photo consists of.

I have a digital stills camera that can take a photograph with a resolution 1920 pixels wide and 1080 pixels high – that's just over 2 million pixels or 2 **Megapixels**. In order to represent all the colours and degrees of brightness the screen can display we need to use three bytes of digital data for each pixel (red, green and blue in the range 0-255 each). So, to store a bitmap of that photo the camera needs to use 6 million bytes – about 6Mb.

A bitmap is a very inefficient means of storing picture data, although it is the most accurate. Most photographs are going to have areas that are exactly the same colour and brightness so you can start compressing the information by defining areas of the image that have the same value. If you aren't too fussy about the meaning of "same value" or very fine detail you can compress most photos by quite a lot. Far better compression schemes are possible using more advanced mathematics, of course. The highly popular **Jpeg** scheme, for example, uses Discrete Cosine Transformation, which I'm not going to attempt to explain as I'm not sure I understand it sufficiently myself!

Video as digital files

A very inefficient way to store a video picture is as a series of bitmaps, each one defining one frame. For good quality video you need at least 24 bitmaps for each second of video playback. There is a format that stores video in this manner; it's called Uncompressed AVI (Audio Video Interleave). As the acronym implies, AVI files contain audio as well as video data, and as you might guess, they are pretty big. A program I use to create animations, iClone, produces high definition uncompressed AVI files and 1 second of video needs 178Mbytes of memory to store. These types of files are so large that they cannot be fetched from the hard disc of a computer quickly enough to be displayed in real time.

I've already pointed out that there are perfectly good ways to compress individual pictures, so it seems obvious that compressing each frame using a method such as Jpeg encoding is going to make video files smaller. This is called Intraframe encoding because all the compression is applied within the individual frames. The most common example of an Intraframe video compression scheme is DV-AVI – the first digital video cameras available to consumers. Here each frame is compressed, but a DV-AVI file contains each individual frame as a separate image.

Intraframe video compression

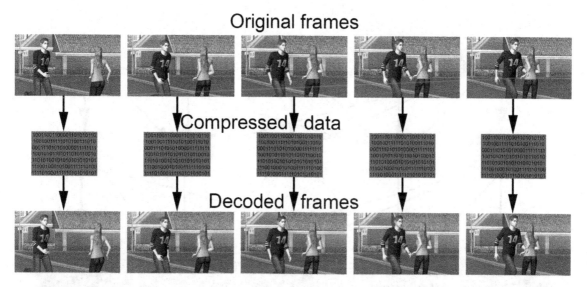

DV-AVI files are only "standard" definition, with the same number of pixels in each frame as regular TV broadcasts, and the compression applied to the individual frames is such that the pictures don't quite meet the high standards required by most broadcasters – although DV cameras are used for news gathering. The files are still big, but not so big that they can't be read from a computer hard disk in less than real-time – so they can be played back smoothly.

The compression applied to the individual frames of video is relatively light as well, comfortably within the power of a computer to decode and re-encode without significantly slowing down playback.

Interframe compression

DV-AVI files and similar intraframe compression methods still produce files that are too big to be sent over the Internet or via transmitters – there is just too much data. The next step in compression techniques for video looks at the similarity between adjacent frames in much the same way as still picture compression looks at the similarities between adjacent areas. Imagine a video of a newsreader sitting at a desk with a picture behind them. The only differences between the subsequent frames are small movements of the newsreader's head. So, by only recording the *differences* between frames, the amount of data needed is reduced enormously. This is a very extreme example; video with lots of movement, either by the subject or the camera, can't be compressed so much, but there are still savings to be made.

Simplified interframe compression scheme with a GOP of 4 frames

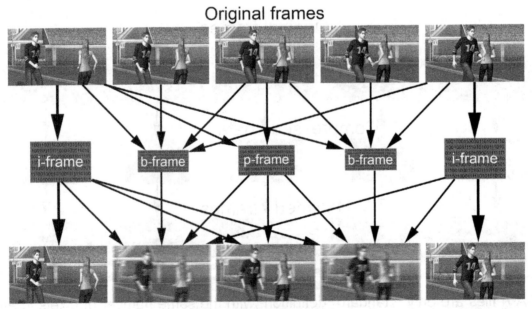

The most popular form of interframe compression is currently MPEG-2. The video consists of Groups of Pictures" (GOPs). These are generally around 12 to 15 frames in length. The first frame is called an I-frame, and, although compressed, holds all the data needed to reconstruct that frame. I-frame stands for intra-coded frame – all the compression is within the frame just as in DV-AVI. The rest of the GOP is made up of P-frames and B-frames. P-frames (Predictive-coded frames) refer to data from the previous I or P frame when compressing data. There are normally 3 or 4 P-frames in a GOP. B-frames (Bidirectionally-predictive frames) refer to data from frames both before and after it.

If, like me, you struggle with the concept of how that all works, the important point to grasp is that for MPEG-2, there is only one high quality, accurately compressed frame every half second or so. Every eighth of a second, there is reasonable quality data in the shape of a P-frame. The rest is the result of a very sophisticated compression scheme. Or, if you prefer, Smoke and Mirrors.

Another useful fact to know is that MPEG-2 compression works by dividing frames up into blocks of pixels. Sometimes it can look at two successive frames and say "the block of 16x16 pixels that were in the top left corner of the frame have now moved five pixels right and two pixels down". The difference between them is all that needs to be recorded. Even if the blocks aren't exactly the same, the principle can be applied. Clever, eh?

This fact explains why, when MPEG-2 compression is very high or has gone wrong, the video picture tends to turn into square, blurred blocks.

Bitrates

When compressing a video file, the resolution and frame rate may be fixed but you can vary the amount of compression by altering the **bitrate** – the number of digital data bits used to represent a second's worth of video.

MPEG-2 can use variable compression. If the video gets a lot of movement, it can reduce the compression to try to keep up with the large changes. You can also specify the bitrate of the compression to suit your own purposes.

DVD quality MPEG-2 video uses about 6000 Kilobits to represent a second's worth of video, although this may vary depending on the content if the encoding uses variable bitrate – compressing video with less movement more than sections with lots of movement.

Sometimes the words **"Data Rate"** are used instead of bitrate just to confuse us. That might not be measured in bits, but bytes or something else. So when we look at data rates, let's make sure we are comparing like with like. A Kb is a kilobit. A KB is a Kilobyte - eight times more, so be sure to check if the b is upper or lower case. Some people just love trying to confuse the general public, and whoever came up with those abbreviations wasn't trying to make it easy!

MP4, H.264 and beyond

MPEG-2 is still too big to use over the internet and get decent quality. Other formats, including MP4 video, use more advanced compression schemes with a correspondingly larger need for computer power to encode and decode the images. The current favourite for compression is a scheme called H.264, used by AVCHD cameras, Blu-ray discs and much more. Although specialist hardware can handle this format relatively easily it can put a great deal of strain on a normal computer's CPU, making smooth playback difficult. It's particularly tough for editing programs to extract single frames, which media playing software doesn't need to do. If you are puzzled that Windows Media Player can play back your new camera footage smoothly, but your editing software can't, that's why.

The highest level of H.264 encoding, 5.2, is employed by Sony for the XAVC standard, and Studio 19 can handle the S variant of that format intended for consumer use.

Recent computer hardware and software have caught up with the requirements of H.264, although 4K video can still be a strain, but technical advances and the desire for higher resolution video mean that a new standard – H 265 – is on its way. This aims to halve the bitrate of video for a given resolution and quality. At the time of writing dedicated hardware encoders and decoders are being made available, but the current generation of CPU based hardware may have to rely on proxy editing to handle the video smoothly.

Containing file types

I have often read – and answered questions about – video file types that don't behave properly within a video editing package. Media playing software has a great advantage because it only needs to partially decode the files – and often you don't realise that you have to wait quite a while for the playback to get going. Another reason, though, is that two files may appear to be of the same type, but contain radically different content. Even an old format such as AVI is just a **Container** – the streams of data within it can use different compression methods. These schemes –

known as **CODECS** (compression/decompression) may not be compatible with the editing software of your choice. Even DV-AVI has two types.

MP4 and M2TS (Sometimes abbreviated to MTS) are two types of container that can use, amongst other schemes, MPEG-2, MP4 (simple) and H.264 compression. MOV, the Apple format, is even more indiscriminate, and may be a **Wrapper** for many combinations of video and audio compressions schemes.

Time to start editing…

I've singled out the above topics from experience of answering questions about consumer video editing over the years; they are the areas that cause the most confusion. There are many other bits of technical knowledge that you may find interesting (or at least useful!) when you use an editing program, but I will introduce those as and when they are relevant to the functions under discussion. Let's launch Pinnacle Studio 19!

Introducing Studio and Simple Timeline Editing

In this chapter I will introduce you to the basic layout of Pinnacle Studio 19 Plus and Ultimate before moving swiftly on to describe the main Movie Editing interface. You will then begin to create a project using video that is already on your computer, using just one track and simple editing tools. During this process you will be introduced to many features of the Edit Mode. I also hope you will have a little bit of fun at the same time!

Getting Started

I'm going to assume that you have successfully installed Pinnacle Studio 19 Plus or Ultimate, and probably used it a bit, which means there may be a number of small differences in what you see in comparison to the screenshots in this chapter. Mostly, though, you will see just more items in the Library windows. If you want to start from scratch, you can reset your installation by following the steps in the Understanding Studio chapter on page 517.

Run Studio and look at the top of the program window. We can divide the top black bar of the program into three areas. On the left are Windows-style drop-down menus, with a few extra icons. In the centre are five tab style buttons, called the **Main Control Bar**. On the right are the usual Windows-style size control icons, plus another one that looks like a shopping trolley. It *is* a shopping trolley, by the way.

The top of the Program window.

The first drop-down menu item on the left is *File*. Here you will find a few commands that can't be carried out in any another fashion. This will vary with which tab is open, but you will always find *New...* there, with a choice of starting a new *Movie* or a new *Disc*.

The File menu

Let's start a *New Movie* right now, by selecting the **File** drop-down option *New* and then *Movie*. Regardless of which Mode tab you are in, if you have an unsaved movie open, you will be prompted to save it. Once you deal with that, Studio switches to the central Edit tab and presents you with an empty movie project.

OK, now we should all be looking at the same thing – the Movie Editor Window. The top of the Program window is still as I described it. Click on the **File** menu (It should now match the screenshot) and take a look at the options available when you are using the Movie Editor.

The File menu

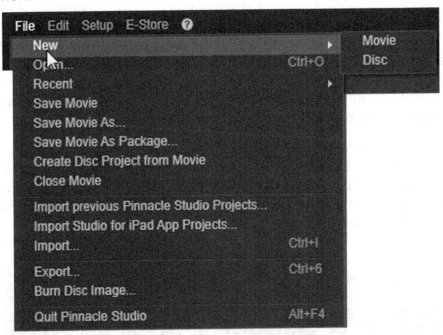

Most of the upper group should be simple to understand – here you can open, save and close projects. *Create Disc Project From Movie…* indicates something also hinted at by the tabs – there is a different editor window for Disc Projects called *Author*. If you want to put a movie on an optical disc and also include a menu you will need to use the Disc Editor by opening the Author tab.

The next section of the **File** menu shows the Import options. It is possible to load projects from Pinnacle 18, 17, 16 and Avid Studio simply by opening them. In this book I'll refer to those programs as Next Gen Studio (the working title during development and still the process name). If the version was Studio 15 or earlier (as far back as version 10) you can use the *Import previous Pinnacle Studio Projects* option. I'll refer to those programs a Classic Studio. Your success at this will depend on the complexity of the project, the version of Studio and what effects and other features you have used. You will also need to have the project folder present, not just the project file.

You can also import projects created with the Studio for iPad application.

The *Import* option will have the same effect as clicking the Import tab – a new window will open over the Movie Editor offering a comprehensive array of options to get media into Studio. If you have moved up from an earlier version of Studio you might expect to see a *Quick Import* option here, but with the introduction of Project Bins it is no longer a menu option in Studio 19, although it is still available and I will describe how to use it shortly.

The *Export* command opens another Window – the same action as selecting the Export tab. Another comprehensive set of choices await you.

File/Burn Disc Image opens up a dialogue box that offers one option that can't be achieved elsewhere – you can burn files and folders to an optical disc. The final option of the *File* menu closes Studio.

The Edit menu

The next two drop-down commands are rather sparsely populated. **Edit** only ever contains the Windows edit commands that are also available as keyboard shortcuts. Two of them are considered important enough to also have additional control icons – the Undo and Redo commands which are the two looping arrows nestling below the **File** and **Edit** menu headers. Having these commands so readily available is a good thing. I find that some of the more complex editing features in Studio are hard to remember – "Should I use the ALT or the CTRL key for what I'm trying to do?" Often it is

quicker to try something, and if the result is a disaster, hitting CTRL-Z or the Undo button puts everything back to how it was. Redo is mostly used because I have pressed Undo too many times!

One thing to remember if you rely on Undo a lot – a saved project doesn't have an undo history, so do a mental check before you actually save or close a movie that you aren't going to want to undo anything at a later date.

Setup only has the one option – to open the Control Panel. We will be visiting this often in the course of this book, I use it a great deal, but I still forget to use the

CTRL-ALT-C shortcut. In the next few pages you might be asked to check various settings here. The panel has a series of sections selected from the list on the left. The features are covered in detail in the Understanding Studio chapter.

E-Store offers you the chance to give more money to Pinnacle, as does the shopping trolley icon over to the right. While there are some things that Studio can't do, much of what is on offer from the store is to save you work creating stuff from scratch. I've yet to feel the need to buy any extras, but your mileage may vary and you might find just the right menu for that DVD, saving you hours of work.

The Help Menu

The Help Menu

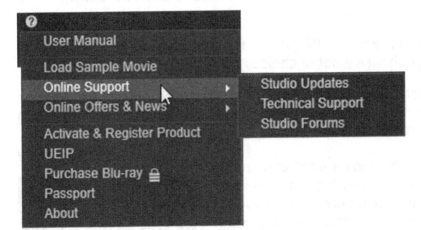

The final menu command is a question mark. It not only leads to *Help*, but also to lots of other information and tools.

The main function is to load the user manual. This is an online link, so you should get the latest version.

You can reload the sample movie *The-Sky-is-the-Limit*, while the next option *Online Support* allows you to check if an update for the program is available, open the Pinnacle support main website page, or visit the Studio forums. *Online Offers and News* sells you stuff and takes you to the Facebook page. You can also open the activation dialogue (perhaps to enter a new serial number).

UEIP is a feature that sends data to Pinnacle about your usage of the program and any crashes you might experience. It only uploads every 10 days, so it's not going to be a drain on your Internet bandwidth should you decide to participate.

Pinnacle used to absorb the cost of buying a Blu-ray licence in earlier versions of Studio, but no longer do so. Therefore you can buy a Blu-ray licence so that you can burn HD movies, with menus, to a Blu-ray disc. Without the licence you can still create AVCHD discs and files.

Passport tells you the current serial number in use and the passport key that associates it with the hardware it is running on. If you install Studio on a different computer, you will get a different passport.

About not only shows the credits, but displays the actual build you are using - handy to check if you are running the latest version. Sometimes the automatic update check may not inform you of this, so you can check your version against support website.

The Main Control Bar tabs

The Main Control Bar is the best way to switch between modes. The two tabs to the right open **Import** and **Export** windows, and the three central ones switch between **Organize**, **Edit** and **Author**. In Pinnacle Studio 16 these tabs were called Library, Movie and Disc, and throughout the menus and context menus in PS19 the areas they lead to are still called the Library, Movie Editor and Disc Editor respectively. I will often use the "old" name for the windows as it describes them more effectively.

Have a quick look at the Library by clicking on the Organize tab; it's a somewhat different layout to Edit and Author. We aren't going to use that mode in this chapter, so switch back to Edit.

The Minimise, Restore Down/Maximise and Close icons far right let you control the Pinnacle Studio Window in the same way as any other Windows program. The only limitation is that you can't run more than one copy of Studio at the same time. Neither can you run a copy of an earlier versions of Next Gen Studio at the same time as version 19. If you are lucky enough to have two monitors you can also stretch the window across both displays.

Another global feature of Studio is the generous provision of tool tips. Hovering your mouse over most parts of the program window will bring up a message telling you either what a control does, or giving you more information about the item you are pointing at. Try it now with the Mode tabs – you will also see it tells you what the keyboard shortcut is for a particular function if one exists.

The Movie Editor Layout

We are going to spend a lot of time looking at the Movie Editor, so it is important that we use the correct names for the parts. I have labelled the screen shot overleaf..

The **Compact Library** and **Player Windows** are side by side below the Mode Tabs. To begin with there may only be one Player Window. Spanning the screen below them is the **Timeline Window,** which when you first start using Studio may only consist of the **Movie Editor Timeline** and not include the **Navigator**.

Each of the three main areas can be varied in size at the expense of the other areas. The main control is the inverted "T" handle at the junction of the Compact Library, Player Window and Timeline area labelled as the *Layout control* in the screenshot. Hover your mouse over this now and a four-way arrow will replace the standard mouse pointer. Click and hold down the left mouse button and you can now drag the junction point around the screen, changing the area allocated to each section.

The Movie Editor Window with the main areas labelled

You should get into the habit of adjusting the Window layout to suit your current task. If you have a simple movie on the timeline with few different assets, then expand the Preview. If you have a complex multitrack project in the making, expand the height of the timeline. Don't struggle!

Your view of the timeline section may differ from the illustration, as you could have a **Storyboard** display instead of the **Navigator** display below the row of buttons along the top. By default you won't have either, which gives you the most flexibility for sizing windows. I'm going to cover the uses of these two optional displays in detail later, but for now, if you can't see them turn them on briefly by clicking on the Display icon that I have labelled. To turn them back off, you click on the icon again. To change between Navigator and Storyboard use the small drop-down menu to the right of the icon.

One other difference could show up in your Player Window, because in Pinnacle Studio 18 Plus and above it is possible to have two Player Windows in Dual Mode, although you may only see one. While two Players are useful in many circumstances, we will only be using one for the next few chapters, so switch to a single display, by clicking on the icon in the extreme top right of the Player Window.

Now that you know how to adjust the areas, what do they do? The first one I shall demonstrate is the Compact Library top left, which holds all the assets you might use in making a Movie. It's the smaller version of what you saw when we switched to the Library Tab. Most of what you can do in the Main Library can be done here. I'm going to get you to add something to the Library with the Quick Import function.

Introducing Project Bins

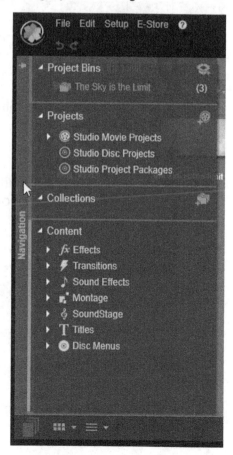

Opening up the Navigation sidebar

Studio 19 brings a new concept to using the Library – Project Bins. If you have used earlier versions of Next Gen Studio, don't worry, because the old features – Media tabs and Watchfolders – exist, they just aren't enabled by default. I'd encourage you to try out the Bins concept as it is simple to use and understand.

You add any media you want to use in a project to the bin before you add it to the movie itself. You might want to add everything at the start, or as and when you need it. Media – video, photos and audio - can be in more than one bin at a time. It's important to realise that the items in a Project bin are just shortcuts and the real items are still stored on your hard disc. If you have six bins all containing the same video clip, there is still only one clip. You can also add other content you might want quick access to a Project Bin, such as a particular title or transition.

You aren't limited to adding media to your current movie from the bin associated with it, but it is good practice.

Creating a new Project Bin

I'll explain the management of bins in detail in the Library chapter, but for now I just want you to create a bin to use with the new project.

Hover over on the side bar labelled **Navigation** to the left of the Compact Library as shown on the previous page. A flyout window opens with a list of Project Bins at the top, and alongside the title is an icon that resembles an open box.

The New Bin tool

Click on the icon and a small dialogue box appears allowing you to provide a name for the Bin you are about

to create. Enter *Project 1* and click on *OK*.

Naming a new Bin

Open up the sidebar again and you will see the new bin listed, so click on it to select it. The Bin will "open" in the Compact Library with a tab at the top highlighted in orange showing the name of the new tab. The window below will be empty.

Further notes on working with Bins starts on page 121.

Adding media to a Bin

There are numerous ways of putting something in the bin we have just created, and I'll explore them all later in the book, but for now let's use the simplest one of all, the **Quick Import** tool.

The Quick Import tool in the Compact Library

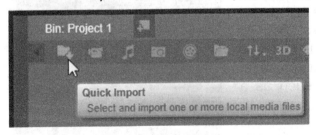

I'm going to ask you to find a file that has already been added by Pinnacle to a Project bin, but let's add it to our new bin

The tool for this is a folder icon with a downward arrow top left of the Compact Library. Click on it and a

Windows Open dialogue appears titled Import Media files. It only shows items that you can add to a Project Bin. But all the usual Windows features are there to help you find files.

Using the Import Media dialogue

The Import Media window

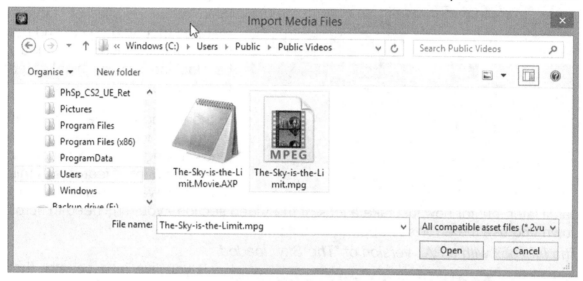

Use the left pane to browse to *C:/Users/Public/Public Videos* and double-click on the file *The-Sky-is-the –Limit.mpg*. After the brief appearance of an Import popup bottom right the file will appear in the Project 1 Bin.

I've deliberately chosen this file because everyone should have it, and therefore you can get started quickly. If you still can't find the file, you could have deleted it, or you might be using a later version of Studio that provides a different sample. See Appendix 1 regarding how you can get another copy of the video.

Click on the new source to highlight it and the first frame of the video should appear in the Preview window to the right.

The Compact Library

Thumbnail View tool

So, are you seeing the file in the bin as a thumbnail or as a filename? If you aren't seeing thumbnails, select the Thumbnail view using the icon at the bottom of the browser second from the left as shown in the screenshot.

If the thumbnail is too small or too large for your taste or screen size, there is a slider control bottom right of the Browser so you can adjust the size.

Thumbnail icons

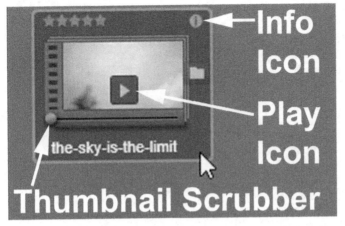

Now that we have sight of the file I want you to work with, let's just look at a couple of Library features that help you to find out more about the video. You should be looking at a highlighted thumbnail of the *Sky* video.

In the top right corner is a small information icon. If you click that a now it brings up a box of details. There are a lot of features in this box which we will look at in more detail later, but for now just take a look at the Video section - you may need to scroll down and use the arrows to open that section.

The Info box with a PAL version of "The-Sky" loaded.

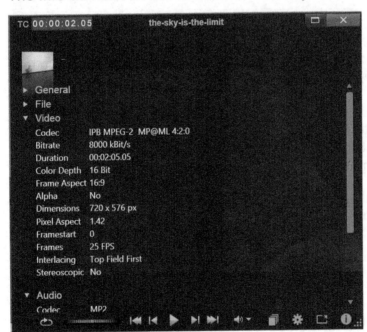

If you live in a country that uses the NTSC video standard, the dimensions of the video will be 720x480 pixels and the frame rate should be 29.97 FPS. If you live in a PAL country the figures will be 720x576 and 25 FPS. I'll explain these differences and the consequences in detail later in the book, but for now, just make a mental note.

You might be wondering how the program knows which type of sample video to install, particularly if you have bought a download version.

It takes information from your country setup in Windows. If you entered the wrong country when you set up your computer, you might get the wrong video format. Apart from the sample video, the other difference will be the default project settings, which are easily over-ridden. You can close the info box now.

The other icons on the thumbnail of immediate interest to us at the moment don't appear until you hover your mouse over it. When you do so a small scrubber bar appears underneath the thumbnail. Grab it with the mouse and you can explore the file by dragging and watching the thumbnail – the larger you have made the thumbnail the more accurate the scrubbing. Wherever you happen to leave the scrubber, that's what continues to be displayed as the thumbnail - so if a file rather unhelpfully happens to start with a black frame, you can alter the frame that is displayed to remind you of the files' contents.

However, this isn't the way you are expected to do any serious work on the file. You will have noticed a play arrow also pops up over the thumbnail, and when you click on that, the video plays - but in the Player window to the right.

Using the Player Window

You will meet this tool in many editing modes, with some different features and controls depending on how you bring up the Window. It is really worthwhile learning the basics of controlling the Player and becoming familiar with some of the keyboard shortcuts that can control preview. In some of the Player windows you may even find keyboard shortcuts work where there isn't an icon for that function.

Above the video preview window are two tabs. Currently *Source* should be selected and you should see the *Sky* video. Click on *Timeline* and the preview will switch to what is currently on the timeline – in our case, nothing. You can also use the keyboard shortcut **H** if you want to switch tabs.

Notice that when you are viewing the timeline, some of the controls under the video disappear – because they aren't available in Timeline Preview. Switch back to Source. If for some reason you aren't seeing pictures check that the V (for Video) icon bottom left of the player is highlighted orange – click it if it isn't. If you want to be sure of including Audio, the A (for Audio) icon needs to be highlighted as well.

If your Player Window doesn't seem to have as many features as shown above, then it is possible that you have made the window too small for Studio to be able to display everything. Use the layout control to increase the size until you see them all. Some of the player controls you can see at the moment are designed to allow you to pre-edit clips before you send them to the timeline. This isn't a workflow I want you to explore at the moment and we will look at it later in the chapter. Let's start with the transport controls, and right in the centre with the Play control – the rightwards pointing triangle. Click it now and the video should play.

When the video is playing, the Play icon turns into a Pause icon, meaning you can stop the video anywhere without losing your place. Hovering you mouse over the icon will bring up a tool tip showing you a really useful shortcut – something I hope you consider using all the time – ***pressing the Space Bar starts and pauses playback***. This shortcut works in almost any circumstance and even if you normally avoid keyboard shortcuts, you might find yourself using it. You may also spot that the tool tip indicates that the L key has the same effect, but this is part of a more powerful set of controls I'll show you in just a moment.

The Player Window in Source mode

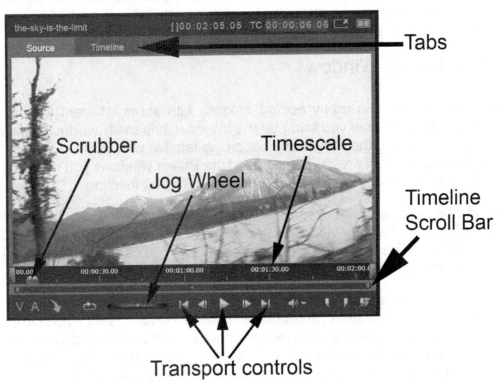

Either side of the Play Button are controls to step one frame backwards or forwards. Try them now and note that the movement is a **single frame** – the smallest amount possible. Once you start working accurately you will appreciate these and the keyboard shortcuts that go with them – the ***Left and Right Keyboard Arrows***. If you are used to a different editor program or are using a keyboard without arrow keys then you can use **Z** and **X**. If you happen to be using a keyboard other than a QWERTY keyboard you may have to check these shortcuts - in an AZERTY keyboard, for example, you need to use W instead of Z. The keys are mapped to the physical positions.

The action of moving one frame at a time is often called jogging – I'll sometimes suggest you "jog to the frame where…" when we are looking for a specific point in a video clip.

Although these jog buttons won't appear on every player window you come across, you may well find that the keyboard shortcuts do work. For example the arrow keys even work on the Library Browser thumbnails if you have selected the scrubber below the thumbnails! We will see another use for them when working in the Main Library.

Jogging can also be achieved with the mouse if yours has a scroll wheel. When you use the wheel while hovering over the source or timeline preview windows, it always jogs one frame at a time. If you hover your mouse over the timeline, it will jog the timeline scrubber, and therefore the player, either 10 seconds, 1 second, 10 frames or 1 frame at a time depending on how wide your timeline view is arranged. Holding down the Shift key will force it to always work in single frame increments.

The final transport icons currently on view in the Source preview player are Jump Forward and Back. Hit them once and they will take you to the start or end of the currently displayed video clip. If you have any other clips in the Library Browser, hitting them again will move you to the previous or next clip.

These *Jump to* controls are particularly useful when working on the timeline, and they have keyboard shortcuts which you will find helpful as well. You can use Page Up/Down, D/F or CTRL and the Left/RIght keys. They are particularly helpful for lining the cursor up with the beginning or end of the clip that the cursor is over.

There are two further controls if you switch to the timeline tab – Go to Start and Go to End which should be self-explanatory.

To the left of the Player controls is a small wheel that mimics the actions of a jog/shuttle wheel. Click and hold, then drag your mouse left and right. With a little practice you will be able to navigate your way around the video at variable speed. I'll be honest and say I'm not a huge fan of this control – not only do I find it hard to use, but I think there is a far better method available from the keyboard.

Playing the video with the **J**, **K** and **L** keys takes a little practice, but gives very precise control. **L** plays the video forward, as if you had clicked Play or the space bar. **K** stops the playback. Now press **L** twice in succession – and the video plays at 2X speed. Again – 4X. **K** still stops the playback. **J** works in the same way, but for reverse playback.

Now for the really good bit. Press **L** until you are spooling through the clip at 4X, and then press **J**. It cuts the forward speed to 2X. Once more, and you are back to normal playback. Hit the key once more, and you are playing backwards. The method works in both directions. Ah, but what about jogging? With the other hand - one frame forward – the **X** key. One frame back – the **Y** key. It's worth playing with this for a few minutes to understand how powerful it can be. Placing your index finger on the **J**, middle finger on the **K** and fourth finger on the **L**, you should soon be able to navigate through the video file very efficiently.

There is a further refinement to using the keys to navigate your way around a video clip. The **SHIFT** key, when used in conjunction with J-K-L, plays video in slow motion - and subsequent key presses slow down or speed up the video down even more.

Below the Preview window there is a timescale with a **scrubber**. The scrubber is always placed over the frame of video currently in view in the preview window.

Using the mouse to drag the scrubber across the timescale is another way of searching through the currently displayed clip. If your mouse isn't over the scrubber and you click and drag you may see a clock type mouse pointer appear. If it doesn't, check the Control Panel. In Project Settings there is a checkbox for *Ruler Zooming*. When Ruler Zooming is enabled, clicking and dragging left or right expands or contracts the timescale. This feature is useful, but you may prefer to switch it off if you find it interferes with scrubbing.

Immediately below the timescale is another bar which is easy to miss called the *Timeline Scrollbar*, which is a slightly confusing name because it doesn't effect the large Timeline Window in the lower half of the program window, but the size and position of the timescale above it. Grab one end of the scrollbar with the mouse and move it toward the centre to see the effect – the timescale effectively "zooms in" to a section of the clip as if you have altered the timescale with the clock pointer. Now you can grab the whole bar and move it left and right. Scrubbing the clip is therefore limited to a smaller area, but gives you greater accuracy. On a two minute long clip like the one we are working with here it's not as useful as when you have a very long video loaded.

To restore the timeline scrollbar in the Player to full width, double-click on it.

The top of the Player Window above the preview screen has some text details above the tabs. On the left is the name of the asset you are currently viewing – at the moment it is the *Sky* video. If you switch tabs over to the Timeline view, it will change to the project name. Over to the right are two sets of figures. The first shows the overall duration of what is contained in the preview window. The second shows the timecode for the current scrubber position (and therefore the currently displayed frame). Both are shown in hours, minutes, seconds and frames. Note the use of colons as a separator, except between seconds and frames, when the convention is to use a period.

The Loop control indicated by an arrow

There are two more icons that are common to most incarnations of the player window. The *Loop Playback* button to the left of the scrubber causes playback to loop continuously. When used on the timeline it will play the

highlighted clip or clips, or from the first to the last highlighted clip if there are gaps between them.

Audio monitoring

The *System Volume and Mute* control affects the monitoring levels of the audio and **not the actual audio of the project**. Clicking on the down arrow reveals a slider to control the volume and clicking on the speaker mutes the sound that is going to your speakers from your preview window .

Full screen preview icon

At the top right of the player window there are two small icons that switch the Player window display. I've already described the

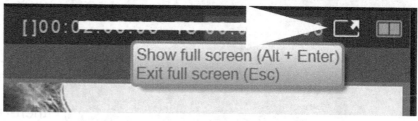

Show full screen (Alt + Enter)
Exit full screen (Esc)

function of the one on the furthest right - it switches on Dual View. The icon to its left controls Full Screen preview. The tooltip shows the keyboard shortcut - **Alt+Enter.** If you have one monitor, you are likely to use this mode for reviewing edits and whole movies. Don't forget that the keyboard shortcuts will work when in Full Screen view. To exit full screen playback you use the Escape key. You can also switch to full screen by double clicking on the window.

If you are lucky enough to have two monitors I'll discuss the advantages of using the second one for full screen preview when we discuss the Control Panel.

I suggest you try a few of the methods I've outlined above to find a particular frame of video. Look for the moment that the lad with the beanie hat shuts the camper van door and then try out the various techniques for finding the exact frame when the door shuts.

If you make it 25 seconds 23 frames, you are using the PAL video. If it comes out at 25 seconds 27 frames, then you have the NTSC footage. One final method – set the scrubber to the start of the video and then click on the Timecode box and enter the timecode of the door slamming frame – now *that's* a quick way to find a frame!

The Timeline area

At last it is time to begin using the Timeline – and we aren't far from doing some actual editing! It's been quite a few pages since I told you to use the *File/New Movie* command. If the timeline isn't empty, do that now.

Track headers, Timescale, Scrubber Handles and Timeline Scrollbar

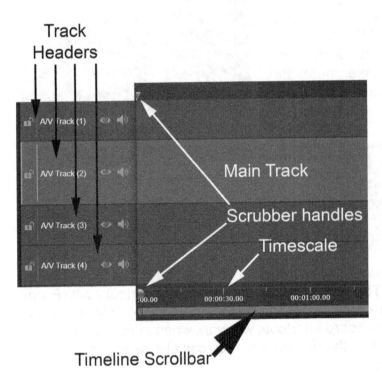

Track Headers

Main Track

Scrubber handles

Timescale

:00.00   00:00:30.00   00:01:00.00

Timeline Scrollbar

The area in which you are about to start building your first project has four track headers on the left – labelled A/V Track (1) to (4). The second track down is taller than the others; it is a lighter grey and the orange bar far left indicates it is the selected track. This is because Pinnacle have good reasons to want you to use it as the main track, and although there is no reason to obey them every time, let's go with the flow for now. If you want to change the track that is active, just click anywhere on the header that doesn't contain a control.

At the very bottom of the window is a timeline scrollbar that works just like the one in the Player. Immediately above the scrollbar is a Timescale that marks the time in hours, minutes, seconds and frames, and again this behaves in the same manner as the one in the Player, including the use of the clock style mouse pointer to evoke Ruler Zooming if that is enabled in the Control Panel. It also has a very useful context menu if you right click on it. You can choose the scale of the display at a number of useful increments from 1 second to 1 hour.

The scrubber has two handles, one above and the other below the tracks, and a red line extends between them - you can grab either handle to drag the scrubber along the timeline. By the way, when you use the scrubber on the movie timeline, if the view currently displayed is zoomed a long way in, you will see two red lines - the left, solid one indicates the start of the current frame, the right dotted one the end.

Every project will start on the left and build to the right – like reading a sentence from left to right. The timescale reads zero at the far left edge of the project, and the numbering shows how far into the duration of the project you are.

Now click and hold on the *The-Sky-is-the-Limit.mpg* video file in the Library Browser and drag it down to the middle of A/V Track (2) and keep holding down the mouse button. As the timeline is empty, and because a feature called *Magnetic Snapping* is normally turned on, the clip will jump to the left side of the timeline. Let go of the mouse button and the clip will appear on the timeline. If snapping happens to be off, the start of the video will be where your mouse cursor is – along with a green dotted line. Try to place the start of the video at the far left of the track and release the mouse button. If you don't quite succeed, don't worry, just grab the video again and drag it left so that it bumps up against the start of the track and then release it. If we left a gap, your movie wouldn't have any content at the very start. On some occasions you might want to do this, but not at the moment.

If snapping is off, I suggest you turn it on - it is discussed on page 44.

The first clip loaded onto the timeline

You may not be able to see the whole clip. All of the thumbnail for the first frame is visible, but the end frame may fall off the end of the track. This is where the Scrollbar comes into play. Double-click anywhere along its length and the timeline will rescale its display so that you can see the whole project and a bit more.

Timescale context menu

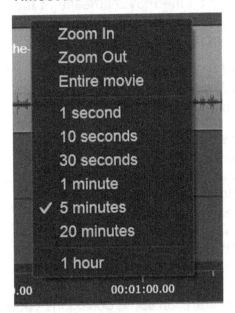

As I mentioned earlier, another way to change the size of the area displayed is to click and hold on the timescale below the tracks. The mouse pointer will turn into a clock icon and you can expand or contract your view by dragging it right and left respectively - if it isn't working remember that the checkbox in the *Control Panel/Project settings* controls this function.

Experiment a little to see how the scrollbar and timescale interact - you can adjust the scale by stretching the timescale. If you grab either end of the scrollbar you can also adjust the scale, and by grabbing the middle of the scrollbar you can move it to view to any section of the timeline.

Right-clicking on the timescale below the timeline brings up a context menu where you can chose specific display sizes - handy if you want a consistent display size.

There are keyboard shortcuts, of course. You can use the + and - keys on your numerical keypad to zoom in and out. I find these keys particularly useful because they are easy to find. A more sophisticated control is provided by the square bracket keys [and]. Not only do they zoom in and out, but **CTRL-]** zooms the timeline right into the frame level, while **CTRL-[** zooms it out to fit the entire project into the window.

When you have explored how to adjust the view to your satisfaction, use the **CTRL-[** key to fit the clip to the window, and we will continue editing.

A Brief Introduction to Background Rendering

When you first put the clip on the timeline, it's quite possible that a Preview Optimisation process began. The evidence is a brown coloured bar immediately above the timeline tracks, that changes colour to green as the render process occurs, finally vanishing when the render is complete.

Because this feature is on by default, don't think that it always needs to be turned on. Editing MPEG-2 video on a reasonable computer with a few simple transitions and titles should be quite painless without it on its full setting - and you might even be able to turn it off completely. When the effects get complex, or the source material is more heavily compressed - particularly HD AVCHD - then you will need set it higher in order to preview smoothly.

I will go into what settings you might want to use in depth in the Understanding Studio chapter. For now, this rendering process distracts you or seems to cause the computer to slow down, you can either wait for it to finish before continuing, or go into the Control Panel, select the Export and Preview tab and reduce the slider from the 100% *Aggressive* setting to around the 20% mark. If you then find that later on you can't preview smoothly, you might want to increase the level.

Setting up a Project

Our movie project now has some content, so let's talk about **Project Settings.** Pinnacle Studio is set up by default to try to guess the correct settings for the project from the first clip you put on the timeline. That is normally what you want to happen, so why worry? Well, you could be starting a project that is going to contain both older, Standard Definition, and newer, High Definition video. If you start with the Standard Definition video, and therefore with a project that has Standard Definition settings, then any High Definition video is going to be downgraded to match the older video when you make your movie. One major advance over the earlier Classic Pinnacle Studio is that you can change project settings even after you have done some work, so if you don't start with the correct settings it is not a huge problem.

Tooltip showing the project settings

We can discover what settings the current project has adopted by using the settings icon top left of the Timeline Window – it looks like a pair of gearwheels. Hover you mouse over it and read the tool tip.

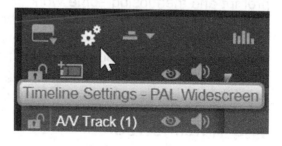

If you haven't changed any Control Panel settings in Studio you should see either NTSC Widescreen or PAL Widescreen pop up, depending on where you live and therefore what type of video you have put on the timeline – we checked the video parameters earlier, but check again if you wish using the *Display Information* function in the Library.

How do we change the settings if they are wrong? Click on the gearwheel icon, and you will see a box entitled *Timeline Settings* appear which allows you to change the settings. If you have the **NTSC** footage, select *Widescreen (16:9)* as the **Aspect**, *NTSC Widescreen* as the **Size**, and *30(60i)* as the **Framerate**. If you have the **PAL** footage, **Aspect** should be the same, *PAL Widescreen* should be the **Size** and *25(50i)* the **Framerate**.

The Timeline Settings menu.

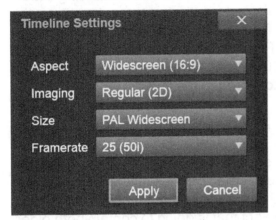

The settings are interactive, so you can't choose an invalid combination such as PAL at 30 frames a second. There is also a setting for Imaging, where you can switch to a 3D project. We will stick with 2D for now!

More information about what all these figures mean is given later in the book, when we look at importing, exporting and the things you can do to optimise Studio. If you are seeing the area above track one changing colour even if you have set the Preview Optimisation to a low level, then some type of rendering is occurring which shouldn't be happening at this stage. Check your project and video properties again.

We should give our project a proper name and save it. When you start a new project, Pinnacle Studio gives it a name such as "New Movie (x).AXP" and after a few of those, you won't know which project is which. Studio won't let you quit a project without asking you if you want to save it, but I'll hold my hand up to ignoring this prompt and then losing some work. If your computer crashes, you will normally be able resume editing where you were before the problem, but this isn't a guarantee. So, it is good practice to save your project at various stages, giving it incremental names so you can go back to an earlier stage. Open the *File* drop-down menu, select *Save Movie As...* and in the save dialogue enter the file name **Project 1_0**. You don't need to add the file extensions *Movie.AXP* as Studio does this for you.

The Timeline Toolbar

At the top of the Timeline area is a toolbar. We have already used the *Timeline Settings* icon. To its left is an icon that it's difficult to describe, but when you hover your mouse over it, the tooltip *Customize Toolbar* appears, so we know what it does! Click on it now to reveal the panel shown below and then click the *Select All* checkbox. You will then enable all the toolbar icons.

I'm going to introduce the use of these controls as and when you need to use them in the projects to follow. If you are impatient to find out what they do then check out the tooltips that appear when you hover over them. Use the index to find where in the book the function of each tool is described.

The Customize Toolbar panel

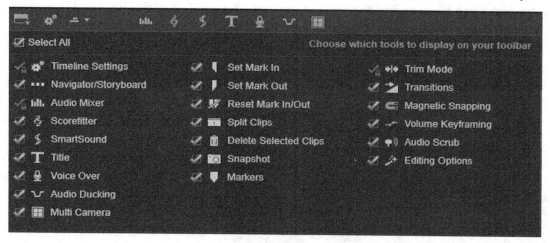

Near the centre of the screen, there is an icon that looks like a razor blade and it's called the **Split Clips** tool. We can use this to divide any clip on the timeline into two parts.

The Plot of our first project

I'm going to take a short break from describing the layout and functions of the Movie Editor in order to explain the story of Project 1. You've probable seen all the footage in the Sky clip by now – four happy young people going for a drive in their camper van, finding some countryside so the boys can impress the girls with their BMX skills and then have fun in the sunset. Could we use this video to tell a different story - perhaps one with a comedic twist? I thought there was probably just about enough footage to do that.

To speed things along, I've named our players Fred, Daphne, Velma and Shaggy – and we could also call the VW camper van The Mystery Machine so that you fully understand my reference. Fred (the driver) and Daphne (the redhead) have been possessed by an evil spirit (although it probably was the fairground owner all along). They see Velma (the blond girl) and Shaggy (with the baseball cap) out cycling and decide to carry out a dastardly deed…

Performing the first edit

At last it is time to actually perform our first edit. Make sure the timeline is active by clicking on the clip once so that it is highlighted with an orange border. The preview window will automatically switch to the Timeline tab. Now use the player controls or the timeline scrubber to find the shot at around 15 seconds of the driver of the camper van looking out of the window after it has stopped.

The target frame for the first edit - PAL version

Then use more accurate controls such as the jog buttons, mouse wheel or the arrow keys to park the scrubber on the very first frame of the next shot, looking into the sky through the trees. The timecode should read 16 seconds 01 frames if you are using the NTSC video, 16 seconds 02 frames for the PAL video. Leave the scrubber there and use the mouse to click on the razor blade icon.

What have we done? Zoom the view in so you can study the thumbnails either side of the cut as displayed in the screenshot below.

Splitting the clip on the timeline

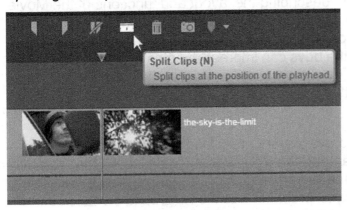

The frame to the left should be of the driver, the one to the right, the sky. If it isn't, either you didn't line up the scrubber correctly, or have moved it by accident before splitting the clip. If this has happened, "Undo"!

We have divided the single clip on the timeline into two clips. You may have noticed the tooltip for the razor blade icon – it indicates that the keyboard shortcut is the "N" key.

Keys or Mouse? There is no right or wrong answer to this. It's almost impossible to use Pinnacle Studio without a mouse, but I tend to use keys for many of the more common actions. *Split clip* is one of these, and in the classic versions of Pinnacle Studio the shortcut was the Insert key. I thought it would take some time for me to get used to the new key allocation, but for a regularly used function, the re-learning doesn't seem to take long. It is worth trying to get used to using the keys even if you don't use them every time.

Let us make another split in the clip using the keyboard. The next point I want you to find is the start of the second shot of a bike – it's the close-up of the red bike frame at about 45 seconds in.

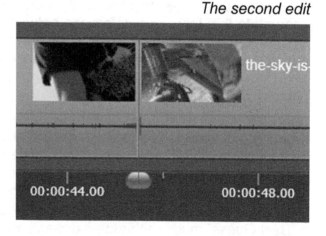

The second edit

Use your navigation skills to find it and use the keyboard to split the second clip on the timeline there. You should create an edit that looks like the screenshot. The timecode is 45.13 NTSC, 45.12 PAL

Although we have done hardly any work on the project, over the next few pages I'm going to ask you to do a lot of experimentation. So that you have a good point to return to, perform a *File/Save Movie* command now.

The icon on the toolbar to the right of the razor blade is a **Trash Can**, and we use it to delete items from the timeline. Whatever is highlighted with an orange border on the timeline will be removed when you click this icon, or use its keyboard shortcut **Delete**. There are three clips currently on the timeline. Select just the middle one by clicking on it and use the trash can or Delete key and the clip disappears from the project.

Click the undo icon underneath the *File* menu, or press CTRL-z and the clip should return.

Windows shortcuts for the selection of clips work on the timeline (and other areas such as the Library browser), so if you hold down the CTRL key and click on the first and last clip, both of those can be selected. Now when you perform a Delete, those two clips disappear and the centre one stays. Undo again to restore all the clips.

Splitting clips and deleting the unwanted parts isn't a particularly sophisticated way of editing, but it is very similar to the process of physically editing film. We will see how we can trim the ends of clips and split up clips before we send them to the timeline later, but for fast editing I find myself splitting clips all the time.

There is one important point about splitting clips that isn't immediately obvious. If you select and highlight a clip *before* you split it, after the split **both** halves of the clip are highlighted. If the clip you split *isn't* highlighted, then after the split operation **only the second half** of the clip will be highlighted.

And why is this important? If you are splitting a clip because you want to delete the second part, then doing so to a clip that isn't highlighted means you can just click the trash can or press Delete. This is no advantage if you are trying to cut off the beginning of a clip, but it is worth bearing in mind. Much more importantly, I want you to appreciate that there is a difference between how Split Clip behaves on a clip that is, or is not, highlighted because when you start to use multi-track editing **there are more fundamental differences**. We will explore those differences later.

Introducing Smart Editing

When you deleted the centre clip, did the last clip move up to take up the space left by the middle clip? It most probably did. There will be circumstances when you don't want this to happen, though. Pinnacle Studio makes use of a technique called Smart Mode, where it normally carries out the action you are most likely to want to happen. This doesn't just apply to deletion, but *all* the editing tasks. You could also call this a "Best Guess" mode, although it doesn't have the same marketing appeal.

If deleting the middle clip left a gap in the timeline, you probably haven't got the Smart mode enabled – although it should be selected by default every time you start a new project.

The editing modes

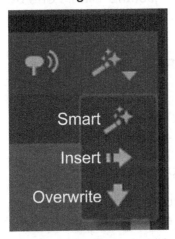

The button that controls Smart mode is at the far right-hand end of the timeline toolbar. It should look like a magic wand. The drop-down arrow alongside allows you to switch to two other modes. Insert mode is symbolised by a right pointing arrow. When you are deleting objects from a track in Smart Mode, it's the same as being in Insert mode, so if you were to switch to that mode and delete the middle clip, there would be no gap left behind. Overwrite mode is symbolised by a downwards point arrow. I'd like you to select that now and try deleting the middle clip again – and it should leave a hole in the timeline track of the same duration of the clip you deleted.

Leaving a gap by using Delete in Overwrite mode

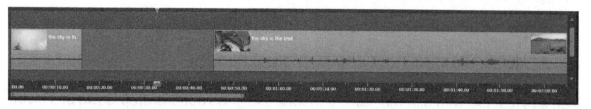

Press Undo and switch back to Smart mode. Surely it has to be a bit tiresome if you need to go through that process to switch modes all the time? Pinnacle have thought of that. The ALT key is your friend. In general, if you want to swap the behaviour that is carried out in Smart mode for the "other" one, hold down the ALT key. Try it now. Select the middle clip, hold down ALT and click the trash can icon. There you are, a gap! Sadly, this doesn't work with the keyboard shortcut Delete.

Smart mode doesn't always just choose an "insert" or "overwrite" function. In more complex multi-track situations it may also adopt a more helpful course of action. In general, holding down ALT defeats this helpful attitude.

"Insert" and "Overwrite" aren't the most obvious names for the choice of leaving or not leaving a gap when deleting, but they are much more obvious as descriptions for what I'm just about to show you. With Smart mode re-enabled and a gap in the timeline, hover the mouse over what is now the second clip on the timeline, click and hold down the left mouse key and start to drag the mouse left. The first thing you will notice is that the mouse pointer turns into a hand and the clip moves left with your action. When it gets into close proximity with the first clip, it should "snap" left to accurately close up the gap, but don't release the mouse key – keep dragging left. The clip will "unsnap" itself and start to insert itself into the first clip. Look at the right hand end of the timeline and you will see the displaced part of the first clip appearing at the end of the second clip. Release the mouse button and the moved clip stays there, splitting the first clip in two. Yes indeed, this is **Insert**.

Dragging a clip in Insert mode

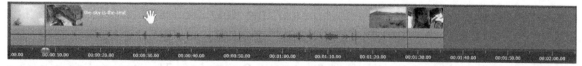

Let us look at Overwrite - reset the timeline with the Undo command, hold down the ALT key and repeat the dragging experiment. On this occasion the displaced section of the first clip **doesn't** appear at the end of the second clip – it is being **Overwritten**.

Dragging a clip in Overwrite mode

You can test this with different editing modes using the options drop-down box if you wish. If you want to do a lot of overwriting, you can change the mode until you want to return to Smart mode. Again, the ALT key is your friend – when you are in Insert mode, holding it down switches to Overwrite, and vice versa.

My workflow is not to change the mode away from Smart unless I'm getting very confused – I use the ALT key as and when required. I'm going to adopt that throughout the book, so unless I specifically tell you otherwise, assume that all operations are carried out in Smart mode.

It can be easy to overlook a really useful behaviour associated with the ALT key. Even when described as "The action that occurs when you release the mouse key reflects the state of the ALT key at the time", it isn't that clear until you start experimenting with pressing the key once you have *already* started a dragging operation. You begin to drag a clip left and it become apparent that you *should* have pressed the ALT key because you wanted to overwrite, not insert. Don't panic – press down the ALT key, move your mouse a little more and the timeline changes to what it would have been like if you have been holding down ALT from the very beginning.

This behaviour is very useful because it allows you to begin to make an alteration to your project **without being 100% sure if you are in the correct mode**. Once you have a visual clue that what you are doing is incorrect you don't need to undo your action, just press the ALT key. The casual observer will even think that is probably what you meant to do all along!

The Magnet

Looking to the left of the mode selection tool, the next two icons concern audio (I'm assuming you have selected all the tools, as I suggested earlier). The third icon that looks like a magnet is extremely important. Hover your mouse over it and you will see a pop up tool tip naming the icon **Magnetic Snapping**. The description is pretty accurate as well - "automatically snaps to cuts and markers when dragging". If, when you tried the above dragging experiments you didn't experience the "sticky" behaviour, then you must have had this control disabled - it should be highlighted in orange.

The Magnet icon

It is possible that you weren't that aware of the magnet's effect; it seems quite natural. Zoom the view of the timescale in a bit to

see it more accurately. Turn off the magnet, either by clicking the icon or using the keyboard shortcut **P**. Now when you drag the clips around you will see how difficult it actually is to get the clips lined up exactly, because it is very easy to end up with a small sliver of one clip left at the end of the other. In Insert mode at least you have a small visual clue, but in Overwrite (Smart+ALT) with a wide view of the timeline it's getting on for impossible to see if you have exactly aligned the end of the first clip with the start of the second without accidentally overwriting a frame or two of the first clip.

Although you will occasionally need the accuracy of positioning that can be achieved with the magnet **off**, I recommend that you leave it **on** by default – if you switch it off for a particularly tricky editing task, get into the habit of turning it back on as soon as you have finished the task. If you don't, then like me, you will almost certainly find the occasional unexpected "flash frame" marring your projects – and you rarely spot them until you have wasted a DVD!

Time to tell the story

After all that trial and error, the project may be in a bit of disarray by now.. If you aren't confident that you have returned the project to its original condition before we began deleting stuff, open the *File* menu and hover you mouse over *Recent*. A list of projects should appear to the right, with the saved version of your current movie at the top of the list. Double click on the name, decline the offer to save the project that is open in the timeline and you should be returned to the project in the state it was when you saved it several pages back.

Highlight the centre clip and delete it, *without* leaving a gap.

At this point, despite me only having described less than half the buttons on the timeline toolbar, you have enough knowledge to start trimming and re-arranging the video file *The-Sky-is-the-Limit* into our new story. We have the clip in the Compact Library and a version with a few splits in the timeline window below.

The first section of the video shows all four characters driving along in the camper van. The next section shows them all riding bikes, before the girls decide just to watch.

The first task I'm going to set you is to edit out the presence of Velma (the blond girl) and Shaggy (in the baseball cap) from the first section.

Find the first frame of Velma inside the van and split the clip (08.29 NTSC 09.00 PAL). Scrub through the clip and find the last frame of Shaggy, move forward one frame so that we are looking at the steering wheel, then split the clip (11.01 NTSC 11.02 PAL). There are now four clips in total on the timeline and the second one starts with the first frame of Velma and ends with the last frame of Shaggy, both inside the van. Highlight and then delete the second clip – you should be in Smart mode and no gap will be left because the clips to the right move left. If you rearrange your timeline view you can compare your middle four thumbnails with those below to check your movie. If the shot of Fred looking out of the window is missing, it could be that you need to to adjust the timescale. Try right-clicking and selecting 30 seconds from the context menu.

The four central thumbnails for the current state of the movie

Play the timeline from the beginning up until the point where Fred looks out of the window. What do you think? Is there anyone else in the van? Yes, actually, because you can see Velma's hand in the foreground of Daphne's shot. What's more, it is the only shot we have of Daphne inside the van, so we really need to use it. What can we do?

Before people owned VCRs and DVD players with slow motion and pause buttons, there was a lot that you could get away with. If I show you a photograph for only a short period of time, you won't register all the detail. Perhaps if we shorten the shot of Daphne, most viewers won't notice the hand. So that is my plan. As I mentioned before, Pinnacle Studio has much more powerful tools for editing clips than Split and Delete, and it is nearly time to show you them.

Arranging the tracks

Before I show you the simplest way of trimming a clip without splitting it, it will help if we rearrange our view a little. Given that we are only using one track, couldn't it be a bit bigger? Right click on the grey area where the track name A/V Track (2) is and a context menu with six entries will pop up.

The first two are *Insert New Track* and *Delete track*. You can chose to insert a new track either above or below the current track. An additional way of adding a new track is a small icon above the track headers - but it only adds a track at the top of the pile. *Delete* removes the track and its contents. You don't get asked "Are you sure?" before the track disappears, but if you do so in error, Undo and the CTRL-Z key works. Even so, use this with care, just to save you from panic attacks!

The track header context menu

Next is *Edit Track Name* and we may as well try it out. Click to select it and the name of the track becomes highlighted; use the keyboard to edit the name to *Main Track* and return.

Tool for adding a new track to the top

The option we want is *Track Size*. Select *Large* from the submenu. Even with the smallest screen, that shouldn't be too big. You might need to adjust the proportion of the screen allocated to the timeline, and a scroll bar may have appeared to the right so that you can adjust the view to see the whole height of the timeline.

The other track menu options are *All Track Sizes* which lets you change all the track heights at once, and *View Waveforms* which switch on and off the squiggly lines drawn underneath the thumbnails that represent the audio. Turning waveforms off doesn't give us bigger thumbnails and we will need them later, so leave the check box ticked.

You can adjust the track layout with the mouse. If you hover over the lower edge of a track – and it doesn't need to be in the header – you generate a two-headed handle that lets you click and drag the height of the track. You can also rearrange the order of the tracks. You need to use the track header area for this – Click, hold and drag up or down and a small white circle and line shows where you can drop the whole track and its contents. If you decide that you have put everything on the wrong track, you can move it up or down the order using this method.

Make sure you are happy that you are seeing as much of the main track as you are comfortable with on your particular screen size. Zoom in with the timescale so that the edit between Daphne and the shot of the steering wheel is clearly displayed.

Introducing Quick Trimming

I mentioned earlier that splitting clips and then deleting the sections we don't want isn't the most sophisticated way of editing, although it has speed and simplicity on it side.

A lot of editing operations consist of altering the start or end of a clip, and sometimes you might want to add material, not just take it away. This is called trimming. Pinnacle Studio has two trimming modes, and we will start with the simplest, which I call Quick Trimming.

An Out point handle (enlarged)

Its time to do a bit more mouse hovering. When you hover near the centre of a clip, the name of that clip appears, along with a figure that turns out to be the duration of the clip as it appears on the timeline. The first clip should be 8 seconds 29 frames NTSC or 9 seconds 0 frames PAL in duration. The second one should be exactly 5 seconds duration in either video standard.

Move the mouse very close to the junction of the two clips below the level of the thumbnails. If you are just to the left of the junction an Out Point handle will appear - a right pointing arrow with a bar to its right – as shown in the screenshot. If you hover to the right of a junction you will get an In Point handle – a left pointing arrow with a bar to its left.

An In point handle (enlarged even more)

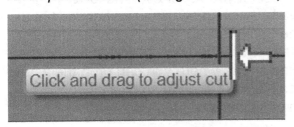

If you see a tooltip that is longer than that shown in the screenshots, then there is another option that should be off by default but could confuse matters if it is turned on. If, when you click and release an In or Out point handle a yellow bar appears at the junction of the clips, you have Advanced Trim mode becoming activated when clicking near cuts. **We don't want to do that yet**. Advanced trimming is powerful but can be complex and is unnecessary for the tasks I have for you in this chapter. I want you to turn that feature off for now. In the Control Panel, go to Project Settings and uncheck the box that controls the feature.

Control Panel option for setting Advanced trim mode by clicking

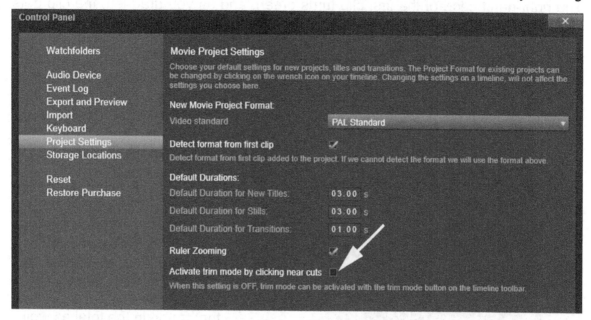

You may also generate another type of handle when hovering you mouse in this area. Go too high and you will get a fold-over effect used for creating transition - which we aren't trying to do yet. If you hover over the green line in the lower half of the track, it is possible you will generate a small speaker icon. This is for adjusting the audio levels, and again, we don't want to do that. To stop this type of control appearing, you need to turn off Volume Keyframing, controlled by an icon on the toolbar to the right of the Magnet (illustrated on page 77). Switch it off now - it should be off by default.

Trimming an Out point

So, for Quick trimming, click, hold and ***drag straight away***. When you are using quick trimming you will see a **green** bar on the edge that is being trimmed.

The action we are about to try out is illustrated below. Hover your mouse just to the left of the junction between the first

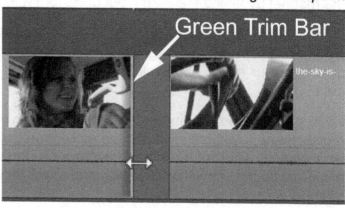

and second clips to generate an Out point handle. Click, hold and slowly drag the mouse left.

The right-hand edge of the first clip turns green, and as you drag left, the clip gets shorter. The player and the thumbnail at the end of the clip update as you change the Out point. If you drag too far, you will eventually stray into the previous shot of Fred, so drag right again. I think we should end on the shot before Daphne looks ahead again and I settled on a point at 8 seconds exactly. Glancing at the timecode top right of the Player window will tell you when you have found this point - 00:00:08.00 both NTSC and PAL– and when you do, release the mouse button.

The modified Out point shown in the player window

Check the new duration of the first clip by hovering your mouse over it. It should be 08.01 NTSC and PAL. If you are puzzled by the 1 frame difference between that and the Timecode, remember that the first frame is numbered as zero and we have to include that frame in the total as well.

If you can't achieve this level of accuracy when dragging the edge of the clip, you probably don't have the timeline zoomed in enough and the effect of the magnet is getting in the way. The keyboard shortcuts can come to your rescue – the number pad + and – keys zoom the timeline view in and out. You can use them **even while you are holding down the mouse button**. Of course, you could also turn off the magnet by hitting the P key, but don't forget to turn it back on again.

If you are about to embark on a lot of fiddly one or two frame adjustments you might well want to turn off the magnet, but the advanced trimming mode might be better suited to your needs. You will have to wait a few chapters before I explain that in detail.

Have a look at the timeline again. Oh dear, we have left a gap - when you play the movie, there is a second of nothing more than black video. In the current project, it would be the work of a moment to drag the other two clips left – you could even multiple select them with CTRL-click and move them together. Not such a trivial task if there is a lot of other stuff after the edit. to say nothing of what would happen if there was video or something else on the other tracks.

I'll show you a useful short cut that can help in these and other circumstances. Hold down **Ctrl** and **Shift** at the same time and click on the second clip. Notice that **both** clips to the right are selected Now drag them to the left to close the gap. This is useful, but more importantly, if there were clips on other tracks, and they to were to the right of the clip you selected, those clips would have been added to the selection as well.

A new feature was added in into Studio 18 but has now be modified so that it can now be used to achieve the same thing. Use *undo* to restore the gap, right click on the gap and a context menu offers the option to *Close Gap*. Do that now to pull the other clips right. (I don't recommend this feature for multi-track projects, but I'll explain why on page 107)

The new Close Gap function

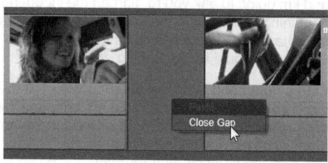

In Quick trim, you can see now that Smart mode gives you **Overwrite** behaviour. From a few paragraphs back you will know how to swap the mode – by holding down the ALT key. Use Undo three times to reset the trim and try again, this time holding down ALT – remember you don't even have to hold it down to begin with. This time, the following two shots maintain their position relative to the last frame of the first shot, which saves us the work of rearranging them after the trim.

So, you have a choice of how to carry out such operations. You can use the (automatically selected) overwrite mode and if you want to then eliminate the gap, use Ctrl-Shift click and dragging or the Close Gap function. Alternatively, if you switch to Insert mode by holding down the ALT while trimming, the gap in the timeline doesn't occur. I will just mention now that you will only affect the track you are editing - if you are working with multiple tracks and want to work in Insert mode, you will find Advanced trim mode more powerful. More about that later.

Ok, back to the storytelling. Take a look at what you have done. *We* know that Velma's hand is there, but would someone else notice? If you have someone nearby, ask them. Play them the first two clips and then casually ask them how many people were in the van. With a little bit of luck they will say "two".

That hand in the foreground *could* actually belong to Fred, using it to hold the steering wheel. (Let's assume the pink sleeve is some kind of fashion statement.) You need to study the shot for a few moments before you realise that Daphne is sat in the *back* of the van and there is a bicycle brake handle in the foreground. Why did we get away with what is such an obvious cheat? I think it is the head movements and directions in which they are looking. Fred turns to look back, and then we cut to Daphne who then appears to look at him. We haven't given the viewer time to make other assumptions or start looking around the frame for clues about the real geography. I also think we can help the illusion a little more by adjusting the next shot.

Editing Terminology

I'd like to establish a little bit of terminology first. The edit we are about to adjust again consists of two shots. The first is called the **Outgoing**, the second the **Incoming**, and I'm going to ask you to "tighten the incoming" by trimming some frames from the beginning so we cut to the second shot at the same place in relation to the timeline, but it has moved on a little in time. If we were to cut to the shot when the action was earlier, we would be "loosening" it.

Fred's right hand is on the steering wheel at the start of the incoming shot, so let's trim it so that his right hand is out of frame and the left one is about to enter. Generate an In point handle to the right of the cut by hovering your mouse, click and hold, press and hold down the ALT key and begin to drag the mouse to the right. The green trim bar should show you that you are doing the correct thing. Watch the preview window, and once the left hand disappears out of shot, drag left and right a couple of times to ensure you have got the very first clean frame. Again, if you aren't able to get enough accuracy, try zooming in the timeline a little.

Quick trimming the incoming video

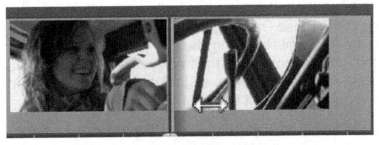

You should have noticed the material to the right keeping station – no gap this time. The timecode doesn't help us on this occasion, but o nce you have chosen your frame and released the mouse button, hover over the clip and check that duration. It should be 4 seconds 15 frames NTSC. 4 seconds 13 frames PAL.

One more trim might help the illusion even more. In the final movie, I'm hoping to make it appear that Evil Fred has deliberately swerved the Mystery Machine into the path of Shaggy and Velma. We can help this by shortening the next shot of the sky so that it is already rotating when we cut to it – the swerve would have started when Fred turned the wheel.

First we need to split the second clip again at the junction between the shot of the wheel and the shot of the sky - 08.29 NTSC, 08.24 PAL. Now we are going to tighten the incoming shot of the sky. Although it is exactly the same process as before, you are looking for a point when the shot begins to rotate and this might be a bit harder for us to agree on.

On this occasion don't hold down the ALT key – quick trim the incoming shot by dragging left and leaving a gap. You can keep an eye on the timecode now, and by sliding the mouse left and right we can agree that the first frame where there is a suggestion that the camera is starting to tilt is at 09.18 NTSC 09.15 PAL.

First frame of clip three after the tighten

Release the mouse key, press down Ctrl-Shift and click on the third clip to select both clips to the right of the gap, and then slide the clips left to fill the gap.

The duration of what is now the third clip should be 02.28 NTSC, 02.24 PAL, and the first frame of the third clip on the timeline should look exactly like the screenshot - study the right lower edge in particular. The overall movie duration should be 1:31.20 NTSC 1:31.16 PAL

Using Quick trim to loosen an edit

All of the above actions are aimed at tightening up material, but the major advantage of Non-Linear editing is that we can change our mind. What happens if we use Quick Trimming to **loosen** an In or Out point? It is well worth trying out a few experiments to help fix in your mind how Pinnacle Studio behaves, but before we do, let's **Save** the current movie rather than relying on the Undo command.

Look at the edit between clips 1 and 2 and try lengthening the incoming video – that is, the clip that shows the steering wheel. Hover your mouse to create an In point handle at the left edge of the second clip. Click and drag right and a gap appears in the timeline as before. We are in Smart mode, but it is working in Overwrite mode. Now drag slowly left and observe the timeline thumbnails. First we close up the gap. Each frame you drag left, the In point of clip 2 is loosened. Once the In point of clip

2 reaches the Out point of clip 1, we begin to see that the frames of the Out point of clip 1 are overwritten. You may have to drag quite slowly to see the thumbnails update. When you have dragged sufficiently left, the outgoing shot of Daphne is completely overwritten and the shot of Fred appears. Also, we run out of incoming frames of the steering wheel, and Shaggy appears as the incoming shot. Drag the mouse back right a bit so at least we have the correct pictures and release the mouse button.

What have we done, and why would we want to do it? The first thing to consider is the rest of the movie after the edit point – nothing has moved, so the movie has the same duration. Each time we add a frame to the Incoming, we subtract one from the Outgoing, so the total duration of clips 1 and 2 remains the same.

OK, that is one reason why we might want to use this type of trimming. A more artistic motive is to maintain the **Continuity**. A good example of this might be a shot of one person throwing a ball and another shot of someone catching it. When we edit these two shots together we can't have the ball appearing in mid air in the incoming shot before it has left the hands of the thrower in the outgoing shot. Once we have established a good cutting point between the two shots the viewer will believe the edit. If we then want to change the cutting point by shortening the outgoing shot, lengthening the incoming shot by an equal amount maintains the timing between the two shots.

I'll discuss Continuity editing in greater detail in a moment as well as in later chapters.

Having messed up our original edit, we can't put it right by altering the In point again – if we use the ALT key to invoke Insert mode clip 2 can be shortened but clip 1 is unaffected. Let us try lengthening the Out point of clip 1 instead. Hover the mouse to the left of the edit point to get an Out point handle, click and drag right – ah that does it! As the Out point of clip 1 is loosened, the In point of clip 2 is tightened by the same amount. With a bit of care, you should be able to restore the edit to how it was before we began experimenting.

What if you want to loosen an In point without changing the corresponding Out point of the previous clip? Well we need to be in Insert mode, and as you should be fast beginning to realise, the quick way to achieve this is to hit the ALT key. Generate an In point handle for the steering wheel shot, click and hold the mouse button then hold down ALT and drag left. The steering wheel clip has frames added to the beginning and gets longer, while the following video is pushed down the timeline.

Now try the same with the Out point of Daphne's shot, just to be sure it is clear in your mind how the other shots aren't shortened, but moved later to make room for the extra frames.

I'll just remind you that in this chapter we are only using the Quick trim methods on the timeline, so be prepared for more powerful features when we meet Advanced trimming.

Video Grammar

To restore the movie back to how it was at the start of the previous section. reload it using the File menu - you should find it in the list of recent projects - and play what we have done so far to remind yourself where we got to.

For the moment, the first part is working OK. We now need some shots of the cyclists from the rest of the footage. Before we turn to that, I'd like to do a bit of Film School 101.

The point I would like to cover is explained in one book on my shelves as *"...the creation of a continuity of time over two shots involves temporal marking because continuity of time in an edited sequence is a synthetic product not at all identical to the time in which the events are actually placed"* (D. W. Griffith and the Origins of American Narrative Film. The Early Years at Biograph. Tom Gunning University of Illinois Press 1991).

Put a little more bluntly, we are going to cheat. The point that Tom Gunning is making is that an edited sequence can give the *impression* of real time, even though the sequence doesn't exactly mimic it. We can contract (or even expand) the passing of real time to suit our purposes.

Another phrase that is used to describe what we are going to do is Continuity Editing. In the very early days of people trying to tell a story from filmed sequences, the passage of time wasn't always shown in a linear manner. The most notable example is an Edison film shot by Edwin S. Porter, *The Life of an American Fireman (1903)*. In one version of the film, a sequence at the end shows a room on fire, a fireman entering through a window, rescuing a woman and leaving. Some moments later, he returns and rescues a child. The next (and last) shot of the film repeats the same action from outside, including a story point not already seen – the woman pleading with the fireman to return to rescue the child. This is a controversial example, as two versions of the film exist, one "corrected" to intercut the interior and exterior shots in the manner a modern audience would expect. It is argued by many that the first version is the incorrect one, but other examples of this way of storytelling from the early days of film also exist. Time was not always portrayed in a linear manner. Nowadays, apart from the use of flashbacks (or occasionally flashforwards) which are signalled as such, it normally is.

Another convention that dates from the early days of film and is so common that some people may not be consciously aware of it is the "180 degree" rule. When two people are in the same shot and are looking at each other, one faces left, the other right. If we decide to produce two closer single shots, we would arrange the camera positions so that they still look the same way on screen. This is why we naturally assume that Fred and Daphne are looking at each other in their two single shots in the first sequence. If you want to ensure you never break this rule you must keep your camera positions within a 180 degree arc so that you never "cross the line" – an imaginary line you can draw between the two subjects.

The same convention applies to movement. A sequence of shots of a policeman and an escaping criminal will make more sense if they are both running in the same direction across screen – one is chasing the other even if we can't see them in the same shot. The opposite applies if you want to give the impression that two people are moving towards each other. If the camper van is travelling left to right, and the cyclists are travelling right to left, a hundred years of cinematic convention and grammar tells us that the two are moving towards each other.

Of course, there a dozens of ways to get around these conventions. A shot of the van moving straight towards the camera has no "line" to cross. The two shots of Fred and Daphne in the van have a line of their own – the "eyeline" between them.

The practical upshot of this is that because in our sequence the van is predominantly travelling left to right, if we have a choice of shots of the cyclist, we want to use the ones where they are travelling right to left.

First shot of Velma

When you look at the available shots of Velma and Shaggy cycling, you will realise that they are rather sparse, but at least the direction of travel happens to be OK. However, the above theory might influence the order in which we use them.

Use the scrubber to investigate the video on the timeline at about 15 seconds in.

There is a brief shot of Velma that pans across to Shaggy. Split the video at the start of the shot (15.00 NTSC and PAL) and the start of the next shot (16.11 NTSC. 16.09

PAL). The clip we have isolated has a duration of 1 second 11 frames NTSC, 1 second 09 frames PAL. Next look for a sequence of three shots of the girls cycling on their own at around 26 seconds.

Second shot of Velma

In the third shot of this sequence first Daphne and then Velma cycle right to left through frame. Find the first moment where Velma is completely on her own – the timecode should be 28.21 NTSC, 28.18 PAL. Split the clip at this point, then find the first frame of the next shot – 29.24 NTSC, 29.20 PAL – and split again.

I don't think two shots are going to be enough. There is a very brief moment starting at 19.27 NTSC 19.23 PAL where Shaggy is almost on his own – a bit of Fred's arm in shot, but let's try to use it anyway. Split the clip at the timecode I have just given you and again at the start of the next shot, 20.24 NTSC, 20.20 PAL.

Shaggy almost alone

We have three shots now; we might need more but it would be good to see how things are shaping up. First, I want you to tidy up the timeline by deleting the shots we aren't going to use. up until the swerve. Use **Ctrl-[** so the project fills the timeline. Count the separate shots – you should have 10. CTRL-Click on shots 4, 6, 8 and 10 to highlight all four clips, then delete them. You should be left with 6 clips and a total duration of 15.07 NTSC, 15.06 PAL.

At this point, I'm going to ask you to perform an incremental save. Use the *File/Save As* menu command to use a new project name, **Project_1_1**.

Using Drag and Drop

I want to move the shot of Velma and Shaggy cycling – currently the fourth on the timeline, in between the shot of the van wheel and the view across the lake which starts at 5.21 NTSC, 5.18 PAL. Have a look at that point to identify it. Now, we could put a split in there, but this is a good time to explore some options you have for rearranging the timeline using drag and drop.

The Timeline Player

Click and hold the fourth shot and start to drag it to the left.. Watch the preview window or the thumbnail to the left of the clip you are dragging. I hope you are in Smart mode – if you are the clip you are dragging will be inserting itself into the other clips and the length of material on the timeline won't be changing. What you are seeing in preview and in the thumbnail is the frame before the place you would put the dragged clip if you were to release the mouse button.

The Timeline during Drag and drop

Eventually you will see the wheel of the camper van on the road. If you go too far the same shot will appear as a thumbnail at the other side of the Velma shot. Slide left again to see the shot across the lake. The timecode will be 05.20.NTSC 05.17 PAL Release the mouse key and you will have dropped the old clip 4 into a newly created split in clip 1.

How was that for you? I tend to use this technique for less accurate adjustments. In the current example you need to be frame accurate otherwise you will get a flash frame or two because you are trying to place the cycling shot exactly between two other shots. However, you can keep your eyes on the clip thumbnails either side of the clip you are dragging as well to help - so this is another case of life being easier with the correctly scaled view.

The split created by inserting the clip is now permanent – if you delete the new clip you will see the edit point in the original clip. If you try this, use undo to put the clip back.

OK, so if by using the above operation you have created a split anyway, why didn't you just split the clip at a pre-chosen point anyway and made life a bit easier? The clip would have snapped into place because of the magnet. Well, the new method is actually a bit quicker, and more importantly it will be far more convenient once you start working with multiple tracks.

Using Markers

An alternative to splitting a clip involves the use of **Markers**. These have many other uses as well. Using a marker isn't as destructive as splitting a clip - for example you could mark a position on the timeline where you *think* it might be good to insert something else, but haven't decided quite what yet. When you find a shot that fits the bill, you can add it exactly where the marker is, or perhaps change your mind a little either way based on what you have chosen as the new material.

We are going to use a marker to indicate accurately where we want to move the first cycling shot too. Use undo to restore the project to the point before we started moving the clip around. Better still, load the saved project that you named **Project_1_1**.

Find the target point where you would have split the first clip – 05.21 NTSC, 05.18 PAL. With the scrubber parked there, click on the orange icon to the left of the trash can on the timeline toolbar - it is indicated by the white arrow in the screenshot below.

A marker at 5:18 (PAL Project) with the Marker panel open

An orange marker will appear on the timescale at the same place as the scrubber, as shown by the black arrow below. Now repeat the dragging operation with clip 4, and you will find that as you get into the near vicinity of the marker, the clip will snap into place. That was easy, wasn't it?

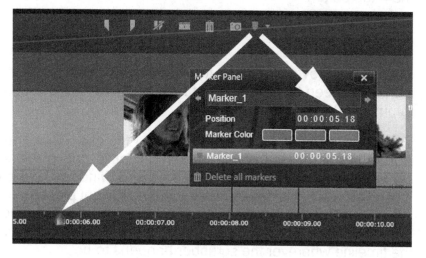

Adding markers can also be done by pressing the "**M**" key. Neither method stops playback if it is running, so it is a great way to make a quick note of a point in the movie you want to come back to. I use this feature a lot to mark the beat of a music track I want to edit in time with, for example.

You can alter the position of a marker by dragging it with the mouse. To delete it, when the scrubber is exactly aligned with the marker, the marker tool acquires a line through it. Clicking it now deletes the marker above the scrubber, as does pressing the M shortcut.

More sophistication can be achieved when you open the Marker Panel with the drop-down arrow alongside the Marker icon. Here you have a choice of three colours so that you can use different colours to mean different things. As you add markers you build up a list which also displays the timecode for each marker position.

Clicking on this list takes the timeline scrubber to the timecode of the marker. Alongside a highlighted marker is a trash can. At the top of the panel is a box where you can edit the marker's name. Scroll buttons either side of the box let you step through the markers, and below is a box where you can type in a timecode to alter the marker's position. When you finally want to tidy up the display, *Delete All Markers* is available at the bottom of the panel.

This example might seem a trivial use of a complex feature, but markers are one of the things in Pinnacle Studio that will grow on you. We will see later that you can also add markers to the clips themselves, and there will come a point in a complex project where the only alternative to adding a marker might be actually to write down the timecode of a point you need to line up to, so the sooner you get in the habit of using them the better!

Using Cut and Paste

Back to the movie. I'm going to suggest you move the clip of Velma cycling on her own in between the two shots of Fred and Daphne looking at each other. We need to put it at 08.18 NTSC, 08.16 PAL.

Yes, there is yet *another* way of moving the clip – **Cut and Paste**. Remember the *Edit* menu at the top of the screen? That is one place that you can find these commands, along with **Copy**. The standard Windows keyboard shortcuts also work. If you **Cut** a clip it is deleted from the timeline but placed on the Windows clipboard. When you **Copy** a clip the original is left in place but another copy is placed on the clipboard. Now, when you use **Paste**, the contents of the clipboard are inserted into the timeline wherever the scrubber happens to be.

Let's do it now. Highlight the shot of Velma on her own - currently the last clip on the timeline - and select *Cut* from the *Edit* menu, or just press CTRL-x. Move the scrubber to the timecode given above and then *Paste* (or CTRL-v). Job done.

The timeline after the Cut and Paste operation

One thing to note is that *Paste* to the timeline places the clipboard contents onto the track from which it has been copied, and not the one highlighted as active. When copying multiple tracks you may be grateful of this behaviour, but it may not be what you expect.

Cut (or Copy) and Paste are very useful in lots of circumstances. If you already have a clear idea of what you are doing they can save a lot of time. They can also be used to move items from the Library or even between projects. However, as part of the creative process I prefer drag and drop because it is clearer what you are doing. If your thought process is interrupted after you cut but before you paste, who knows what is on the clipboard?

The Storyboard Feature

The final rearrangement of the current shots is to drag the shot of Shaggy up to 10.14 NTSC 10.11 PAL. There is already a cut here – between Daphne and the steering wheel shot, so we could just use a simple Drag and Drop. However, I think that this is a good time to introduce the **Storyboard**.

If you have used a storyboard before, particularly if you have graduated from Classic Pinnacle Studio, then you won't find the Pinnacle Studio 19 Storyboard quite the same as you might be expecting. If you are unfamiliar with the concept, then you deserve a brief explanation.

Normally, a series of still pictures arranged left to right, top to bottom on a page represents each distinct shot used to tell a story. You read the story in the same manner as a comic book. Sometimes a shot that develops may be represented by a series of still frames - perhaps indication the opening and closing frame of a shot. The duration that each shot shot lasts on screen isn't indicated. When a director plans a complex sequence - one he will almost certainly have to shoot out of sequence - he may draw the shots in the order that he intends them to appear in the final cut of the movie.

In Pinnacle Studio and other video editing programs the storyboarding process is extended to using shots that have already been shot, and perhaps trimmed to contain only the useful parts. These are dragged and dropped onto a storyboard area and can be played in sequence to check if the story is working in the most effective way. If the director or editor is unhappy with the result then shots can be rearranged by dragging and dropping.

Timeline editing is far more sophisticated, but can mask the underlying structure that is made more obvious with bold thumbnails telling the story.

Pinnacle Studio 19 has a form of storyboard that is limited to a single strip along the top of the timeline, but offers a clearer view of the story and makes drag and drop much easier to use.

So, let's turn on the storyboard now. The third icon from the left on the toolbar may show as two strips or as three "frames". To change the control, use the drop -down arrow and select the lower storyboard "frames" icon. Now, when you click on the Chose Display icon, you alternatively switch the storyboard display on and off. (The strip icon switches to the Navigator display, a tool of real use only when using multiple tracks. We will look at that later.)

Enabling the storyboard

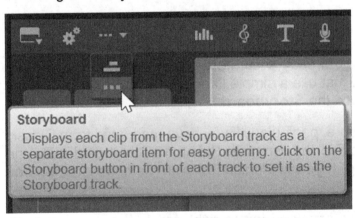

To adjust the height of the storyboard generate a double headed arrow by hovering your mouse over the bottom edge of the storyboard area. Click and drag to make the storyboard a decent size.

If there are no thumbnails displayed when you first open up the storyboard then you need to select which track is being displayed.

You may notice a small icon has appeared on the track headers. Click on this to make it the active storyboard track.

Setting the track for storyboarding

The storyboard uses a very nice "Touch Screen" style interface. If the thumbnails aren't all displayed, you can scroll the strip left and right by clicking and then *immediately* dragging, or using the scroll arrows that materialise when you just hover over the storyboard. Notice that the durations of each shot are displayed on each thumbnail.

If you click on a storyboard thumbnail and then pause for a moment, the hand pointer turns into a normal mouse pointer, the thumbnail below becomes highlighted, and you can drag the shot itself, rather than the whole storyboard, left or right to reposition it relative to the other shots.

Please do that now with the final shot currently on the timeline (and the storyboard), dragging it from the end position to between the shot of Daphne and the steering wheel, as shown in the screenshot, then releasing the mouse button.

Repositioning a clip in the movie with the aid of the storyboard

Because any form of storyboard was missing in Avid Studio, and I rarely used it in the Classic versions Pinnacle Studio, it wasn't part of my normal workflow. However, I'm increasingly becoming a fan of the feature. Where you might find it very useful is in the early stages of building up a project, particularly one that might consist of photos rather than video. It is possible to add transitions as well. We will look at the storyboard again on a number of occasions later in the book, so check the index if you want to know more, including the use of transitions.

Reviewing the Story So Far...

OK, time to play back what you have compiled. Put the scrubber at the start of the timeline and press play on the Timeline preview player. We have established Fred and Daphne driving along, and Velma and Shaggy appear to be cycling towards them because they are travelling in the opposite direction across the screen. Fred throws a look at Daphne. We "see" what he and Daphne can see, and she throws a look to Fred. There is a shot of Shaggy - Fred's intended victim, and then Fred swerves the van.

By the way, did you get distracted by the way the storyboard scrolled across the top of the timeline? I do. I suggest you turn it off for now. We will re-enable it when required.

Review the movie again. At this point we clearly need some more shots to depict the "dastardly deed", but before we find those, let's polish up what we have done so far.

I think the sixth clip in the sequence - Shaggy on his own - could benefit from a bit of shortening. It might help the pace. A convention that is often used to build up tension is to increase the pace of cutting between shots as we approach a dramatic moment. If we take a little off the top of the shot then we will also see less of Fred's arm on the right of frame.

I have taken 8 NTSC frames or 7 PAL frames from the beginning of the shot. It should end up as 19 frames NTSC or 15 frames PAL in duration – slightly shorter than the preceding shot.

If you were just making a project of your own, rather that having to match my numbers, you could just do a Quick trim on the In point with the ALT key held down. When the shot of Shaggy looks to be taking up slightly less space on the timeline than the shot of Daphne, you could let go and preview the effect. In fact, try that now and see how you get on!

Unfortunately, because we need our projects to match, if you don't succeed at first it may be easier to jog the scrubber the required number of frames into the clip, split and then delete the first part.

Duration adjustment

Have another look at the video. I haven't obeyed the rule I set myself about the building up of the pace with the duration of the shot of the steering wheel, have I? That really needs to be slightly shorter than the previous shot. Because I'm happy with the In point, I'm going to tighten the Out point. I have already have decided that I want to make the clip 17 frames NTSC 14 frames PAL long. I'm therefore going to show you how to alter the duration of a clip by typing in the numbers.

When you are cutting moving video, you often make decision about duration depending on the content, choosing the In and Out points with care. If you just want to shorten or lengthen a shot by adjusting the Out point, you might consider using

Adjust duration. If you were making a slideshow from photographs, there is no downside at all, because the In and Out points are going to look the same, regardless.

The Timeline Clip context menu

To find the Adjust Duration box, you need to right-click on the clip you want to change – in this case the shot of the steering wheel. This is just the beginning of the operation, as it will bring up the clip context menu.

The menu has lots of interesting commands, so try not to be distracted by them – they will all be explained when we need them.

Some, such as Delete, Cut, Copy and Paste are just alternatives to other methods, because you expect to find those sorts of commands in context menus.

Adjust duration is the fifth option down so click on it now. A simple box opens which contains the current duration of the selected clip. Enter 00:00:00.17 frames if you are making a NTSC project or 00:00:00.14 if you are making a PAL one. When you click on OK the box closes and the clip shrinks from the right. Assuming you are in Smart or Insert mode, the clips to the right move up as well.

The seventh clip's duration being altered to 14 frames (PAL Project)

It's that easy, and I use it quite a bit when adjusting still pictures and items such as titles.

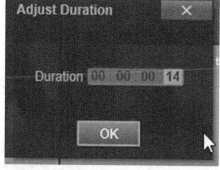

Check out the movie again, and I think you will agree that the tighten does help make the sequence more dramatic.

Adding more shots

There are still some clips needed to finish telling our story, but we have run out of shots on the timeline. There is no rule that says we can't drag another copy of the source file down to the end of the timeline to extract a few more shots from it. However, this is a good time to introduce you to another way of adding items to the timeline which will lead us to a more sophisticated workflow.

Firstly, you may need to find the Source video in the Compact Library again - chances are it is still on display, but if it isn't then use the tabs at the top of the Compact Library to select the Project 1 bin. If that tab has been lost, open the Navigation side bar and select the bin from the Project Bin area.

The Library clip context menu

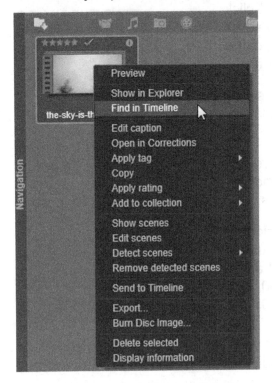

Having used the right-click context menu on a timeline clip, you might want to see what happens if you use it on the clip that is now displayed in the Compact Library. Have a look and you will see a somewhat daunting array of choices.

Preview sends the clip to the Preview player and starts playback. **Show in Explorer** opens a Windows Explorer window open at the location of the file. **Find in Timeline** highlights all uses of the clip in the current timeline.

The middle section relates to Library operations that we will explore in detail later. At the very bottom **Delete Selected** allows you to remove an item from the Library and **Display Information** has the same effect as clicking on the small "i" icon discussed earlier.

Near the bottom there is an option to **Send to Timeline**, though. If you use this it places the selected clip at the point on the timeline occupied by the scrubber. Useful as an accurate replacement to drag and drop, but not essential. Try it now if you like, then use Undo or just delete the new clip.

Using the Source Preview window

Source Preview controls

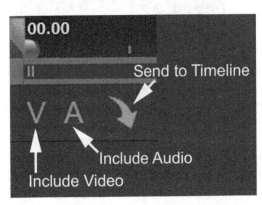

What I want to demonstrate now is a feature of the Source preview window that we glossed over earlier in the chapter. It's a way of selecting a section of a source file *before* we send it to the timeline scrubber position.

When Source is the selected tab at the top of the Player window, there are six additional buttons either side of the transport controls. The **V** and **A** determine if we are previewing

Video, Audio, or if they are both highlighted, both. Make sure they are both orange. Next to the right is a downwards curving arrow. We will use this to send the clip in the window to the timeline in a moment. Notice the tool tip, which tells us that the keyboard shortcut is **B**.

Setting the In and Out point callipers

To the right of the transport controls are three buttons that relate to the orange callipers that appear at either end of the Player window timescale. The callipers are used to mark In and Out points for the clip, with the left-hand one being the In point and the right one being the Out point. The final button resets both markers to the original positions.

You can use a number of strategies to set the In and Out points. Dragging the callipers themselves is easy enough, as long as the timescale is adjusted correctly. More control can be achieved by using the conventional scrubbing and jogging controls, including the keyboard shortcuts, until you locate the desired point and then click the relevant button, or the **I** to set an In point or the **O** to set an Out point.

Highlight the *Sky* video in the Library so that it appears in the Source viewer and scrub along to 1 minutes 5 seconds. Here is a shot of Fred skidding his bike right towards the camera, ideal for the collision if only Velma or Shaggy were on the bike. However, if we start the shot after most of Fred's torso has left the top of frame I think we can use it. Locate the frame where you think this might be with the scrubber and click the In point marker. The calliper moves right to mark the new In point. (00:01:06.25 NTSC, 00:01:06.21 PAL)

For the end we can use almost all of the shot, except the eagle eyed viewer might spot Shaggy emerging in the background just at the end. Jog back a few frames so that he is still masked and set the Out point (00:01:07.14 NTSC, 00:01:07.12 PAL).

Notice how close together the callipers are in the full view of the clip, so for the screenshot I have zoomed in using the timeline scrollbar control.

You can instantly tell the duration of the pre-edited clip by looking at the timecode after the "[ ]" symbol at the top of the preview window.

Now we want to put what is in the Source preview player window into the middle of the shot of the van driving straight towards camera. Select the timeline tab of the Player and park the scrubber at 12.19 NTSC, 12.15 PAL. How will Studio know which track you want to send the clip to? It assumes that you want to send it to the currently active track, so if the Main Track doesn't have the orange line at the left of it's header then click on an empty part of the header to make it active. Switch back to source, and you will see the new clip is still there, with its In and Out points intact. Click the *Send to timeline* button. Resist the temptation to preview the edit if you can - things will be more impressive once we have added another shot.

The In and Out points we have set for the source clip are remembered by the Library, not only if you select another clip then return, but even if you load another project - they will even survive closing down Studio.

To reset the callipers use the Clear button to the right of the Mark In and Out buttons, or use the shortcut Shift-U.

The next shot is going to come from the sequence where the boys are performing jumps. At 00:01:26.19 NTSC, 00:01:26.16 PAL there is the start of a great shot as a bike flies through the air. Silhouetted against the sky, you would have no idea who is on the bike. Mark that as the In point and find the last frame at 00:01:27.16 NTSC, 00:01:27.13 PAL and mark it as the Out point

This time I'm going to ask you to drag and drop the shot in the preview window straight to the timeline. I want you to put it between the close shot of the van and Fred looking out of the window (00:00:14.03 NTSC 00:00:14.03 PAL).

Make sure the Storyboard isn't open before you try. Click on the preview window and hold down the mouse button, then drag in the clip towards the timeline. When you get over the track, the preview window will begin to display the current frame that the green dotted cursor is hovering over.

You shouldn't need to look at the timecodes to find the junction we are aiming for. The frame underneath the scrubber will be in the preview window, and with the correct level of timeline zooming, you can see the Out point of the previous clip - still the front of the van - on the timeline, and the first frame of Fred looking out of the window in the Timeline preview window.

Slide the mouse left and right a little to check you have the exact frame. When you are happy, release the mouse button and the new clip will take its place in the timeline.

The source clip dragged to the timeline

Now you can preview the edits. Turn the sound down first, because that draws attention to some of the dodgy joins. Watch from the beginning, and don't show it to anyone else yet.

OK, I think we have all the right shots, and they probably are in the right order, but it is a bit lame at the end. We are going to help with the sound, but it's not quite as dramatic as it could be. In my opinion, we can make some big improvements with just a few small tweaks to the last few shots.

I suggest you save your project before working on the moment of "impact" as it is possible to get a bit carried away and lose track of where you started from.

After experimenting a good deal with shortening the last shot of the van moving to camera I also felt that the shot of the bike skidding into the camera needed to be shortened as well. I would encourage you to experiment yourself to see how you can improve things. In the end, I shortened both shots to 12 NTSC or 10 PAL frames each, leaving the In points as before and taking the frames off the end of each shot.

If you follow the above recipe then I hope you will agree it has more of an "Impact"!

We are now in the area of creative judgements where there isn't an actual correct answer. Even when I've talked you through what I think will help, you may have a better idea. The odd frame adjustment here and there can make a significant difference. One area you might want to look at is the issue of the continuity of the van. Because we have split the shot, there is a certain amount of *double action*.

Feel free to trim a few frames of the start of the shot and add them to the end of the second shot of the van - and you can even play around with the shot of the skidding bike with the proviso that the total duration of both shots combined is 24 frames NTSC or 20 frames PAL. By the way, when we meet the Advanced trimming tools I'll show you a simple and powerful way of altering the In and Out points without changing the duration of a clip.

Adding an ending to the story

The other thing that could be expanded on is the storytelling. I think a couple of shots of Fred and Daphne at the end might make their evil intentions a bit clearer and give us a less sudden end to the movie.

We can use the shot of Daphne emerging from the back of the van first. Use the Source preview to set the In point to 28.02 NTSC and PAL and the Out point to 31.01 NTSC and PAL. Drop this shot on the end of the current movie.

Although it is a huge time jump, you will be amazed at what the audience are willing to accept. If I'd suggested we used the shot of Fred slamming the door first, however, the jump may have been too severe for most people to accept. We had seen him in the van, and then he would have jumped out. By putting the Shot of Daphne first, we can use it now. Mark the In point as 25.15 NTSC, 25.13 PAL and the end point as the end as 28.02 NTSC and PAL.

Have a look at the whole project, with the sound turned down. I hope you will agree that we have done something interesting, even if it is just a bit of fun. In the next chapter I'm going to show you how we can use the sound track to enhance the movie. It will to be your first introduction to using more than one track as well.

I'm going to add a checkpoint here, because there could be a few small differences between our projects and we will need to have the same material to work on in the next chapter. My version has 14 shots. The easiest way to count yours is to open the storyboard - if you have any "flash frames" they will show up clearly here. The NTSC version has a duration of 21 seconds, the PAL version 20 seconds and 23 frames. A few frames here or there isn't a problem - in fact I'd be surprise if we managed to match up exactly after all this time - but if the difference is more than 10 frames or more, you should load the PAL or NTSC version from the website or data DVD and compare the projects. You can cheat and just use my version if you want, because this isn't a test!

When you are happy that we are telling the story in the same way, save your movie as **Project 1_2**. We will move on to the next chapter using that as the starting point.

Audio and Multi-track editing

In the previous chapter, we have been creating our movie by assembling, splitting, trimming, and re-ordering clips of video on a single track. I've paid scant attention to the sound that comes with the shots. It is very natural for a "film maker" to think about the pictures that tell the story and worry about the sound afterwards – as any professional television or film sound recording engineer is only too aware. Of course we definitely need to hear clearly any dialogue that is required to tell the story, and if that dialogue takes place "in vision" the movement of the speaker's lips must be in sync with what we hear. However, it's just as important that the background audio or "atmosphere" is believable as well, and that cutting between different background sounds doesn't jar – or if it does, it is because we *want* it to jar.

This chapter is going to show you much more than how to fix and enhance audio, though, because later on it explains the basics for all projects that use more than one track, even if those extra tracks are video, stills or titles. We need extra controls and options once we are working with multiple tracks, and in Pinnacle Studio those controls are consistent regardless of the type of media the tracks contain.

Even the simplest of home movies may need to use the natural sound recorded at the same time as the pictures, whether it is your cute child gurgling away, or the roar of an aircraft at a flying display. However, both examples may have sections that are too loud or too quiet, or include distractions such as people talking in the background that make editing difficult.

In the project we have created, we could take the "silent film" approach, remove all the natural audio and plaster some music on. A sophisticated silent film score might even have something to highlight the moment of impact – a crescendo or cymbal crash, for example. In fact, by the end of this chapter, I will have resorted to both those tricks, but as an enhancement rather than a replacement for getting the sound right in the first place.

Listening to the audio

Before you start making any judgments regarding the quality and levels of audio, it's a good idea to "calibrate" how you listen to your sound. I'm hoping you have a reasonable pair of stereo speakers attached to your computer, and that the left channel comes out of the left speaker and the right comes out of the right one! If you don't, or you have to use your computer in a noisy environment (or need to keep the noise down out of respect for others) then consider using a pair of headphones. Play some music with Windows Media Player or get Windows to make some noises and set the volume of your speakers fairly high. Click on the small speaker icon you should have at the bottom of your Windows task bar and make sure that playback levels are high. Each open application can have its own volume setting that you can reach by right clicking on the speaker and opening the Volume mixer.

Windows volume levels.

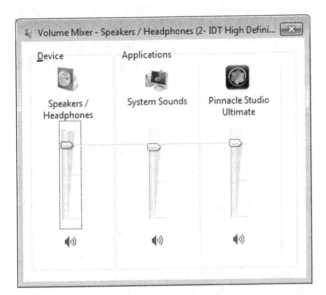

In the previous chapter, I showed you how you could adjust the level at which you monitored audio in the Player window – the speaker icon and popup volume slider. Just to re-iterate, any adjustment you make using these controls doesn't affect the movie. I suggest you set the volume slider to about 80%. Now, if you want to check a quiet section of the movie you can temporarily lift the monitoring level. If you want to play video without listening to the sound, get into the habit of using the mute option.

Now you have established a baseline, load Project 1_2 and scrub to last clip, the one where Fred slams the van door. Highlight the clip on the timeline by selecting it, then click on the loop play button and listen. If the sound of the door slam is reasonably loud without deafening you, then things are well set up.

Master Volume

At the bottom left of the program window, below the track headers, is a meter that monitors the audio playing. This will show the levels either of the source preview, or the timeline.

The Master Audio Meter

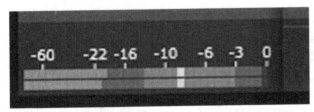

The meter is calibrated in **decibels** (dBs) and as you can see from the numbers, these units aren't linear. The meter responds to peaks of input, and then takes time to "decay" – that is, to fall back - to zero. This helps you read the levels. The coloured bands indicate the safe areas – normal noises should register in the yellow area, loud peaks should get into the orange and only on very rare occasions should you see the red area light up. The penalty for going into or above the red is distortion – the horrible, squared off sound you get from overdriving any audio device (popular with some guitarists). In the past, sending too high a level could be even more of a problem – in the very early days of radio you could actually blow up a transmitter if the signals were too high!

The Mixing Panel tools

To get to the mixing controls, we need to click on the tool bar icon that looks a little like a bar graph. Each track header will be expanded to show three additional controls and have a track meter added to the header area.

The knob that appears at the bottom alongside the master meter controls the combined levels of all the tracks, as sent to the final file or disc when you export a movie. It's best to keep this set to the 0dB setting while you make your project, and only if you want to make a change to the final product should you alter the level. The tracks and all their individual level settings relative to each other are affected globally, so your "mix" will remain the same, but *everything* will get a boost or a reduction.

The knob is a graphic representation, which you don't have to "twist". Hover your mouse over it and you generate a horizontal double-headed arrow; click and drag left and right to make alterations. Play the door slam and try altering the level; at +12dB the meter should go into the red. Single clicking on the knob makes the text box active, and you can enter a value. Double clicking sets it to maximum.

The Audio Mixer

Reset the master volume to 0dB but leave the meter panel open to observe the effect of the next set of controls. The left-most control in each header is the master **track** volume. This applies to the whole track, and if you adjust it you will see the meter levels rise and fall and hear a change in level, but there is no other visual indication that you have changed anything. It too should be set to 0dB at the beginning of a project, giving you leeway to increase as well as reduce the overall level of that track.

For example, you may have placed some music on a new track and then made some subtle changes at various points. When you review your work, you might think the whole level needs reducing, in which case you could alter the master track level.

Before we start using the next control, take a look at the project on the timeline. Make the Main Track even taller if you can. The top of each clip is occupied by video thumbnails, and the lower half is a visual representation of the audio. A green line indicates the level each clip's audio is set to, and by default that is set to 0dB, with the green line three-quarter of the way up. A blue line indicates the stereo positioning (which we will come to later) and is half way up the area, centred over and slightly obscuring the audio waveform. The first half of the project is fairly quiet and the waveform only just peeks out from behind the blue line. The last two clips have louder audio, and the peaks are getting to about 50%. A waveform that goes above 90% is in danger of distorting.

So how do we alter the level setting of a clip? Place the timeline scrubber somewhere in the second clip – Velma and Shaggy cycling – and then adjust the second knob on the main track with the green scale . "Adjust the volume at the current position on the clip" is what the tooltip says, and indeed that is what happens. As you increase the setting to +12dB the whole of the green line moves up until it reaches the maximum height of the audio section. Drag the knob to the left and the level indication line drops to zero. Release the knob and then double click on it and the setting reverts to 0dB.

Altering the level at the scrubber position

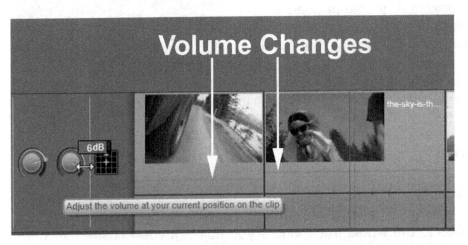

Let's use the control to increase the level of the second clip. The scrunch of bike wheels on gravel contrasts nicely with the noise of the van, so let's bump it up a little to 6dB.

Notice that although the green line moves, the *waveform* of the audio doesn't change in magnitude.

Volume Keyframing

The Volume keyframing button

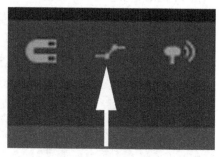

You can drag the green line with your mouse by switching on Volume Keyframing. This is controlled by a button to the right of the magnet, so switch it on (making it orange rather than grey) now.

Move the scrubber to clip 4 – another shot of Velma cycling – and hover your mouse over the green volume level. The line turns white and a small speaker icon appears along with a tooltip. Click and drag the line higher and try to set the level to 6dB as well – the green line will end up at the same height as the one in clip 2. Not so easy as using the knob - there is no indication of level and the line keeps sticking at the "zero" level. When you release the mouse button the volume knob moves to reflect the new position and with the cursor placed over the clip you can check the level by hovering your mouse. If you struggle to do this, use the knob instead.

I would only use this feature if I was setting a clip level very high or low or just lining it up with the previous or next clip. In other circumstances it's a bit too inaccurate for my tastes. However, we aren't yet using the full power of keyframes, because we haven't added any yet.

Before we investigate Keyframing, I'm going to suggest you close the Mixer, but before you do I'll briefly mention the third control. It's the Surround Sound and Stereo Panner. You need to click this to open the Panner box. If you are just working in Stereo, dragging the the blue dot left and right alters the position of the track and the result is reflected on the timeline. You can add keyframes here as well.

If you are making a project that is going to use surround sound, further control is possible from back to front, along with surround options. There are further details in the More Advanced Tools chapter.

If you opened the Panner to take a look, it will close when you shut down the mixer. Play the movie from the top and listen carefully. The first four shots are all contained in clip 1, and the audio that goes with them seems OK. We have slightly boosted the level of the cycling shot , but the next clip contains two shots, the first of which has OK audio. The second shot's audio really jars though – suddenly a radio is playing and someone is laughing and it's clearly not Fred. For now, I'm going to mute the audio here and find something else to replace it with later on. We could split the clip into its two different shots, but this is a good place to introduce the real power of Volume Keyframes.

The Audio Scrubbing tool

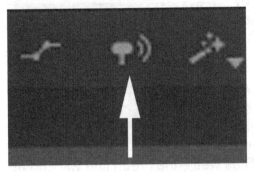

Expand the timeline so that clip 3 occupies most of the width of the timeline. Drag the scrubber along the clip and find the video cut between the two shots. This is where we want the audio to cut. What if you were looking for an audio point and the video didn't have any clues? If the waveform isn't big or different enough for you to identify the change, then you need to turn on Audio Scrub – the button to the right of Volume Keyframing.

Do this now and try scrubbing. If you drag the scrubber quickly you can hear audio as normal, and even slowly it's quite easy to identify where the radio starts playing. When you have found the correct point, you can either just leave the scrubber there or drop a marker on the timeline.

Hover your mouse over the same point so the green line turns white, then click and release. A square green block appears on the volume indication line – it's a keyframe. Now move the mouse slightly to the right and just click to grab the line, then without releasing the mouse, drag it all the way to the bottom of the track and then as far left as you can. Notice that another keyframe is created as you do so.

Keyframing the audio

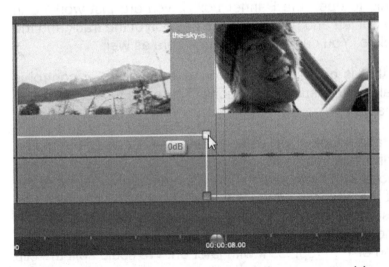

If you drag the scrubber along the clip now, you won't hear any change, but try playing the clip at normal speed with the Space bar or Player controls and the audio should cut out completely at the point we changed the level.

Do you still hear the first note on the radio? I do if I make the level change on the video cut using the PAL video. This is because the audio isn't quite in sync. If you hear the same problem, drag both keyframes to the left one frame. As you are moving the keyframes you may notice that a small tooltip appears telling you the current volume setting.

So the projects match, move the keyframes one frame left even if you are making a NTSC project so the drop in volume happens at 7.27 NTSC, 7.23 PAL.

Volume keyframe context menu.

Adding just two keyframes can be useful, but adding more opens up some powerful options. The easiest way to add them is to click as before, but if you right click on the volume line a small context menu appears that allows you to add a keyframe, delete a keyframe if it is under the mouse cursor, or delete all the keyframes in the current clip.

Move to the first clip of the movie and arrange the timeline for a good view – you could enlarge the track height to its maximum if you haven't already done so. The clip has four shots with four distinctly different audio backgrounds. I'm going to get you to first put a fade up at the beginning, and then boost the level of the second and fourth shots.

Using two keyframes to create a fade up

The first shot is about 2 seconds long. Create a keyframe at about one second into the clip, then create second one to the left. Pull it left and down so it lines up with the first frame of the clip, creating an upwardly sloping line. We have created a roughly one second fade up of the audio – have a listen and I hope you agree it gives a slightly gentler introduction to the movie.

Having created the fade, it's easy to adjust simply by clicking, then holding and dragging either of the two keyframes – you can change the position at which the fade starts by dragging the first keyframe right – or even have the audio start at partial volume by dragging it higher. The duration and final level of the fade is adjustable by moving the second keyframe. A fade down is easy to create by starting with a high level and making the second keyframe lower.

You can also adjust the position of the fade without affecting the levels or duration. When you hover, click and drag on the volume **line**, rather than a keyframe, you can drag the line itself. There are two differing behaviours here. If the line is sloping or vertical, you can only drag it left or right, effectively moving the **position** of the level change.

Dragging the whole fade to the right

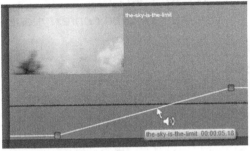

However, if the line is *completely* horizontal, you can only move it up or down, changing the **amount** of the level change.

The best way to get an understanding of this is to have a little mess around. Drag the sloping line of our fade up to the left and right to see the effect – when you can't move the fade any earlier, Studio makes the line steeper, and therefore the fade shorter. Put it back to about 1 second and then add another keyframe about a second from the end of the clip, dragging it down to the bottom to create a fade out. Now see how dragging the downward sloping line affects the position of the fade out. Even if you make the line completely vertical, you can still drag it, so we could use the technique to alter the position of the "cut" we added to the volume of clip three.

OK, that's sloping lines, so now let's create a **horizontal** line. Right click on the new keyframe and delete it using the context menu and we will be left just with the fade up. Now drag the remaining fade up back to end at the 1 second position. Use the scrubber to locate the cut between the view out of the window to the shot of Fred driving – it's at 01:27 NTSC, 01:23 PAL. Click on the volume line to add a keyframe, and then search for the next shot change, back to the view of the trees at 03.08 NTSC 03.07 PAL, and add another.

Now grab the centre of the line between the two new keyframes and try to drag it. It won't go sideways, but it will go up and down – creating another pair of keyframes in the process. Now we can adjust the level just for that shot.

Adjusting a horizontal volume line

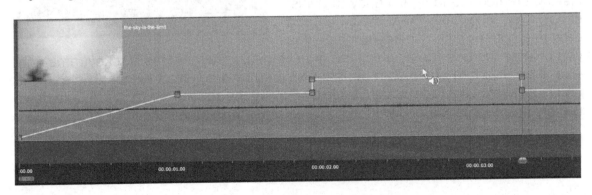

The next trick is a neat way of adjusting levels subjectively, rather than by looking at the waveforms and volume levels and making repeated guesses. You can adjust levels "on the fly" while the clip is playing in loop playback mode. Make sure the first clip is highlighted so that only that clip is looped and then click the loop button in the player. Now grab the horizontal volume line with the mouse. You can adjust it while the clip is playing, and even though the changes don't happen immediately, on the next pass you can hear the result of the new setting. As you are adjusting the levels, take a look at the track meter – even if you push the line up to 12dB, the levels aren't getting into to the orange section, so you can safely set it at full volume.

I'd like you to also boost the level of the fourth shot's audio, starting at 04.15 NTSC, 04.13 PAL. In this case we don't need to add a second keyframe because the clip ends on the same shot. Keyframes aren't needed at clip boundaries. Push it up to +12dB as well.

When you listen back carefully to the whole clip now, you might hear a small but disturbingly harsh "click" at one or more of the abrupt level changes. This is possibly the result of our level change not exactly lining up with the audio cutting in the source video. Fixing it is easy – we transform the "cut" to a very fast fade.

Softening the level changes

Zoom the timeline in so that you are seeing single frame increments on the timescale, then drag the outgoing volume keyframe one frame to the left and the incoming keyframe one frame to the right. Try this on the last two level changes of the clip and you will soften the level change just a little. You could make the fade longer if you wish, but if you make it too slow the effect becomes a little odd.

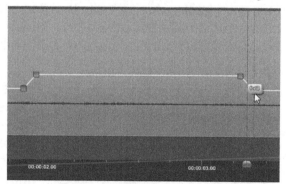

Subtle Keyframe adjustments

You may have noticed that lines tend to snap away from, and back to, their original position. This is always the case when dragging lines, even with magnetic snapping turned off. If you want to make subtle changes you have to drag the keyframes themselves, and even then you need to hold down the ALT key to override the snapping behaviour. If you are trying to join two identical pieces of audio together without the listener being able to spot the join, then you will need to work in steps smaller than that allowed by the snapping, so remember to use the ALT key, and work with the keyframes themselves.

So, that is the basic mechanism for making level adjustments. If you want you can always bring the volume knob into play as well – it will still adjust the level at the current scrubber position even with keyframes in place, where it has the same effect as dragging vertically, but with the extra function that when placed on a sloping line it adds an additional keyframe. For me, the rotary control is less sensitive than the mouse, so unless you actually want to type in the levels via the text box, I'd suggest you work with the volume indication lines themselves.

Something that it is worth getting into the habit of is remembering to switch off the volume keyframing icon once you have finished making adjustments. It is a little too easy to grab or create an audio keyframe when you are intending to do something else with the clip. The snapping behaviour normally lets you repair any accidental damage to your project easily, but it's better that it doesn't happen in the first place!

Detaching the audio

I think we have reached the point where there isn't much we can do with the audio unless we can edit it separately from the video. Pinnacle Studio can do this in a couple of ways but I'll start with the most logical one, specifically designed for audio work.

Our main track contains a clip that has both video and audio, and at the moment any editing action affects both equally. However, it is possible to switch to a mode where you can apply operations to one *or* the other without completely splitting up the clips.

The Detach Audio command

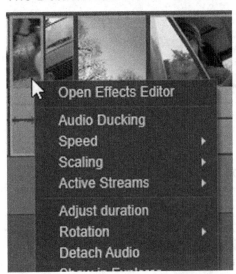

Have a look and a listen to the movie at around 12 seconds onwards. The bike skids towards camera and we cut away from the video before it stops moving. Because we cut away from the audio at the same point, we get a very unfortunate result – what could be a very useful sound effect is cut off in mid flow and just sounds like a mistake. Cast your mind back to when we included the shot – we chose the Out point so as not to see Shaggy emerging in the background - and then shortened the shot even more to improve the pace of the editing. We really don't want to cut off the video any later, but it would be good to hang on to the audio even just for a few frames. So rather than compromise either the video or the audio, let me show you how to split the tracks and edit them separately.

You may hear of this type of edit called a number of things – *Split A/V* (audio/video), *leading the video* or a *L-cut* (you will understand this last term a little better in a moment).

Highlight the ninth and tenth clips together (CTRL-Click) and then right click on one of them to bring up the context menu. We have seen this briefly before when we used Adjust Duration, but now select the next option, Detach Audio. You will see a dramatic change to the appearance to the timeline, although at this point nothing has been altered in our movie.

How the timeline appears after using Detach Audio.

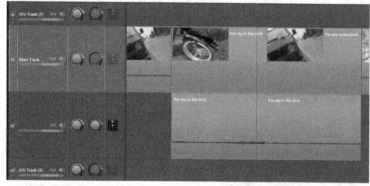

What we had labelled as the Main Track has been divided horizontally into two tracks, with audio from the selected clips moved to the new track immediately below. The video clips that were selected have lost their audio waveforms. These two tracks are more closely linked than if they were two separate tracks – have a look at the space between them and there is no gap. If you try to change the order of tracks by dragging the track header vertically you will see both tracks stick together, and slightly different things happen if you select a clip by clicking on it. Click on the video and both the video **and** audio section below are selected.

If you click on the video again, the audio is deselected. So, the first time you click, both clips are treated as one. Clicking on the audio selects just that clip.

Creating a split A/V edit

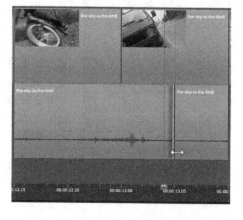

I've a lot to explain now that we have introduced another track into our movie. Before I do, let's perform the edit on the audio. Using Quick Trim, loosen the out point for clip nine's audio track by 6 frames NTSC, 5 frames PAL. With Smart edit on, this will overwrite six frames of the next clip – the audio of the van. In doing so, you will have replaced it with the audio waveform associated with the bike skidding to a halt.

Play the edit and I think you will agree it's clearer now what the sound is. There is nothing wrong with hearing something happening that we can't actually see – it occurs in real life, after all.

You should see now why some people call this an "L" cut – the edited audio clip forms the lower half of a letter L when looked at in conjunction with its video clip.

If you open up the audio mixer, you will see that both the video track and the new audio track have volume controls associated with them. We have left most of the clips unchanged so we need a way to control the sound levels still locked to the video. Drag your scrubber along the timeline and you will see the green volume controls enable and disable themselves depending on the presence of audio on the two tracks that they control.

Video and Audio Track Monitoring

Track monitoring

You may have noticed another change to the track headers. There are two icons to the left of the track names that we haven't used yet. The first looks like an eye and when you click on it you turn off video monitoring. Note that unlike the case with audio in the player window, Timeline Monitoring means inclusion in the final product, so switching off the eye means not only that no video on that track is shown in preview, but it is *also excluded from the final movie*.

Studio has automatically turned off the video monitoring for the lower track and shows this with a red line through the icon. In most circumstances this is a good idea, although on rare occasions you might want to re-enable it by clicking on it again, removing the red line.

To the right is a speaker icon, and this controls the audio monitoring for each track. It actually works like a mute button and you can see the track volume control grey out when you click it. Try it now on the lower track and when you play the section we have just edited, you won't hear any audio over clips 9 and 10. If you were to make a file of the movie as it currently stands, there wouldn't be any audio for this section on that, either.

If you look at the top of the track headers, you can also see the eye and speaker icons that control all the tracks at the same time. If you have turned some video and audio tracks off, you can re-enable them by toggling these controls off and then back on, or if you decide you just want to just export the video or the audio to a movie file, these controls work globally.

There is a powerful tool hidden in the context menu for clips. It is named **Active Streams**. Open it now by right clicking on clip 8, which ends with the first shot of the van approaching - and hover over the option. A submenu shows that both Video and Audio are checked. Now look at the setting for the video section of clip 9, and you will see the Video is activated and greyed out (you can't turn it off) but Audio isn't checked. Check it now and you will see the audio waveform re-appear underneath the video thumbnail. We have put the audio back! Now check out the audio clip below – Video is disabled and if you enable it, video thumbnails appear on the second track as well. After experimenting, return clip 9 to it's previous state.

The Active Streams command

So, with the *Active Streams* option we can turn the video or audio off on any clip. We cannot switch off both, but I cannot think of a reason why we would want to. This is going to be more useful when we start using additional tracks, but it is worth bearing in mind when using *Detach Audio* because although we can't "re-attach" audio, we **can** re-enable it as an active stream to the video only track, which is in

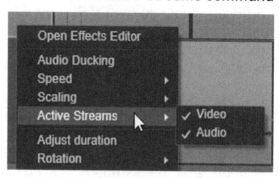

effect the same thing. All we have to do then is delete the detached audio track using the track header context menu and we are back to square one.

By the way, if you have applied any volume changes to the audio of an A/V clip, they **are** transferred to the detached audio track. If you re-enable audio on a video only clip, the original volume changes will be restored, but any changes you made to the detached audio **won't** be transferred back.

The penultimate shot of Daphne at the back of the van at around 16 seconds has more than two people laughing and talking. This is distracting. Let's use the Active streams control to disable the audio. Although it is slightly more long-winded than using the mouse to alter the volume level to nothing, it removes the waveforms from the clips, giving a clearer display.

Now let's turn our attention to finding some replacement audio. The last clip has a door slam followed by the sound of one girl giving a bit of a laugh or snigger. I think this might work over the previous shot.

We now need to make a copy of this audio. Begin the process by detaching the audio from the last clip on the timeline.

Copying Clips on the Timeline

The next technique I'm going to demonstrate is very useful. It doesn't just apply to audio either – you will find it just as useful for making duplicate video clips, stills or titles.

I want to duplicate the laugh from the last shot. I could go through a few hoops and extract the audio from the source file in the Library. I could use the Windows style Copy and Paste controls but I might struggle to place the copy where I want to. A better option is to use a modified version of Drag and Drop – **Copy**, Drag and Drop.

The difference is in the CTRL key. Click on the detached audio of the last shot to make sure it the only thing highlighted and then hold down CTRL, before clicking again on the audio and dragging it left. Note the "double" mouse pointer that indicates you are copying a clip. Don't let go of the mouse button until I tell you to!

Oh dear – although we have created two copies of the same clip, the original has shifted position to the right to make sure there is room for the new one. Smart editing is working in Insert mode. What's more, because Smart mode takes into account the content of all the tracks, the Video track above is disrupted as well in order to keep the shots after the disruption in sync.. Keep dragging left and eventually the copied clip finds enough free space for this disruption

Dragging a copied clip in Smart mode

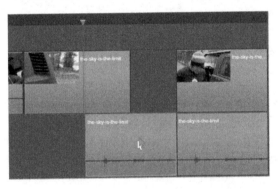 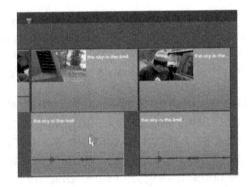

A new Smart mode feature

If version 19 is the first version of Next Gen Studio you have used, then the fact that Smart mode Drag and Drop (and Copy and Paste on the timeline) has changed is of no interest to you. However, if you have used an earlier version then you will have encountered problems trying to re-arrange the timeline once it contains items on more than one track. It was all too easy to disrupt the sync between items.

The new Smart mode is much more user friendly and eliminates many of the issues from the past. I'll look in detail at Smart mode later in the book, but for now let me show you just one example of how earlier versions used to work.

Dragging an item from the Library to the timeline using Smart mode creates a sufficiently large gap on **all** the tracks so that the relationship of the items after the point you are adding the new media stays the same. However, in the past if you dragged an item that was on the **timeline** to a new position, Smart mode worked exactly the same as Insert mode, so only the track that you were moving an item on was affected. Worse still, if you were moving multiple items of different sizes on multiple tracks, differing size gaps would be created, disrupting the sync even more. There were ways of working around this problem, but now with Studio 19, you don't have to!

To see what happened in the "bad old days" you can switch to Insert mode.

Delete the copy of the last clip's audio that we placed under the penultimate shot and use the Edit mode drop-down at the end of the toolbar to switch to Insert mode – the left pointing arrow icon. Now try the above operation again. Notice that as soon as you create the copy, the original audio clip jumps to the right the same amount as the new clip's duration. It's now lining up with the end, rather than the beginning, of the associated video. That means it is out of sync.

Using Insert mode only displaces the audio track

Remember that in the new Smart mode both the audio and video were displaced. Dragging the new audio clip left in Insert mode doesn't pull up the unwanted gap, either. In earlier versions of Studio I would have recommended using Overwrite for the copy operation. Let's try that now.

Use Undo to clear up the mess and try again. Switch back to Smart mode. Let's override Smart by holding down the **ALT**

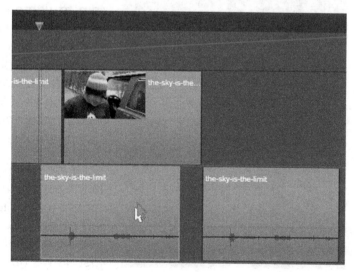

key **as well as CTRL**. Now, when you click and start to drag the audio copy to the left, the original stays where it is and is partially overwritten by the new copy. If you wander into the video track you will see the audio clip overwriting the video - we have flipped the Smart behaviour to Overwrite.

Copying the clip in Overwrite mode

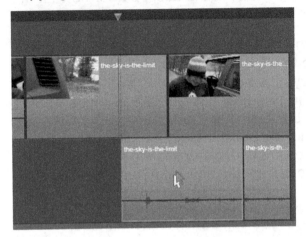

Continue to drag the copy so it clicks into place on the detached audio track with the left edge aligned with the left edge of the penultimate video clip - the result will be the same as working in the new Smart mode as shown on the previous page.

By the way, many keyboards have AltGr key, which will have the same effect as holding down CTRL and ALT at the same time.

With the new Smart mode behaviour it is more likely that you won't need to use overwrite so often but it is still a useful tool. Remember the point I made earlier - if you set about an operation and find yourself in the wrong mode, using ALT works "on the fly" - press the key, drag a little more and you are doing what you intended to do in the first place.

Trimming off the door slam

Play what we have and it is very obvious that the clip has been duplicated. First of all, use Quick trim to tighten the In point of the new audio – don't hold down Alt though as it will pull up the second clip as well, destroying the synchronisation of the the second door slam. Trim off the first door slam we have added to clip 13 – you should be able to do this just using the visual reference of the waveform. If you are having trouble, zoom the timeline in.

Now, it's a lucky coincidence that the start of the laugh seems in concurrence with Daphne's head movement. If it didn't, we could slide the audio left or right to make it coincide. I don't know if you agree, but to me that is a pretty good cheat just as we have it – it really looks like the laugh is sync audio! There is silence at both the start and end of the video now. Let's try to fix the end first. Cast your mind back to dropping the shot of Fred slamming the door into the timeline. I got you to tighten the beginning, so there may be some useable audio before the In point. Using Quick trim again, drag the In point of the last audio clip to the left so that it joins up with the out point of the previous audio.

Review the section – not a bad solution, I think. What about the second laugh in the second audio clip? My first thought was to cut it out completely, but let's try using Volume Keyframes again. After the door slam, create a gentle fade down to -22 dB that finishes just before the laugh. Reducing the volume makes a difference to our perception – we have cheated the "perspective" so the sound seems further away, and because it is lower in level it's not instantly recognisable as the one we used earlier.

Audio edits at the end of the movie

Automatically filling a gap

We need a bit of background audio to fill the silence at the start of the shot of Daphne. There is wind noise all over the rest of the audio, so a bit of wind noise would do the job. We should be able to find something on the original source material. It has been a while since we have used the Compact Library so you may need to switch to the Project 1 Bin. Now bring up the original source video in the Player window by clicking on it in the Compact Library. A quick search reveals the last shot has plenty of wind noise! After our friends have dropped the bikes on the beach, clear the current In and Out points using the player tool or Shift-U and then mark an In point at 00:01.55.00. Switch off the Video by deselecting the V icon bottom left of the player. Now we are ready to put it on the timeline

When we used Send to Timeline before, the clip was placed on the currently selected track. Now that we have a choice we need to click on the audio track header to make it active. Put the scrubber where we want our new audio to start, which is the beginning of the penultimate shot; remember that CTRL-Left and Right Arrow is a good way to navigate to the start of each clip. Now switch the preview back to Source and use the *Send To* button.

What you are seeing is Pinnacle Studio's Smart Mode being *very* smart indeed. It has made an assumption that you want to **fill a gap** with the clip in the source player, and has placed the start of the clip in line with the scrubber but it hasn't overwritten the following clip. Neither has it displaced the following clip to make room for the whole duration of your source clip. It is behaving like Overwrite where there is a gap, but not overwriting any video or audio that is already on the timeline.

That's a very handy feature that saves you time - you only have to define the In point of the new clip and Studio does the rest. However, what if you did actually want to insert? You can defeat Smart mode when using the Send to Timeline button by using the ALT key. However, if we use drag and drop, it's much clearer to demonstrate.

Use Undo and then try the same operation by dragging from the Source preview window. If you aren't aware of what Studio is trying to do, you might get very confused, but once you are aware of the "Gap filling" feature, it makes sense. Drag your clip to a gap in the timeline and it fills it if it can, but never overwrites any other material - here we are seeing Smart Mode do something that you can't do in either of the other conventional modes.

Filling a gap with Drag and Drop

the-sky-is-the-limit   the-sky-is-the-lir

If you don't drag the clip into a **gap** but somewhere that already has a clip, Smart Mode behaves in the same manner as before and creates a gap in all the timeline tracks and ripples the remaining shots right as well. If you hold down the Alt key, Smart is disabled and the drag and drop reverts to Overwrite mode.

The start of the gap is defined as the current cursor position. If you look at the mouse cursor it displays as a "+" sign and an outlined frame.

If we had a suitable untrimmed clip available in the Compact Library, we could also perform this trick using that as a source. It is *very* smart, because as long as we are happy with the start of a clip, Studio automatically makes it fit a gap. If you want to choose a new In point, though, you need to use the Source preview

Please let me stress this again – *this isn't just an audio feature*. There is a further example in the next project where I use it as an example of 3-point editing. If you have a gap on a Video timeline that you want fill, Drag and Drop from the Source viewer or Compact Library is a great way of doing it. You can't use the same trick from the timeline – you would have to trim the clip so it was shorter than the gap, drag it into the gap in Smart or Insert mode and then Quick trim the out point back to the exact duration of the gap. There is a conceptual difference to how a clip behaves depending on where you drag it from, which is an important point to remember.

Don't Panic

Even as I write this, I can remember my own growing confusion when I first began working with Avid Studio, the first version of Next Gen Studio. My predominate editing experience was with Classic Pinnacle Studio and I suspect that even after this length of time some readers of this book may be moving on from that software as well. If you are starting to feel a bit swamped because I'm introducing concepts such as Smart Editing, Overwrite and Insert as part of a narrative please stay calm! These will be summarised and expanded on with further examples in Chapter 6.

Automatically replacing a clip

Replace Clip operation

I want to show you another of Studio's clever tricks. You can drag a clip from the Compact Library or the Source Preview window and get it to **replace** another clip. The new clip will take on the duration of the old clip. As an example, I'm going to change the audio for clip 5 – Daphne in the van – because it has the radio playing in the background.

- Detach the audio of clip 5.

- Switch to the Preview Source tab and make sure the "Sky" footage is selected.

- Make the Preview Video Stream active – the V button as well as the A button.

- Clear the current In/Out points.

- Scrub to the second shot from the beginning where the camera starts on Fred's arm as he is driving the van.

- Set the In point to 00:00:02.00 but don't bother with the Out point.

The keypress that you that need to remember for a *replace* operation is **SHIFT**. Hold it down and then drag from the Preview window to the timeline. Wherever you put the cursor the shot underneath is replaced with the one from the Source Viewer. When you have had enough of trying this out, drop the clip on the detached audio under clip 5.

I asked you to switch the Video stream on in the Source Player window because the effect of using replace is more clearly demonstrated with a video clip. Deselect the video now by right clicking on the new clip and unchecking the video stream.

There are a number of points worth making about the replace operation:

- You can select SHIFT *after* you start the dragging operation in the same manner as ALT, so changing your mind is easy.

- You can replace timeline clips with either video or audio from the Source viewer or Library even if either the Video or Audio stream for that clip is not active, as long as you aren't trying to put a video only clip onto a detached audio track.

- You cannot swap a photo for a video or vice versa.

- If an effect has been added to a clip, that effect is inherited by the replacement.

Using Track Monitoring

There is one gap still to fill in the audio. We lowered the level of the sound in clip 3 over the picture of Fred and we need the same sort of atmosphere as we have just laid under Daphne's shot. I will use this as an opportunity to show you when you might want to use the track monitoring features. Use Ctrl-Alt Drag and Drop to drag a copy of the audio we have just put under clip 5 and position it under clip 3, lining up the start with the level drop on the audio track above. It isn't quite the correct duration, but don't bother trimming it exactly for now. When you play the timeline it is pretty obvious that we have repeated exactly the same audio. I'm going to try and shift it a little by finding the end of the usable audio and lining this up with the end of Fred's shot, then trimming the start instead.

Extend the Out point of our "new" audio using Quick trim so that it nearly reaches the next audio clip and play it again. At this point we really can't hear properly, so switch off the Video Main Track audio by clicking on the speaker icon on the track header. *Now* we can hear that it has been extended too far – the atmosphere changes to exterior.

You can use Audio scrub now to find the correct out point – you can even hear audio as you use Quick trim, so there is no need to mark the Out point, just set it with the green trim bar.

Creating new audio for clip 3

Now drag the whole clip left so that the new Out point aligns with the end of the third clip. The magnet doesn't help you here as it doesn't work on the ends of clips – in fact it might be making life harder as it will keep trying to align the In points, so switch it off.

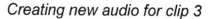
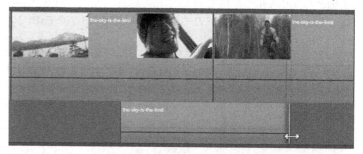

With the out point aligned, trim the beginning of the clip so it aligns with the drop in volume of the clip above.

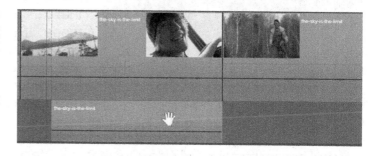

As a final tweak to make it sound a little different, bump up the volume level a few dBs as well. Switch the audio monitoring back on again and have a final listen. Not bad considering what we had to work with. There is a little bit of background radio under the steering wheel shot, but I'm happy to let that go for now. What we need now are some sound effects!

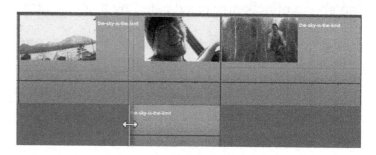

A quick trip to the Library

Any media that you want to include in a project needs to come from the Library. There is a whole chapter dedicated to this powerful feature of Pinnacle Studio later in the book, so for now I'm just going to guide you through the steps to find the two sound effects required and how to add them to the *Project 1* bin.

At the top of the Compact Library are a series of tabs. I can't be sure how many tabs you might have open at the moment, but you should have *Bin:Project 1* available as one tab. If there any others present, then remove them by clicking on the x symbol at the end of each tab. Now create a new tab by using the **Add new tab** button to the right of the *Bin: Project 1* tab. The resultant new tab will be called *Bin: The Sky is the Limit*, which is the default new tab. (This may change in later version of Studio 19, but whatever appears,don't worry as we are going to change it anyway).

Hover the mouse or click on the sidebar that says "Navigation". This will open a tree view which we have used before, but for the next step I want the Navigation area to remain in place when you move you mouse away.

The Library Pin tool

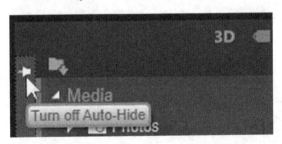

It is possible that you have already discovered a feature of the Compact Library Navigation bar - a small pin icon that can be used to switch off the Auto-Hide mode. If that is the case, you may have already turned that off and the tree is permanently displayed. If you haven't, do so now by clicking on the pin. In normal use you might want to use the auto-hide function as it saves some screen space, but this next demo will be much easier with in off.

You will notice the coloured side bars that indicate the type of assets - Content, where the sound effects are, is indicated by a yellow stripe.

Navigate by opening branches of the tree and scrolling down to find Sound Effects/UFX vehicles 2 and click on it. The current tab changes to yellow and displays the contents in the window below. There should be a set of audio icons or a list of files and I want you to highlight the one called Car Crash. In the preview window you should see an audio waveform appear. Click the play button or space bar to listen to what we have loaded.

It is possible that a small window opens telling you about a render operation – that is just Studio converting the audio for use if this is the first time you have used it, so wait a moment.

Now, we could use this effect straight from the content folder, but it's very good practice to put it into the *Project 1* bin and there are a number of ways of doing this. One would be to use Quick Import as we did with the footage we are using, assuming we could find it on the hard disc. We could also use the Main Import tab. However there are three easier ways.

The Context menu for all items has an option to Add to Project bin. Right click on the Car Crash thumbnail and select Add to Project Bin. You are offered a choice of bins, so select *Project 1*.

You can also Drag and Drop. The other sound effect I want you to use later on is in the Cartoons folder and called *Bedspring*. Locate it,Scroll the navigation tree up to the top so that the *Project 1* bin is in view, then Drag and Drop *Bedspring* into the bin's title. Be warned though - if you are trying to drag and drop from a Project Bin or Collection, be sure to hold down the CTRL key to force the operation to **Copy**, rather than **Move**, the item. This is because these are linked locations, rather than permanent ones.

There is another way - Copy and Paste. You can right click and select *Copy* from the context menu, then switch to the target bin by selecting the tab at the top of the library. Now right click on an empty area and select *Paste*.

New content in the Project 1 bin

Let's now work on the Car Crash effect. Highlight it so that it opens up in the source preview.

You can use the waveform, in conjunction with your ears, to set In and Out points. We don't want the car approaching, just the squeal (04.15 NTSC, 04.13 PAL), and you can trim the end to just after the last bit of falling debris – (08:09 NTSC, 08.07 PAL). We are going to use another timeline track for this effect; drag it from the source viewer to A/V track (3) so that the beginning lines up with the shot of the trees beginning to tilt - the eighth clip on the Main Track.

Let's be tidy. Right click on the track header and use Edit Track Name to change the title of the track to Audio FX 1. This doesn't mean that we can't put anything else on this track, but as we don't have to, we won't! In a more complex project you might want to keep all your tracks bunched up so they will fit on the screen, and a track might contain different types of media for different parts of the movie.

We could put our audio on any track that was free – all the audio gets mixed together so you hear everything. I've not used track one for a good reason though - Video handling is different to Audio. If you imagine the tracks as layers of paper on your desk, you will only **see** what is on the top layer. Because the video we have fills the entire screen, we can't see anything placed below it. If I wanted to overlay a title or logo on the video, to see it over the main track, it would have to be on a track above – in this case A/V Track (1). So it is good practice to leave that track empty.

Back to our sound effect. If you preview the movie around the crash area, I think you will agree that the sound effect isn't working. A bit of analysis leads me to the conclusion that the actual bang is happening far too early. Drag it right and you will see the Timeline Preview keeping up with the scrubber so it should be easy to line it up with the cut within clip 8 of the van approaching. Listen again. I think it's too late this time - the crash happens when the bike is already in mid-air. We want it to happen just a fraction after we cut away from the skidding bike shot.

There are a number of strategies you could use to get this right. You could use trial and error to drag the sound effect left a bit and see if you get it right. When we look at advanced trimming you will discover another approach. What I am going to talk through now though is a "quick and dirty" method.

Multi-track clip splitting

Audio scrub through the timeline until you think you have located the start of the crash. Make sure no clips are highlighted by clicking on a bit of grey timeline background. Now I want you to split the clip – so click the razor or press the N key. What happened? Not only did the Audio clip get split but the Video clip above was also divided into two.

Here is a new behaviour that I alluded to earlier when I mentioned that clip selection was important when splitting clips. If no clips under the scrubber are selected, when you use Split Clip, **everything** under the scrubber gets split.

Use Undo and select only the sound effect, then split again. That's better, just the audio clip got cut into two parts.

You might want to try a quick experiment to see what happens if there are three (or more) clips under the scrubber. Move the scrubber right to around 16 seconds where three clips all stack up, then select any two of the clips and use the split command. Yes – **both** the selected clips are split. Use Undo to mend the splits.

Back to the audio on track 3. Select and delete the first part, then switch the magnet off because we want frame level accuracy. Grab the sound effect and start to drag it left; watch the preview window because the scrubber is now showing the frame before the one where the clip is going to be dropped. When you see the first frame of the van approaching camera, release the clip.

If you play the timeline now, the crash occurs an instant after we cut away from the bike skidding, and is decaying by the time the bike is in the air. We have placed the audio in the optimum position, I think. However, by using "Split clip" as a way of marking, we have cut off the squeal, and it would be good to get that back. Simple – Quick trim to loosen to the In point.

The sound effect in its final position

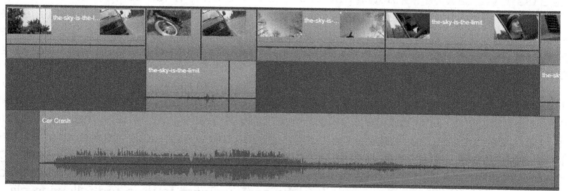

Create a handle to the **right** of the beginning of the sound effect and drag **left** to reveal the waveform. With audio scrub turned on, you will hear the screech getting quieter. You should end up with a new In point about a third of the way into the "trees" shot. Scrubbing does tend to slow down some editing functions, so don't forget to turn it off again.

Overtrimming

If you drag way too far, you will see the audio clip that is revealed is a darker colour. This is to indicate that you have *overtrimmed* the clip. If some of a clip is displaying as a different colour then you are trying to use a part that doesn't exist. In the case of audio you will get silence, for video you will get a still frame. It's probably easier to trim the Out point to see this on the current audio clip. Later in the book I may refer to the result of overtrimming as "dead meat".

Now that the tyre squeal is restored, review the timeline again to check your work. At this point I think the whole crash effect is too loud relative to the other audio. A glance at the main meter shows it nearly going into the red, so reduce the overall level of the clip to -12dB for now.

Trimming Gaps

Now, I was very specific about how to trim the clip because you may have been tempted to try and trim using an Out point handle to the **left** of the clip. That's not a bad instinct, but because of Smart Mode you might have got a bit of a surprise as to what actually would happen. I'm going to get you to try a few experiments now, so let's do an incremental *Save as...* of the project in its current state, calling it Project 1_3.

Pinnacle Studio sees the area to the left of the sound effect on the Audio FX 1 track as a **Gap**. We saw earlier how a gap is treated differently when using Drag and Drop. When you generate an In or Out point handle in a grey area of unoccupied timeline you are about to trim the gap and not the clips either side. When you use Smart Mode to trim a gap, it works in **Insert** mode (when you Quick trim a clip it works in Overwrite mode).

This behaviour is actually very helpful, as long as you remind yourself that it is a gap you are trimming. This will be clearer if we look at a situation where there are clips at both sides of the gap. Take a look at the gap in the Main audio track at around the 14 second mark. There are a number ways of making the gap smaller – loosening the Out point of the audio before or the In point of the audio after, or drag and dropping the audio clips. If we trim the gap, it works as if we were to drag the following clips to the left. This shortens the gap and I'd like you to try it now. Generate an Out point handle for the gap and do a Quick trim operation to tighten the gap - the three audio clips move left (and lose sync with the video above). Try quick trimming the In point of the gap and exactly the same thing happens. Loosening the gap has the same effect, so you should be able to put the three audio clips back where they were.

If you want to trim a gap in overwrite mode, hold down the ALT key. We could have used that technique to extend the sound effect on track 3 using a Out point handle to the left of the clip, but hopefully now you understand the reason why you would need to hold down the ALT key!

By the way, this Smart mode behaviour also occurs if you are only using a single track. You may not have noticed it yet (I haven't asked you to use it) as it seems quite intuitive in those circumstances.

Multi-track deletion

While we are on the subject of Smart Mode, now is a good time to demonstrate the different behaviour you get with Delete when there are multiple overlapping tracks.

If you delete a clip from a single track, the gap is automatically closed in Smart mode. Delete clip 2 to see the effect – everything to the right is moved up. However, if there is something on another track above or below that overlaps the clip you delete, that gap is only reduced as much as is possible without removing any more material. So if you try to delete the bike skidding shot (the ninth clip on the Main track), nothing moves at all.

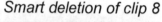
Smart deletion of clip 8

Even more interesting is what happens if you try to delete the shot that starts with the sky rotating (the eighth clip). A *little* of the gap is closed up, but we don't lose any of the sound effect. This is very Smart indeed!

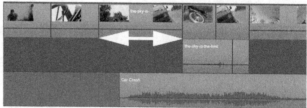

As usual, to override Smart, you hold down ALT – and there will be no attempt to pull up the gap. (Remember ALT needs to be used with the Trash icon to delete, the Delete key doesn't work with ALT).

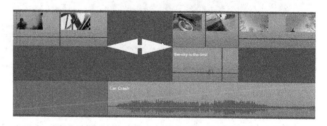

If you switch to Insert mode, the gap is pulled up with no regard to the other track – they stay where they are and any synchronisation you had is lost.

You have probably made quite a mess of the timeline by now, so try a few more deletions to get the hang of this, then reload the project as saved. One more question may pop into to your mind. "What if I wanted to exclude one track from all this automatic behaviour?" A good question, the answer to which is *padlocks*.

Using the Track Locks

At the far left of the track headers are a row of buttons that look like unlocked padlocks. Click on one of them and that track becomes locked and no editing operations can effect it. A locked track is indicated by grey hatching.

Try locking the audio effects track and applying a split where three tracks are occupied – if you hadn't selected any clips you would normally split all of them, but in this case the sound effect is left alone. Now delete clip 2 – again the audio moves up with the video because we are in Smart mode, but the sound effect on track 3 is unaffected by the Smart operation. Repair the damage with a couple of undos.

Three locked tracks, with only Audio effects enabled for editing

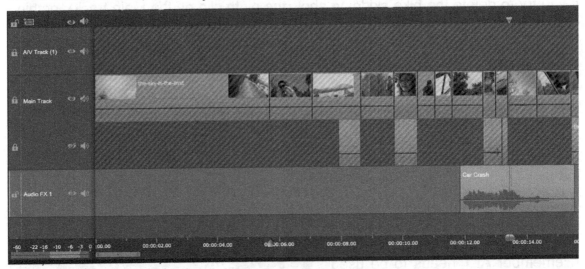

Locks can be very useful at times. Let's say you are building up a music video that included titles that displayed the lyrics of the song. You don't want either the music or titles to move in any circumstances, and if you continue to add video to other tracks in Smart mode, Studio will be constantly trying to maintain synchronisation of tracks by splitting the music and moving the titles. You could switch off Smart mode and lose the advantages on the tracks you are editing, but much better would be to lock the music and the title track and carry on using Smart mode on the remaining tracks.

Top left of the track headers is another lock that is global. If you click it, all the padlocks are closed on all the tracks. Click again, they are all released. Now, with all the locks on, the whole of the content on the timeline is covered in hatched lines and you can't perform any operations on it at all. This is handy to stop you making changes by mistake, but not much else. Where global locking can be useful is on a complex project where you can't see all the tracks. Locking everything and then unlocking just the track you want to modify ensures that you don't forget a track currently scrolled off the bottom of the timeline window.

The Navigator

Another aid to working with more than a few tracks is the Navigator. I've been putting off opening this until we have a complex enough timeline to justify using it. The toolbar item used to enable Storyboard view can also be used to bring up the Navigator display. Use the drop-down arrow to select the strip icon, and then click on the icon to display the Navigator.

What you see now is a very upmarket timeline scrubber that takes into account multiple tracks. The Navigator has a fixed height, unlike the Storyboard; the more tracks your project displays, the thinner the representation of those tracks. Each clip is coloured to represent the type of media, so Video is blue, for example. The currently selected clips are shown as bright orange, regardless of the type.

The Navigator and context menu

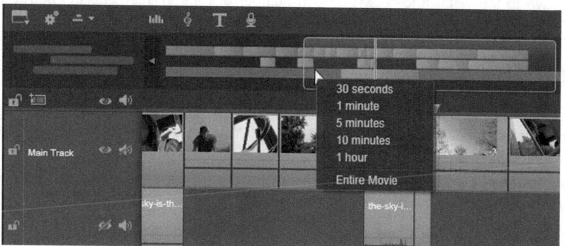

Even for projects with just a couple of tracks there are some good reasons to consider using the Navigator, particularly if it is a lengthy one. Right-click on any part of the Navigator and you can choose how much time occupies the full width of the timeline from the menu. Arrows at either end allow you to scroll, and you can also drag the viewing area left or right with the mouse. A double click on the shaded area will fill the display with the entire movie.

This feature is of particular use when you run out of display real estate. Either your project has grown a lot of tracks, you are working with a small display, perhaps on a laptop, or a combination of both. As in the screenshot, some tracks may be scrolled off the display, but the Navigator is there to remind you what content is on the lower tracks. If you don't have a massive screen, leave the navigator enabled while you work through the next part of the chapter as it will help you to see the full effects of the actions I'm going to demonstrate.

Clip selection and detached audio

New rules apply to Studio 19.1 and above. When you click on a video clip, any audio on the detached track below which overlaps the video **and has originally come from the same video file** will be added to the selection. If you have a sound effect, music or audio from another file on the detached audio track then that will **not** be automatically selected.

It's important to realise that when audio is associated with the video above it isn't necessarily in sync – we can prove this by shifting the clips a little and observing the door slam. If you want to restore exact sync you can always make the audio stream active to the video track – we have a number of clips in this condition and it is impossible to spoil the audio synchronisation – at the expense of not being able to perform a split A/V edit.

Multiple clip selection

I've mentioned how you can select a group of clips by using CTRL-click. You can also draw a box around clips to select them all. You can even use those commands together to build up quite complicated selections.

Another Windows selection method that works is CTRL-A – Select All. Try this on your project and all the clips will be highlighted.

Once a group of clips is selected you can de-select individual clips by CTRL-clicking them.

In Windows, selecting an object then holding down Shift and selecting another object adds every object between the select objects to the group. The same happens on the Studio timeline. (In version 19.0 this was not the case so if the following example doesn't work, check that you have patched to the latest version.)

Click on clip 1 and then Shift-click on clip 4. The two video clips in between are included in the group. The new behaviour in version 19.1 means that the detached audio below clip 3 is also selected. Even though it isn't in sync, it is from the same source as the clip above.

Shift selection on a single track showing the behavior of detached audio

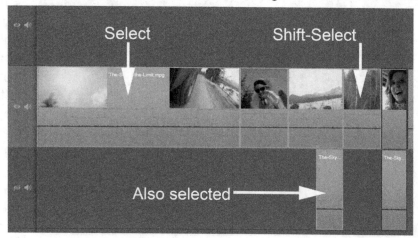

Shift selection can also span tracks. If you click on clip 1 and then Shift-click on the Car Crash sound effect on the Audio Effects track, all the clips that start before the end of the sound effect (and their associated audio clips) will be selected.

Shift selection across tracks

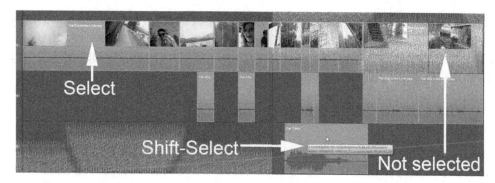

Selecting everything to the right

Pinnacle Studio has a further timeline function for selection that is potentially very useful. If you hold down CTRL *and* Shift then click on a clip, the clip and everything to the right, on all the tracks, is selected. Try it out on clip 8, the tree tilting shot. Everything that starts at the same point or later is added to the selection. Now try clip 10 (13.01). In this case the Car Crash sound effect and the extended audio from the bike skid isn't included because although they are active at the same time as the start of clip 10, they begin earlier.

Selecting all the clips to the right

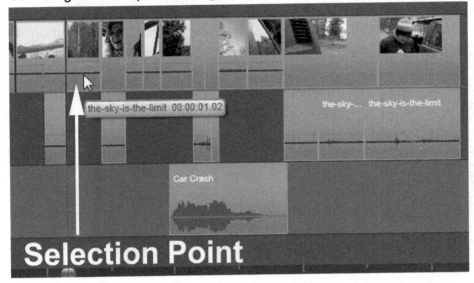

This feature is great for shuffling everything right to make space for a new clip, or left to close a gap, while making sure you are moving everything needed to maintain sync.

Use the CTRL-Shift click option then click and drag the whole selection. You can even move the group up or down the track layout, until you try to put it somewhere that there aren't enough tracks, when the group snaps back to the original position.

If you drag the selection into the area of the project that already has content, you will see that the new Smart mode Drag and Drop works correctly, creating the same size gap in all the tracks as the largest track in the dragged selection. If you want Overwrite, hold down the ALT key as usual.

Moving clips in a multi-track project

In the past dragging a group of clips from one part of the timeline to another didn't do wonders for our sync. The new Smart mode behaviour solves all that.

If you want to work in Insert or Overwrite mode, however, the workflow required to perform this kind of operation without destroying the sync isn't too difficult. First, switch to your chosen mode then make a gap after clip 1 that is big enough to accommodate the clips we want to move. Do this by CTRL-Shift clicking on clip 2 and dragging the whole group 5 seconds to the right.

Now select the last clip including its audio and drag it left into the gap. If you are in Insert mode the audio to the right is shifting more than the video, so hold down ALT and drag a little. Good – now both the audio tracks have popped back into sync. IN this particular case the magnet makes lining up the clip we are moving with the first clip a bit tricky, so drop the clips in the gap, zoom the timeline in and then drag them again to line up the edges of the video. The audio will overlap under the first clip. Drop the clips there then double click the navigator to see the whole project and then CTRL-Shift click in what is now the third video clip to select everything that needs to be pulled up and drag the group to align with clip 2. That wasn't too hard, was it?

Making a gap before moving a clip selection

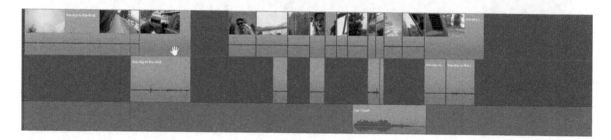

Dragging from the Album or Player

Smart mode does have another useful feature to help you build up multi-track projects without constantly having to re-build the sync between clips. When dragging a new clip from the Compact Library or Source Preview in Smart mode, Insert mode is applied to **all** the tracks, not just the one you place the clip on.

Try this. Load the saved project **Project 1_3**, then right click on the first clip to bring up the context menu. Select Find in Library and the Sky footage should appear in the Compact Library. I'm going to suggest you add another shot between Fred looking out of the window and Daphne appearing at the back of the van. At 24 seconds exactly there is a bit of panning left through the trees. Mark that as the In point, then find the last frame, which is less than half a second later, and mark it as the Out. Drag it from the Source Player window to the timeline and try to insert it between the shots of Fred and Daphne at around 14 seconds into the project.

Insertion from the Source viewer in Smart mode

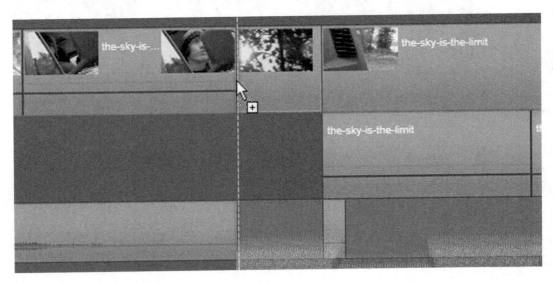

Notice how a suitable gap is made for the clip. When you have it located correctly, Smart mode even splits the sound effect on track 3 for you. Drop it in place and review the result.

OK, so it doesn't really have the affect I thought it might, but it was easy to insert! The door slam is still in sync. If you reselect the clip and delete it, we are almost back to how we were, except a split has been added to the sound effect. It is only a short overhang, so you may as well delete it – perhaps that is where we should have ended in the first place, but having the overlap helped the demonstrations earlier.

Grouping

A new feature introduced in Studio 18 allows you to define a selection of clips as a group. This in effect turns them into a single clip for the purposes of selection.

This feature is useful for both Video and Audio. If you have added a title to particular video clip, or perhaps something more complex such as a Video overlay, then grouping is a way of ensuring that when you select one asset, the other gets selected as well.

Forming a group of clips

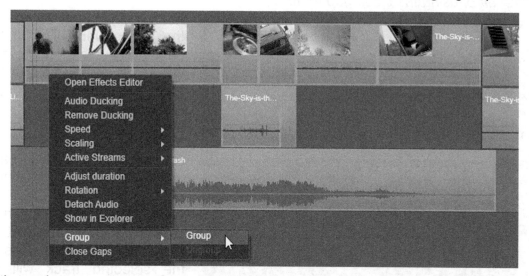

Let's see how we can use Grouping to help keep the audio and video together. Hover just above Video clip 6, click and draw a box around the 7 video clips and 3 audio clips that make up the collision. Now right-click on any of the highlighted clips and select Group from the context menu, then select Group from the submenu.

Deselect the clips and now try to select just one of them. You will find that all of them are selected automatically. Now drag the group around the timeline – and you will see how it behaves just as if you has multi-selected the clips.

Put the grouped clips right at the end of the timeline and experiment with something else. Select a single clip from elsewhere on the timeline and drag it into the group of clips. The clips will be disrupted in the same manner as if they weren't grouped. It's important to understand that grouping doesn't convey any special qualities to the selection of clips other than selection. The components of the group aren't locked into sync with each other and can be split just like a single clip.

Closing Gaps

Another recently added feature is the *Close Gap* command. You can find this by right-clicking on any gap in the timeline.

Close Gap has been improved in PS19. but it's still a bit of a dangerous function to use on multi-track projects. Firstly, it acts on just one track, and secondly it doesn't respect grouping. To demonstrate the function, right click on the gap between the first and second clips on the detached audio track of Project 1 and select Close Gap.

The result of using the close gap feature

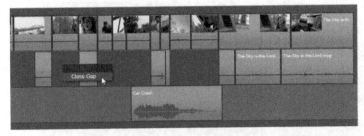

From this you can see that all the subsequent clips in the detached audio track are also pulled left by the size of the gap, destroying the relationship between the tracks.

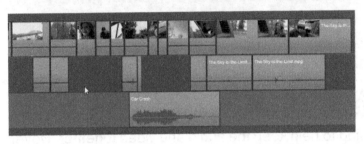

A more complex, and potentially timesaving version of this feature is *Close All Gaps*. This appears if you right click on the empty space at the end of a track. All the gaps on the selected track will be removed, and all the clips will end up at the beginning of the timeline. If you go through a long clip on the timeline snipping out sections you don't need, then this command will remove all the gaps left behind with two mouse clicks.

The result of using Close All Gaps on the detached audio track

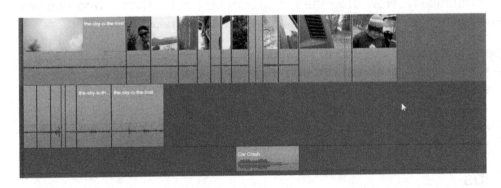

We have certainly covered a lot of ground regarding multi-track working in the last few sections. There are further examples of using Smart mode later. Before we return to the project in hand, let me stress once more that these multi-track techniques are aimed at both video and audio – making a mess of the sync between clips is very obvious with audio, but can also be critical with video, as we will see.

Lightening the mood

Now, I don't expect we are going to fool many people into thinking that crash was real. The sound effect is too exaggerated. I did say "comedic" when describing the project, so let's try to make it a bit more lighthearted. Reload **Project 1_3** if you aren't sure you can restore it to it's correct layout.

Adding the Bedspring effect

Go to the Project 1 bin and select the Bedspring effect we added earlier so that appears in the source preview.

Set the In point using the waveform to trim off the silent frames from the beginning.

Now drag the sound effect from the Player Window down to track 4 to line up with the start of the shot of the bike flying through the air. Have a listen to the levels. Maybe down a bit? I've set the volume to -6dB.

Adding Scorefitter Music

I'm going to add one last embellishment. This has little to do with timeline editing and all to do with adding some polish. You may be disappointed that some of our audio work has been covered up – extending the bike skidding sound for example - but I'm going to cover it up a little more now. There is still that steering wheel shot with a random radio playing in the background, and a little mood music might help the atmosphere.

We have nearly run out of tracks. We could put the music on track 1, but as I explained earlier, it's best to leave that free for titles. Let's add another track at the bottom. Right-click on the track header of track 4 and select *Insert New Track/Below*. I'd like to think you were tidy-minded enough while we are here to rename track 4 as **Audio FX 2** and track 5 as **Music**. Even track 1 as **Titles**?

Are you having trouble seeing everything on screen? Try *All Track Sizes/Small*. Still a bit of a squeeze? You can manually adjust the tracks to be a little thinner that the Small size, but I like to keep the Main Video track a bit bigger. There is a "hidden" boundary between the Video and Audio sections of Main Track, so you can increase the height of the video section without enlarging the audio.

Our project could do with a piece of copyright free music, slightly sinister, and 21 seconds long. You could compose it yourself, or find a composer to do it for you. Another option is to use Scorefitter. Ultimate knows 74 basic tunes, Plus somewhat less (unless you buy some more) but it can create up to eight or so variations of each tune to virtually any duration you like. Best of all, using it in *any type of production* with *total worldwide clearance* is completely free.

The Scorefitter tool

You open Scorefitter by clicking on the treble clef icon to the right of the audio mixer button.

The duration box allows you to enter the duration of music you require to be composed for you, and choosing a short duration can limit the variations available.

What is very handy is that if you have selected some clips on the timeline the duration will automatically be entered into the box. Close the Scorefitter box, click on the timeline and use CTRL-A to select the entire movie. While you are there put the scrubber at the beginning of the timeline and click on the music track header so that it becomes the selected track. Now re-open the Scorefitter box. You should see the movie duration in the duration box.

There are eleven fairly self-explanatory categories in the left-hand box, and the songs in each *Category* are listed in the *Song* box. It's handy to use the mouse tooltips here, as hovering over each song title gives a very full description of each piece.

Version on the right contains just that. Short durations offer fewer versions, and below 4 seconds some will only produce silence, but short music stings can make interesting punctuation in a movie.

Click on *Preview* to hear your selection. It's important to note that there may be quite noticeable differences in how songs are arranged for different durations – drumbeats and codas are often added to get the correct duration, rather than varying the tempo.

Have a listen to what is on offer. My choice is *Electronica/Reaction Time/Transit Blur*.

You can save your choice as an audio project to the Library with the ability to change the suggested name. This project can then be retrieved from the Library as a Scorefitter track.

The Scorefitter dialogue

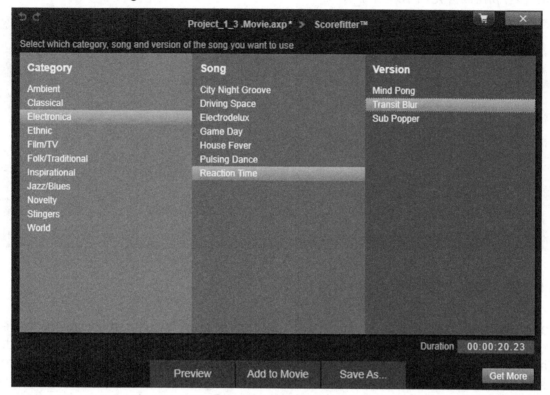

Clicking on Add to Movie places the composition onto the currently selected track at the scrubber position. You can't add to a locked track. Send the track to the Movie and if you got the setup right it should occupy the bottom track starting at the beginning of the movie. If it isn't in the right place it is the work of a moment to drag it to the correct position.

I'm not sure what colour you would call a Scorefitter track on the timeline. Khaki? Anyway, if you double click on it or use the context menu to *Edit Music*, the Scorefitter box reopens, giving you the chance to change the selection and re-send your new choice back to its original location.

How about the final levels? When I first made this project in Pinnacle Studio 16.0, the levels seemed a bit low, but the changes in version 16.1 and now 17 seem to have changed the defaults. I've set the music to -6db and the master level to +3dB, but you might want to tweak things a bit more. Just make sure the levels don't go into the red. Now save the movie with a new name, **Project 1_4**.

The final timeline for Project 1_4

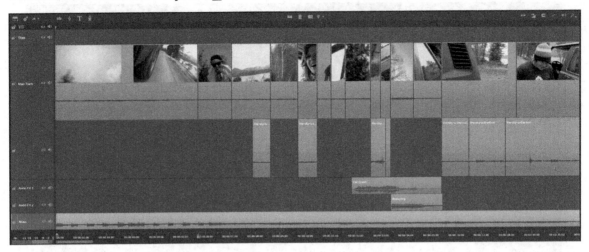

A note about SmartSounds

Many experienced users of Pinnacle Studio prefer to use a program called Smartsounds for automatic music generation, which was included with the older Classic Studio programs. They prefer the quality of the music and may have invested in additional discs. Studio 17.5 came with a free plug-in which will be inherited if you upgraded to S19, or you can buy the plug-in from Smartsounds.

While the basic Quicktracks interface that comes with the plug-in is similar to Scorefitter, you can also pay extra to enable the Sonicfire pro interface, which offers full scoring features. I've used this successfully in the past to create some great music. One downside is the cost, and I'm disappointed that even when you have paid a lot of money, YouTube often claims that you don't have the rights to use the track you have made. It's up to you to prove that you have bought a licence. Fortunately this doesn't apply to Vimeo.

If music is important in your projects, then it's well worth investigating Sonicfire Pro, but it's a complex program that falls well outside the scope of this book.

Simple Exporting

I'm going to stress again that a normal Pinnacle format movie file doesn't contain any video or audio. It is possible to save you movie as a project package, containing the required source files, but even that can't be played by someone without a copy of the editing program.

The Export function deserves its own Chapter, so If you want to skip forward for a full summary, do so now. Otherwise you can follow this quick recipe. Want to make a file to send in Windows Media Player or upload to the internet? The best choice in PS19 for standard definition video is probably MP4, which now uses the latest codecs.

- Click on the Export button top right of the screen.

- Select *File* as Export type, Settings type: *MPEG-4,* Preset *Full Size SD (best quality)*

- Click on Start Export

- In the Save As window browse to a location - the Windows Library *My Video*

- Enter a file name - *Mystery Machine*

- Click Save

- Wait a bit...

Exporting the file

…and your file will be create in the location you specified. You will then be presented with a choice of media player with which to play the exported file.

There are many subjects still to cover in later chapters. In particular, studying the Advanced Trimming feature will pay you good rewards. We haven't looked at adding transitions, titles or effects or the complex issue of making DVD or Blu-ray discs. However, you have made a movie that tells a simple story.

Next I'm going to introduce the Importer, Library and Exporter so that we can add, find and output assets. I'll then turn to the more advanced editing features. If you want to skip ahead, please do so, but there are some powerful features described in the next few chapters that you may not know about.

Using the Library

In the next part of the book we will explore in detail how to import, store and export content before returning to editing itself.

In this chapter I'm going explain how to quickly link items that are already stored on your computer to the Library; we can then go on to understand how the Library works. I'll then expand on more complex and powerful Import functions, including the use of Analogue, DV or DVD sources in the following chapter.

What is a Library?

Computers store data within various folders on their hard discs and in the past you had to obey the folder structure. Windows has moved on to introduce Libraries – places where a user can find all their documents, music and so on without having to address the actual folders which contain the data. Libraries are easier to search and organise – your *My Music* library (or iTunes Library) only contains music. Tracks are rated, can be sorted by criteria such as *Artist* and you can generate playlists.

The Library concept used by Pinnacle Studio 19 takes this a step further. It is a database that contains any items that you may want to include in your project. Some of these items are put there by default – Transitions, for example. Other items such as captured video, music tracks and photos will be unique to you. You can choose which of these are included in the Library. The items are still stored in the same place on your hard disk, but their locations are tracked in the Library database.

If you can't see the advantage in this and are comfortable with organising your assets within folders the way you have always done, it is possible just use the Library as a clever search facility, far better than any Windows based *"Open…"* dialogue box. There are a couple of steps you need to take in order to work that way and I'll show you how to do that beginning on page 120.

The two Library sizes

The Library exists in two forms:

The Main Library – this is the program window that opens when you click on the *Organize* tab on Main Control Bar. The whole screen is dedicated to displaying the contents of the Library.

When you open one of the other main tabs – Edit or Author, the Library shrinks into **The Compact Library** – the window that occupies the top left portion of the screen when you are using the Movie Editor or Disc Editor. In addition the Title Editor, Menu Editor and Montage Editor also display the Compact Library. The Compact Library is where you pick all the items that you wish to use in any of those editors.

There are some functional differences between the two forms, but they are essentially the same feature. I'll flag up the detailed differences of the Compact Library later, but for now let's just say that the majority are to save space on the screen. You can do almost everything you might find useful in the Compact Library, but for complete control and a better view you may prefer to use the Main Library. The changes you make to your view are retained when you switch from the Main to the Compact Library, and vice versa.

Media Assets

I'd like reiterate an important concept. **You cannot include any video, photos or audio in any project if it isn't already in the Library.** You, or the Studio program, need to have checked it into the Library before it can be used. This is also the case when you want to include media in titles, menus or montages.

If that sounds a tiresome thing to have to do, compare how you would find a video file in Classic Studio. You would look in the Album, and if it wasn't there, you would have to use the *Browse To* icon to open up the hard disc folder location where the asset was stored. It would then be displayed in the Album so you could drag it to the timeline.

In Studio 19, if the video file isn't in the Library, you can use the Quick Import tool, as described earlier, to find the file. When you open it, the file is displayed in the open window of the Compact Library so you can drag it to the timeline. In addition the file is now registered with the Library until you choose to remove it.

To seasoned computer users this might seem like an unnecessary restriction but it has important advantages – all the media you might want to include can be accessed, searched and categorised in the same way, and any items you don't want to clutter up your view can be excluded.

The program itself can examine items added to the Library before you start to use them – so you can avoid using media that might cause problems.

The way you arrange the media on your computer can be as organised, or as chaotic, as you wish. If your video and audio files are already orderly then you can see that in the Library. If they aren't, then you can bring organization to the chaos using Library features.

There are three main ways of "checking in" media items to the Library: Quick Import, the Import Tab and Watchfolders. We have briefly looked at Quick Import on page 26, the Import Tab and Watchfolders are covered in detail in the next chapter, but in Pinnacle Studio 19 Watchfolders are disabled by default.

Project Bins vs. Watchfolders

Pinnacle Studio 19 introduces a new feature to the Library – Project Bins – and downgrades an old one – Watchfolders. If you have installed Studio 19 as an upgrade over an earlier version where Watchfolders were used, you will inherit the settings from before but they won't be enabled to add more media. Everything will be the same except that the Project Bins feature will be added and the Media category in the Library will be renamed as Library Media.

If you have installed Studio 19 cleanly but used Watchfolders in the past, you can enable them using the Control Panel.

If you are new to NextGen Studio you can ignore the old way of working and just use Project Bins. However, you won't see the Library Media category in the Library. If you want a broader view, it is possible to restore it. Before I tell you how, it will help if I give a bit of background information.

The Watchfolder system allows you to define a number of hard disc locations that are constantly monitored for valid content – they are "watched" – and if new items are found they are automatically added to the Library. By default, the monitored locations were the current user's Media locations. So if you used Windows or another program to place a video file in "My Video", it would automatically appear in the Pinnacle Studio Library. Sophisticated users of Watchfolders could customise the list of locations that were watched. Those users never needed to manually Import anything, even though sometimes things were imported that perhaps they wished hadn't been.

There were issues with using Watchfolders, however. They do add another background process to the running of Studio, and although the impact on performance was normally minimal, it could slow things down in some circumstances. More fundamentally, if a file that wasn't fully compatible with Pinnacle Studio was automatically added to the Library it could bring Studio to a grinding halt. Sometimes it might not even be possible to relaunch the program without resetting the Library.

In older version of Next Gen Studio I worked with Video Watchfolders turned off. Corel seemed to have decided that this is a more reliable way of working as well, and now all Watchfolders are disabled by default. Instead, they introduced Project Bins. These are much simpler to understand but somewhat labour intensive. They coincide with Corel's other video editing package VideoStudio. To some extent they are a duplication of features, because the Library also has Collections that do the same thing (and more), but at least Collections have not been removed.

However, in order to encourage you to use only Project Bins, on a new installation of PS19, Corel's programmers have disabled Watchfolders and also hidden the full library listing of media assets that are available in older versions of NextGen Studio's Library. Fortunately, it's possible to see a full listing of your Library media with a simple workaround.

How to see all your Library Media

If you want all of the media in your Library displayed as part of the tree view of your Library Navigation structure but don't want the Watchfolder process to be running, the following steps need to be taken.

- Open the Control Panel (under the Setup menu) and select the Watchfolders tab on the left.

- Click on the Enable tab

Enabling Watchfolders without any folders listed

- If there are any folders listed as being watched use the Remove All button to delete them from the list.

- Click on OK.

You may be asked if you want items to be removed from the Library. Don't worry that saying Yes will delete them from your hard drive – It won't. Incidentally, if you have folders listed as being watched but the feature disabled, the Library Media tab will still appear.

The Library Media category in the Navigation bar

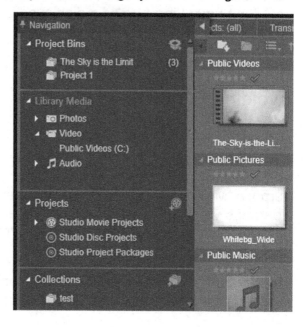

Using Project Bins

I introduced you to Project Bins on page 25. The idea behind them is that when you start work on a project, you create a bin and place items in there for use on that specific project. You can add further items later on if or when you realise you want to use them.

Because the items remain in their original hard disc location, placing them in a bin is almost instantaneous, and doesn't cause duplication of the same data which would take up additional disc space. It's perfectly OK to add the same clip to a number of different Project BIns.

A nice feature of bins is that if you hover over a clip in the Library Browser, the titles of all Project Bins that contain that clip light up green in the Asset Tree window.

If the material needs to be imported from a camera it has to be added to the hard disc first and then linked to a bin. In these and other circumstances you may want to create bins that aren't project specific to give you easy access to the media on your hard disc, but my advice is that you should also consider the use of Collections in these circumstances and use Project bins for just that - the intended contents of a project.

Managing Project Bins

We saw on page 26 how to add a new Project Bin using the Create tool alongside the category name. Once you have created a new bin, right clicking on its name offers you the chance to rename or remove it. If you do try remove it you will be warned if it is not empty. You need not worry that any bin content will get removed from your hard disc - it won't. However, if this is the only place that links to a particular clip and you don't have Library media displayed as a category you might lose track of that clip.

Incidentally, the default bin *The Sky is the Limit,* is indestructible!

Avoiding Project Bins

If you don't want to work with Project Bins, then you can do so, but the worst possible way of working is just to throw everything into the default Bin - The Sky is the Limit - and add it to any project from there. Alternatively you might just create one general purpose "My Project Bin" and use that for everything. I can understand the temptation - perhaps you want to do a very simple edit to quickly create a movie and have no intention of saving the project, but once Project Bins get cluttered up they are worse than not having them at all.

My recommendation in these circumstances is to work from the Library Media category in the Navigation bar. If you haven't got that displayed, refer back to page 120.

Quick Import into a Project Bin

Adding Video, Photos and Audio to the Library quickly is often best done by using Quick Import. You can add items that are already stored on the hard disc of your computer as long as the items are recognised media types.The option is available from the Main and Compact Library.

The Quick Import icon in the Main Library

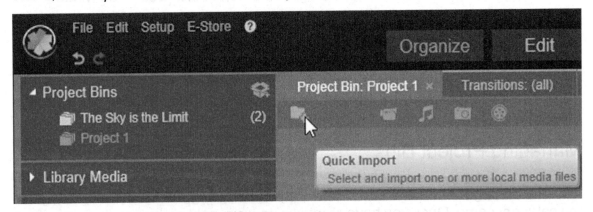

The Quick Import tool can be found at the top left of the Library when you open the Organize tab. Firstly select the Bin you wish to add the item to. If you are in the Compact Library you may need to open out the Navigation side bar to do this. Now click on on the Quick Import tool and an Import Media Files windows opens (shown on page 27). One point not mentioned when we used Quick Import before is that you can use the normal Windows multi-selection tools to import more than one file from a folder at the same time. Once you have found the file or files you want to add, highlight them, click OK, and the items are added to the current Bin.

Quick Import into Library Media

You can also import directly into the Library Media category (if it is displayed) by using the same Quick Import icon. If you select the main category itself then the Import box will offer you all valid media types, but if you have selected one of the subcategories of Photos, Video or Audio then the items will be filtered

So, if Audio (or a subcategory of Audio) was being displayed in the Library when you clicked on the Quick Import icon, you would only be offered a choice of audio files. To circumvent this, you can override the file type selection in the Import Media Files dialogue box.

The Import Media dialogue looking for just audio files

Note that when you Quick Import into Library Media the item doesn't go into the category that is currently being displayed. A path is created to the actual location and added to Library Media as a sub category, but the item is also added to the Latest Import collection, and that *is* displayed.

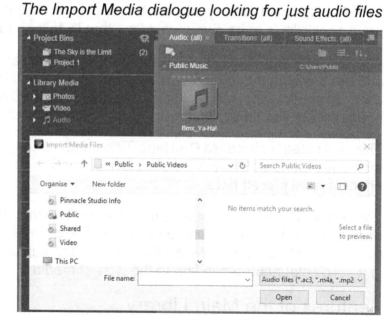

So, just to reiterate, when you use Quick Import, the file stays in exactly the same place on your computer. It isn't moved, nor is a copy made. All that happens is that an entry is made in the Library database logging the existence and location of the file. Any changes you subsequently make to the item in the Library aren't made to the file. For example, it is possible to rename a Library item – but when you do this the original file is **not** renamed.

Alternatives to Quick Import

A slight different approach to linking items to the Library is possible using Browsing. If you have lots of items to import you can scan locations. If they are stored on media that could become disconnected from your computer then you need to consider copying rather than linking. You might want to use Watchfolders. There is also the complex subject of capturing video from cards, tape or DVD. All this and more is discussed in the Import chapter.

Displaying assets other than media

As well as being the place to find your useful media, Pinnacle Studio uses the Library as a gateway to all the other assets you might want to use.

In addition to **Project Bins** and **Library Media**, the Library also allows you access to **Projects**. You can open a Movie or Disc project from the Library by double-clicking it, and it will open in the relevant editor. You can also drag and drop Movie projects from the Compact Library into another Movie or Disc project. This opens up some great possibilities to help your workflow that I'll talk about in detail later.

Also available from the Library are **Collections**. You can have numerous Collections and put anything into them that you want. This is similar to features in other editors such as project bins and racks, but arguably more powerful. If you don't think you need most of the Library features, I urge you at least to read about Collections.

The final category is called **Content**. Titles and menus, video effects, transitions and montages along with audio assets such Sound Stage music generation and sound effects are all placed here.

The Studio 19 Library helps you find these items with the addition of coloured lines on the tabs and sidebars - Orange for Project Bins, Blue for Media, Purple for Projects, Green for Collections and Yellow for Content. The currently selected tab is highlighted in a solid colour corresponding to the type of media.

Features of the Main Library

Let's start by giving some names to the areas of the Main Library. Take a look at the screenshot over the page.

If your Browser Window is not as shown, but consists of a list of file names, then you are looking at Details View. Click the Thumbnails View icon on the Library Toolbar and your display should now resemble the Main Library screenshot. I'll describe the rest of the toolbar later.

Browsing with Tabs

The top row of the Library has a series of **Tabs**, similar to those you would find in a web browser. Click on any of the tabs and the contents of the **Browser Window** change to show the contents of your new tab selection. The **Asset Tree** Window is on the left. This tree structure is the primary way to control what appears in the Browser Window of each tab.

The Main Library

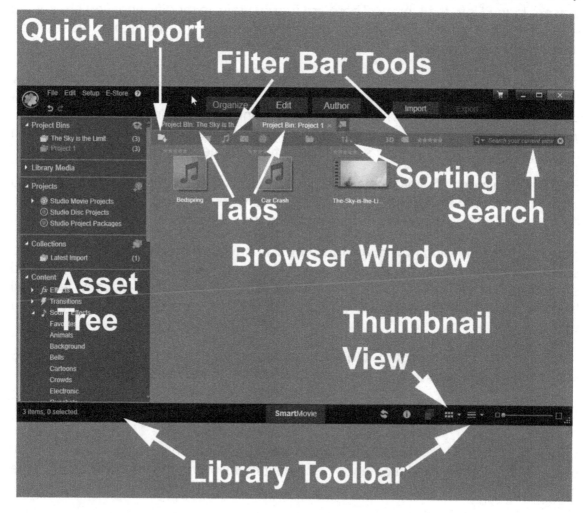

When you first install Pinnacle Studio there is just one tab, open at the only Project Bin, but tabs are very easy to **add**, **modify** or **delete**. The currently selected tab is indicated by being the fully coloured, the others just have a stripe at the top that indicates what type of tab they are. The Asset Tree Window has the location of the currently displayed tab highlighted in orange.

To the right of the row of tabs there is a smaller icon that has a + sign beside a folder. This is how you **add** a new tab. Click on it now – a new default tab entitled *Project Bin:The Sky is the Limit* appears to the right of the other tabs.

To **modify** the new tab, look at the Asset Tree Window on the left of the screen. Using your mouse, click on the small arrow alongside *Projects* and then click on *Studio Movie Projects*. The name of the tab changes to *Studio Movie Projects (all)* and the contents of the Browser View Window changes to show you all the projects that are logged into the Library. There are further ways to modify what you are seeing when the tab is open, but it always bears the name of the highlighted Asset Tree category or sub-category.

To **delete** a tab all you have to do is click the small X on the right side of the tab. Try that with your recently added and modified Projects tab. You should now be back down to however many you had to start with. Think twice before deleting tabs; if you want to clear the current view and look at something else, it's just as quick to switch tabs, and you may have spent some time setting up the current tab for a purpose.

Each tab is almost infinitely customisable. You can set each one up exactly how you want to, then browse across to another tab, and when you re-select the original tab it will be just as you displayed it. This includes the addition of a Search filter.

You may be wondering how many tabs you can have. When you fill up the available space across the top of the screen a small navigation arrows appears at either end so you can scroll to find more tabs. There doesn't appear to be any technical limitations, so if you have a good memory then by all means create as many as you wish!

If you like using the keyboard, then you can navigate across the tabs with the TAB key to move right, and the Alt-TAB key combination to move back to the start.

Using the Asset Tree Window

Let's look at the **Asset Tree Window** in more detail now. Before we do, if you currently can't see the Library Media category, enable it by following the instructions on page 120.

Click on Library Media in the Asset tree to switch the current tab to display the contents. Now expand the Library Media tree more by clicking the white arrowhead. It rotates to point downwards, and you should have at least three types of media below – **Photos**, **Video** and **Audio**. There may be a fourth – **Missing Media** – if you have "lost" some items in the Library.

The Browser open at the Library Media tab

In the Browser Window that occupies most of the screen there will be groups of thumbnails separated by darker grey headers. Even if you haven't imported anything yet the sample movie media consists of a music clip, a video clip and a still picture. You can reveal and hide the thumbnails with the orange arrow for each header. Look at the middle of each header and you will see the actual hard disc location for each group; they are ordered alphabetically – so my list starts with *Public Music* which is a folder in **c:/users/public** on my hard disc.

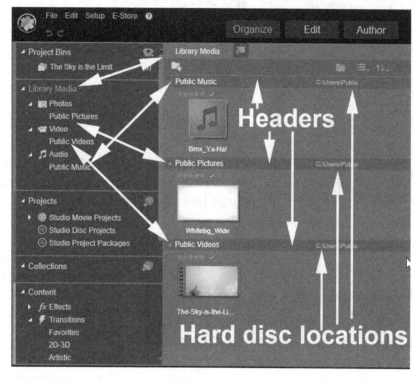

Note the important difference here between a Windows Explorer view and what you see in the Library View Window. **Only folders that hold media that has been imported into your Library are displayed**. The parent directories are not shown. This applies to Media, Projects and Content. Project Bins and Collections behave even more differently than Windows Explorer, as we will see later.

Asset Tree tools

Apart from the arrowheads for expanding and contracting the categories and the scroll bar, there are a few other features to the Asset tree. If you like using the keyboard, you can navigate up and down the Asset Tree Window entries using the Up and Down arrows on your keyboard.

Tools for creating new Bins, Projects and Collections

There are also icons that allow you to to create new Project Bins, Projects and Collections using icons opposite the appropriate headers.

There are only context menus available for the Project Bin section of the Asset Tree (allowing you to rename or remove bins). The other sections offer you nothing when you right click on them.

The Browser Window Toolbar

The first icon top left of the Browser window is the Quick Import tool I've talked about so much. This tool is not present if you have a Collection or Content selected.

Media Filters for Project Bins

The next three icons will only be present if you have a Project Bin open, so select one now. By un-highlighting the icons you can excluded the type of media the icon represents from being displayed in the Project Bins.

The central group of tools with a Library Media tab open

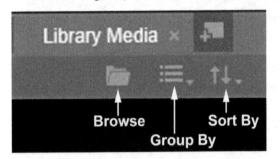

The Browse tool is a simple folder in the centre of the toolbar, which is an advanced way of importing media, covered in the Import chapter.

The Group by tool

The next icon - Group by - will not be present when you have a Project Bin, Collection or Content folder open. This controls how the Browser Window groups the display of assets.

Clicking the tool gives the option to group your media or projects by Date Created, Folder, Rating, or File type. If you wanted to only look at photo files that were Jpegs, you could select "file type" and then select the group ".jpg".

The Group By tool choices

Change the grouping and observe the changes in the way items are displayed. The Browser Window still shows the assets arranged into groups that can be opened and closed with the aid of the orange arrows. My default choice here is to group files by *Folder* because I'm in the habit if keeping my media reasonably well organised, but you might want to choose *Date created* instead.

If you click on your choice of grouping twice, then the sections are displayed in the reverse order. For example, if the the view is already grouped by Folder in A-Z order, clicking on Folder again will change the sort order to Z-A.

The Sort by tool

The other option for the Browser display defines how the assets are displayed within the groups.

The Sort options

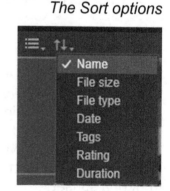

There are even more options here to help you arrange the assets. **Date** is particularly useful as it doesn't just use the date, but also the time. Duration might also be of use in some situations. There are also a number of choices that only appear when certain locations are open - photo resolution, video frame rate, album, artist and Genre for music and even Missing Media.

If you want to sort in the reverse order, click again on the chosen order, and it will be reversed.

You can also reach the Sort options from the Browser Window context menu. Right click on an unoccupied space in the window and you also get a shortcut to Quick Import if the particular tab supports it.

Sorting by date - a problem with video

You may notice an inconsistency with the wording when trying to sort by date. In the Library Media section, you will be offered *Date Taken* and in the Bins *Date Created* and for photos this works well. However, for video files this isn't really the best field to sort by, as it gets changed if you copy the media to the date of the copying. To work round this issue, see page 170.

More Filter tools

To the right of the Toolbar are three filtering options. Regardless of whatever tab you have selected, grouped in any manner you have chosen, in any view, it can be further refined here.

The Filter bar

There four powerful methods of finding the media you want. 3D, Tags, Ratings and a very good textual search.

3D filter

If you are making stereoscopic video projects, then this filter is for you. By selecting it, only assets that have 3D properties will be shown.

Tags

You may be familiar with the idea of tags from software photo albums or even Facebook, where you can apply tags to pictures – for example, the names of people. A picture with 3 people in it might have tags for Tom, Dick and Harry. A picture of Tom on his own would only have a tag for Tom. Then you can search your collection for all pictures that have Tom and Harry together. Any pictures of a sunset can have a Sunset tag, and then you might be able to search for a picture of Harry standing in front of a sunset.

The Tags sidebar

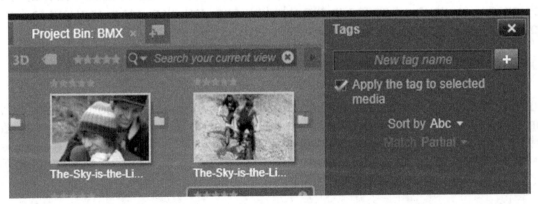

Before you work with tags, it's a good idea to create some. The first step is to click on the Tags Icon on the filter bar - it looks like a luggage label. When you do so, a new sidebar opens to the right of the browser. If you are working in the Compact Library, a small new movable window opens up over the top left of the screen.

Working with tags is best demonstrated with a tutorial. For this we need some source pictures and Pinnacle should have provided some for you when you installed Studio.

Create a Project Bin called *BMX* and use the Quick Import function to add the eight *The-Sky-is-the-Limit* Jpeg photos that are in the Public Pictures location *C:\Users\Public\Public Pictures*. If you can't find them, they are on the DTVPro website and data DVD. Make sure the bin is sorted by Name.

Type "bicycle" into the text box as a tag name and click on the + sign. Tag names aren't case sensitive, so "Bicycle" and "bicycle" count as the same tag. You can use the Add icon alongside or the enter key to create the tag.

You can apply a tag in a number of ways. By checking the box labelled "Apply the tag…" underneath the name creation box, any items that happen to be selected when you create the tag will have the tag applied. There are three ways to add tags that have already been created to new items. Right-click on the first picture – the 01.jpg – and you should see **Apply Tag** available in the context menu. Hover your mouse over that command and a list of potential tags should appear. We only have one choice, so select "bicycle".

A tag icon will appear alongside the first thumbnail, (If there isn't, it's possible you have switched off the Tag Indicator in the Thumbnails view selection menu - see page 138). Hovering over the tag icon lists the tags given to the picture (still only one at the moment) and the option to "remove all". Hovering over the tag name itself opens up the option to delete the tags individually.

Pictures 2, 3, 4, 6 and 7 all have bicycles in them. CTRL-Click all of them to select them as a group. Right click on one of the highlighted pictures and from the context menu, apply the "bicycle" tag; it gets applied to all the selected photos.

I think that the second way of applying a tag is neat. To demonstrate that, we need some more tags. If you haven't made the first project yet, you might not know the names I've given to the four people - Fred, Daphne, Velma and Shaggy. Return to the sidebar and create a tag each for them.

Daphne is the girl with red hair. Drag and drop the *Daphne* tag from the side bar to the first picture with her in. Notice the graphic that reminds you of the tag name as you drag it.

To tag the rest, use the third way, which is quicker. Multi-select the remaining four pictures which she is in and click on the tag name in the side bar. Notice the number of items has gone from 1 to 5.

Velma is the blond girl. Multi-select all her photos and click on her tag. Both the boys are in pictures 1, 2, 5, 7 and 8. Multi-select those pictures. Now try this – click on Fred's tag, then click on Shaggy's. Both tags should have been added to the selected pictures.

Leave the pictures selected and click on Fred's tag again - whoops, we have deleted the tags! Click again, and they're back.

To complete our tagging, the fourth picture needs a Shaggy tag. When you have done that, select each picture in turn and observe the highlighting in the sidebar – all the tags "owned" by each photo are highlighted as you step through.

Remember that you can navigate around the Library with the arrow keys. In conjunction with the mouse, you might find this a convenient way of adding multiple tags to items as you work through the latest folder of imported photographs.

At the top of the list of tags are two drop-down selection lists. *Sort by* only dictates how the tags are ordered in the tag sidebar. The *ABC* choice is obvious, but *Relevance* not so. It could be called popularity, or even "how many items are tagged with this tag", so when you choose Relevance, Bike and Shaggy top the list because those tags are attached to the most photos.

To see what the Match choice does, we need to select some tags. You may have noticed the icon to the right of each tag name in the sidebar that looks like a magnifying glass looking at a tag. Click on *Bicycle* and the familiar "filtering by" orange bar appears at the top of the browser and we only see photos tagged as *Bicycle*. Add another tag, *Daphne* and the photos of her will be added as long as **Match** is set to **Partial**. The three settings behave like logic gates And, Or and Nor, if that is a concept familiar to you.

- Full - the view will be filtered to show all the photos that have a Bike **and** Daphne in (And)

- Partial - all the photos that have a Bike, **or** Daphne, **or both** are displayed (Or)

- None – only the photos **without** a Bike **or** Daphne are displayed (Nor).

Closing the Tags sidebar by clicking on the tag icon leaves the tag filters in place. The Library warns you that you have a filter in place by placing an orange bar across the top of the current View Window. The quickest way to clear the filter is to click on the "x" at the right end of the orange filter bar.

To manage the tags, you hover over them. Two icons appear. You can rename the tag, and all the items that have this tag are adjusted accordingly. Change "Bicycle" to "Bike" to observe the results. You can also delete the tag, removing it from all the items and the list.

Ratings

Ratings are the simple way of sorting your media, projects or creative elements by how important they are to you. Let's use the example of a series of still photos that you take on a day out. When you import them into the computer, some are going to be "must haves" and some are a bit poor. It's very easy to give each picture "stars out of 5" for its content and technical merit. When you start to put together a slide show of your day out, you are going to put in all the five star pictures. However, when you watch it back, you might realise that it looks as if Grandma wasn't with you that day. Perhaps in most of the pictures of her she was being shy, or you got your thumb over the lens. Lower the rating and you'll find those pictures, and include them, perhaps with some corrections to improve them technically.

Using ratings is pretty simple. I'm going to use transitions as the basis of a demonstration. Even though Pinnacle have now introduced Favourites categories for Content, I like to rate transitions, because it offers more choice. Even if you haven't bought any extra content, you probably are overwhelmed with the choice Pinnacle Studio gives you. However if your editing preferences are similar to mine, most of the time you will use a simple crossfade. So, let's start by giving that transition a 5 star rating.

In the tree, locate Content, expand the tree by using the arrowhead and open Transitions, Standard Transitions, and then 2D Transitions. Now, if you are viewing thumbnails in the browser you should have a choice of at least 83 transitions. Scroll down until you find the Cross Dissolve. Above each thumbnail should be 5 grey stars. (If you aren't seeing stars, then check that the *Thumbnail View* drop-down selection as shown on page {Ref} has *Ratings* checked. If the transitions don't appear to be in alphabetical order, check the sort order as described on page 129.

Now hover over the stars at the top left of the Cross Dissolve transition and they will turn orange to show you are in the right area. Clicking on the furthest right star and then moving your mouse away turns all five stars white. Do that now and you have given Cross Dissolve the highest rating. Clicking on any other star changes the rating to that level. If you really want to "un-rate" something, click on the currently selected star again. Make sure that the Cross Dissolve has 5 stars.

Add a few 4-star and 3-star ratings to some of the other transitions in the 2D Transitions folder so you can see the next effect. Now use the tree to select the Alpha Magic group of transitions and rate a few more with 4 or 3 stars. Using the tree, change the current tab again, so that you are looking at all the of the Transitions. Lots of them, aren't there? Make the thumbnails as small as you like and it's still a huge amount. Now that some are rated, we can use the ratings to find our favourites.

The first way to use Ratings is to use the Filter Bar. There are 5 stars after the label "Rating filter", and if you click on the fifth star, you should now only see the Cross Dissolve transition. Change the view by clicking on the fourth star, and you will see all the transitions that you rated with four stars *or above.* Click on the third star and you will see all the 3, 4 and 5-star rated transitions. Note that the transitions are still in their groups.

Viewing transitions filtered and sorted by ratings

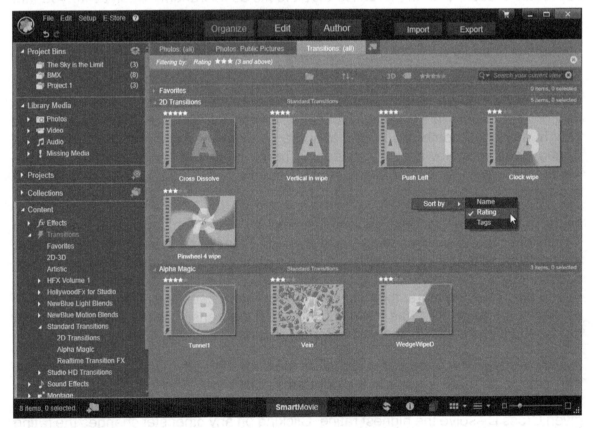

Again, the Library warns you that you have a filter in place by placing an orange bar across the top of the current View Window. In the current case you will see the text *"Filtering by:* Rating ***" on the left of the bar, and a close icon on the far right.

Notice that the transitions are still in alphabetic order within their groups. If you use the Sort by functions, you can force each group to be shown in ratings order.

One very useful feature of Pinnacle Studio is that when you import photos that you have given a rating to in your Windows Picture Library, that rating is transferred to the Pinnacle Studio Library as well. The ratings remain separate after that point, so changing the number of stars you have given in one Library doesn't affect the rating in another.

The Search Box

Searching for "Push" in Transitions

The final item on the filter bar is the **Search Box**. Here you can enter words that will filter your browser view by the caption, or title or name. This basically means the text underneath the thumbnail – different assets have different conventions. You can edit the caption of a media asset so that it is no longer identified by its filename, but you can't do that to a project – you have to rename it. Any Content has an un-editable title. Whatever the convention, it's the text underneath the thumbnail, or in the name fields of details view that is searched.

As you type the search word, the number of items shown is refined. Enter a second word in the box, and then you have the choice of if you want to match either word, or only see items that have both words. You change the setting with the drop-down arrow to the left of the text box. Select Content/Transitions in the Asset Tree, clear any existing filters and type "push" into the box. I'm left with 12 items that all have the word "push" in their text. (You may have less of you have Studio Plus)

Changing the search logic

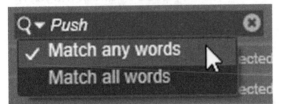

Open the drop-down box with the arrow and check "match any word", then type a space and then "left". I now have a view in the browser of 56 items – they either have push **or** left in the text.

Change the search setting to "match all words" and we see the only items in transitions that has both words – the 2D Push Left transition, and if you have New Blue installed, two further versions in Roll and Shredder. You may not have even known you had such a choice!

The search box is in my opinion the most useful of the filters. I know there is a "Old Film" Effect somewhere, and rather than browsing for it, the simple act of typing those words into the search box narrows down the browser view very quickly. OK, there are a couple of effects with the word "gold" in the text, because it contains "old", but That's not too bad, really!

Combining filters

Using more than one filter gives you even more power. You can switch ratings and tags on and off, even when there are words on the search box, so you can apply all the filter techniques at once. When a filter is applied, the orange bar across the top of the browser lists all the filters in place. You can deselect the Rating filter by double clicking on any star, Tags by clicking on the tag icon and text searching by using the close x to the right of the search box a very good search facility.

The Library Toolbar

You may have already used one of the buttons on the toolbar at the bottom of the Library window to ensure that you are looking at Thumbnails View in the Browser Window. Let's look at the rest of the toolbar in detail.

On the far left, the number of items currently on view in the Browser Window and how many are selected are displayed. Item selection is indicated by orange highlighting in the Browser View Window itself.

Library toolbar tools

In the middle of the toolbar is a button for **SmartMovie**, the automated movie creator. You work with this functions from the Library view, so this is why you enter it from here.

Five controls grace the right of the toolbar. The **Information** button opens a small window at the bottom of the screen giving you information about the currently selected item. This is a summary of the more important information you get when you open the information box for a particular asset. I rarely sacrifice the screen space by opening the information window, but there is one feature that you may want to access using this window - the **Comment** field.

You have the chance to attach comments to every asset by typing them into the box here or in the Information window. Leaving the information window open allows you to see any comments you may have made.

Alongside the Information button is the **Scenes View** button. It may well be greyed out at the moment. Scenes are a feature in Pinnacle used as a way of dividing up video files; once they are divided up you can choose to view them with this control. To access this view you need to have a video file highlighted. A "scene" in Pinnacle isn't the equivalent of a "scene" in a film or TV script - it is normally just one single shot, but can be just part of a single shot or a series of single shots depending on how you detect them.

Highlight *The Sky is the Limit* Project Bin and click on the clip in the Browser to select it and the Scenes View button will become white. Click on this to get a sample of Scenes – the orange bar across the top of the Browser View window and the Scene view button also turning orange warn you that you are in a different mode. Depending on what clip you chose, you may see one thumbnail, or a whole host of them.

We will look at Scenes starting at page 277. Disable the view for now – if you aren't likely to use Scenes in your projects at least you now know when you have the wrong view selected!

The next two icons to the right control how the items are displayed in the Browser View Window. I've already mentioned the first, **Thumbnail View**. It ensures we are seeing Pictures, not text details, but it also can control what else appears around the thumbnails. Click the drop-down arrow on the right of the button and you will see the choices. A tick indicates if that option will be displayed, and I tend to work with most of them turned on – but you may find some of them distracting and wish to switch them off.

Thumbnail view display options

Rating - Five stars show the item's rating. These are placed top left of the thumbnail

Stereoscopic - if the media has stereoscopic properties, a "3D" symbol appears after the rating stars

Information - The "i" icon top right that opens the Media information window.

Correction – This is more significant. If you have sent a media item to the Corrections Editor and applied a correction it will be indicated with a gearwheel icon below the Info icon. Whenever you use a media item from the library in a project, it will have the correction automatically added. Note that turning off the indicator isn't the same as removing the correction. I always leave this one turned on.

Collections – Shows a folder icon below the Corrections icon if the item is part of at least one collection.

Tag – This is one of the indicators you might want to turn off, because all it shows is if a tag has been applied, not what it is. The indicator is a small "luggage label" icon placed to the right of the thumbnail.

Used Media - If the item represented by the thumbnail is in use in an **open** project, a checkmark appears. The checkmark is green if the item is part of the currently displayed project, grey if part of the project in the other tab - for example you have the Movie project editor open but the item is only part of the project in the Disc project editor. When the Main Library is displayed, the checkmark will always be grey if present in either project. The "tick" appears to the right of the rating stars.

Name – Switches on and off the caption below the thumbnail. For items in the All Media category, you can edit this caption by right clicking on the thumbnail and selecting Edit Caption. This doesn't alter the item's filename, so if you are stuck with a load of clips with unhelpful names (Video_01.mpg, Video_02.mpg) and the thumbnails also don't do much to identify them, it's a good idea to label them with something more helpful. The filename can always be found using a number of methods.

Shortcut – Sometimes the thumbnail doesn't lead to a real file, but is a shortcut to another file. The icon appears on the top left of the thumbnail. You are most likely to see this indicator when you work with Scenes or create your own Library Shortcuts.

Details View options

Details view options

Clicking the main part of this button switches the View Window to a textual display. It might look boring, but it can be very useful.

The available fields can be selected in the drop-down menu and are the same as those of the Sort by tool - **Name** (which will be the edited caption if you have changed it, the file name if you haven't), **File Size**, **File Type**, **Date**, **Tags**, **Rating** and **Duration**. Name is always displayed, but you can enable and disable which of the other fields are displayed with the drop-down arrow alongside the Details View button. Unless you have a small screen and like to use very long names, you may as well leave all the items selected.

Thumbnail size slider

The final control on the far right of the Library toolbar only has an affect when you are in Thumbnail View. Switch to that view now, select a tab that has a number of thumbnails. If you haven't imported much into the Library yet, try Transitions. Now adjust the slider and you'll see the size of the thumbnails alter in response. I find myself using this control a good deal. With a small view in the Compact Library you will want to find a compromise between being able to recognise the thumbnails and fitting in as many as possible.

The Browser View Window selection and sorting

From now on, I'm going to refer to the Browser Window as simply the browser, and the Asset Tree Window as the tree. We have already established that there are two styles the browser can take. While you might ignore the **Details View** most of the time, it does have it's uses.

Use the Tree View to switch the current tab to some photos – All Media>Photos>Public should bring up at least the ones that Pinnacle Studio installed. Now switch to Details View using the button on the Library toolbar. Most of the view is self explanatory. Each field can be resized by dragging the field boundaries at the top of the list, but Details View's most useful feature is allowing you to sort the list. Take a look at the line of labels showing the field names and click on *File size*.

Details view sorted by File ascending file size

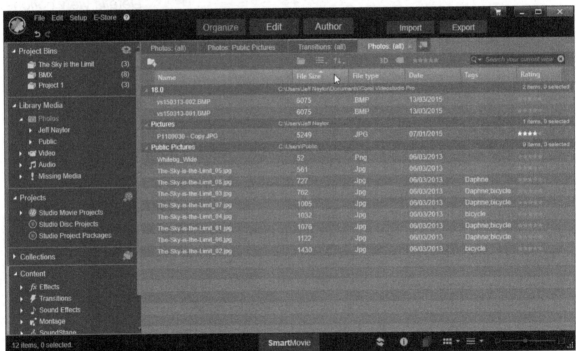

The small arrowhead in the File size field shows the current sort field, and because it is pointing up the group is sorted low to high, ascending or A to Z. Click the field heading and the arrow head will point the other way and the sort order will reverse. You can click any of the field headers and sort them low to high or high to low.

This sorting only applies *within* the groups, and is independent of how the categories are grouped. You can now achieve this type of sorting in Thumbnail view, but the column layout of Details view makes it much clearer what is going on.

If you are looking for a particular tag, date or file size it's also much easier in Details view.

Apart from this, Details view has the same functionality as **Thumbnail View**, so we will explore them both together.

Using the Browser Window

If you have too many items to fit on the screen (and you can't or don't want to make the thumbnails smaller) there will be a standard Windows scroll bar at the right of the browser. If you have a mouse scroll wheel, that will also work. Clicking on an item will highlight it to show that you have selected it, and you can then use the keyboard arrow keys to move around the view, highlighting details or thumbnails as you move around the screen.

You will want to perform multiple selections at times. The standard Windows controls work for this. Click on one item to select it, then hold down CTRL and click another to add it to the selection. Instead of CTRL, use SHIFT and all the items between the first and second item are added to the selection as well.

If you want to select everything that is in the current view, even if it is currently scrolled off the screen, then use CTRL-A (for ALL). I mentioned earlier that the individual groups displayed in the browser can be opened and closed with the orange arrows on the left of the group headings. If you use Select All, even items in the closed groups get selected, so take care using this feature. You might find yourself handling far more items than you think!

If you want to "draw" boxes around items with your mouse to group them in a selection this works just like Windows too.

Once an item or items are selected, then you can do something with them. What is possible will depend on the type of item, and whenever you are in the Main or Compact Library. What you can't do is drag and drop items **within** the Library View.

Browser Functions

Apart from finding stuff to put into projects, there are other functions that we can carry out on assets. It's time to explore these functions. Some of them can be accessed by means other than right-clicking to bring up the Context menu.

When you hover over a Thumbnail in the browser, one additional control always shows up - an icon at the bottom centre, overlapping the picture. This performs a **Preview** action when clicked, opening the asset in the appropriate preview window. When using the Compact Library the Player Window is used. In the Main Library a dedicated preview window is opened, tailored to suit the type of asset. If the asset is a still photo, the icon looks a little different to indicate that you won't get a video player window.

Thumbnail controls

If you just want to play the thumbnail without opening a player window, you can do so by holding down ALT and then clicking on the preview button.

Another control that may appear is the **thumbnail scrubber**. This only appears if the asset would have a timescale - it's no use on a still photo, for example You can use this to choose which frame is displayed, or for a quick reminder of what the clip is about - perhaps the opening frame is black and you want to set it to something more obvious.

You will also find the scrubber available for Transitions, Effects (even those which aren't keyframed), Montages and Audio.

Another browser function that can be achieved without the context menu is **Open In..** which can be achieved by **double-clicking**. This varies a good deal with the type of asset. Photos, Video and Audio open in the Corrections Editor, projects open in the Movie or Disc Editor, Titles, Montages and Soundstage assets open in their respective Editors. By the way, Scorefitter is a subset of Soundstage - I believe Pinnacle are leaving room for other audio creation editors in the future.

The Delete dialogue box

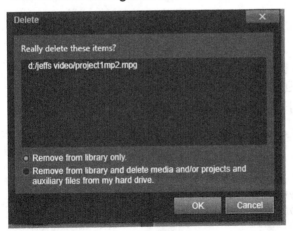

Project Packages, which contain all the media assets of a project, responds to the double-click option by extracting the media and project files which you can then open separately.

The **Delete** key works as a shortcut in the Library. Content can't be removed, unless they are ones you have created yourself such as My Titles and Menus. Using the delete key when working with Project Bins or Collections removes the item from that location and nothing else – you don't even get a chance to wipe it from your hard disc.

Last Chance Saloon for deletion

Deleting any item in the All Media or Projects Categories results in a dialogue box like the one shown in the screenshot. In the case of a media item, or a selection of items, then the choice is clear. Do you want to remove the item just from the library, or **also** delete it from your hard disc?

Removal from the Library only is harmless. If you forgot that you had a project that used that item, the program will automatically search for it when you open the project, and if it finds it where it was before, puts it back in the Library.

If you select the second option then any selected media item will be removed from the Library **and** the hard disk where they are stored on your computer.

If the list of items includes projects they will be removed from the Library and the project file and any auxiliary render files associated with that project will be deleted from the hard disc. (That's according to Pinnacle - in my experience the auxiliary files aren't removed.)

If you click OK, before that happens you will get a second chance and a further description of what you are about to do.

DANGER - if you are the sort of person that relies on Windows having a recycle bin, then be warned that Pinnacle Studio doesn't put your deleted items in the bin for possible retrieval. It deletes them outright.

If you are deleting a project, then be reassured that although the project itself will disappear, none of the Media items included in the project will be deleted, either from the Library or the computer hard disc.

Double clicking and Delete also work in Details view, but for Preview you will have to use the Context Menu.

Browser items Context menu

When you right-click on an item in the Browser window an extensive Context menu appears. Some functions will be available in all ciirconstances others will depend on which Library format you are using and the type of asset.

Let's work through the Project Bin asset Context menu, noting differences with other types as we go.

The Context menu for a video item in the Compact Library

Preview opens whatever the asset in the appropriate preview window as discussed above. Every type of asset has this option apart from Project Packages.

Show In Explorer opens the asset in a new Windows Explorer window - useful for tracking down where an item actually is on your hard disc. This option doesn't appear for Content.

Find in Timeline is a function that is only possible when the Compact Library is open in a Movie or Disc Editor and the asset is on the timeline. It will highlight all the occurrences of the chosen media asset

Rename is only available for Movie or Disc projects and lets you do a renaming operation without having to worry about the file extensions that you would have to take care of if you performed the rename outside of Studio.

Edit Caption can be applied to all assets except Content. As mentioned before, it allows you to alter the name given to an asset and used by the Library for searching and filtering. It doesn't affect the underlying file name of the asset.

Open In... is the same function as double-clicking, described in detail above.

Unpack Project Package only displays for Project Packages and has the same effect as double clicking. Project Packages are discussed in the Understanding Studio Chapter.

Add to Favourites will be present for all content, unless the item is already a favourite, in which case you will see **Remove from Favourties**.

Apply tag, Apply rating ,Add to collection and **Add to Project Bin** are common to every Context menu.

Copy adds the selected object to the Paste buffer

Remove from collection will be available for any item that is already in a collection.

Show scenes, **Edit scenes** and **Detect scenes** all work only with video. If you look closely at a thumbnail that has been split into scenes you will see three thin frame borders to distinguish it. Scenes are a complex subject that require a full section later in the book.

Send To Timeline - you will only see this option in the Compact Library. It is an alternative to dragging and dropping. The item is placed at the current scrubber position on the currently selected track using the current edit mode. Transitions have this option, but only work in certain circumstances.

Burn Disc Image can apply to Media or Projects, opening the Burn to Disc dialogue. Here you can export files to optical media in the form of a data disc as well as make DVD and Blu-ray discs from projects.

Delete selected duplicates the function of the delete key, just discussed.

Remove from Project Bin is only valid for Project Bin items and does just that.

Display information brings up the info box we have seen earlier in the book.

Favourites

Adding a transition to the Transition Favourite section

This is a new feature (added in PS 18.5) that allows you to nominate any content as a favourite, so it then appears in the Favourites section under the relevant content category.

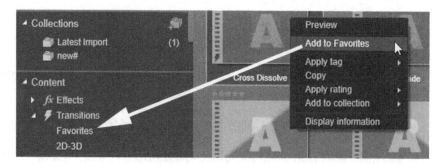

This function is only available from the context menu, so you can't drag and drop. To remove an item from Favourites, you just open the context menu again and select *Remove from Favourites*.

This is a simple way of organising some of the vast array of content into an easy to find location. If you want a more general purpose tool that is far more powerful, you should consider Collections.

Collections

One feature I have skipped over until now is the Collection category. To some extent they have been superceded by Project Bins and My Favourites, but I still think the Collections is a far better function.

If I wanted to carry out some repairs on a fence at the front of my house and all the tools and materials were at the back of my garage, then although I can't be sure exactly what I'll need, it's a good idea to collect together the items I'm likely to use and carry them round in one go. In reality I may already have a suitable set of tools containing a hammer, screwdriver and small saw in a toolbox, and I'd also put some likely looking nails and screws in another box, stick some wood under my arm and then walk round to the front of the house. I'll almost certainly have to go back for something else, but at least I'm a *bit* organised.

That's like starting to edit together a movie with a collection of clips you are most likely to want to use in one collection (or a Project Bin), and a set of your favourite transitions in another (or in the Favourites folder).

Like most analogies, this has a flaw. If I've only got one hammer, it can only be in one toolbox. But I can have 10 different Collections with the same video clip in them. What's more, the video clip hasn't even moved – it's still safely tucked away in its original location on my hard drive.

So –

- You can have as many different Collections as you wish.

- Any type of asset in your Library can be put in any Collection, and they can be in as many different collections of them as you wish.

- Anything you put in a Collection isn't moved from its real location on your computer.

Let's create and populate a Collection using the tree. Click on the icon alongside the Collections category. This looks like a group of folders and a + sign. A very simple box will pop up that is asking you to name the New Collection. Enter "Testing" into the box and click OK.

Now let's put something in the "Testing" Collection. Unfortunately Pinnacle have removed the Quick Import function from the Collection category. It is possible to use the Browser import method which I'll describe in the Import chapter.

I'm going to use the photos supplied by Pinnacle. If you created the BMX bin to try out tags then you will already have imported them, otherwise follow the instructions on page 131.

Adding photos to a Collection

Open the BMX bin, select all the thumbnails and right click on one of them. From the context menu select *Add to Collection/Testing.* Now switch to the Testing collection

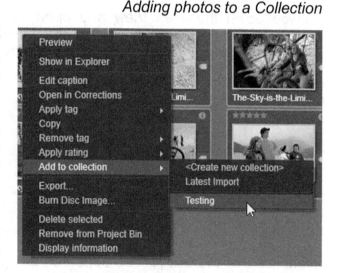

Right, I hope you are seeing the same as me. In the browser there should be thumbnails of all the pictures you chose to import.

Now we have created a collection, let's see how to manage it. Right-click on "testing" in the Tree View and four options present themselves.

The Collections Context Menu

Rename – Change the name of the collection.

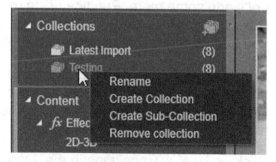

Create Collection – We have just done that, but here is another way to do it.

Create Sub-Collection – Yes, you can create a collection within a collection, but it is more powerful than just that.

Remove Collection – Deletes the currently highlighted collection.

I want to work through the first four options in order to demonstrate a number of important features regarding collections. Let's start by renaming the "testing" collection. Right-click on "Testing" and select Rename, enter "Photos" over the top of "Testing" and press return.

Now, create a new collection using the right-click option. Call it "Today's Project". Notice that the list of collections is being maintained in alphabetical order. If you want to test that, create "Another Project" and it will appear at the top of the list.

Subcollections

I'd urge you not to skip over sub-collections, because they aren't as obvious as they may sound. Right-click on "Today's Project" and create a sub-collection called "Useful Transitions".

Browse down the Tree View and open *Transitions, Standard Transitions, 2D Transitions*. All the transitions in that category should now be shown as thumbnails in the View Window, listed in alphabetical order.

Adding a transition to a collection

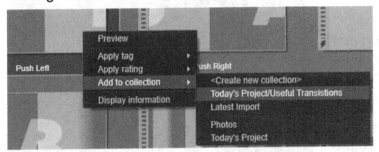

If they aren't in that order, use the browser context menu to sort them. Scroll down to the "Push" transitions and right click on Push Left. Use the Context menu to add it to the *Today's Project/Useful Transitions* Collection. You will notice that the text *(1)* has appeared alongside the Useful Transitions name in the list of collections.

Let's add some more. Practice using multiple selections by using CTRL-click to select Push Down, Right and Up. Right click on any of them and the context menu will let you add them all to a collection at once.

An even neater way of adding items to a collection is by **drag and drop**. Let's scroll up the 2D transitions group to find the most useful transition of all, Cross Dissolve. Click on it, hold and drag it across to the collection name in the tree, then release the mouse. The item count goes up to 5.

Click on Useful Transitions in the Tree View and you will see the 5 items it is said to contain. Its *Parent* collection, Today's Project, isn't showing that it contains **any** items. But when you click on Today's Project you might be surprised to see the five transitions are showing in the View window.

This is an important point. If this was a Windows folder structure, all you would see was the sub-folder, not its contents. That's not that case with collections – you see all the individual items regardless if they are contained in sub-collections or not.

The next trick up Collection's sleeve is drag and drop within the tree. Oh, dear, I created the *Photos* collection before *Today's Project* whereas I should have put all those photos in a subfolder of *Today's Project*, really. No need to recreate photos as a sub-collection though. Click and hold on Photos and drag it on top of Today's Project. Brilliant! Photos are now a sub-collection, and if we view Today's Project there are 13 items in view.

What if you are looking at a parent collection, and want to know which sub collection a particular item is in? Hover your mouse over any item in the browser. If the item isn't in the parent directory, then the sub collection which contains it lights up Green - the colour of collections. What's more, if that particular item happens to be in another collection, that collection's name will highlight as well.

This feature works when you hover over an item in its home location as well – go to the 2D transitions folder, hover over one of the Push transitions and Useful transitions will highlight.(Incidentally, this also happens with Project Bins.)

The Collection indicator tooltip

I mentioned the **Collections** indicator when we looked at the Thumbnails View selections. If an item is included in one or more collections and you have the indicator enabled, hovering your mouse over it produces a list of collections that includes the item along with options to remove the item from all the collections. This 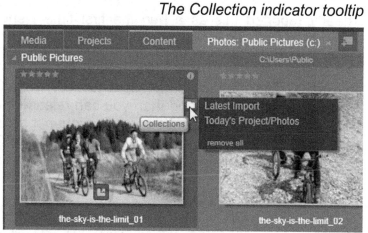 is more useful than the tree highlight feature if you haven't expanded all the collections in the tree.

Sub-Subcollections, anyone?

Yes, yes, I'm getting the idea, I hear you thinking. It might seem there are so many options that I'm trying to turn you into someone who spends their entire time rearranging their tool shed and not actually doing anything useful. Bear with me...

Create a sub collection under Useful Transitions called Pushes. Add, don't drag and drop, the four push transitions in Useful Transitions to the Pushes sub-collection. So, now the Push transitions are in both "Useful Transitions" *and* "Pushes"

Open the Pushes collection and there are 4 items. Now open Useful Transitions and it is still showing 5 items. You might expect to see two instances of the Push transitions, **but any view of a collection ignores duplicate items** that may be included in some of the sub-collections. This actually let's you be *less* organised, because if you have created a number of collections with overlapping themes and therefore items, you'll only ever see one version of each item.

When you used the right-click on the Push transitions, you might have spotted another option – Remove from collections. Let's remove the duplicate items from the parent directory. We could use the Collections icon method described above, but the context menu will work in all circumstances, even Details View.

Multi-select the four Push transitions and use the right-click option to remove them, or just hit the Delete key. The number of items in Useful Transitions has dropped down to 1, but there are still 5 thumbnails on view. Try to delete one of the pushes again and you can't.

I nearly reported this as a bug the first time I encountered it, because I didn't understand how different Collections were to Windows. Silly me…..

Promoting sub-collections to collections is easy when you know how. Click and hold on Useful Transitions and drag it up to just below the Collection category title. A thin highlight bar will appear and then you can release the mouse button. Because the list is maintained in alphabetic order, it might not be immediately obvious what has happened, but look again and you will see that Useful Transitions is no longer a child of Today's project, while Pushes is still a sub-collection, but only of Useful Transition.

Re-arranging collections

This is made much easier with two tools – **drag and drop** and **copy and paste**.

What if you decide that you have put an item in the wrong collection? Let's try **drag and drop** to return the four Push transitions to the Useful Transitions folder. Select the Pushes sub-collection, select all four transitions, and drag one of them over the Useful Transitions entry in the tree. Now Pushes is empty and Useful Transitions has 5 items.

To try out **copy and paste**, multi-select the 4 pushes again in the Useful Transitions collection and use either the edit/copy command from the top menu, or CTRL-C, switch to the Pushes sub-collection and use edit/paste or CTRL-V. You should now have the four push transitions in both collections. This would be most useful when you are making a new collection from an old one, but don't actually want to alter the old one. You can also use cut and paste, but this has the same effect as drag and drop.

I hope you now understand enough about viewing Collections to realise why you don't normally see those grey dividing bars that subdivide the browser into Folders, Rating, Date or File Type when looking at the other categories.

If you want to find items in a Collection there are a number of strategies you can use. Consider switching to the Details View or using the filter options which I'll describe soon. Most importantly, keep in mind that if something is in a Collection, it **must** also be listed in the Library under one of the other categories.

I hope that this section explains why I think Collections are in a different league to Bins and My Favourites.

Special Collections

You have probably noticed on your own screen and the screenshots a collection called **Latest Import**. You can delete this collection anytime you like, and every time you use either Quick or the full Importer it will reappear containing the media items that you imported – even if you put them into a collection at the time of the import. It's a very useful feature, because if you don't pay much attention when you bring items into the Library it's there to remind you, like a post-it note stuck on the desk.

However, like that scrap of paper, I can't recommend that you rely on it being there after the cleaner has been in overnight. Using Quick Import, the contents will build up each time, but if you use the main Importer, the collection gets reset each time.

You can still find the items you have imported because they will be somewhere in the All Media category, but to avoid that trouble, I suggest that you get in the habit of renaming Latest Imports to something else if you haven't imported them straight into another collection at the same time.

Another useful automatically generated collection is the **Latest Smart Creation** collection. Every time you preview a SmartMovie, the collection is changed to reflect the contents of the previewed Smart creation.

The Compact Library

For most of the time spent editing with Pinnacle Studio you will be using the Movie Editor, and you will be doing little more with the Compact Library than dragging and dropping assets to the timeline, or selecting them to appear in the Source viewer. However, time spent organising the Main library will save you work when finding the assets you need. Apart from a few small changes, the Main and Compact Library are functionally the same.

When the Library is displayed within editing windows in it's Compact form, it needs to save space, but even in it's smallest incarnation almost all of the features are there. Tabs run along the top, with the Filter Bar underneath and a truncated Toolbar at the bottom. The Information window can't be opened, which is no great loss as you can open a separate Information window with one click.

We have seen the navigation bar in action already on page 94 . It opens when clicked on to bring up the tree view. If you aren't running Studio full screen, the navigation bar will still use all the available screen space. You can also set the Auto-Hide option to off to keep the tree view in place. The pin icon to the right of the title Navigation controls this.

You won't just find the Compact Library in the Movie Editor; it's in the Disc, Title, Montage and Menu Editors as well.

Missing Media

The Library will lose track of assets if they get moved by you or another program. If they get moved from their original location to a Watchfolder, or to a subfolder within a Watchfolder, Studio should track them down and re-add them to the Library, but you will continue to see Missing Media items in the Library asset tree relating to the original location.

Missing Media in the Library

If the file has been moved to a non-watched location, or has been deleted, the asset tree will continue to show Missing Media and the item will display a red exclamation mark. If you are happy to lose the file, you can delete the thumbnail from the library to unclutter the display. If you want to restore the item you can manually relink it with the context menu option. A Windows style dialogue lets you browse to the new location and find the file. If you don't know where it has gone you can use the search feature in Windows.

If the file has been deleted, the first place to look is the recycle bin. Use the right click menu there to restore the file. You can then manually re link the file, but if it has been restored to its original location, Studio will find it again the next time you re-open the program. So, if you had a moment of madness and stuck loads of files in the bin, it's probably quicker to restore the contents of the recycle bin and then just close and re-open Studio.

You can also experience messages about missing media when you open a project if you have moved the files since you last worked on the project. It is also likely to happen if a project has come from another computer and you didn't use Project Packages. Using the project files associated with this book is an obvious example of that because you might not have copied the assets to an identical location to the one that I used when building the project.

So, if you open a project and get yellow clips with exclamation marks, that means it contains missing media. If you don't see a dialogue box offering you the chance to relink the media, try reopening the project and the dialogue should appear. Alternatively, use the *Find in Library* option on the yellow clips and you should be taken to the Missing Media in the Library where you can relink as described above.

If you choose to relink when you first see the warning, the same browser lets you search for the file that is missing. If the file has been renamed, you can force a new file name on the project, as long as the new file has the correct file extension. It's possible to load the wrong file – Studio doesn't check that the file is actually identical. There are occasions where you might find this feature useful, but there are other times that it might cause all sorts of problems!

Strategies for using the Library

There are many ways of using the Library, and how you do so may depend on how you tend to organise your computer.

If you are relatively new to video editing, or are installing Pinnacle Studio on a clean computer, then the way the Library is set up on installation may well suit you. You can use Project Bins for each project you make, and possibly use Collections to keep track of any clip you have imported but not included in a bin.

It would be better if you enable the Library Media category so that you can see everything that you have. That is discussed on page 120.

At this point, if you don't intend to use ratings, tags or collections on a long term basis, you are ready to go. If you want to start adding useful metadata to your Library or carry out some of my suggestions such as setting up a Useful Transitions collection, you should consider backing up the Library regularly – and I'll show you how in a minute.

The next consideration is whether you want to use Watchfolders. This can slow down performance a bit and might lead to problems when adding unusual items to the computer. If you turn them off you can't use Windows as a way of importing without the second step of adding the items to the Studio Library as well.

My method is to use Watchfolders for My Pictures and My Music, to take advantage of the Windows Library functions (automatically ripping CDs and adding the track information, for example). Video is a different matter for me because adding large video files is a more time consuming task and therefore has a great impact on a computer performance when working in the background.

It is always recommended that you keep video on a separate hard drive if you can. Even if you use a separate partition of the same physical drive this can have some advantages – less fragmentation, and easier backups, for example.

Employing a second physical drive – even an external one – has further advantages in that the Operating System doesn't need to interrupt the reading and writing of video to carry out its own background tasks.

If you still prefer to have your video in a Windows Library, you can add locations on another drive to the Windows Library. You can then add a further Watchfolder to that location and set your default Import locations accordingly.

If you have media already scattered all over your computer and want to find and add it to the Studio Library, consider using Scan for Assets as a one-shot solution.

However, I keep my videos on a separate hard drive in folders with meaningful names. I don't let Watchfolders look for video. When installing Pinnacle Studio, I used the importer to physically add the whole of the video drive to the Studio Library with the *My computer* function. I then discipline myself to always use Studio's Import routines.

You may want to go further or vary from those recommendations, but once you have set up a decent Library structure you will almost certainly want to take advantage of metadata and collections. The major issue in doing that is the possibility of losing your work, which brings us on to backups.

Refreshing your Library

Sometimes you may issues with content not working correctly in the Library or even appearing to be missing. There is now a Refresh button on the lower toolbar of the main Library that will refresh the Library for you, hopefully fixing any errors in the process.

The Library Refresh tool

Using this feature is non-destructive, but it takes a little time to work. When you first click on the tool items disappear from your Library - Favourites and Content that has been added to collections, for example. Don't panic, though, because the refresh isn't complete until the tool icon ceases to be greyed out and becomes available again.

Protecting your the Library

Pinnacle Studio 19 should have a function that lets you backup the Library – possibly even save and load different Library setups. However, it doesn't. Perhaps Pinnacle Studio 20 will have.

In the meantime, I strongly recommend that if you put any effort into organising your library in any sort of complex way, or start using metadata or collections, that you back up the Library manually. Sometimes I have known Studio to crash and corrupt or even destroy the Library database. It's happened just enough times to make me careful.

In addition to backing up your Library, the technique can be used to back up your settings file, which although less time-consuming to reset after a crash is still a nuisance

Before you embark on this task, please note a few provisos - don't experiment while you have important unfinished projects, don't blame me, blah blah blah :-). If you have any doubts, back up your computer before trying this for the first time.

Pinnacle Studio stores its settings and Library database, along with a number of other important files, in a location that is hidden from prying eyes on many computers. The first thing we need to do is reveal the location.

Revealing Hidden Files and Folders

You can to do this in Windows Explorer. To reveal the hidden files and folders in Windows 7 or Vista go to **Tools/ Folder options/View** and set **Hidden Files and folders** to **Show hidden files, folders and drives.**

In Windows 8 and 10, click on the **View** menu, select **Options** and it will bring up the **Folder options**, select the **View tab** then set the properties as for Win 7.

You should now be able to see the files that Windows doesn't normally let you see.

Backup

To backup the current Library and settings using Windows Explorer:

- Go to your boot drive (normally C:)

- Navigate to *Users/Your profile name/App data/Local/Pinnacle_Studio_19/Studio*

- Copy the whole of the *19.0* folder to save the Library, Effects list and Settings

- Alternatively, if you just wish to save the Library, open the *19.0* folder and copy the *NGDatabase* folder

- Navigate to a safe backup location of your choice and paste the folder there.

The Library data location

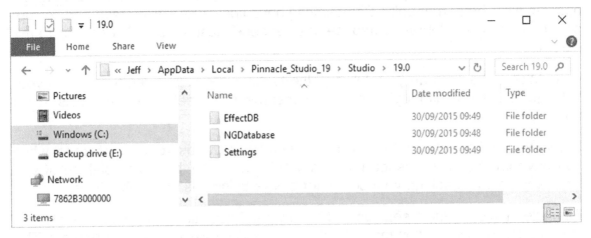

Restore

To restore the saved Library and settings

- Close Pinnacle Studio

- Go to the safe backup location you used to save the data and copy the *NGDatabase* folder if you just wish to restore the Library or the *19.0* folder if you wish to restore the setting and effects list as well

- Go to your boot drive

- If you have copied the 19.0 folder navigate to *Users/Your profile name/App data/Local/Pinnacle_Studio_19/Studio/* and delete the whole of the current *19.0* Folder

- If you have copied the *NGDatabase* folder navigate to *Users/Your profile name/App data/Local/Pinnacle_Studio_19/Studio/19.0* and delete the whole of the current *NGDatabase* Folder

- Paste the saved Pinnacle folder from the clipboard to the current location.

That's it. You could extend the technique to keeping different versions of the Library database and settings for different situations.

Importing a Library from an earlier version

If you have used an earlier version of NGStudio and built up a large Library, you might be disappointed that when you install Studio 19 your old Library isn't made available to you.

It is possible to exchange the NGDatabase folder used by earlier versions of Studio with that used by 19 - in all the above instructions you will find the the 17 or 18 folders by using 17 or 18 in the paths instead of 19. Studio 16 and Avid Studio Library data lies in a plain Avid folder.

Please test any Library imported from another version very thoroughly! I've tested this with Studio 18 and 19, but not extensively using large Libraries, so it is possible that you might get a crash.

Importing and Linking

As I've said a couple of times already, if you want to add clips to the Library that are already stored in a reliable location on your computer the fastest way is to use **Quick Import**. This adds a link to the imported file's location in the Library database so that it appears in the Media Library. You can Quick Import more than one file from the same folder at a time, and choose to place it in a Project Bin or just add it to the Library Media listing. In either case it also gets added to the Latest Import collection.

I demonstrated Quick Import on pages 122 and 123.

Browsing

Pinnacle Studio 19 offers another way of linking media to the Library. You can drag and drop any file from a Windows environment into the Library Browser. This includes a Windows Explorer window, the Desktop, or even the standard file dialogue of another program.

This feature is made easier with the Browse tool, which exists in the middle of the Browser Window toolbar. Clicking on it opens a new, suitably placed, Windows Explorer window for you to drag and drop from. You can use all the power of Explorer to locate the assets you are looking for, including Recent Files in Windows 10.

The Browse Explorer window when first opened

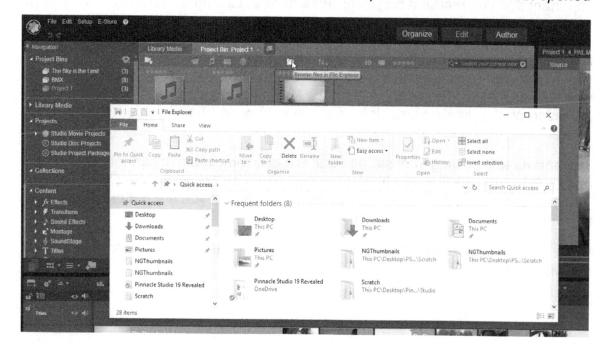

Of course, you can also harness the Windows search power from the Import Media Files dialogue that you get when Quick Importing, so you might wonder what advantage Drag and Drop offers. One is that you can choose where you want the imported file to end up. If you drag it from Windows to a Project Bin, that's where it goes. If you drag it anywhere else it just appears in the relevant branch of the Library Media tree. Another advantage is that if you have a second monitor you can leave a number of customised Browse windows open and drag media into the program at will.

When not to use Quick Import or Browsing

People often have more than one hard disc on their computer. If the extra drives are internal, then linking to a file doesn't create any issues – it will always be available. Many people's extra drives are external - plugged into a USB or possibly a Firewire port - and can be easily removed or even swapped for other drives. Some people may have drive caddies to allow them to change drives.

Even in these circumstances you may still find Quick Import sufficient for your needs. If you have added an external drive so that you have space to store lots of video files, you aren't going to remove the drive and still expect to be able to access the video files.

Because you can use Quick Import on removable media on your computer, it is very important that you realise it only ever **links** to files. Linking to a file that is on a USB memory stick that happens to be plugged into your computer isn't a good idea unless you are prepared to leave the stick in place while you perform the editing. Worse still, linking to a video file that was on a DVD in the optical drive on your computer has two drawbacks, because not only do you have to leave the disc in place, but Studio won't be able to read the video file from the DVD fast enough for you to scrub through the video on the timeline smoothly. The same may be true of some memory cards as well.

The answer to importing from storage that is easily removable or cannot be read very quickly is to copy the files to a hard disc drive. *You can't do this with Quick Import.* You can work round the problem by using Windows, but you are better off using the full import features of Pinnacle Studio.

Even if you only want to link to files, rather than copy them, the Importer is a more powerful tool.

Importer terminology

Before we open the Importer window to investigate it fully I'd like to clear up a few terms. The Importer can be used for any of the following functions:

Importing – Link mode, where a digital file that is already stored on your computer is linked to the Library.

Importing - Copy mode, where a digital file is acquired from a source – a DVD disc, a camera or removable media – and stored on your hard disc and a link added to the Library. Some minor format changes may also be made.

Ingesting (digital capture), where the source is digital tape and you end up with a digital file on your hard disc, and a link added to the Library.

Digitising (analogue capture), where the source is an analogue signal, and you end up with a digital file on your hard drive and a link added to the Library.

Opening the Importer

OK, now you can open the Importer window either by using the File menu or clicking the Import button on the Main Control bar. The Window opens over the top of the current display and is re sizable and moveable – use the usual Windows methods. The top of the Importer window has a close button on the right.

Import From and Tree view

Opening Tree View

At the top left is a box with the name **Import from**. If you don't have an analogue capture device the first entry may say *(no device found)*. If you have a File based camera attached, it will appear next in the list. Below

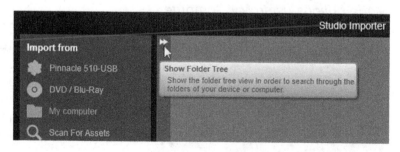

those sources is an entry for DVD/Blu-ray import. These types of import will be discussed later in this chapter.

We are interested in **My computer**. Click to select and the button will light up orange.

If you don't see the Tree view on the right, you need to click on the small double arrowhead at the top of the Tree view bar. This isn't normally an issue for *My computer*, as it should open automatically, but can cause confusion when trying to import DVD and Blu-ray images.

Tree view open

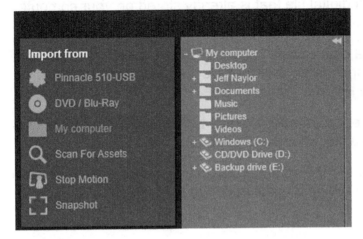

From the Tree view you can navigate to any location on your computer. You click on the + symbols to open up subfolders like the branches of a tree.

There will be three further entries in the Import from box.

Scan for Assets is an other way of linking assets to the Library, while Stop Motion and Snapshot are forms of analogue capture.

Mode

In the right-hand top corner is another box entitled **Mode**. The options available in the Mode box will depend on which choice has been made.

With *My computer* selected to import from, the first item you will see in the mode box is **Import mode**, and you have a choice of *Copy* or *Link*. Switch between the two options and you will see that in Copy mode an extra couple of boxes appears below.

Mode options using My Computer.

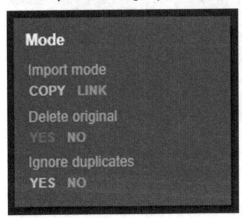

With *My computer* as the **Import from** choice and *Link* as the **Import mode**, we are looking at a grown up version of Quick Import. Notice the second line of the Mode box is *Delete Original*, but if you try to select *YES*, you can't – because we don't want to delete something we are only linking to!

The final selection in the Import box is "Ignore Duplicates" and it might not do exactly what you would expect. I'll come back to it in a moment.

The area between the *Import from* and *Mode* boxes should be filled with two sections. To the right is a browser area, where the media items are displayed, and to the left is the Tree view, (if it is expanded), with scroll bars to help you display some of the longer paths.

We should have at least one item in the Library from Chapter 1 – you probably have got a lot more. Let's navigate to *The-Sky is the Limit* clip which should be in your C: drive, under *Users/Public/Public Videos*. Open the branches of the tree as required and highlight the *Public Videos* folder, and a thumbnail of the sample video should appear in the browser window.

It's possible you can't see the video. You may have deleted it, but more likely is that you have filtered the view. A dark bar runs below the tree view and browser and at the left edge is a small drop-down menu.

Browser view selection

Here you can select the type of files displayed, and you will need *Video files* or *All compatible asset files* selected to see the Sky footage. At the other side of the bar is a slider that alters the size of the thumbnails. Use this to make the Thumbnail a decent size.

Once you have the video in the browser window, move back to the Mode box and toggle between the *Yes* and *No* choices under *Ignore duplicates*. If the Sky video is already in your Library (and it should be) the check box top right of the thumbnail will disappear when you click *Yes*.

So, *Ignore duplicates* doesn't exclude any files from being displayed in the browser – it just controls if a check box is available. With *Yes* selected, you can't select any files that are already in the Library.

Look again at the lower bar. *Check all* and *Uncheck all* gives to the chance to select or deselect the whole array of files on view – provided they have a checkbox. The thumbnails that have the box can also be selected or deselected individually by clicking on the checkboxes themselves.

If the above example isn't working for you, then for some reason the Sky video isn't in the Library. In any case, let's re-import it by selecting the *No* option for *Ignore duplicates,* checking the box on it's thumbnail and unchecking any other assets on view.

Before we click on the Start Import button at the bottom of the Importer window there is a further box to consider.

Import to (in link mode)

In Link mode, PS19 only allows you to Import into a Project Bin. To many people this may seem like an artificial restriction and I agree. However, it's possible to work round that simply by allowing Studio to generate a bin and then delete that bin - the items will still be present in the Library Media category.

Import to lists the available bins and also has the *Create Bin* icon. Before opening the Importer, selecting where you want to import to means that location is highlighted. If you choose Library Media, no bin is selected.

Import to in Link mode and the Create Bin tool

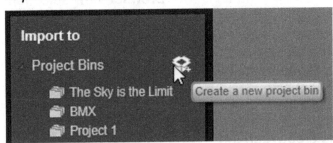

Importing into an existing bin is pretty straightforward. You select the target bin before opening the Importer, or if you forget, you select it from the list. If you want a new bin, then you can create that from within the Importer too.

If no bin is selected, then Studio creates one for you. It will have today's date in the format yyyy-mm-dd as the bin title, but you can always rename it. If you continue to create new bins rather than use the one that has just been created each subsequent bin will have the suffix (2), (3) and so on.

One slight anomaly of the early releases of S19 is that you can highlight the default The Sky is the Limit bin, even though the Importer refuses to put the imported clips into the folder and creates a new one instead. Hopefully that won't confuse you too much!

So, to test the function, create a new bin called *test* so that the Import we are about to perform doesn't spoil any bins you have in place

Linking an asset to the Library

OK, now you can click on *Start Import* at the bottom of the Importer window. The window will close and you will be returned to the main program. In the bottom right corner of the screen a small progress bar will pop up with messages about the import.

In this example its appearance will be so brief you may miss it entirely. At other times it may take some time. However, if you have to wait, you can carry on editing while you do so.

The Import completing in the background of the main program

Once complete, the new *test* bin will show up in Project Bins and open in the Library Browser, containing the Sky sample footage.

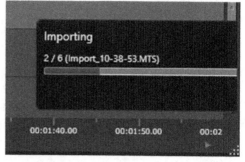

Something else occurs. If you look in the Collections category a Latest Import collection will have been created with a number (1) after it. Open that collection and you will also see the newly imported clip. In addition, the clip will have been added to Library Media in the appropriate location. In the case of the Sky sample it was already there, but any new clips would appear too.

There is a little more functionality to look at in the browser. Re-open the Importer and hover your mouse over the Sky thumbnail again. A scroll bar at the bottom can be used to scrub through the file and the thumbnail displays the video. Over the lower area of the thumbnail is a small Play button that you can use to play the clip.

Preview controls at the bottom of the Importer

This is where the two remaining icons on the lower bar of the browser come in useful – the speaker icon controls audio monitoring levels, and the full-screen button furthest right expands playback to full screen. That control will only be available once you start to play the clip – use the **Esc** key to quit.

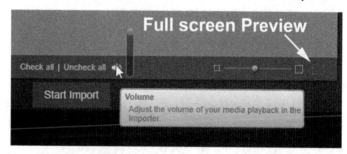

One further feature is that you can again use the normal multi-select Windows methods to highlight selections of thumbnails in the browser, but the only operation that you can carry out on a group of thumbnails is to select or deselect the check boxes.

There is another Import function that works in Link mode, but we will look at that after studying Import from My computer fully.

Recent Import Collection - a warning!

Don't rely on this collection, even if you don't want to use bins. It will disappear when you use the importer again. If you want to use collections for your imports or your projects, rename the collection straight away or move the contents into a collection that you are already using.

Copy Mode

Open the Importer and ensure the *Import from* My Computer function is selected. Switch the *Mode* to Copy. This means that the file will be copied to a new location, and **then** linked to. The most obvious reason for this is if the file is on removable media.

When you switch to Copy mode, a number of things change. The YES option of *Delete original* becomes available, two new boxes appear on the right of the screen and the Import to box on the left changes appearance. You are going to copy a media file, and Studio wants you to choose where to store it, what you want it to be called and what Metadata to add to it.

Import to (in copy mode)

Changing the Import to locations

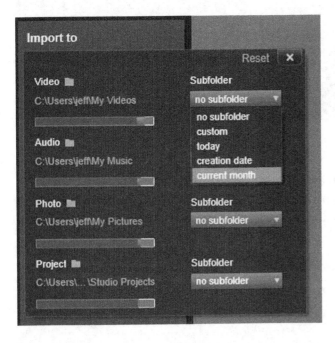

The *Import from* box no longer shows a list of Project Bins. Instead, four locations are shown, one each for the three types of media and another for Projects. If you haven't changed any of the default settings, then video files will be copied into *C:\Users\Your User Name\My Videos*, for example. If you only have one hard disc, then this is as good a place to put them as anywhere, but notice that you have the option to set subfolders for the location.

The bars underneath each location indicate how much free space on that hard disc.

There are a number of ways of changing the locations and subfolders used for storing items. You can change the hard disc and folder simply by clicking on the folder icon after each media type.

Clicking the "More Settings" arrow or the *set subfolder* text opens up a comprehensive set of options as shown in the screenshot - including a reset button. Another place to define the default locations is in the *Setup/Control Panel/Import* menu, where Directories and subfolders are amongst the options.

Subfolders can have one of five types. *No subfolder* places the import directly into the selected folder. *Custom* allows you to specify a folder name into which items are placed – you just type the name of your choice in the box provided. *Today* automatically creates a subfolder with the current day's date, in the format *yyyy-mm-dd*. *Creation date* uses the date on which the files you are trying to import were created – according to Windows. *Current Month* offers another way of you organising your imports so that they are grouped into the months in which you imported them.

Metadata

Below the Import from box there is another box called Metadata. This is also present when importing from sources other than My computer that force you into Copy mode.

The Metadata options

Metadata is the collective term for Collections, Tags and Ratings. You can automatically add items to a Collection and apply a Tag at the time of import.

If you start to type a name into the top text box a list will drop-down of the names of already created Collections. You can automatically add the asset you are about to import to one of these Collections by selecting it. If you type in a name that doesn't exist, then a new Collection will be created.

The lower text box has the same function for automatically adding a Tag to the assets.

Filenames

Having decided where you want to put the files you are about to copy or create, you also have a choice of what filename you want to use courtesy of the Filename box that has appeared beneath the Metadata box. The choices available for filenames are similar to that for folders,

Filename custom options

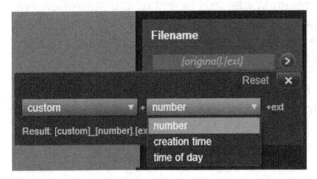

You can use the original name, or if you use a custom name you can add a second part that is either a number (incrementing for each file imported), the creation time in hours minutes and seconds (which in the case of a video file is the time you started shooting) or the time of day that the import process happened.

The Copy process

When you click on Start Import in Copy mode, again the Import window closes and you are returned to the main program.

The end of a Import session in Copy mode

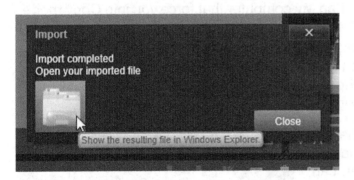

The same small progress box will indicate how the copy process is performing. Obviously this is going to be slower than linking, and you can carry on working while it happens, but the program performance may be impacted on. When the copying is complete, a window opens offering the chance to open the storage location in Windows Explorer.

Copying from other devices

If you have a file based camera that you can connect to your computer, there is a good chance that when you do so it will appear as a source in the Import from box. Pinnacle Studio might not recognise all cameras, but should pick up the presence as long as it is detected by Windows. If you plug your camera in and open the relevant *Import from* box, you should go straight to the location in the camera's memory where the files are stored.

One issue might be if you use a stills camera to shoot video, or a video camera to shoot stills. I have a Digital SLR that shoots great video, but Windows thinks it is a stills camera. Pinnacle Studio can't find the Video files unless I use the memory card in a card reader instead of straight from the camera. I also have a video camera that shoots still photos, and in this case stores them in a different location on it's memory card. In this case I need to open up the tree view mentioned earlier and browse to where the photos are stored, or use a memory card reader.

If a camera uses a card, rather than internal memory or a hard disc drive, putting the card in a card reader on your computer may have the same effect as plugging in the camera. I can't test every situation, but I assume this is because Studio recognises the card structure and name.

If all else fails and a device doesn't get it's own entry in the Import from box when you plug it in, then if Windows has recognised the device as a drive location you can use the My computer option in conjunction with the tree view to find the assets, or use any software that came with your camera to transfer the clips.

It's possible that someone has sent you some files on a memory stick, an external hard drive or as data files on an optical CD, DVD or Blu-ray disc. Again, the My computer Import from box should be your chosen route to these files. However, if the optical discs are formatted as DVD or Blu-ray discs suitable for playing on a standalone player, Pinnacle Studio has a better option for importing the files, more of which in a moment.

Displaying old thumbnails when importing camera files

There may be an issue when importing into PS19 from a file based camera that doesn't use continuous file numbering. If, when you delete files or format a card the camera starts its file numbering from the beginning again, when you try to import new files with the same filename as you have previously imported, the thumbnails from the old file will be displayed. If you have Ignore Duplicates checked, you won't be able to import them either.

Now, this can be extremely confusing if you don't know about the problem. There are two ways of solving the issue:

1 – Just ignore the fact that the thumbnails are wrong, uncheck *Ignore Duplicates* and import the files anyway. They will be suitably renumbered and you can then look at the imports with the correct thumbnails and manage them as normal.

2 – Delete the cache of thumbnails before trying to Import.

To do the latter, you need to ensure that you can see hidden files and folders in Windows (see page 156) and then to delete the Thumbnails, close Studio and use Windows Explorer to navigate to:

C:*Users/ Your profile name*
/Appdata/Local/Pinnacle_Studio_19/Studio/Scratch/NGThumbnails

Select all the folders with CTRL-A and delete them. When you open Studio will have to regenerate all the thumbnails, which may mean you have to wait briefly as the thumbnails are created when they need to be displayed. This does mean that when you try to import a camera file that has the same filename as one previously imported the old thumbnail won't be displayed.

Sorting by date issue with video files

As mentioned on page 129, Studio's Library looks at the date a video file was created, so if you have copied across the files, either with Windows or with the Importer, the original shooting date and time will be lost. The time that you stopped shooting is stored in the Modified field, but this isn't accessed by Studio.

Your camera may have a software utility that will move the files for you, or you could risk using the Move command in Windows, but that is a little risky as you will wipe out the original files on the camera. The next section describes a way of working that avoids the loss of the video shooting date and time.

A strategy for camera files

I recognise that we all have different ways of working, but I would like to suggest a workflow for you to use when importing files from your own cameras.

Although I have a separate, internal hard drive to store my media assets, you don't need one to follow this idea - where I refer to "Media drive" you can just as well use the default Windows library locations.

In my media drive I have a folder called Video and under that a folder for each type of camera I use. When I import from my file based Panasonic SD10 I use the customised location Media drive\SD10\creation date and the customised filename SD10_[creation time]. When I import, all my video files can be found both by date and time of shooting. They are arranged in a folder for each day, and the time of shooting is appended to the file name. Even if I imported from a couple of different cards, and do so in the wrong order, alphabetically sorting the filenames will restore them to shooting order.

Scan for Assets

There is a further feature of the Import that only works in Link mode that is worth considering. If you switch the **Import from** selection to *Scan for Assets* you will notice that the Mode box has lost all its functions, the Metadata box has appeared and the bar at the bottom of the screen has changed. The collapsible tree view is still there, but the browser window only contains a message which explains the function.

Scan for Assets with Video format selection

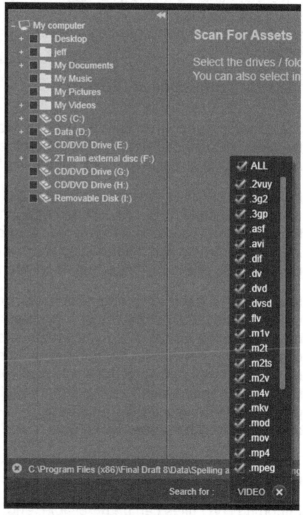

Checkboxes will have appeared in the tree view. Selecting a particular box doesn't cause the contents to be displayed. You can select whole drives or folders, but if you expand each drive or folder you can see subfolders, each with its own checkbox.

These checkboxes allow you to be very selective about what folders you want to include in the pending scan operation.

The control bar at the bottom of the Import window contains three further selections – click on Video and a tree opens listing all the types of files Studio can import, each with its own checkbox. If you want to only scan for AVI files, for example, uncheck the ALL box and then just check the .avi box. If you don't want to scan for audio or photos, then deselect the ALL checkboxes for these categories.

Still nothing will have appeared in the browser. In fact nothing will, even when you click on Scan and Import at the very bottom of the window. The message "Are you sure" will appear, because if you begin the scan you will be starting a background process that will take some time and use computer resources that could otherwise be used for editing.

When you do confirm that you want the process to start, the Importer closes and you are returned to the main program. In the background, the specified folders are scanned for the specified file types, and every one that is found is added to the Library. You are kept informed of the progress by messages at the bottom right of the screen.

So, in this respect, the process is a more powerful form of Watchfolders, but it's a one-shot function – the specified folders aren't monitored for any other items added at a later time. I would recommend using Scan for Assets function when you are first setting up your installation of Pinnacle Studio, or perhaps after plugging in an external drive that contains media you might want to use. It is an all-inclusive process, so if you think you might find yourself going into the Library and removing some items after Scan and Import, consider using Import from My computer or even Quick Import instead.

Import from optical media

Just to remind you - if an optical disc has been burned in a data format, you can use the methods previously outlined to import the files. You will want to copy, rather than link to the files because that disc isn't going to be in the drive forever!

If the DVD or Blu-ray disc has been made for playing on a DVD or Blu-ray player, you should use DVD/Blu-ray option in the Import from box. This includes DVD discs that have been recorded on camcorders or other DVD recorders as well as created in Pinnacle Studio and other editing programs. Pinnacle Studio doesn't allow you to import DVDs or Blu-ray discs that have been copy protected.

Inserting a suitable disc into your DVD or Blu-ray drive on your computer and switching the the DVD/Blu-ray option will start the process of reading the disc in the drive. Once the disc is read (which may take a little time) the number of thumbnails displayed will depend on the number of Titles on the disc - one thumbnail per title, so you don't have to import the whole disc. On some discs you get proper thumbnails that you can preview and even scrub through. However, on other discs you may get generic video placeholder thumbnails. This bug appears to be somewhat random although it may be related to the type of audio that the disc contains.

The name of the disc pre-populates the Filename box, although you can change that if you wish.

Importing DVD titles can be unreliable, and Pinnacle Studio, along with most other programs I've tried, fails with certain discs, particularly if a standalone DVD recorder has generated them. The problem often doesn't show up with a DVD import until you try to to re-render it into another format. I would urge you to test any imports by making a test file from them before you put mountains of work into a project that uses these files as source material. The most notable issue is a gradual loss of audio sync.

Having said that, Pinnacle Studio 19 is better at importing problem discs than earlier Pinnacle products. Check the Pinnacle site for patches and hot fixes on this subject as DVD recorder manufacturers don't always follow the standards that they should!

Importing titles follows the same pattern as copying other files, and you will end up with a Pinnacle Studio compatible MPEG-2 or H.264 video file in the location you choose, and the items added to the Library as well.

Importing from a DVD Image stored on a hard disc

One thing that may not be immediately obvious is how to import from a disc image, rather than an actual disc. Once you open up the tree view the the right of the Import from box, however, it becomes clear how to browse to any location on your hard drives where an image might be stored.

If you run Windows 8 or 10, then you can also easily import DVD images created as ISO files, by using the Mount

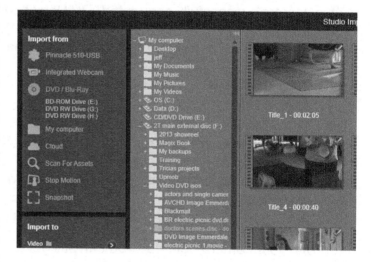

command to turn them into a virtual drive that will show up in Studio's Importer.

DV and HDV

Two video formats that have been popular for years with consumers and prosumers are the original Standard Definition and later High Definition DV (Digital Video) and HDV tape-based cameras. While they are no longer sold widely, many people still use them, even in the semi-professional market.

The video that these cameras record is normally stored on Digital Tape, and as I mentioned earlier, importing that kind of data is called *ingesting*. Video information stored on a tape is of no use to a computer, but a relatively simple digital transfer can be used to ingest the data without degrading it in any way and place it in a file suitable for editing.

One disadvantage of this form of storage is that you can only play back from the tape in real time; another is that mechanical issues can cause poor tracking, leading to data that is incomplete. However, in comparison to analogue formats such as VHS it is far superior.

DV and HDV cameras normally connect via Firewire (otherwise called an IEEE 1394 port) even if your camera also has a USB port. If your computer doesn't have FireWire built in, expansion cards for desktop computers and PC slot adaptors for laptops are available. Some of Pinnacle's capture hardware also includes a FireWire port. (There are a few rare DV cameras that can pass video via USB, but you will need to use the software supplied with the camera to import from those).

With a camera successfully connected, *DV Device* will become available in the *Import From* source panel top left of the Import Window. Select it and it will highlight in an orange colour. The DV transport controls will appear below the preview screen.

Failed to get video from device?

I find that to be sure of Studio picking up my DV camera, it is best to connect it up via the FireWire port **before** starting Studio. This should not be required, but I think my camera can be a bit of a law unto itself. If you are a Windows 7 or above user, you may have some issues with generic FireWire devices. If you are having trouble getting your computer to see your camera, you may need to investigate if you need to install a Legacy device driver. You can find details on the Microsoft website.

Even with your camera detected you can still get an error detecting the actual video, even if you can control the camera. This can be caused by a faulty firewire cable, but more likely it's to do with the order of connection or a prior unsuccessful connection attempt. I've seen this happen a couple of times with S19, Windows 10 and a USB 510 capture device, and re-booting the computer, making sure the camera is connected and then launching Studio has always cleared the problem for me.

DV Capture settings

The choices you have in the *Mode* box on the right side of the preview window determine how the file will be stored on your computer. For DV tape, the obvious choice is to ingest the data from the tape in the same format - DV-AVI. DV is DV; that's it – it's a fixed format.

Choosing MPEG-2 will cause the DV format to be re-encoded during capture to a more compressed format. HDV cameras use MPEG-2 as their basic format anyway,

DV-AVI cannot be used to contain high definition video. Custom setting allow you to vary the standard definition MPEG-2 settings if you wish, but unless you have a particular requirement, stick with the default settings that will match the best quality from the camera.

Scene detection is an option that allows you to generate a data file at the time of capture. This file contains information as to how Pinnacle Studio can subdivide the file it is working on into a series of scenes. When capturing from DV or HDV you can choose to detect scenes by Time and Date – which effectively means a scene break is added each time the camera was stopped and started again. The second option adds a scene break when there is a noticeable change in the video content. This will often be the same place as you pausing the recording, but can also be triggered by sudden changes such as a camera flash going off. This option is of more use on video that doesn't have the embedded timecode of Digital Video.

Automatic, every xx seconds isn't an option I use much, but if it suits your workflow, it's worth noting that there is very little advantage in doing so at the time of capture. Scene detection by interval is a simple mathematical operation, so it happens very quickly if you decide to detect scenes in this way after the capture.

Manually, by pressing space bar has its uses if you are "minding" a capture and want to mark certain sections. The scene points will only be as accurate as your reflexes, but will help you find parts of a tape you noticed and marked by pressing the spacebar at the time of capture.

The *Stop at tape end* option should be fairly explanatory – except I don't know why anyone would want to continue capturing after a tape had come to the end! The Tape end signal is generated because the tape has physically come to the end, not because the tape is blank.

Having set the source - where we are ingesting from - and how we want to store the video, we now can set **where** we want Studio to store the file in the *Import to* box. This is the same as Copy mode, except you only have to define where you want to put video.

For DV capture/ingest, Studio offers controls on a par with fully professional NLE programs. On the more organised TV or film shoots, shots are logged with a relevant time code and duration. It is then the job of the edit assistant to ingest the takes marked as good into the system once the tape reaches the edit suite. Using the Start, Duration and End boxes this can be done automatically. Below that, are a set of controls for the DV camera, for the less organised amongst us!

Note that the speaker icon only affects preview volume, not that on the final file.

HDV Capture

HDV capture differs in that the end result is always a set of MPEG-2 files because that is how the files are stored on tape. Otherwise the process is the same as a DV camera although some HDV cameras need to be switched to HDV mode before you can extract HD video from them.

Dropped Frames

There is one serious error message you might see during the Capture process - under "Recorded" you may see "Dropped Frames". If you do, then you may have a damaged tape, a camera that needs its heads cleaned, or a more fundamental computer issue.

Hard disc data rates – a capture bottleneck?

Let's presume you have a solid, working FireWire connection to your camera, which is playing the DV tape successfully. You are capturing in the DV-AVI format, so no fancy processor work is involved. However, after a few seconds of successful capture, the Dropped frames counter starts to register losses. This is a Very Bad Thing.

The ingest process is pretty straightforward. When I perform DV capture the CPU usage in the Task Manager/Performance tab hardly gets into double figures. The one time-critical task is storing the file onto hard disc. It doesn't go straight there – it is buffered through the computer's random access memory to start with – but the disc needs to be able to keep up in the long term.

Consider the DV-AVI file size. It consists of 3,600KBytes for every second of video, so even on the most well equipped computer it won't take long to fill up the spare RAM. That data needs to be written to the hard disc at the same speed it is being generated from the DV tape – over 3 and a half million bytes a second.

Modern hard discs can achieve this speed with ease. Real life drives can peak at over 20 times that data rate. What can possibly go wrong?

One of the recommendations for video work is to use a separate drive for storing files. The main reason for this is that the operating system which occupies the C: drive (in most circumstances) is never really idle, and it is accessing files it has stored, not just as data, but parts of itself that aren't stored in RAM. Windows also uses a paging file that serves as an adjunct to its random access memory, and that too is on the C: drive. If the OS is working on files on one part of the hard disc and Studio is trying to store files somewhere else, much time is wasted as the heads fly up and down the disc platters trying to do two or more things at once. Having a separate drive for video means it isn't being constantly interrupted by other access demands. This affects playback and capture.

What if you only have one drive? Well, capture should still be easily possible if the drive is in good shape. Windows stores files in an increasingly random pattern as the drive fills up. If a large number of small files are deleted, the OS may decide to fill up the empty space with one large file split into smaller parts. The process is called Fragmentation. When it occurs on conventional Hard Disc Drives it lowers the performance of the computer.

Basic defragmentation tools are available in Windows, although Windows 8 seems to keep your drives in good enough shape automatically. Other tools are available that claim to do a better job, but you don't need to go over the top – if a drive is reported to have less than 10% fragmentation it's highly unlikely that it is causing dropped frames.

Compression and Indexing checkboxes

It's not just the Operating System that may be accessing the main drive – other background programs can be using it as well. Some programs could even be scanning or indexing other drives, so it pays to keep a check on what is going on behind your back.

It's possible to automatically compress hard disc drives in some circumstances. Newer operating systems have introduced automatic indexing to speed up searching. Both processes can disrupt smooth data transfer. I'd recommend you turn both off on any drive you wish to capture to. In Windows/My Computer, right-click on the icon for the particular drive and select properties. I've drawn an arrow pointing to the two boxes that need to remain unchecked on the screenshot.

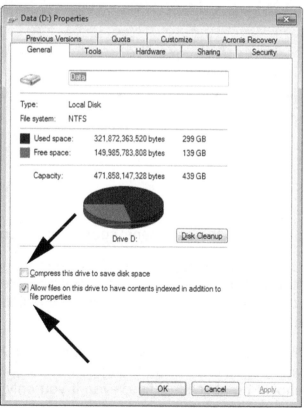

On older computer systems the next thing to check would be what transfer mode your capture drive is working in. Because Pinnacle Studio only works on Vista and higher, it isn't likely that your hard drive is working in a mode called PIO. DVD drives can be put into PIO mode by a bad disc, for hard drives it is normally the sign of an internal fault in the drive.

You might want to check the speed your drive achieves. You can find the **Resource Monitor** in Windows *Start/All Programs/Accessories/System Tools/*. It provides a running graph of disc activity and the transfer speeds achieved. The screenshot shows the graphs generated by playing back DV-AVI video in Studio from an external hard drive.

The Windows Resource Monitor

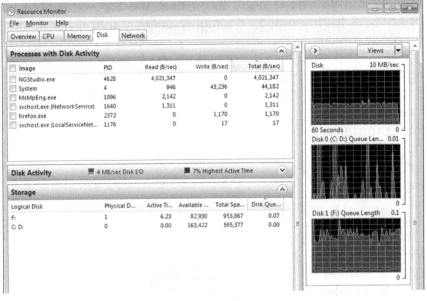

If you have an external hard disc connected by FireWire, or more likely USB 2.0, another source of problems can be that the external connection is clashing with other devices. Check the data rates and make sure that they aren't sharing a hub connection. The best way to do this is to plug them directly into the back panel sockets of the computer.

One final thing that can affect disc performance is power management software. This is unlikely to be affecting the hard disc of a desktop machine, but a laptop, particularly running on battery power, could be affected by general slow running, including the disc drives.

In the "bad old days" trying to capture to a hard disc using DMA mode 1 access, it was possible to cause a dropped frame just by moving the mouse. Modern discs should be absolutely fine, even if you only have one, but a culmination of factors might still lead to dropped frames.

These aren't the only causes of poor capture, but the others are more likely to cause problems with analogue video, so let's move on to that.

Analogue capture

Ah, those crumbling VHS tapes in the loft, mocking your promise to transfer them to DVDs. One day, one day...

If you have decided to bite the bullet, you are going to need some hardware to convert the analogue signals sent out by the VHS player to a digital file.

If you are familiar with analogue video principles and what digital actually means, you can skip the next few sections, but if you're not really sure how an audio or video picture can be passed down a single wire, take a deep breath. I'm going to go quite a long way back.....

An analogue video primer

Let's start with Audio and how an electrical signal can represent it. Before I can explain that, I had better define what sound actually is.

It's a variation of air pressure. A bell passes its mechanical vibration to the surrounding air. The sound of my voice is created by my vocal chords by vibrating the air as it passes through them. When that air vibration reaches your ears, it moves your eardrum, which translates the signal into nerve pulses that are deciphered by your brain.

The human ear can hear vibrations of varying speeds. A slow vibration – let's say 50 times a second – will be heard as a very low note, and a fast vibration – perhaps 16000 times a second - as a very high note. If that vibration is pure and at one frequency, it will be a clear sound like the tone of a tuning fork. All other sounds are a mixture of frequencies.

In order that we can pass sounds down wires, over the airwaves or record them onto electronic devices, we first convert them into an electrical signal that consists of electrons moving around a circuit. They can do that at all the frequencies we can hear, as well as very much higher ones.

So, a graph of a sound wave against time will look the same as the voltage present in an audio circuit. Both will look similar to the waveforms that Studio draws on its audio timelines. If you use the Preview window to look at the waveform and zoom right in, it still only gives a rough idea of the changes in sound pressure or the electrical signal – although other programs can look closer.

For high quality sound, the components of any system need to carry nearly all the frequencies humans perceive as sound equally – and you may have heard of the term Frequency Response as a measure of how good an audio system is.

OK, I need to define vision next. The human eye sees light reflected off objects around us. This light – a very high frequency radio wave – enters our eyes through a lens and hits light sensitive cells at the back of the eyeball where it is converted into nerve signals. These signals are sent to the brain and deciphered. The slightly different frequencies of the light waves are what we perceive as colour.

When we look at a TV set, the "trick" that fools us into believing we are seeing a true moving image is the same today as it was hundreds of years ago when people made novelty devices such as zoetropes or a set of flick cards . A series of still pictures displayed in rapid succession will appear to the human brain as fluid motion. This is often called the *persistence of vision*, but in fact more recent research shows it is a brain function known as the *Beta Movement Phenomena*. Whatever you want to call it, a flip book of drawings or 16 photographs projected within a second is seen to be smooth movement and this led to the invention of film. Even with further advances, the standard for film projection is still only 24 frames per second.

Television *(from the Greek **Tele** (far) and Latin **Viso** (to see))* needed a way of turning this fast succession of pictures into an electrical signal that could be passed down wires, or transmitted over the airwaves. The solution is still with us today, and involves scanning an image to create an analogue Video signal.

A frame is divided up into a series of lines, and these are scanned, starting at the top, from left to right. To produce a monochrome signal, the brightness would be measured along the scanned line and represented as a variable electrical signal. At the end of the line, a new one is scanned from slightly lower, and the process repeated until the whole frame is scanned. Then the next frame is scanned, and so on. Negative pulses are added to the signal to indicate the start of a new line, and larger ones for the start of a new frame.

Ah, but that's only black and white, I hear you say. A colour TV picture is made by mixing the three (additive) primary colours – Red, Green and Blue. If you can get those colours pure enough, then by mixing them, you can reproduce any other colour. The original cathode ray tubes fired electrons at phosphors. LCD displays use liquid crystals to filter light. Plasma displays contain tiny fluorescent light sources. All of them mix the three primary colours – and a full dose of each will produce white.

Three signals can give us the full colour range, and some Video connections are indeed **component**. A two wire system (**S-Video**) consists of a luminance (black and white) signal, and another which encodes the hue (colour) and saturation (how much) into one signal know as chrominance. Finally, a **composite** video signal needs only one wire, as the chrominance signal is modulated onto the luminance signal in a similar manner to radio signals.

The single composite video signal also has to have audio modulated onto it in order to be transmitted through the airwaves on a single transmission frequency. The result is the complex, fragile signal that has been used to transmit and receive analogue television pictures since the introduction of colour TV in the 1950s. It has only just been phased out in some parts of the world, and will be around for many years to come in other parts. What's more, it's what comes out of the back of a VHS machine!

Interlacing, frame rates and digital compression.

Having described the complexities of analogue signals, I can now refer you to the first chapter of the book where you should find the rest of the information you need to understand the process of how video is manipulated and stored in the digital realm. One we get the fragile analogue signals converted to digital files, the biggest threat to the quality is over-compressing the files.

Capture hardware

If all that theory has left you a little dizzy, let's return to more practical matters.

To import analogue video directly into Studio, you are most likely going to need a Pinnacle capture device. Pinnacle Studio only supports the newer capture devices or a DV Firewire input.

Pinnacle used to make capture device that fits inside a desktop computer. Sadly even the latest models don't work on 64-bit operating systems if you have 2Gb or more of memory – which defeats the object of having a 64-bit OS.

USB connected devices are easier to fit, and are also suitable for laptops. The USB Pinnacle branded models Moviebox/USB 500/510 and Moviebox Plus/Ultimate/700/710 (the latter models can output video) are still available on eBay and some other retail outlets but beware that many of the earlier models used Moviebox in their name somewhere and won't be compatible with the newer operating systems - check the Pinnacle website carefully!

The remaining USB capture devices are branded as Dazzle products, and marketed as low cost solutions – often without full versions of the Studio software. The models that will work on the latest operating systems are the DVC 101 (DVD Recorder), DVC 103 (Video Creator) and DVC 107 (Video Creator Platinum). they can capture full resolution, standard definition video at good bitrates.

The only third party devices that may work with Pinnacle Studio are ones that connect via FireWire. Canopus make a range of these, but I haven't had the chance to test one. If you own one, you will need to use the DV camera import option.

A neat Analogue Capture alternative

If you own a DV camcorder that you can connect via FireWire, you might be able to use it to capture an analogue signal. This will depend on the model – it's a feature that is more likely to be provided on high-end camcorders.

Check the manual to see if it has Analogue In and is capable of DV pass-through. Some models of camera may have this feature in the North American versions, but have it disabled on the European version to comply with import quota restrictions. You might be able to get a "crippled" European model modified to work.

If you have the correct equipment, you can use the DV capture mode to capture the analogue signal plugged into the camera. One stumbling block could appear to be that when you click capture, the camera starts playing its DV tape. The answer to this is to remove the tape and close the tape housing door.

Sometimes, this method may require a long run up time – the camera needs to obtain a stable signal before it can tell Studio's DV capture routines it is ready – so recording the first few seconds of an analogue tape may be problematic. Once working, though, the quality should be as good as any other capture device and you are capturing straight to DV-AVI.

Firing up the device

With your capture device plugged in and installed, switch to Import Mode and in the *Import from* setting box, select your analogue capture device.

Open the fly out panel by clicking the forward arrow to see the options available. Your particular device may not have all the options shown. First will be a choice of connection - Composite or S-video.

A brief word about connections

S-video uses a four-pin connector carrying two analogue video signals, chrominance and luminance, down two separate wires. This offers better quality as the final combination of colour and luminance is not required. If your analogue source has an output socket providing S-video it is better to connect up to your capture device using this if you have suitable cables.

One important warning – the front panel RCA sockets on VCRs, DVD recorders and TV sets are almost always for input only – you won't get a signal out of them to feed your capture device. Some TV sets may have output RCA sockets at the back.

In Europe, you will be used to the presence of SCART sockets on VCRs, TVs and DVD machines. These connectors are normally bi-directional, but if you have a SCART plug with only one set of leads, there is a 50/50 chance the leads are for input **to** the SCART. If you need to buy a SCART lead or adaptor, I'd recommend you get one with an input/output switch.

The Import settings for analogue

Another word of warning about SCARTs – the sockets of a particular machine may not necessarily output a S-Video signal. If it is capable of doing so, you may have to operate a switch on the back panel, or a menu option on the machine itself. If in doubt, consult the manual. A muddle in this area is a major cause of only getting a black and white picture.

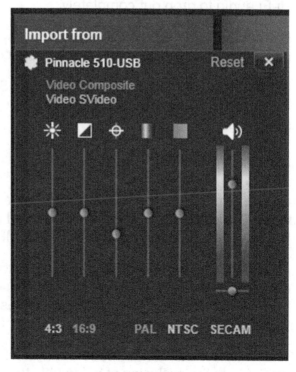

Once you have a capture device hooked up, you can return to the settings panel knowing what the Video Composite and Video S-video options are for!

Adjusting the input

Five virtual sliders control the brightness, contrast, sharpness, hue and colour saturation of the video input signal. Unless there is something significantly wrong with the video signal, I find it is best to leave these in the middle positions. If you are sure that the whole of what you are about to capture needs to have, for example, the brightness lifted, then it will save you time if you make the adjustment during capture, but smaller adjustments are best left to the edit stage. Hue will have no effect if you are using the PAL standard.

To the right of the panel are the audio controls. The vertical slider controls the input level, and you can see the effect on the meter to the right of the preview window. The horizontal slider will control stereo balance if that works on your particular hardware.

I've lost count of the number of times I have had to restart a capture because I forgot to set the audio levels. Always play your source material so that you sample the loudest section of audio, and set the level control so that only the loudest parts light up the yellow section. You don't want any red showing. Use your ears as well – listen for distortion and if you hear it when the meter peaks, turn down the levels.

A tip about capturing audio from VCRs - if your playback machine has a Hi-Fi symbol, it should have two audio systems. The conventional method records an audio stripe along the tape, but the Hi-Fi method encodes the audio signal amongst the video. Look for an option to switch between the two; if Hi-Fi is available, use it as the audio will sound much better. The only potential issue is that tape disturbances can cause Hi-Fi audio to drop out completely.

Bottom left of the box are selections for aspect ratio - 4:3 and 16:9, otherwise known as Standard and Widescreen. Select the correct shape for your source material.

Finally, you can select PAL, NTSC and SECAM. These are the European, North American or French TV standards and you should select the one that matches your source video.

Mode selection

On the right side of the preview screen the Mode box varies a little from that offered when DV is selected. The presets offered here will differ between capture devices. For my 510 USB I have a choice of DV, MPEG or Custom.

I suggest you use DV in many circumstances, particularly if you have plenty of hard disc space. Using MPEG capture is discussed in the previous section about capturing from DV cameras as well, and may be best if you want to make DVD discs quickly. Custom may offer other options, although MJPEG is no longer offered in S18.

The other controls in the mode box are for Scene detection, which are the same as for DV, with the exclusion of being able to use the time and date. My recommendation for analogue capture is to set scene detection to *automatic based on content*, but we will see later that you can this during the edit process.

The final two boxes for analogue capture are identical in function to the ones for DV capture and Copy - setting where you want the file stored, and what you want to call it.

Mode selection set to MPEG-2

Ready to record? You need to start the VCR, camera or other analogue source playing manually – Studio can't control it like a DV camera. Set the tape up a little earlier than you want the capture to start and press Play a moment or two before clicking Start capture. Another option is to set up the VCR so it is paused on the first good frame and then press play once capture has started. Which is best will depend on how stable your playback source is, and

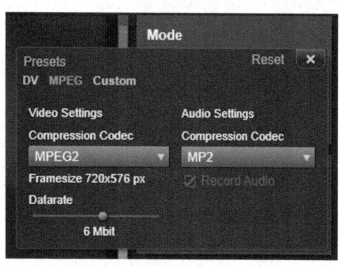

how close to the beginning of the recording you need to capture video from.

If all is well, the album area will fill up with thumbnails, you will capture your video and audio, stopping when it's all in the computer, switch to the Edit Mode and get on with the creative bit. If you have dropped some frames or Studio refuses to capture, then review the information about DV capture, and then read on.

More Analogue Capture issues.

One major cause of dropping frames is the Hard Disc bottleneck described earlier. It's easy to check for, so it should be the first thing on the list when troubleshooting capture issues. If the problem occurs using the DV setting, but goes away when you choose MPEG, then it almost certainly is the hard disc access speeds. Even if it doesn't, it is still worth looking at the disc performance as mentioned earlier. If that doesn't solve your problem, let us start looking for the problem at the start of the signal chain.

Most analogue capture is likely to be from domestic video recordings – VHS or Betamax VCRs or analogue camcorders. I'd wager that the tapes you are trying to record from aren't fresh either. To eliminate the cause of the dropped frames being unstable playback from tape, try recording a more stable video signal - the video picture from a camcorder, the off air signal from a TV or the output from a DVD player should all be very stable. If you drop frames with these, then the next section about tape playback can be skimmed through, but still introduces some good practices.

If you can, use the same VCR or camcorder to play back the tape that recorded it. That may not be possible, particularly if you are doing a favour for someone else! The next best bet is a VCR with a timebase correction feature, although some of the simpler ones can cause "flash" frames (a single frame in an incorrect place) when used in conjunction with the top end capture devices. My VCR has a "Video Stabilizer" feature that has exactly that effect. It is good to have the choice, though.

I have boxes of VHS tapes which I'm still supposed to be digitising, and I have to admit to not storing them in ideal conditions. It is worth spending a little time making sure you are getting the most stable playback you can. If the tape has been stored somewhere like a basement or loft (or particularly a garage!), leave it in the house for a least a few hours to let it acclimatise - preferably longer. Then put it in the playback machine and spool it (fast forward and rewind, as opposed to play) up and down its entire length a couple of times to even up the tension. Finally, run a cleaning tape through the playback machine.

When you start playback to set the audio levels, either let the machine automatically adjust its tracking, or if you have manual control, adjust it for best playback. This is best done on a TV if you can connect to one. If you still see disturbances on playback, it is likely to cause dropped frames, particularly with the simpler capture devices. The newer upmarket capture hardware incorporates more sophisticated electronics.

If you still experience dropped frames, the next suspect to investigate is another computer process interfering with the stream of data. The cheaper devices use software and the computer's CPU for capture. Open up the task manager at the performance tab and have a look at CPU usage when capture is running. If it's peaking over 50%, check for background processes. Disconnect your Internet connection and shut down all the anti-virus, anti-spam security clutter which clobbers the performance of your computer.

Another possible culprit is the interface between the capture device and the computer. I assume you didn't get any error messages when following the install procedure - if you did you will need to follow them up. PCI cards may, in rare circumstances clash with other PCI devices, and one solution in the past was to switch the capture card to another slot, but I've rarely heard this reported in recent years. If you have a choice, put the card in the first slot.

USB (Universal Serial Bus) is another matter, though. There are 3 standards, but USB 2,0 is the most common. It can transfer at data rates up to 480Mbits a second – more than enough – but USB 1.1 has a maximum data transfer rate of 12Mbits a second. That's not very good – the standard is obsolete. Most high speed devices will complain if they are connected via this standard, but you also need to be suspicious if don't find the word *Enhanced* in the Hardware Manager/Universal Serial Bus Controllers entry in the Device Manager.

None of the devices that work with Pinnacle Studio can take advantage of USB 3.0 at the time of writing. I'm holding out hope that a USB 3.0 HD capture card will be available one day!

Connection via a USB hub can cause conflicts, and for capture devices that take their power via USB, be warned that some USB ports are limited in the amount of power they can provide.

So, eliminate all unneeded USB devices, and plug your capture device into a back panel USB socket on your desktop or tower computer. If you are using a laptop, don't use a socket on the front edge, and make sure you are running on mains power.

If you think you have tried everything, see if you can try another computer – there is always the possibility that the device itself is faulty!

What Capture setting should I use?

Given that analogue capture in Studio is currently restricted to Standard Definition video, and that even DV-AVI files are manageable with a decent sized hard drive, why settle for less and capture at a lower quality than the maximum?

Pinnacle Studio used to use Direct Stream Copy for mpeg-2 files, so there were some advantages in speed and avoiding two lots of encoding by capturing to a DVD compatible format that could be "SmartRendered"

With faster computers, the DVD render times aren't anywhere so long now, and Pinnacle appear to have dropped all forms of Direct Stream copy for DVD video, so the main advantage of capturing to mpeg-2 is if that is going to be your final format, you aren't going to carry out any editing or transfer them to Video-DVD.

Webcam Capture

One "live" video source that you can capture apart from those plugged into a working analogue capture device is a webcam. A useful function in some circumstances - you might just want to send a short video message, but with the chance to edit or add captions. Most webcams are rather low quality, but if you have one built into the lid of your laptop, it's a shame not to be able to record the output.

Settings are similar to other analogue and digital capture sources.

Stopmotion and Snapshot

Two additional import functions exist at the bottom of the Import from box. Both use a video input - Webcam, DV or analogue - to capture video stills or video frames.

Stopmotion can be quite a bit of fun. I fired it up to test it for this chapter, and ended up animating my coffee cup all around my desk. You can capture 8 or 12 fps animations, which is to say that you need to capture either 8 or 12 pictures for 1 second of video. The most useful feature is the "Onion skin" preview that shows a ghost image of the previous capture to help alignment.

When you have built up your animation, Studio saves it as an MJPEG AVI video file, a series of photos, or both.

The **Snapshot** feature captures still frames from a video source and saves them as Jpegs.

Screen Capture

The Live Screen Capture tool

An increasingly common requirement is for some way of capturing what is happening on the screen of your computer. Pinnacle have addressed this need by providing a standalone program. It's the same tool that Pinnacle's parent company supply with their other video editing program, VideoStudio.

There are other screen capture programs available, some of which may be more suitable for capturing gameplay or other fast moving screen images, but in my experience the output from these programs can sometimes be problematic to edit.

 FRAPS in particular can use a very lightly compressed codec that may choke your computer when you try to edit it. Others such as Bandicam may create variable frame rates which can cause havoc when editing. So if you want to be sure that you can work with your screen capture files in Pinnacle Studio, I'd highly recommend you use Live Screen Capture.

You run the program from your Desktop or Metro interface. Once open, you are presented with a small, moveable interface. It looks pretty simple, but open up the Settings drop-down and you get quite a few choices.

The Settings for Screen Capture

In **File Settings**, the first few options are straightforward – what you want the file to be called, where to save it, if you want it included in the Library and if so, in which folder. This last option does not appear to work in Pinnacle's version of the program.

Frame rate is the usual NTSC/PAL choice between 30 or 25 fps, or the option of 15 fps, which would give you smaller files but that might look a bit choppy. Notice that it doesn't matter what framerate your PC display might be achieving, because you are going to end up with a file that will work correctly in an editing program.

In **Audio settings** you can choose to record the PC's system sounds, a microphone plugged into the PC or both. The sound check button will help you set up the microphone but you may need to dive into the Windows recording settings to get enough level, using the Boost control. Refer to the Voice Over tool on page 420 for further details.

Control settings offers you a *Mouse click animation* feature that adds an enlarged graphic of mouse operations to the video capture, making it easier to see what the user is getting up to on the screen. F10 and F11 are normally enabled as keyboard shortcuts to *Stop*, or *Pause* and *Resume* recording, but if they clash with another program you can disable them. If you have two monitors attached to your PC, the **Monitor Settings** will allow you to choose which monitor display is captured.

There are further choices of what you capture available to the right of the Record and Stop buttons at the top of the program window, and these are still available when the Settings area is closed.

By default, *Full screen* is shown in the drop down selection box, but if you open it, you also have a choice of *Custom*, or any of the other Windows that are active, so you can choose an application even if it isn't full screen. Selecting any of these options will cause a cyan border to by drawn around the area that is to be captured.

The recording countdown

Capturing a custom area of the screen requires you to set up the area using the Freehand selection tool. Clicking on this adds handles to the cyan border so that you can resize the area, and a button in the middle of the area allows you to move it. If you want to alter the aspect ratio of the capture area, click on the little link icon between the width and height parameter boxes. You can also type values into these boxes if you wish to.

ScreenCap icon in the taskbar

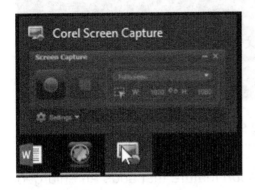

To begin recording, just click on the red record button. Don't worry if the Screen capture tool is currently obscuring part of the screen you wish to capture – after a 3-2-1 countdown it will minimise itself down to the task bar.

If you kept the function key setting enabled, you can just use F10 and F11 to pause/restart or stop recording, otherwise just click on the program icon in the taskbar to restore the capture tool back to its original position.

Once you have stopped recording, the resultant file will be saved in your specified location,

Watchfolders

Pinnacle Studio has a feature that automates the Quick Importing of items. Again, it's best to think of this as *linking* because all that I've said about Quick Import applies

– if the storage location is temporary or slow to access it's not really a suitable place to link to. I've described the system in the Library chapter section Project Bins vs. Watchfolders starting on page 119.

When you first install and run Studio 19 Watchfolders will be disabled and most newcomers to Studio are likely to choose to leave the settings as they are. Having read about the pros and cons, if you decide you do want to use Watchfolders, they can be enabled in the Control Panel.

In the main program drop-down menus the *Setup* drop-down has the option to open the *Control Panel* (or you can use the shortcut CTRL-ALT-C). Clicking on the first option on the left opens up the Watchfolders control panel.

Creating a Watchfolder setup

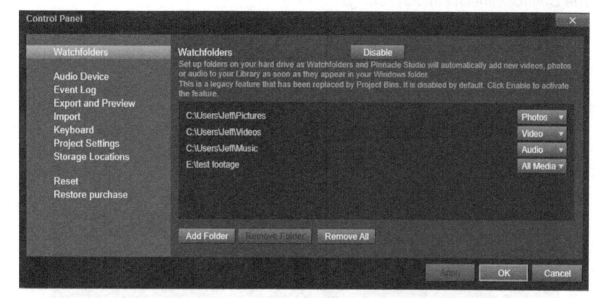

Here you can add new Watchfolders using the button bottom left. Any folder you add will also have any subfolders monitored as well, so in the case of My Photos, all the subfolders named by date are also scanned. Once you have chosen your new folder it is added to the list, where to the right a small drop-down menu lets you choose what type of media to scan for – so for My Photos it would be logical to scan only for photos. Any other items that have found their way into the folder are probably in the wrong place.

Removing unwanted Watchfolders from the list is obviously the function of the *Remove Folder* button. Neither of these functions do anything until you either click on the apply changes button (giving you the chance to make further changes) or you click on OK. When you do, if you have removed a Watchfolder from the list you are given the choice whether to remove the items in that folder from the Library

Control Panel Import settings

Using the Setup/Control Panel function, you can change all of the default settings for Import by selecting the section with that name from the left hand panel.

Not only do all the locations and subfolder options appear here, but you can control settings for Snapshots, (where you create a photo of from the content of the timeline or the Corrections Editor), the default scene detection method and the Stopmotion Import mode.

The Control Panel for import settings

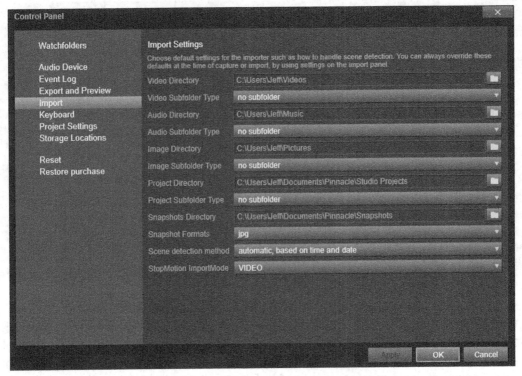

Import problems

There are occasions when importing a file fails. The problem may get reported by the import process, although you are unlikely to get any clues as to why the failure has occurred. There are two types of thumbnails that can indicate a failure. The padlock grey thumbnail indicates that the video file uses a codec that is either unavailable or incompatible with Studio.

A "locked" video file

In the past, some codecs would require an extra licence fee to be paid, and this might come about in the future as well for "Pro" codecs. So the first thing to check is if there is an activation required.

Studio comes with it's own set of codecs, and by default only those codes can be used. If the video file seems to be recognised by Windows then the correct codec might well be in place on the system but not enabled in Studio.

Enabling Third Party Codecs in the Control Panel

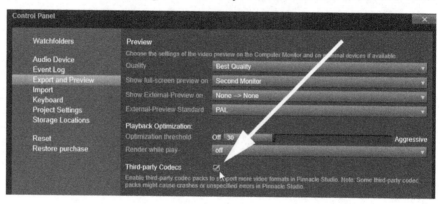

Studio 19 offers a new feature in the Export and Preview section of the Control Panel that allows Studio to use any third-party codecs installed on your computer. This comes with a big warning though - they will not have been tested, so you may experience unusual behaviour or even crashing.

A red thumbnail is the more serious. This may indicate that the file is corrupt or that it's contents don't match the information in the header.

Cineform

One special case is a codec used by GoPro in their editing software for high quality output. Pinnacle will work with most GoPro Cineform files, but you need to install the codec first. This can be done by simply downloading and installing GoPro Studio editing software, which is free.

Export

At the end of the first project I made the distinction between a video file and a project file, and talked you through a simple export process to turn the project into file. In this chapter I'm going to talk through all the Export functions, discuss file formats in more detail and look at the problems that might affect you when exporting to disc.

The Export Window

The fifth tab across the top of the Program window is labelled Export. Clicking on it brings up a whole new re-sizable window over the top of the current mode. This is the same type of window as Import but with one difference. In Import, the linking of items to the library and some copying functions can carry on in the background and return you to the main program. However, all the export functions require the full attention of your computer, even the routines that upload to the Internet. Some export functions can take a long time.

The Export Window in File Mode

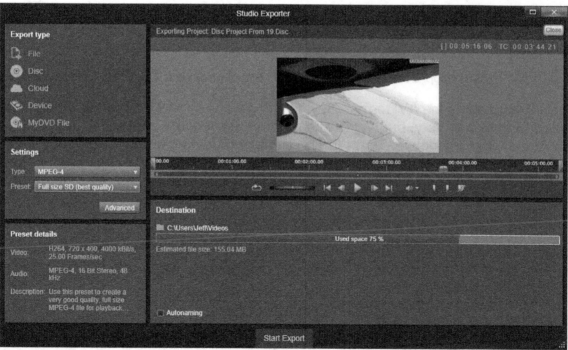

The Export window has five areas. To the left are three boxes labelled Export type, Settings and Preset details. To the right there is a Player window above and a Destination box below. The Destination box changes significantly when you change the Export type and the player takes on a different appearance when you have a Disc project loaded for Export to Disc.

Export to File

I'm going to start with the File export type and walk through exporting a DV-AVI file. This will produce the highest quality file possible of a Standard Definition project, with the least compression. If you wanted a reference file for later work on any standard definition project, this would be the one to choose unless you were concerned about disc size.

In the Movie tab, open the project we made in chapters 2 and 3 the book. If you didn't make it, you can download it from the DTVPro website or copy it from the Data DVD, or you can use any other SD file of short duration that is at hand - The Sky sample footage is fine. Now use the Export tab to open the window and in the Export type select File.

The Settings box is where you choose the actual file format you want to use. There is a vast array available and I'll talk you through the most common types in a moment, but for now select AVI.

Open the Preset drop-down, and you will still see 6 choices. Select Full screen (DV)

A brief word about the AVI format. Saying that a file is an AVI means very little. Most video formats can vary, but AVI is one of the most variable of them all. AVI stands for Audio Video Interleave. That's it. The audio and Video data are interwoven in the same file, but there is no further standards we can guarantee and the data can be encoded in a multitude of ways. So you should never assume that all AVIs are the same. Later we will use the term "Wrapper" to describe some other common file formats that can contain a wide range of data types.

Having chosen the file type and preset, you will see basic details you have chosen in the Preset details box below along with a brief description of what the chosen preset is best suited to.

If you want more settings options, there is an Advanced setting button. Open this now to see the array of options. At the bottom of Advanced settings are 4 checkboxes which determine the actions the Pinnacle Studio will take when the export process is complete. As some renders will take a long time, you aren't going to be sitting watching the process at all times, and *Sound audio alarm* can alert you to the fact that the process has finished. Before you ask, no, there doesn't seem to be a way of changing the audio alarm - believe me, I've tried!

Advanced File Export settings

Shut down PC will be handy if the export is going to be a long one and you are going to leave the computer on overnight or while you go out. If you have other programs with unsaved data open, this option won't work, which is a good thing!

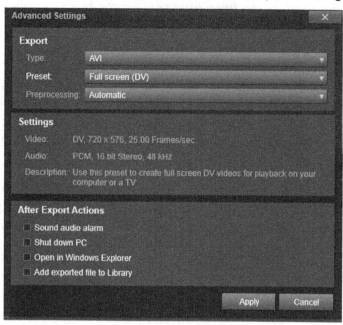

Open in Windows Explorer and *Add exported file to Library* will be useful in many situations, but might be a nuisance at times. I tend to leave the first one unchecked and perform that action manually if I wish because you get offered the option when Export completes.

In the Export box of Advanced Settings you will see a choice of Preprocessing. This will make more sense when I describe the rendering and optimisation processes in Pinnacle Studio. Until we want to troubleshoot an issue, I'd suggest you leave that setting on automatic. If you are experiencing render problems, it is worth forcing the program to use *No Preprocessing*.

Custom options

Let's just open up a can of worms for a moment. In the preset box, select *Custom*. Even with the DV preset still in place there are a number of parameters you can adjust - the interlace and audio settings,and the choice of including video and audio in the file.

For more choice, open the Settings/Video/ Encoding drop-down menu. In earlier versions of Studio there were many more choices, but on a clean installation of S19 there are only three choices - DV, MJPEG and Uncompressed Frames. If you have more, then they may have come from other programs but are unlikely to be reliable.

What's a Codec?

Encoding is often referred to as a Codec (Compression and Decompression method) and various file types - or wrappers - allow a different subset of the codecs available on your computer. If you select MPEG-2 as the file type, for example, you can only have MPEG-2 as the codec, but you can vary the frame size, bitrate and interlacing options.

Just to be clear - once you stray away from the preset encoding methods and settings, there is no cast iron guarantee that the file you produce will be universally acceptable. There isn't even a guarantee that Pinnacle Studio will be able to carry out the export.

I'll demonstrate a custom codec in a moment, but for now, close the Advanced setting box and return to the Full Screen DV preset.

The Player Window in File Export

The In and Out callipers can force a partial export

The player isn't just there for you to check out the project before you export it.

The In and Out point callipers we used in the Source Preview window are also present in the Export player when dealing with files. You can alter them by dragging or using the buttons or the I and O keyboard shortcuts to set them to the current scrubber position.

If you have a long project and are only interested in a part of it, or perhaps you are trying to troubleshoot a render issue, setting the callipers to the desired section restricts the export to that part of the project.

Marker navigation works in the Player window as well. If you are working on a project and decide you want to export a particular section, dropping a couple of markers onto the timeline before you switch to export will allow you to find the section quickly and then set the In and Out points.

Timeline Export callipers

The Edit timeline toolbar also has three icons that mimic the controls available on the Source preview and Export player windows for setting and clearing In and Out points.

If you wish to choose a section of the movie while still in Edit mode you can use these markers, and then when you go to the Export tab they will be waiting for you in the Export player. You can make further changes in the player if you change your mind.

The three timeline export tools are to the left of the central group

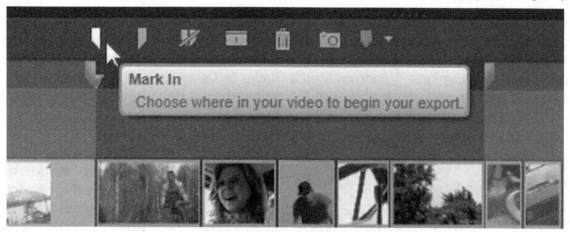

Destination

The top of the Destination box holds a small folder icon with the name of the default location in which Pinnacle Studio is intending to save the file you are just about to create. To change this location, click on the icon and you will get a Windows style dialogue box enabling you to do that.

Below this is a blue/grey bar indicating the amount of used space on your chosen destination drive, beneath which there is a estimated file size.

Why only "estimated"? Well, in the case of DV-AVI, the estimate will be very accurate. DV-AVI is a fixed compression scheme. Other schemes will compress the video more if there is less detail or movement, so estimates can be no more than that.

The final item in the Destination area is an Autonaming checkbox. With this selected the project name will be used, and if you have already saved a file with that name in that location and choose not to overwrite it, an incremental number will be added.

Uncheck the box for now and click on "Start Export". A Windows style "Save as" dialogue allows you to chose the location and filename for your export. Any changes made here will affect the default location.

Once you enter a suitable filename, the process begins. The controls beneath the player preview are replaced with a progress bar and a status message. In the current example you should read the file name and then the information *Exporting frame xxx of xxx at hh:mm:ss:ff.* The movie plays in the player preview as the export proceeds. In the current case it should play very fast unless you have a very slow computer or an issue with your setup.

After not very long at all (about 3 seconds on the computer I'm currently using|), the progress bar will complete its journey to the far end and an Information box will pop up telling you the export has finished. Three icons give you the chance to open the file in Windows Explorer, Windows Media Player or QuickTime Player to check the export. If the file isn't compatible with Quicktime or you don't have it installed, you won't be offered the option.

What you see after a successful file render

So what is happening here? Studio works its way through the project, taking the source material – video, music and whatever other assets we may have added - and then using the instructions contained in the project file writes out a new file called project 1_4.avi (or whatever name you gave it) into the location you specified. This process is called Rendering.

Render Speed

If the project were a lot longer, you might have to wait some time for the file to finish. You might wonder why Studio can't also inform you of precisely how long it will take to complete. The time taken to render each frame depends on the complexity of the operation, thus making a time estimate a little tricky. We haven't included any effects or other assets that would add to that complexity either. You may notice on some projects the rate of rendering varying as the process progresses because Studio is encountering items that take longer to process.

One common question regarding rendering is "What can I do to speed it up?" Well, rendering uses the CPU very heavily. It may also use the Graphics chips in the computer, mainly for rendering transitions or effects but also for encoding complex codecs. Use of the Graphics hardware will also depend on if it is CUDA or Quicksync capable, and the type of codec you are rendering to. Make sure you are using the most suitable Hardware acceleration for your computer - see page 525.

Some rendering routines make better use of multi-core CPUs - it varies with the file type. There are specific circumstances where the hard disc speeds may be important - uncompressed AVI and Smart Rendering. So the only generalised answer I can give is "buy a faster computer". A more specific answer would depend on exactly what type of movies you are making.

If you check the rendered file in WMP, I hope you will agree it looks no worse than the original. The file should be able to play on any computer that has Windows Media Player on it. Use Windows Explorer to examine the file. Yes, it's as big as Studio predicted.

That is a big file considering the duration of the movie, and you wouldn't want to download a long file in that format from the Internet. Another problem the size of the file gives is that in some circumstances you might get jerky playback on a system with a hard disc bottleneck - similar to dropping frames as we discussed in the Import chapter.

Why on earth would I want to make a file so big? The answer would be to maintain as much quality as possible. The file size is large because DV-AVI uses *Intraframe* compression, as discussed in the first chapter, and can never be very efficient.

Let's look at the AVI presets list again. Apart from the full screen DV preset, there are four presets for MJPEG, which is a similar form of compression to DV. You might need these in some circumstances, but not very often.

It's worth looking at the custom settings and choosing Uncompressed. Even before you render, you should take a look at the size estimate - in the case of the project, it is 623MB, instead of 75MB

The new file is estimated to be about 8 times the size of one made with the DV-AVI codec, which makes it even less practical. It does have its uses though; if you are making complex projects that require multiple passes of rendering, it will avoid introducing errors caused even by the light encoding used by DV-AVI. You may want to use this format when exchanging video with specialist effects or 3D animation programs.

If you decide to make an uncompressed file and then try to play it back, you will find the bottleneck is your hard disk - it's unlikely to play back smoothly unless your hard drive is in good shape and free of other tasks, as I explained in Chapter 1.

Just to give you an idea of the practicalities of working with files this big, let's make one. Start Export and give it a new name. When the Make File operation finishes, load the large uncompressed file into the Library, put it on the timeline and see how it behaves.

You will probably find that the file will show up incorrectly as standard, 4:3 aspect ratio - the subjects will look too skinny. I'll show you how to put this right when we discuss Aspect ratio in the Corrections Editor, but just live with it for now and try playing the clip.

If your computer is reasonably new and in good shape, the clip will probably play OK. If I put the video on an external USB 2.0 drive that is quite full and somewhat fragmented, however, playback can become a bit erratic.

The biggest downside of this type of file is its huge size. The file would be nearly too big to fit on a CD optical data disc, and yet it only contains 20 seconds of video! DV-AVI isn't that much better - we wouldn't get 25 minutes of that format on a DVD disc. You can see why the home video industry needed a better way of compressing video.

MPEG-2

Until recently, MPEG-2 was the most important video codec for the consumer video market; it is used by DVD video discs and many digital transmission systems. Recently with the introduction of web streaming and Blu-ray, other more compressed formats have become just as important, but MPEG-2 is still with us in many forms.

MPEG stands for Motion Picture Experts Group, and is the name for a family of standards for compressing video and audio. You have probably heard of MP3 audio – that's one of theirs. It's an Interframe compression method, and I've described the basic principles in the first chapter.

Lets make an MPEG-2 file of the project. Return to the Export mode, set the Type drop-down box to MPEG-2 and the preset to DVD compatible, click Start Export, name the file MPEG2test.mpg or similar and click Save.

The resulting file is more than four times times smaller than the DV-AVI, and over 30 times smaller than the uncompressed AVI! How can it possibly be of comparable quality? Have a look – re-import it into Studio. It's pretty good considering, don't you think? Well, actually, given that it is made from an MPEG-2 file in the first place, it should be, in most places, as good as the original.

Windows 8/10 and MPEG-2

If you have Windows 7, you should be able to play MPEG-2 files in Windows Media Player. However, if you have a consumer version of Windows 8 or 10 you will find that you can't play back MPEG-2 files or DVD discs. This will be a problem if you want to test your exports outside of Studio. You can pay extra money to Microsoft to upgrade, but I can recommend the VLC media player as a free alternative. What's more, you can also use it to read Blu-ray discs or disc images.

Like all "free" programs, take some care. Don't get it from the Windows store, as the version for Win 8 I downloaded doesn't seem to play MPEG-2. Don't use a search engine to find it either – go to http://www.videolan.org/ to be sure you aren't getting a hacked version or one that has had adware grafted on. You might even consider making a donation to help keep these genuine open source projects alive.

You can set VLC to be the default program for opening MPEG-2 files. You can do this by right clicking on any mpeg-2 file in Windows Explorer, selecting *Open with…* and then *Choose default program* and selecting VLC player.

MPEG-2 Quality

I don't want you to get the impression that MPEG-2 is as good as DV-AVI. It doesn't achieve the extra compression without some loss, but that loss is mostly in the movement.

There are two important points here.

The first is "garbage in, garbage out". Rendering the MPEG-2 video back to DV-AVI doesn't improve it, even though the format can store detail more accurately.

Secondly, you may throw your hands in the air in disgust that we are degrading the pictures, but all DVDs use this MPEG-2 codec. If we want to view DV pictures on a

TV at their original quality, we need to use a DV deck or camera, and print projects back to tape. The other alternative is to use High Definition technology, but that involves some compression as well.

MPEG-2 can use variable compression. If the video gets a lot of movement, it can reduce the compression to try to keep up with the large changes. You can also specify the bitrate of the compression to suit your own purposes.

Now let's make an MPEG-2 file that uses much more compression. Go into the settings box and change the Preset to Custom. Open the Advanced box and adjust the Peak and Average Bitrate to 2Mbit/s. Apply the changes, close the advanced window and make a file, giving it a different name – compressed.mpg for example.

MPEG-2 Custom settings

The new file is smaller – about 6Mb, which is around a third of the size of the one made with three times the bitrate. The time taken to make the file should have been about the same.

Now load both the MPEG files into Studio and look for the quality difference on the timeline. Use Full screen preview for the best comparison. You will notice straight away that the shot of the van wheel is far noisier in the second file. Examine some still frames, comparing the second shot with the trees through the van window. You don't have to look that carefully, to see far more "blocky" artefacts on the 2000Kbits/sec file. There is also much more general noise on the lower bitrate picture.

However, I wouldn't say that the smaller file was any where near three times worse than the bigger one. Would you?

Clever people in that Motion Picture Experts Group.....

"So which one is the best to make?" I hear you ask. As we are trading picture quality for file size, if the space a file takes up isn't an issue, then use the highest bitrate. If the file is too big to store on a DVD or send over the Internet, then you need to compromise. However, apart from DVDs, there are better choices of codec if file size is important to you.

I've nearly done with MPEG-2, but there are settings in the Video and Audio section of Custom that deserve attention.

You can choose the pixel dimensions of your file, even choosing ones that don't match any recognised aspect ratio. Most Media players will try to make your rendered file the shape of a normal TV screen, but there may be times when you want an odd shaped file for a web site or some other project.

Interlacing is a tricky subject. I would always keep the setting to match the source footage - de-interlacing or reversing the field order should only be used to rectify problems that already exist in my experience.

Bitrate control is something else to alter with care. Variable bitrate (VBR) will produce a file with a compression scheme that matches the amount of compression to the content of the video, averaging at the preset level. This method gives the best quality for a given file size, but there may be short bursts of high data rates that some devices can't handle – for example, producing stuttery playback on an old model of DVD player. VBR is particularly effective if the codec makes two passes of a project, one to get an estimate, and the second to actually encode the file. Studio doesn't employ two-pass encoding – it is normally used by expensive, professional DVD authoring programs.

Constant bitrate – CBR - none of the above paragraph applies! The compression level is fixed regardless of video content. This is the safe, but inefficient, option.

Audio options allow you to alter a number of aspects of the sound. The two options for MPEG-2 files are mp2 - an audio compression scheme that predates the popular MP3 format, and PCM, a very raw audio codec - in fact it is hardly a codec at all as it is a binary representation of the analogue audio signal - just like a .WAV file.

Because the audio portion of an AV file is only a small proportion of the total file size, choosing lower bit and sample rates has little benefit, but the options are there for specialist purposes.

MP4 files

Moving forward, the next major advance to be widely adopted was the MP4 video standard. In effect, this offers more efficient compression, at the expense of added complexity, so that hardware needs be more powerful to encode and decode the files.

These new standards were again developed by the MPEG standards committee, but released in stages. MP4 is a wrapper that was designed from the outset to be able to contain a increasingly complex set of codecs.

The initial type of MP4 compression was just know as MP4 or "Simple". Unlike earlier versions of NGStudio, S19 doesn't create simple mp4 files unless you go into the custom settings - all the presets for MP4 use the H.246 codec..

H.264 files

The more advanced H.264 codec is used when Studio makes High Definition files and puts them in an MP4 wrapper. Just to confuse us even more, you can have H.264 video in a MOV wrapper, or even in a MPEG-2 TS wrapper - the latter with the file extension M2TS or MTS.

You might want to make an HD file from our project using the MP4 preset. It's not going to be real HD because it will just be like blowing up a small photograph - you will see the grain more clearly - but the file size will be interesting - 30MB. Given that a Full HD picture has 5 times the number of pixels as an SD one, it's remarkable that the HD H.264 file is only twice the size of the SD MPEG-2 file. It's the existence of the H.264 format that has brought HD video to the mainstream and one of the reasons that High Definition video is possible at all in small, cheap consumer cameras.

For better quality the Transport Stream settings offer higher bitrates and more control. These files are put into an MTS wrapper.

Encoding H.264 options

Pinnacle Studio 19 uses Intel Quicksync for encoding and decoding H.264 video. Quicksync specifically can use hardware decoding and this may be an advantage if you have the latest generation Intel CPUs with built in graphics – even if your computer has another graphics card. If you don't have suitable hardware, the routines default to software, but this is still a good situation as the Intel routines seem to be widely praised.

Custom H.264 settings

When you make AVCHD or Blu-ray discs, or MTS files, you have access to the advanced H.264 encoding options by using Custom settings. This gives you the possibility to work with hardware acceleration on, off or automatic. I suggest you leave the decision on automatic unless you have issues. I've yet to use a setup that shows a significant speed difference, but I do have experience of some systems on older versions of Studio that are more stable with hardware acceleration off. So, if you see crashing or strange results when working with H.264– perhaps the famous "Green screen" that indicates render issues – then try custom settings and switching off hardware acceleration in the Advanced settings box. This is a different control to the Hardware acceleration checkbox in the Preview window of the control panel, by the way.

Studio 19 now has a further hardware acceleration rendering control that may interact with these settings. In the *Control Panel/Export and Preview* window you can choose between Intel, Cuda or None. If you have a Intel CPU that has onboard HD graphics then Intel is the obvious choice. If you have a powerful, Cuda-capable Graphics card you may get faster results with Cuda, and if you are experiencing poor renders and crashes try switching to None. See the screenshot on page 525.

There is a further choice of encoding with H.264 – three settings are available in custom mode under the heading Image quality. Fastest Speed, Balanced and Best Quality are fairly self-explanatory. They alter the amount of processing that is carried out during the render process, and in my judgement affect fine detail more than movement rendition. There is a speed trade-off, and normally Studio appears to use the Fastest mode as its default setting.

In tests on various computers, I've found the speed of render ratio to be about 1:2:4 – that is if a file renders in 1 minute in the fast mode, it will take 2 minutes in the balanced mode and 4 minutes in the Best mode.

The quality improvement is much harder to quantify. A lot will depend on the original quality. I carried out some tests with 40Mbit/s DSLR video re-rendering to the same bitrate, where I could see very little difference between the original and the new file created with the Best Setting or the Fast setting. Downgrading the files to 24 Mbit/s showed a greater difference with the original, obviously, but the Fast setting wasn't noticeably worse then the Best setting.

Further tests with 17Mbit/s video upscaled to 24Mbit/s for burning to Blu-ray were a little more conclusive – the Best setting retained more of the fine detail, but I have to say the results were quite marginal.

My recommendation is that if you are considering spending three times longer rendering H.264 video, take a little time setting up a test. If you can see a difference worth the extra time, then do so – after all, you can always leave the render to run and go to bed!

Smart Rendering

There are times when rendering files that Studio uses a technique called "Smart Rendering", otherwise known as Direct Stream Copy. The video is coppied directly from the source file to the export file without being processed. This saves time. It also saves introducing further errors to the video because it hasn't got to reprocess it.

Earlier versions of Pinnacle Studio did offer some form of Smartrender for Mpeg-2 DVD files. However, I can find no evidence that it exists in PS19. It does exist in some forms of H 264 rendering, however.

In order for Smartrender to work on any particular section of a movie, a number of criteria need to be met:

- No Video effects have been added or titles superimposed.

- The original video needs to be encoded with the same codec that Studio is rendering to.

- The compression level of the source material must be the same or lower than the target for the final file.

- What is more, the section needs to start and end of a GOP boundary. If the first frame of the clip isn't an i-frame at the start of a GOP, a "short" GOP needs to be re-rendered, and then smart rendering can continue from the next GOP boundary.

The obvious sign that it is happening is the speed of render - at least twice that of normal file rendering. You will find that often the speed of rending is limited by the transfer rates of your hard disc.

The Smart render export option

Smart and H.264

Smart rendering is a bit limited in Studio 19. Currently MP4, MOV and some MTS files will trigger the option. You can include photos and titles, but if some sections of the movie aren't in a compatible format then you won't be offered the Smart option.

When you open the Export window, you will see a hourglass graphic that warns you to wait while the timeline is scanned. If Studio decides that Smart rendering is possible, an option will be added the the format list allowing you to select Smart.

Settings

Type: Smart

3GPP
Audio
AVI
DivX
DivX Plus HD
FlashVideo
Image
Image Sequence
MOV Video
MPEG-1
MPEG-2
MPEG-4
Smart
Sony XAVC S®
Transport Stream (MTS)
Windows Media

A Smart rendered file always ends up in an MP4 wrapper.

At the time of writing there were a number of issues with the Smart render feature in S19 that didn't exist in S18.5. Hopefully they will be fixed in an early patch.

A list of formats

I'm going to run down the whole list of Formats now, giving pointers to when you might want to use them. I'm not going to explore the custom options, but remember they are there, and also don't expect every combination of parameters to produce a successful render.

3GPP – designed by the Third Generation Partnership, this is a format for mobile phones. It's based on MPEG-4, with variants that use either the Simple version or H.263, a codec designed for low-bitrate video conferencing.

Audio – You can make an audio only file of the project as either a .WAV (otherwise called PCM) or an MP3 (those Expert Group clever clogs again). These are the two most common standards for digital audio. If you delve into the custom settings, you can also make a mp2 file. which is an older form of MP3 and used in making MPEG-2 files.

AVI - we've discussed this fully early in this chapter. DV-AVI or even Uncompressed AVI are the best choices for preserving quality.

DivX – This is a commercial format based on MPEG-4. In Studio, it uses the .AVI file suffix, but it is an interframe compression scheme. There are presets for Xbox and PS3 games consoles as well as High Definition.

DivX Plus HD - a further development of the DivX option that will make files with a .mkv suffix. AVC/H.264 encoding is used.

Flash Video – Adobe's format popular for embedding video into web sites. Studio produces .flv files, one of the basic formats of YouTube and other video sharing sites. There is also a Nintendo Wii preset.

Image - produces a still image of the frame of video at the In point calliper of the Exporter Player Window. There are plenty of choices of format, with even more available in the custom drop-down.

Image Sequence - if you need a sequence of frames saved in a photo format, set the In and Out point to the start and end of the area you need and export them in one of a large choice of formats. This may be one way of getting high quality video data into another program to add complex effects or frame-by-frame retouching.

MOV Video – This is the file type for Apple's QuickTime format. MOV is a wrapper or container that holds video and audio and makes it suitable for playback on Apple hardware and software. The format isn't exclusive to Apple, however, and is used by many NLE's. The type of compression inside the file can be DV, MPEG, MP4 and H.264. Pinnacle Studio is a bit picky with the audio that can be included. For export, ACC is the only audio option.

MPEG-1, 2 and 4 – we have covered these earlier in the chapter. H.264 is used for the HD MP4 presets, but not at as high a bitrate as the MTS format.

Smart - You will only get this option after a successful scan of the project has determined Smart is possible. See my notes earlier about what is possible with this option.

Sony XAVC S® - This proprietary format is the consumer version of XAVC. It uses the highest level of H.264 encoding, and perhaps its most interesting feature it the ability to create UHD 4K files. The files produced by Studio are in an MP4 wrapper

Transport Stream - a decent range of file formats that all use the H.264 codec. Of particular interest is a Standard Definition setting with a 2000kbits/second bitrate which produces pretty good pictures in comparison to the experiment we tried earlier with the same bitrate MPEG-2 video.

Windows Media – This is a proprietary (it is owned by Microsoft) but open (anyone can use it) standard. There are many variations, including codecs designed for slide shows, but Studio makes the most generally accepted type of files. Presets include High Definition, but like Real Media, Windows Media has its own settings box layout and you are restricted to presets. The file type is .wmv, and like most modern codecs, it uses interframe compression.

As Pinnacle Studio develops more file formats are bound to be added, because it is a technology under constant improvement. As hardware gets more powerful, better compression can be achieved and still be coded and decoded in "real time". This means video can be sent via low bandwidth channels such as mobile phone networks. On the other hand, storage space becomes less of an issue, with hard disc sizes getting larger all the time, and high capacity memory cards constantly dropping in price. For high quality video work, there may come a time where even consumers will return to low compression formats.

Playing Back Files

If you ask the question "What format of file should I use so that I can be sure that anyone who receives it can play it back?" you won't get a straight answer. To begin with, not every computer runs Windows, and a significant number of people have Apple computers.

If you are going to send the file on a physical media such as a data disc or memory stick, size isn't too much of an issue, so you might think that you would be safe with MPEG-2 files, but even then the target computer might not have the correct codec installed - basic versions of Windows 8 don't have an MPEG-2 codec, as I noted earlier. With a bit of searching, you can probably find "free" MPEG-2 playback codecs on the Internet or you can install VLC, but your target audience may not want to do that.

So, what do you send people for the best quality? If they run Windows, then a Windows Media Video file should always work. If they have a Mac, you could send them a .MOV file.

As things progress, MP4 H.264 video is becoming the most common format around, and most people will own a computer or tablet that will be perfectly capable of replaying MP4, MOV or MTS containing H.264 video, if not actually editing it.

Remember that Studio limits the bitrate of MP4 files so that they are suitable for sending over the internet. For better quality, MTS offers higher H.264 bitrates but will take longer to send.

Export to Disc

Some Studio users will be more interested in making DVDs or Blu-ray discs than in making files. In this section I'll start by concentrating on Standard Definition DVDs and discuss High Definition optical output options later. Before I show you the steps involved in burning a DVD, let us look at the DVD format.

What exactly is a DVD disc? Like the CD that came before, it is a plastic disc sandwiching a layer of material that has a variable reflectivity. By bouncing a laser light beam off the disc onto a photo-sensitive cell, the playing device can read a series of bits of data - the basis of all digitally stored information. Huge amounts of data can be stored on the disc, but sometimes not all that accurately, so error correction is built into any playback system – something that digital storage achieves quite easily.

The critical difference between DVD and CD is the wavelength of the laser used to read the disc. A shorter wavelength enables a smaller area to represent one bit of data, and therefore more data can be squeezed on a disc. Incidentally, the same applies to Blu-ray - even more data can fit on a disc because the system uses a shorter wavelength still (a blue laser, not a red laser, hence the name Blu-ray).

Two more facts about DVDs – DVD doesn't stand for Digital Video Disc, but Digital Versatile Disc (they can be used to store other forms of data, including audio only), and the data is written from the inside of the disc outwards, unlike vinyl records.

Optical DVD discs fall into three categories:

Read only discs that are pressed from a glass master. These are used for mass distribution and have a type of "DVD-ROM".

Writable discs that contain an organic dye which can have its reflectivity changed when a high powered laser beam is fired at it. A pattern of 1's and 0's is burned on the disc – hence the name burner. A low powered beam doesn't affect the dye, so the disc can be read using the same laser with adjustable power settings.

Re-writable discs that use an alloy instead of the dye, so that the writing process can be reversed – the disc is therefore capable of being erased and reused.

There are 2 sizes of disc – 12cm and 8cm, although 12cm disc are far more common. Discs can also be double sided – they need to be read from both sides - and Dual layer, where the laser focuses on different layers at different depths in the disc.

Writable and re-writable discs come in a number of formats. There are three basic standards - DVD+R, DVD-R and DVD RAM. DVD RAM is a more flexible format, but only a limited number of stand alone players can read the discs.

This leaves +R and –R. For overall compatibility, -R probably has the edge. I'll discuss compatibility – a thorny subject for many people – at greater length later.

Getting ready to burn

At the risk of stating the obvious, you need a DVD burner fitted to your computer to burn a DVD. Pinnacle Studio 19 can burn a DVD image to a CD disc, but you won't be able to play it on most DVD players.

If you have a DVD burner in your computer that is fairly up to date, then it can probably burn most types of discs, so you will have to make a choice about which type of blank disc to use. If it's an old burner your choices and the speed at which it can burn, may be limited.

The first few times you make a DVD, I'd recommend using a rewritable DVD as a test. You will eventually want to buy some of the –R or +R discs that are a one-shot deal. They are much less expensive nowadays, but it's still a shame to waste them on experiments. Regarding disc quality, see my comments on page 225

What, No Menu?

You don't have to make a disc project that includes a menu in order to burn a Video DVD. Because Menus add a layer of complexity and potential compatibility issues I'm going to give them their own chapter. If you haven't made a DVD before, burning something nice and simple will be a good exercise in proving that you can make a DVD that works. So, if you don't have a suitable disc project yet, or are trying to find out why your DVDs won't play properly, you can work through the following pages with a simple project. For the example here, I've used a 10 minute MPEG-2 file and put it on the Main track of a new project in the Movie Editor. If you want to work through the steps, you can also use the *project1mp2 PAL* file from the data DVD or the website, or chose a suitable file of your own.

NTSC vs PAL

Pinnacle Studio makes either PAL (50fps) or NTSC (29.97fps) DVDs. Not all DVD players are multi standard. Most PAL players can play NTSC discs. Most NTSC DVD players *cannot* play PAL discs.

The format chosen by Pinnacle Studio normally matches the project format. If the timeline you have opened when you select Export contains a PAL, 25 or 50 frames per second project, Export will produce a PAL disc. If the frame rate is reported as 29.97, 30, 59.98 or 60, then the resultant DVD will be in the NTSC format. Disc authoring in Studio isn't sophisticated enough to produce discs with a mixture of formats.

This isn't to be confused with region encoding. There are nine regional settings to help DVD distributors attempt to stop grey imports. All the DVDs that Studio makes are set to Region 0 – an informal term meaning "Worldwide".

In the vast majority of cases you will end up with the correct format DVD, but it is possible to have the incorrect project format for your type of footage, so before opening export it is a good idea to check the format by opening the Project Settings icon - the gearwheel second left on the timeline toolbar, as described on page 37.

Disc Export Window

Upon opening the Export window, (see overleaf) selecting the Disc Export type results in a change of view. With a Movie project as the source, the preview window won't differ from the File mode, but if you have come to Export from a Disc project, even one without a menu, then you will see the Disc Simulator window. This works in the same way as the simulator in the Disc Editor I'll look at in detail later, but for now, think of this as the last chance to check your project before embarking on a lengthy render process.

In the File preview style window, note you still have the chance for a partial export by setting the In and Out point callipers.

Below the Preview window the previous Destination window has been split. On the left is the Target size setting and below a graphic representation of a disc, divided up as a pie chart. On the right the Destinations settings have changed too.

The Export window with Disc simulator

Disc Settings

The drop-down *Type* box offers either 3 or 4 choices. If you have paid a small licence fee, Studio offers Blu-ray burning. We are concerned with DVD creation in this section, so I have selected that.

Preset allows you 3 choices. It's an important point that Studio only makes DVDs with full resolution although the Video DVD standard allows for lower resolutions. Therefore the quality settings in Studio only affect the bitrate which we discussed when we looked at at MPEG-2 compression. Low bitrates affect moving content

Settings box showing the Preset options

more than the quality of static pictures.

Best Quality will always use the optimum setting regardless if you have space for your entire project. We will look at the other settings later. I've selected Best quality for now.

Before we investigate what the Advanced settings do, I want to walk through a disc creation sequence.

With DVD selected in the Setting box to the left, you should have a choice of 7 different *Target Sizes* in the box to the right. The smallest is a 650Mb CD disc and the largest is Unlimited. If your project is small, you can burn it to a CD disc. The advantage is that blank CDs are a little cheaper than blank DVDs, but the downside can be problems with compatibility. I've not found a DVD or Blu-ray player that recognises a CD as a valid DVD image. It may play on some PCs, but that's not much use.

DVD Target sizes

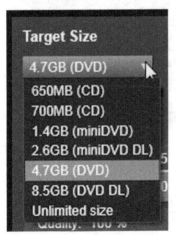

The 4 sizes of DVD are all valid targets. As a generalisation, I have always found Dual layer discs to be more problematic, as well as not such good value for money, but if your project warrants the additional space the option is there.

The choice of Unlimited may seem a bit unusual, but it has two possible uses. A DVD image saved on a hard disc can be played using media player software, so you aren't limited by the physical capacity of an optical disc. The other use allows you to optimise disc quality in certain circumstances, more of which later.

With a Single layer 4.7GB disc as the target and 10 Minutes 28 seconds to be exported, the graphic display shows the space used in orange and the space left in blue. You will note that for some reason Pinnacle have decided to display the durations as minutes to two decimal places, rather than minutes and seconds. The discrepancy between the duration of the project and the time shown that it takes up on disc is because Video DVDs require a number of files and folders to be included to make them valid, and these take up space too.

Destination

In Pinnacle Studio you can't burn straight to disc. An image always needs to be created, and you have to put the image somewhere. The folder icon allows you to specify a location other than the default and the bar underneath shows how much space is available in your chosen destination.

By default, the Discname that will be used to create the image and the disc is that of the project you had open before going to Export. The part of the name that will appear on the disc can be changed by clicking on the text field and typing in a new name.

Device holds a list of your disc burners, so if you have more than one, you can select which you want to use from the drop-down box. An information box alongside shows the media that has been detected in the currently selected burner.

The Creation choices

Three buttons at the bottom of the window show the three possible choices we have at this stage.

Create Image carries out all the steps up to, but not including, the actual process of burning a disc. You can carry out this process without a disc loaded into your burner - in fact, you don't even need a burner attached. While you are creating an image, Pinnacle Studio is locked into the Export window.

Burn Disc goes through the entire Create Image process. If that completes successfully it takes you to the next step of burning the created image to the media in your selected drive. This final part of the process can happen as a background task, so you can return to an editing window or the library to carry on working while the disc is made.

Burn Image takes an image that you have already made with the Create Image button and carries out the final burning process. There are two situations where this process is particularly useful - troubleshooting and making further copies.

Because I want to walk through the process, I'm going for the troubleshooting route of starting with Create Image. I've put a re-writeble DVD in the drive, but it's not needed at this stage.

Clicking Create Image brings up a Browse for Folder dialogue box. We have already seen the pre-selected location under Destination, but if I changed my mind, this would be the last opportunity to do so. Clicking on OK should start the process.

With a simple project containing no effects, the first message you will see is *Creating asset: exporting frame xxxx of xxxx* and a time count of progress. Studio is building up a series of files from the source, but it isn't putting them into the image location.

Exporting render files for disc creation

Exporting Project: new project.disc

00:01:43.20

Status: Creating asset: Exporting frame 2624 of 15693 at 00:01:44:23 (16% done)

Total : 8 % complete

Two files are produced, one video and the other audio, but putting them into a Disc Export folder in the overall Studio Render location defined in the Control Panel.

The message then changes to Creating Disc image. The folder that you have defined for holding the Disc image is created. The temporary video and audio files are combined into Video Object (VOB) files containing both sound and vision and the remaining files that make up a disc image are added. The creation of the VOB files in particular should not take too long, as the temporary files just need combining, not recoding. This process is often called Multiplexing, or Muxing for short.

Assuming no error messages have occurred, You now will have a Disc image on your computer. Although I wouldn't always do this, when troubleshooting, the next stage is to examine the image.

If you can't get past this render stage without the program stopping with a render error message then there are a number of things to try. If your project refuses to render and always stops at the same point, the first thing is to check the project carefully. Sometimes a small gap in the timeline can cause the render to fail. I'm suggesting this because it was a common cause of failure in Pinnacle Studio 15 or earlier and I can't be sure that Pinnacle Studio 19 doesn't suffer from the same problem - although I've not seen it. Other things to look for might be an unusual video effect that might be bugged.

If you can't find an obvious cause or the point at which the program halts seems random, then your options are deleting the render files, enabling *Always re-encode* and as a last resort the *pre-render to file* method I'll discuss in a moment.

Advanced Settings

In the settings box of the Disc Export dialogue there is an Advanced button. Click on it to open the Advanced Setting window. You will notice some choices which will make you curious. Preprocessing is an advanced control that will be easier to explain when I describe the preview optimisation settings in Studio, but in general I suggest it is left on Automatic.

Under the Video Settings, there is a drop-down *Standard* menu that allows you to override the DVD settings - so if for some reason you wanted to make a NTSC disc from a PAL timeline, for example, you could do so here. Again, I suggest you use the default Auto detect setting.

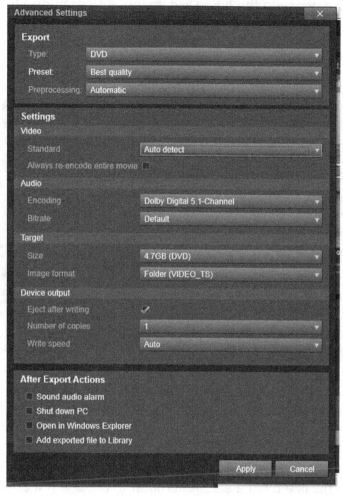

The next checkbox is very useful - *Always re-encode entire movie*. Because Studio tries to save time, it avoids re-encoding video and menus if it can. However, this can lead to errors, particularly with complex projects or those containing video of a less common technical standard.

The first thing *Always re-encode* does is disable the Smartrender process I described earlier. It doesn't take on trust that the MPEG-2 files from the project are completely DVD compatible, and regenerates them to a standard that should be suitable.

That's not all that the checkbox controls, though. If you have already made a disc image so that render files exist, normally the files in the render folder are reused and the Creating asset stage is virtually instantaneous. Better still, if you make a change to one separate part of a DVD and leave others untouched, it's possible that some of the render files may be reused. For example, after a long render process you may spot a spelling mistake on a menu. Changing the menu only and creating the image will often result in only the Menu itself having to be recreated.

Along with Smart Render, this time saving technique can on occasions lead to errors. Checking *Always re-encode* should force Studio to ignore the render files, but if you want to be absolutely sure that nothing from a previous render operation is making it's way into the final Disc image, I recommend that you also delete the render files. You do this by using the Control panel from the Setup menu at the top of the Main program window. Choose Storage Locations and at the bottom of the page you will find a button to Delete render files.

How to delete the render files

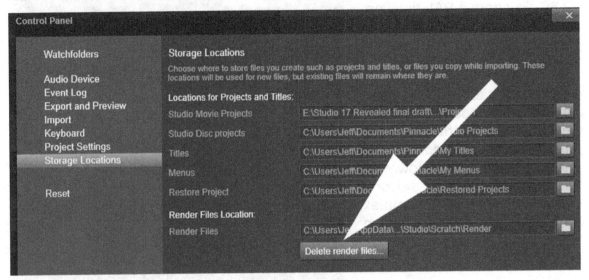

As with pre-processing, the subject of render files will be easier to understand if you read about Preview Optimisation starting at page 522.

Pre-rendering to file

This is a bit of a sledgehammer to crack a nut approach. Sometimes a very complex timeline just refuses to render. If you split it into a number of sections and make a file of that section, then remake the project from the newly made files you may well bypass the issue. For a SD DVD project, I recommend you use the DV-AVI preset. If you are making a HD project for one of the other disc formats, then I would suggest MTS using a preset resolution that matches your project and the bitrate that comes with that preset.

Using MyDVD Files

The idea of pre-rendering to a compatible file is also at the root of using MyDVD, a standalone program supplied by Pinnacle as an alternative to using the Author mode. The Export type *MyDVD File* creates a suitable file for import into MyDVD and there may be circumstances why you can create a MyDVD file and then use that in the Author mode to add Studio menus.

Examining the image

OK, hopefully I've given you enough strategies there to get round render error messages, so once you have a working image, the next stage is to check it carefully.

Assuming you haven't changed any of the default options, when you use Windows Explorer to open the hard disc location of the Image you just created, you will find a folder called Video TS.

Video TS folder contents

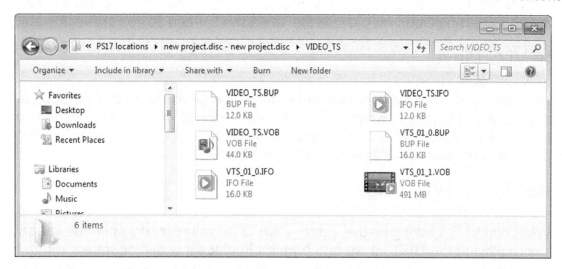

If you examine a DVD disc in your computer drive in the same way, you will also find a folder called Video_TS. There will probably also be a folder called Audio_TS, which is there in case the DVD contains Audio_DVD content. This is rare and more than likely the folder will be empty, even if it exist.

The contents of the Video_TS folder are a structure called a Video Title Set - part of the DVD standard. All Video DVDs will have three types of files in the Video_TS folder.

IFO (information) files contain the information pertinent to the what the DVD contains including what menus and titles it contains, where the chapters start, and much more.

BUP are backup files. If any of the IFO files become unreadable due to damage or bad quality pressing or burning, the player can try to use the backup information instead.

VOB files are the Video Object files that contain the MPEG-2 video, the audio in the chosen format (and possibly with multiple streams for different sound tracks) and any subtitles. All DVDs will have at least two VOB files. In the example I have made, the first one - Video_TS.vob - has to be there for the DVD to work properly, even though it contains no video. If there was a "first run" video such as a copywrite notice that played before the menu, it would be contained in this VOB file. My example then has one further VOB file, which holds the DVD content. VOB files are limited in size to around a Gigabyte (1,048,574 Kbytes to be precise), so even if your DVD has no menu and only one title or chapter, there may be more than one VOB file.

I can play the VOB file in some versions of Windows. My Windows 7 computer has Windows Media Player associated with that file type, and right-clicking on the file name and selecting Open will play the file. Windows 8.1 and 10 don't have the ability.

The VLC Player

If you don't have mpeg-2 playback in Media Player a useful free alternative is to download the VLC player, which is free. It's also a good way to explore DVDs and get Blu-ray playback. Make sure you get it from a reliable source - currently http://www.videolan.org/vlc/download-windows.html.

Exploring a DVD Image

In WMP and VLC, clicking on the Video_TS.IFO file will normally open the image as if it were playing the DVD - if we had a menu in place it would operate through the player controls and we could fully test the image before we waste a blank DVD to test it further.

The first stage of troubleshooting DVD playback should be carried out at this stage. See if the disc plays properly and obeys the menu commands correctly. Don't just play the first bit of the video - check through the disc image for smooth playback, video problems or audio sync issues. If you identify an issue at this stage which wasn't there when you previewed the project itself you need to eliminate that problem before proceeding.

Go back a couple of pages to the Advanced Settings section and apply the Always recode and Delete render files fixes. These are just as relevant to a render process that causes playback issues without stopping the render process with an error.

Has this cured the issue you have with Disc image playback on your computer? If it has, then you can proceed to burning the disc. If it hasn't then your problems are more fundamental.

Menu difficulties are likely to be an issue with the placement of chapter points - these can be very critical to menu operation. Check the web for any patches.

In my experience, playback of video and audio problems at this stage are likely to be caused by using files that appear to be compatible, but aren't properly supported. Some types of MP4 video might fall into this category. Other problem files might have a variable frame rate - video shot by an iPhone, for example. I'd suggest you try making a DVD using a standard video source, and if that succeeds you may need to look at transcoding your source files before using them in Studio. Again the forums should be a good source of advice, and I'll also touch on transcoding later.

In troubleshooting terms, if you cannot produce a proper DVD Image, there is no point in proceeding to the Burn stage.

Burn Image

If you make an image, test it in Windows, then return to Pinnacle Studio and select Burn Disc, the program will assume that you want to burn a disc from the last created image - which in most cases you will. If you don't, then the dialogue box that appears will let you change your mind, but in my case I don't want to. Still, let's look at the options.

Burn Files to disc is a general purpose dialogue box that you will meet in various parts of Pinnacle Studio The *From* box allows you to chose which type of disc you want to make. Files and Folders will create a data DVD holding whatever content you want to put on the disc. The resultant disc won't play as a Video DVD.

Disc Image (Folder) is the mode that takes a folder structure and burns a Video-DVD. It should be pre selected if you come to the Burn dialogue via the route I've just described.

Disc Image (ISO) looks for another type of Image - an ISO file. This type can be created in Studio by selecting it in the Advanced options under the Target heading. The advantage of ISO is that it is a self contained format that is portable, so you can use another burning program with ease. The ISO type isn't limited to Video DVD, so whatever ISO file you select, the type of disc format the ISO contains will be burned to disc. The disadvantage of using it is that it can be much more complicated to explore and test the image before burning in operating systems earlier than Windows 8. Pinnacle currently isn't capable of creating an ISO image for HD disc formats

The small *Source folder* icon allows us to select a different image, files or folders to burn to DVD, and below is a simple browser that lets us edit the choice - of more use in the Files and Folders mode than either of the Image modes.

We can rename the disc that will be created, choose another burning device if we have one fitted, and force the program to eject the disc and close the dialogue when the burning process is complete.

I have to comment that the Burn files dialogue isn't as comprehensive as other disc burning programs, but it serves the purpose. I would like to see the ability to verify a disc added, as in my experience even the best quality discs sometime produce faulty burns.

OK, I'm going to burn a disc from the Video_TS Image., and the Burn dialogue should be automatically set up for me to do that. Clicking on Start burn will immediately tell me if the burner isn't ready - maybe the tray is open or perhaps there isn't a suitable disc in place. If the disc is re-writable, but not blank, the program will warn me and give me a chance to abort before overwriting the disc.

When I choose to proceed there begins a string of messages as the progress bar crosses the screen. Firstly, the disc will be erased if it needs to be. Next a Lead-in area is burned to the disc - required for the laser of the playback device to find the start of the playable area. Writing disc content occurs next, where the files are burned onto the disc to form the digital patterns of 1's and 0's we discussed earlier.

A lead-out area is burnt next - another part of the disc to help players read the disc. In some cases players don't like very short duration DVDs, so if you think that the time taken to write the Lead-out is taking too long, Studio is writing a long lead out in order to make the burned area of the disc a decent size.

OK, if you have successfully burned a DVD, when you re-insert it into the burner you should be offered the choice of playing it in Windows Media Player, or any other DVD playing software you have installed on your computer.

Is all well? Does the disc play smoothly? If it does, then you are on your way to producing DVDs, but sometimes a computer can play a disc that a standalone player struggles with.

If even your computer can't play the disc then something must have gone wrong at the burn stage.

Bad Media?

If you successfully burned the DVD, then the type of disc must be compatible with your burner. DVD drives in computers are a lot more tolerant of bad media than stand alone DVD players, but the occasional bad burn can happen without triggering an error message. Studio doesn't verify discs it has burned. The easiest way to check for a bad burn, probably caused by a poor quality or damaged disc, is to try to copy the contents of the disc to a temporary folder on your hard drive. If you get a Cyclic Redundancy Check error message, or your computer has to try re-reading a particular section, then try burning another disc, preferably of a different brand.

If you've come to this section trying to troubleshoot a burning error that has just started affecting you, even though you are using the same batch of DVDs, let me tell you what happened to me once. I had a spindle of 50 blank DVDs which seemed to be fine. I'd burned about 20 discs successfully, and then I started getting skipping problems. This lasted for about ten discs, and then the problem stopped. Somewhere in the middle of the batch were a small group of DVDs that were faulty. I didn't buy that brand again.

I'm sorry to say that brand names are not always a guarantee of quality. There are only a few disc manufacturers in the world, some with much higher standards (and prices) than others, and a number of the "name" brands buy their discs in from subcontractors – and not always from the same source each time. Another issue is that there are even some fakes around – very poor discs pretending to be made by one of the top names.

For me the good guys are Taiyo Yuden (hard to find except online and now using the JVC brand name) and Mitsubishi Verbatim. To avoid any lawyer's letters, I'll avoid naming brands that haven't worked – after all, they could have been fakes – but I suggest you do some Internet research if you are unsure.

Other burning issues

So, apart from bad media, what else may be the issue?

Don't dismiss the idea that your burner may have developed a fault. Try playing a commercial DVD. If you get jerky playback, the drive may not be able to get data from the disc quickly enough. There is a relatively common cause for this on older computers. It affects hard discs as well, but with DVDs can be triggered by trying to play a faulty DVD. If your burner is having speed issues use the Windows Device Manager to check it isn't running in PIO mode.

What else might be the problem? Well, DVD burners seem to age more than other hardware components – lasers can overheat, mechanical alignments can drift. One way of getting accurate burns is to burn at the slowest speed available. Just because the disc says 16x doesn't mean you have to burn at that speed. Imagine a small boy trying to direct a very powerful fire hose.

You may be able to adjust the burning speed in the Advanced settings box under Device output. If Auto is the only choice available, you could turn to another burning program, but any burner that can't write accurately at it's maximum speed has to be suspect.

Does your burner have the latest firmware? How to check that, and how to update it, is something you should be able to do from the manufacturer's web site.

Another potential culprit is clashing software. There are a number of programs that try to take over control of your DVD burner. If you have packet writing software in particular – sometimes marketed as "Drag and Drop" CD/DVD burning software - it may be running in the background.

DVD player issues

OK – let's assume now that the disc plays back OK on your computer. Put it into your stand alone DVD player. Does it play smoothly on the TV? If the answer is yes, a small smile should creep over your face. If you've got more than one player, a DVD recorder or a games console that plays DVDs, try them. If they all work, allow yourself a proper smile. Try the neighbours? How about the Electronics showroom? I'm sure if you search for long enough, you may find a player that either ignores your disc, or plays back in a jerky manner. Let's look at the problem of recognition first.

Why don't all burned DVDs play on all DVD players? A good question without a simple answer, I'm afraid. We can partly blame the DVD player manufacturers. Some of the oldest players just don't play burned DVDs – they aren't designed to. Others only play some types, +R or –R, rewritable or not. So there are a small group of players that are always going be a problem.

I've got an old DVD player that is very picky. Even though it can play some DVD-RW discs, it can't play every brand. It also doesn't like discs that have a duration of only a few minutes, although most burning programs including Pinnacle Studio now burn a longer lead-out sector to overcome this.

A flat refusal of a DVD player to play a disc – either with a "wrong disc" type of error message or by it just going into a sulk - has a few potential solutions:

- Double check you aren't trying to play a PAL DVD on an NTSC DVD player.

- Try a different disc type – rewritable discs are less likely to work, and more DVD players will play –R discs than +R

- Burn at the lowest speed possible if Studio gives you that option

- Try a different brand

- Use a different burning program

If your reaction to the last suggestion is "I've paid for Studio – why can't it do the job?" then bear in mind that Studio is an editing program that can burn discs. Burning programs will concentrate on burning, and may be better at it. Having said that, there isn't one burning program I've tried that can make my old DVD player accept DVD-RW discs made by one particular manufacturer. I've tried quite a few NLE programs that burn DVDs, and they have all failed as well.

If you want to use a 3rd party burning program and don't have one, I'd suggest you download ImgBurn. It's free, and even Microsoft have been known to recommend it. It is pretty user friendly, if a bit chatty at times. One reason I often use other programs to burn discs is the ability to verify the disc straight after burning, and the better error messages these programs provide. ImgBurn fulfils both these criteria.

I'll show you how to safely install and use ImgBurn to make a DVD from your projects later in this chapter, but let's look at another reason you might want to use it.

A very common question – "What's the best type of DVD to use in order to ensure maximum compatibility?"

The quick answer is to send people one –R and one +R.

The obvious (and unhelpful) answer is to get them pressed for you by a "Glass House". These will be proper DVD-ROM discs, but the process is far too expensive for anything other than a major commercial operation.

A less obvious answer is to disguise the discs as DVD-ROMs. At least then the DVD player won't reject them out of hand. The process required to do this is called Bitsetting and involves altering the Book Type.

The first few sections of a DVD can't be written to. This is where commercial DVDs hold the encryption information that is supposed to protect them from being pirated. Just after that comes data that tells the DVD player what specification the DVD is – its Book Type. On DVD +R discs, with *some* DVD burners installed with *some* firmware and using *some* burning programs, you can set this book type to DVD-ROM!

There are far too many "somes" in that last sentence for me to go into greater detail, but all you need to know is out there on the Internet. I've bought a DVD burner that can do Bit setting when I use ImgBurn, and a player belonging to a family member that couldn't play anything I burned now plays everything I burn.

What if standalone players recognise your DVD, but playback on some or all of them is jerky or skips? As mentioned before, DVD computer drives are pretty robust. However, DVD players are often far less happy trying to read data from burned discs; and don't imagine that the cheap and cheerful player you bought in the supermarket for the kids bedroom is likely to be any worse than a top of the range player – in fact some of the most expensive players can be the most choosy.

All the above points I made about burning apply again. Poor media can cause extra error correction, and some players might have trouble keeping up. Consider another burner or other burning software.

The final suggestion to avoid skipping involves lowering the bitrate of the burned DVD. If a particular player is having issues, you might find that not using 100% quality, but knocking 1000Kbits/sec off the compression bitrate, solves the problem. A small reduction in quality, but it means the player has a little less data to retrieve and error correct in real time. Studio can compress MPEG-2 at bitrates up to 8500Kbits/sec - although it rarely does. You will be unlikely to find these rates on commercial DVDs. The maximum the DVD-Video specification allows is 9800Kbits/sec. You will need to use the custom settings to lower the bitrate of a DVD, so let's look at how to do that.

With only 10 minutes on the timeline, I haven't needed to worry about disc usage. There will come a time when you want to put more than an hour of material on a DVD disc. This is accomplished by compressing the MPEG-2 video at a lower bitrate. You achieve this by selecting options in the Settings/Preset box. The options are:

Best Quality – gives a nominal bitrate of around 9200Kbps (video and sound combined)

If you keep adding video to the timeline, you will eventually get some red figures in the DVD Discometer. If you try to create a disc once the duration is more that Studio estimates will fit on the target DVD, it will offer to truncate the movie for you – cut the end off. Not that helpful, but thanks anyway.

Fit to Disc – this setting estimates what bitrate you need to fit the project onto the target disc.

The estimation can be very conservative. Two reasons in particular are the cause of this. Studio uses a variable compression rate but only does single pass encoding and therefore it can't be sure of the exact size a file will end up. Secondly, it isn't aware if it will be able to use Smart render.

Custom – You choose the bitrate. This is the option you would use to make a DVD with a bitrate of around 6000Kbps - at which you probably won't be able to perceive a drop in quality, but may well play on some of the cranky DVD players out there.

When you opt for the Custom option and open the advanced Settings, you will find a slider in the Video section that you can use to vary the bitrate between 2 and 8Mbits/sec.

Adjusting the bitrate using Custom settings

If you are passionate about getting the best quality you can, this setting can give you hours of fun. You can avoid the inaccuracies of Studio by making an unlimited size DVD image but manually adjusting the bitrate to build an image that will just fit on your chosen DVD size.

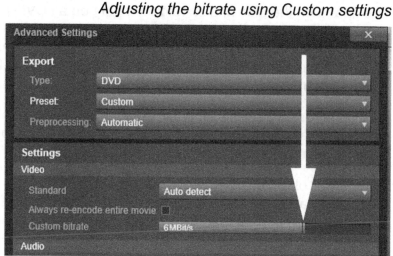

It's not something I've had the inclination to try, because almost all the long projects I've made have used VHS source material.

My rule of thumb is that I can't really see much difference between VHS material burned at 8500 and 5000Kbit/sec. That allows me to make two hour DVDs, which is long enough for anyone to have to endure. With DV footage, I wouldn't want to compromise the bitrate, so I might consider using D/L discs.

If DVDs are used to distribute professional movies, some of them over two hours in length, why don't our movies look like "Hollywood"? Sophisticated 2-pass authoring software means commercial discs can squeeze more duration on a disc, and Special Features are often at a lower bitrate, but it is the original product that is the key. Keeping the image quality as high as possible through the chain using professional cameras and lenses, expert lighting, and time consuming grading make the product look great. However, when it is put on to DVD, it is using exactly the same principle as making a DVD in Studio. Our movies don't look like "Hollywood" because they weren't shot with the same equipment, care and expertise. We can't blame MPEG-2 or Pinnacle.

Audio options

One compatibility issue that may occasionally bite you is audio playback. Because you own Pinnacle Studio, your computer will be able to play back all the audio formats that can be used on a DVD. There are 4 possible options

5.1 Dolby surround should play on all DVD players even if they can't output 5.1 sound. If your project doesn't have surround sound, then using 2 channel Dolby will take up less space on the disc and should also play on all DVD players. The problem might be with playing on a computer or laptop not equipped with a Dolby licence. You have one, but does everyone else? Well, most people will have and I've never heard anyone complaining that they can't hear the audio on a Dolby encoded disc, but it could happen.

MP2 compression takes up the same space as Dolby, won't sound significantly worse and you don't need a licence, but while any computer should be able to play it, there might be some older NTSC DVD players that can't.

PCM is our old friend the Windows Wave (or WAV.) file format. Everything should be able to play it, but the disadvantage is that it takes up significantly more space on the DVD - so much so that the Video compression has to be lowered by 1Mbit/s to make space!

Burning multiple copies

Once you have been successful in making a DVD, there are a number of ways of making a batch of copies. You may have noticed that in Advanced options there is a selection for the number of copies you want. You can select the number of discs you want but this doesn't have any affect in Burn Image mode. One option if you are going to do a long production run is to use a 3rd party piece of software, but you can also use the middle button at the bottom of the Export Disc window.

Burn Disc

You can take advantage of the multiple copies setting with this. If you have come from a successful Create Image session and Always re-encode isn't checked, you won't even have to wait for rendering to reoccur because the old files will be used.

Once you are confident of your DVD burning process, you may want to use the Burn Disc option anyway, even for a one-off disc creation. If you discover that the disc is faulty, you will be able to go back to the image and test it in the manner I described earlier - but you will have wasted a disc

Using Imgburn

I've mentioned using a 3rd party burning program a number of times, and the program I recommend is ImgBurn.

For serious troubleshooting, you may want to build a DVD image from the Video_TS folder that Studio creates, and ImgBurn is capable of that, but you can also employ it for everyday use, burning and then verifying your discs as a separate task while freeing up Studio. The simplest way to use ImgBurn is to get Studio to make an ISO image of your disc. (ISO is a file type for disc images, originally ISO 9660 by the International Organization for Standardization.) When I've finished a project, it's my preferred storage solution to make an ISO image of the final disc to store on my computer - if I then want to make more copies I can load that ISO straight into ImgBurn.

Making an ISO image is just a matter of selecting that type in the Advanced options and proceeding with either Burn Disc or Burn Image. If the disc is already rendered and you don't have Always recode checked, the process is fast.

Acquire a copy of ImgBurn from the official website. To do this, go to www.imgburn.com. Ignore anything that looks like an advert embedded in the site. Download the latest version of the software. At the time of writing this is version 2.5.8.0 and the download link is in the first "News" item - ImgBurn v2.5.8.0 Released! – it reads Click here to download. That link takes you to the download page where there are a number of Mirrors (alternative sites)

ImgBurn is currently free. You might decide to make a donation if you use the program regularly and want to help keep it updated.

My recommendation is to use the ImgBurn mirror for the download, unless you experience speed issues. Clicking on Mirror 7 will simply open a Save File or a Run or Save File dialogue. Choose Save and the file will be placed in the default download location. Open the folder location if it doesn't do so automatically and then double click on **SetupImgBurn_2.5.8.0.exe** to install the program.

ImgBurn is bundled with adware, so it is important that you **don't** use the "Express (recommended)" option to install the program (unless you want the adware!)

Even then, watch out as you will be asked if you want to install additional programs. These may vary from user to user. None of these are required but you have to deliberately uncheck the boxes to stop it happening. **Take care!**

The Write mode selection

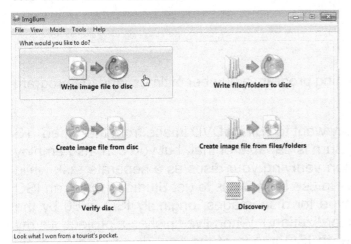

You may read some very negative things about Imgburn installing unwanted programs even if you are careful. It's never happened to me, but if you are very cautious, it is possible to get a clean version of the program that doesn't have the installer responsible. Check out the DTVPro website support page or email me for more details.

When the installation finishes, the ImgBurn website will reopen. Close it and *Finish* the Setup Wizard. ImgBurn will probably run automatically.

When you first run ImgBurn a splash screen appears briefly, then the main window opens in what is called the Ez-Mode Picker. We need to select the Write Image file to disc mode, otherwise called the **Write** mode.

Loading an ISO file

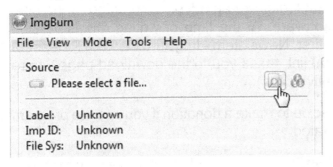

When you are in this mode use the Browse for File folder icon in the Source box to locate the ISO file you created in Studio, and select it.

If you have more than one DVD burner on your system, you need to select the one you want to use from the **Destination** drop-down box. Uncheck Test Mode and check Verify if you want to test your final disc is completely readable before you try it elsewhere. If you are in a hurry, you might want to uncheck it and take the risk.

Bottom left in the setting box you can choose the write speed - you might get more reliable burns if you don't use the maximum available. You can also choose how many copies you want to make.

The next stage is to put a blank DVD into your burner and give ImgBurn a few moments to recognise it. Then click on the Write icon with the Green arrow at the bottom left of the window, and the process will start - or you can select **File/Build** from the menu. Either action will start the process of burning your DVD.

It will take a certain amount of time, but you will be kept informed of progress. One thing that may worry you, but is no cause for concern, is the time spent "Synchronising Cache".

When the burning has finished, the verifying will begin (unless you have unchecked the option). Finally you will get a "Success" message and hear a cheerful (or irritating) little tune.

Labels - a warning

Don't ever stick labels to your DVDs. They might work for a little while, but as the glue ages and the labels peel, you might lose the disc, and even damage the player. Use a CD/DVD marker pen (or Sharpie) to mark up your discs. If you want a better look, buy an inkjet printer that can print directly to printable DVDs.

AVCHD Discs

AVCHD discs are a halfway house between DVD and Blu-ray. You can use normal DVD discs and DVD burners to make the discs, but you can only play them back on a Blu-ray player – and because AVCHD discs aren't part of the official Blu-ray specification, not all Blu-ray players will play them. Because the AVCHD format is promoted by Sony and Panasonic, if you own a Blu-ray player by either of those manufacturers it's very likely to work with these discs. Look for the "AVCHD" logo if you are thinking of buying a Blu-ray player.

There are a number of limitations in comparison to Blu-ray. The maximum bitrate is 18Mbit/s so some of the better AVCHD cameras will have to have their pictures downgraded slightly. Duration is relatively limited – for example, about 35 minutes at best quality on a single layer DVD - and although you can use menus, I've read that the AVCHD Disc format only supports "simple" menus. What that means, I'm not sure, but Studio struggles to create complex menus that are reliable on this format, so I wouldn't recommend you do anything too elaborate.

For me, the medium offers a great low cost way of viewing home-made HD material on my main TV. You may prefer to go the extra step to Blu-ray if you want the last bit of quality or you make long projects. Only recently, since I've bought a camera that shoots at a higher bitrate than 17Mbits/s and the cost of burners has come down have I joined the Blu-ray camp.

The structure of files on an AVCHD disc is completely different to DVD, but the principle is the same – a whole host of files that hold data about the contents and menus, with the Video and audio held in files that can be played separately. The format used is .MTS and you will find it if you drill down into the folder structure – BDMV/Stream.

All of the leading Blu-ray playing software packages can handle AVCHD discs, and VLC can also play them if you ask it to look for Blu-ray. If you just want to check the quality of the rendered video, you can play the .MTS files themselves with most media players, including WMP. Testing the menus without burning a disc can be tricky, but I've converted the Folder Image created by Studio into an ISO file using ImgBurn, then mounted that as a drive in Windows 8

The process of creating a AVCHD disc is almost identical to creating a DVD. In version 18 I've not detected any attempt by the software to Smart Render video – so that takes away one source of potential problems although at the expense of speed. The "Always re-encode" checkbox still controls the re-use of the asset files though. Troubleshooting AVCHD discs should follow the same pattern as DVDs, but bear in mind that your discs are not guaranteed to work on players that don't have an AVCHD logo.

If you remember back a few pages, I talked about the AVCHD rendering options. With the likelihood the Disc projects are going to be of a longer duration than files, there is more chance that the preset options will be best for you as they use the Fastest Speed H.264 render setting, but if ultimate quality is your aim, then you can access the Balanced or Best settings from the Advanced Settings button.

AVCHD 2 Cards

Pinnacle Studio has introduced support for a new output format – AVCHD 2. While this shows up in the Export Disc Settings options, it's not actually for writing to a disc, but to a memory card. The card can then be played on any device that supports playback. AVCHD 2 lifts some of the limits of the older format – you can now use it for 50p and 60p video, and with bitrates up to 28Mpbs. It opens the way for full HD in 3D as well because it uses an extension to the AVC standard - MVC, or Multi-View Coding.

When Studio prepares an image for this format, it uses full resolution HD and a bitrate of 22Mbit/s. Partly because of the increased specification, you can't put this format onto a disc and the Device selection actually looks for a suitable card to write to. If you have a memory card reader or suitable camera connected to your computer, you can select that as the destination, and the command Burn disc will copy the final files to the memory card. Instead of setting the Target disc size, you choose the capacity of the card you intend to write to.

Blu-ray Discs

To make Blu-ray discs, you will need to buy a Blu-ray licence from Pinnacle. It's an option in the Help Menu. Once you buy the licence, make sure you make a note of the email address you used. If you reinstall the program and lose the option, you can use the Restore Purchase option in the Control Panel so that you don't have to pay again!

I mentioned earlier that the Blu-ray disc format uses a higher frequency laser to read and write discs than the DVD format. This allows smaller "pits" to be used, so the disc can store more information. Significantly more, in fact, because a single layer Blu-ray can hold 25Gb of data - over five times as much as single layer DVD.

Although the cost of blank discs is now reasonable, if you have to buy a burner, they are still quite a bit dearer than DVD burners.

Some DSLR cameras produce video at high level bitrates of 40Mbit/s, and, the maximum theoretical video bitrate of Blu-ray is 40Mbit/s, so you will get just over a 80 minutes on a single layer disc. However, the technical limit to the AVCHD standard used by most modern HD cameras is 24Mbits/s. You may have a camera that shoots at 50 or 60p with a bitrate of 28Mbit/s, but some Blu-ray players cannot handle 50 or 60p.

For the Fit to disc setting, Studio uses a maximum of 24Mbit/s, giving a little under 2 hours duration. While this shows a quality of 60%, don't think that your video is being hugely downgraded (unless you are sure it has a bitrate higher than the AVCHD standard). Best quality seems a somewhat buggy setting. In most circumstances Fit to Disc will give a similar end result and is far less likely to crash on you.

Again, the H.264 render setting can be customised between Fastest, Balanced or Best Quality, but consider the additional render time should you choose Balanced or Best.

The Blu-ray standard allows discs to also contain MPEG-2 video as well as or instead of H.264. You will get lower quality for a given bitrate, but the MPEG-2 render might be of interest if you are experiencing pixelation or playback issues with your discs. You can select MPEG-2 using the Advanced settings/Settings/Video/Encoding.

When you use MPEG-2 and Fit to disc, the bitrate chosen starts at 40mbit/s.

If you have a Blu-ray burner it may have come with playback software, so troubleshooting the discs from an image will present no problems, but if you don't have any playback software, the disc structure is similar to AVCHD and you will find the video and audio content in the MD/Stream folder of the image. Alternativly, you can install the free VLC player as mentioned earlier.

Output to Cloud

Export to Cloud

The third option for Export type is Cloud – the Internet, basically. Video sharing sites allow you to upload videos, and Pinnacle Studio helps you automate the process. Each of the services currently implemented have slightly different interfaces within the Export window. But the three video services are essentially the same.

Historically, uploading to YouTube has been a feature of Pinnacle Studio products for a number of years now. I'll walk through how this works in Pinnacle Studio 19.

YouTube upload

The process starts with you selecting YouTube in the Settings box. The only option is Publish, and to begin with the Publish window is divided in two in the same manner as Files export. The player has In and Out point Callipers so you can select a part of the movie or disc, and the lower half has a destination window.

When you click on the *Start Publishing* button at the bottom of the Exporter window you are offered a choice of where to place the render file that will be generated for upload. You can change the location with the usual File Destination folder icon, and the bar shows how much space remains on your chosen hard drive. If you are unhappy with the current choice, you should change it now because you won't be able to after you have logged into YouTube.

Logging into YouTube

Clicking on Start Publishing will open up a Google log-in window unless you are already signed in. Once logged in, the next screen offers you the chance to enter the same details that YouTube allows you to specify in its browser uploader. Title, Description, Tags and Category define the information that will appear about the video. Licence defines what people can do with your video and Privacy gives

you the choice of who can see it. All these settings can be modified at a later stage within your YouTube account once the video has uploaded.

Setting the YouTube format

Format is the important setting. YouTube offers 4 settings which are a simple trade off of render and upload time against final quality. Fastest is 360p - sub-DVD quality. Standard is Standard Definition at 480p (not quite PAL SD, but close), 720p and 1080p are the High Definition settings.

If you choose the highest quality setting, the viewer will have the choice of watching at a lower quality (and therefore faster) setting that may suit their Internet download speed better, but obviously if you choose a fast setting, the viewer won't be able to watch at a higher quality setting.

Having chosen a suitable format, clicking on Start begins a render process, where a file of a suitable quality is rendered to the area specified earlier. The choice of file settings seems to be chosen carefully to make the most of YouTube's qualities, but it is important to note that YouTube will add further compression and optimisation to the files that Studio uploads.

Studio uses MP4 simple codecs for SD and H.264 for HD and bitrates of around 1, 1.5, 3.2 and 7Mbit/s respectively for the 4 resolutions, so you can see immediately that a 1080p video is going to take about 7 times longer to upload than the fastest 360 setting.

Once the file is made, the upload to YouTube begins, and when complete you get a box offering to open your web browser to examine the results. However, you may find that if you do so immediately, YouTube may still be processing your video – this is quite normal.

I do use the YouTube uploader in Studio for convenience, but it doesn't always make sense to. While the video is uploading you are locked out of using Studio. You can match the MP4 settings that are used by Pinnacle using custom. The other point is that if you aren't waiting for the upload to finish, you can afford to use a higher bitrate. I have no positive proof that using the 1080p MP4 file preset (H.264 at 12Mbit/s) gives better results because of YouTube's re-encoding, but the additional time it takes isn't a huge price to pay for the possibility that the end result is just a little better.

Other Cloud services

Uploads to Facebook, Vimeo and Box follow the same pattern and apart from the different log-in and properties boxes, offer the same 4 preset upload sizes.

Output to Device

While some versions of Studio had a number of file output presets that were specific to particular playback devices, they were scattered around the various file types. Pinnacle Studio 19 neatly puts all these presets into a new Export category with sections for various devices of Apple, Microsoft, Nintendo and Sony. The Advanced settings allow some changes similar to File Export but you can't customise the actual file settings - which would rather defeat the object of using what are the recommended setting for each device.

When you have made your file, you will have to manually transfer it to the device in question.

MyDVD

As I mentioned earlier, Pinnacle now provide a secondary standalone program that will create discs for you. It's not intended to replace the Author mode of Studio, but it may offer some advantages.

One is that it is a little easier to understand. The other possible advantage is that it may work when the built-in disc authoring fails. However, if you decide to use it, any work you do on adding menus to your projects before you open My DVD will be lost.

To use My DVD, you start with a completed movie in the Edit or Author tabs, switch to Export and then use the My DVD File option to create a suitable file.

The My DVD File export options

If you allow the exported movies to be placed in the default location, when you open My DVD the program will find the files.

Once you have made the files - one for each title you want on the disc - then you need to use Windows to open the My DVD program.

I don't intend to go into details about My DVD. It's a relatively simplistic "Drag and Drop" program that was originally written by one of Corel's other companies that has been bundled with Studio. It doesn't offer a huge range of menus or navigation options even when you use the Advanced mode, and you really don't get a decent preview of what the disc will look like until you burn it.

Smart Edit, Insert, Overwrite and Trimming

Chapters 2 and 3 of this book cover much of the timeline behaviour in Pinnacle Studio 19, apart from the use of Advanced trimming. In this chapter I'm going back to the beginning to cover some of that ground again in more detail. You can use this chapter as a quick reference for the concepts, while the later part of the chapter looks at the more complex editing tools.

Smart Mode

Pinnacle Studio has three editing modes available and you choose them with the Editing Options tool at the far right of the Timeline toolbar.

Editing Modes

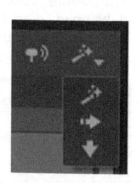

Smart mode is represented by a wand and is the default mode. For most operations I recommend using it, as it is designed to make a "Best Guess" that should speed up your editing. It applies to dragging, dropping, deleting and trimming clips.

Some Smart mode operations use Insert mode, others use Overwrite mode and sometimes Smart mode behaves a bit differently to both, so before we start to examine which type of behaviour occurs in which circumstances I want to define clearly the Insert and Overwrite modes.

Insert mode

You can force Studio to behave in Insert mode all the time by selecting it from the Editing Options drop-down. Insert is represented by a right pointing arrow. I suggest you might want to work through the examples with me - I'm going to start by using *The-Sky-is-the-Limit* video file we used in Project 1 and the *The-Sky-is-the-Limit* photos in the "Today's Project" collection that we created in the Library chapter - so if you have worked through that chapter and haven't deleted that collection then open it now. You should also be able to see what is happening with some random photos of your own choosing.

I've put the "Sky-is-the-Limit" clip on track 2, split it at about 16 seconds where the shot of the sun shining through the trees starts, and then I've deleted the second part of the clip from the timeline.

Next, I've adjusted the timescale so that the clip occupies about three quarters of the timeline.

The original Timeline

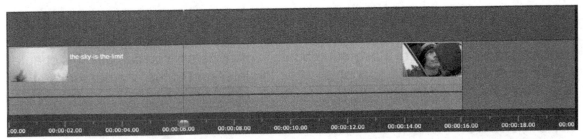

Switching to **Insert mode** by selecting the right pointing arrow icon in the Editing mode tool, I've then selected a photo from the library, clicked on it, held down the mouse button and dragged in down to track two on the timeline.

Even before I release the mouse button the original video clip on the timeline is split at the point I drop the photo, with the second part of the video clip moved to the right. Releasing the mouse button drops the photo in place.

Drag and drop in Insert mode

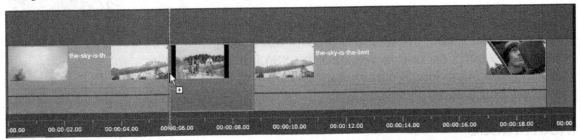

3 seconds of still photo have been **inserted** into the video. All the video is still there and the project is 3 seconds longer.

Now I'm going to use a simple trimming action to lengthen the photo. I hover the mouse over the inside left edge of the photo so that an In point trimming handle appears. Clicking the mouse button down, holding it and dragging the mouse to the left causes a green bar to appear on the left edge of the photo. As I drag the mouse further left the mouse pointer has turned into a double headed arrow. The photo gets longer to indicate I have increased the duration.

All the time this is happening, the second half of the video clip is moving right to make space for the longer duration of the photo.

Trimming in Insert mode

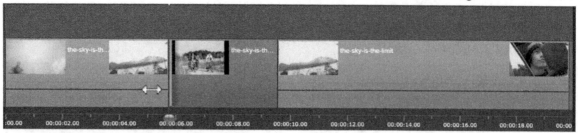

The screenshot shows the end of the second video clip much closer to the end of the timeline window. Releasing the mouse leaves the clip in the same position. The movie is the length of the original clip, plus the 3 seconds of the first insertion plus whatever amount I've stretched the photo duration by - about another second.

The next part takes a little bit of thinking about. If I delete the inserted photograph, what would you expect to happen to the timeline? Because inserting an item into another one has done no damage, removing the item by deleting in Insert mode also does no damage. When I select the middle clip with the mouse and press the Delete key, the photo disappears and leaves no gap behind - the second video clip moves back to the left to fill the gap.

Deleting the photo in Insert mode - no gap!

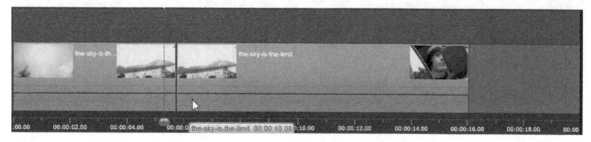

The movie is back to its original length, and the only sign that an edit operation has occurred is that the video is split at the point I dropped the photo into it and split the clip.

Overwrite Mode

While Insert mode is always polite, making room for itself, or closing up any gaps it would otherwise leave behind, Overwrite just barges straight in; it never alters the positions of any other clips it might interfere with - it just deletes anything that gets in its way instead.

First, let's set up a timeline identical to the one we used to examine Insert. If you still have the project open, keep using undo until it is back to a single 16 second clip. I've included the screenshot again to save you turning pages to compare.

The original Timeline - again!

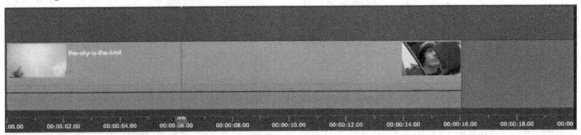

Switch to **Overwrite mode** using the Edit Mode control by selecting the downwards pointing arrow, then drag the photo from the timeline again and observe the result.

The obvious differences here are that the second video clip hasn't moved left, and instead of the In point starting just one frame later than the Out point of the first clip, it is 3 seconds later - the duration of the photo.

The photo being dropped in Overwrite mode

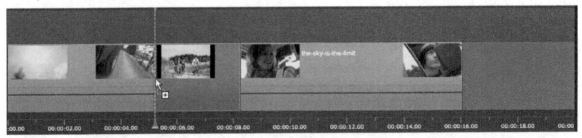

When you release the mouse button, the timeline should remain the same length.

OK, lets now see what happens if we decide to trim the photo to make it longer. Repeat the same operation, forming an In point handle, clicking and dragging left.

The photo duration increased at the expense of the outgoing video

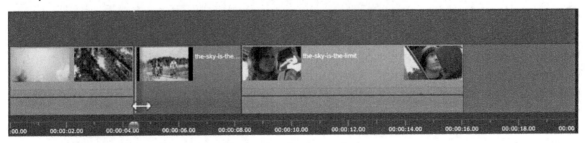

As the screenshot confirms, the timeline duration doesn't alter, and you will notice that the Out point of the first clip changes as you move the In point of the photo. Before you release the mouse button, drag right as well - you will notice that Overwrite mode rather rudely leaves a gap, rather than nice Insert mode that tidies up after itself. Drag back left so that the photo is about a second longer and release the mouse button.

Hopefully by now you will be able to predict what is going to happen when I delete the photo in Overwrite mode. It leaves without a care in the world and doesn't even close the door behind itself.

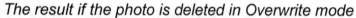

The result if the photo is deleted in Overwrite mode

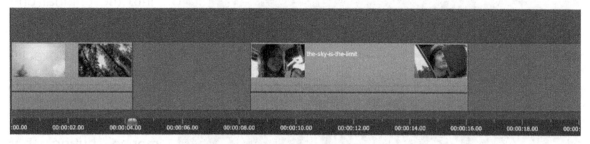

One thing to remind you of is the Alt key modifier. When you are in Insert mode, holding down Alt switches you to Overwrite. When you are Insert, holding down Alt switches you to Overwrite, although for deletions, you have to use the trash icon as the context menu and keyboard shortcut doesn't function with the Alt key.

Smart Mode Drag and Drop

Before we continue, undo the timeline changes to restore the 16 second clip and switch back to **Smart mode**.

If you only have media on one track in Pinnacle Studio, it's easy to predict how Smart Mode will behave when you drag and drop - it uses Insert mode. If you don't want to switch away from Smart mode but want it to Overwrite, then hold down the ALT key before or even during the operation as discussed in the opening chapters.

Smart mode begins to apply it's magic when you have more than one track occupied by media. To demonstrate this I've set up a simple two track example using the sample footage again.

If you want to emulate this, trim the video on track 2 to 9 seconds duration, then drag the portrait shaped photo of Shaggy on the bike to track 1. Line the start of the photo up with the cut to the trees just after 3 seconds, then extend the outpoint a little by trimming to line it up with the end of the shot looking out at the lake. Very crudely,

I've created a sequence where the shots looking out of the van have a still photo of Shaggy on his bicycle superimposed.

Two track sequence

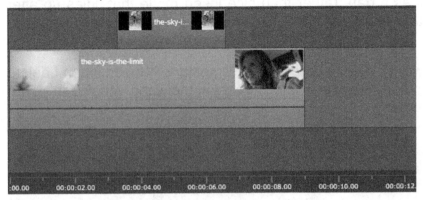

When you select another photo from the Library and drag it down to the middle of the photo on track 1, Smart mode inserts the new photo into the original one but also makes a gap in the video on track 2! The gap is exactly

the same duration as the new photo.

Smart drag and drop to track 1

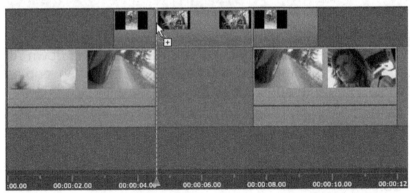

Don't let go of the mouse button, but continue to drag the photo down to the middle of the video on track 2. The same behaviour occurs - the relationship between the first photo and the video is maintained and the picture of

Shaggy is still only overlaid on shots looking out of the van.

Smart drag and drop to track 2

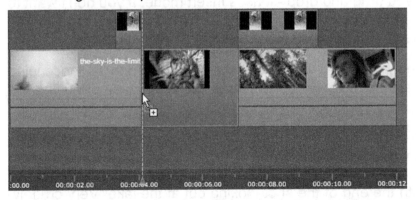

Pulling the new photo further down still to track 3 allows Smart Mode to close up the gap. Releasing the mouse key drops the new photo onto an empty track without disrupting the tracks above.

Smart drag and drop to track 3

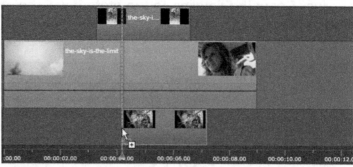

Remember the Alt key? If you were to use it in these circumstances, Smart mode becomes a simple Overwrite. No relationships between clips on the timeline would be altered, but anything underneath your new clip would blotted out.

There is a significant difference in behaviour when you drag an item into a gap using Smart mode, but first we need to look at Drag and Drop on the timeline.

A new Smart mode feature

Pinnacle have listened to customer feedback and changed the Smart behaviour when dragging media that is already on the timeline. In the past, it didn't take into account items on the other tracks, but in PS19 it does. (It could be argued that the old behaviour was a bug, but let's give them the benefit of the doubt.)

If you experimented with the Alt key, reset the timeline to the three items as arranged in the last screenshot. Rescale the timeline view to 30 seconds using the timescale context menu.

Now drag the 3 second photo on track 3 up to track 2 so it sits below the photo on track 1.

Drag and Drop on the timeline creates gaps on all the affected tracks

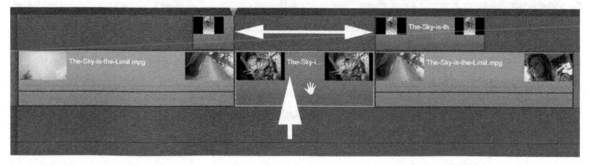

Notice the gap created in the content on track 1. This keeps everything in sync - our superimposed photo still starts and ends in the same places relative to the video on track 2 as it did before - coinciding with the exterior shots.

This new feature gets even more helpful if you want to drag not just one, but a group of clips. Reset the timeline to the state it was before and then use CtRL-Drag and drop to bring a copy of the video on track 2 down to track 4.

A four-track example timeline

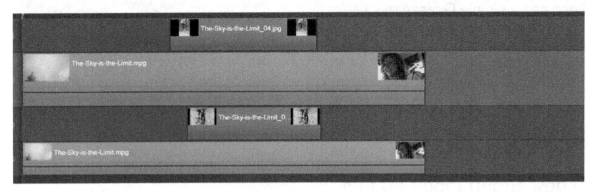

Now select both the photos using Ctrl-Click and drag them both down a drag so that the insert themselves into the video clips.

Smart Drag and drop retaining sync between clips

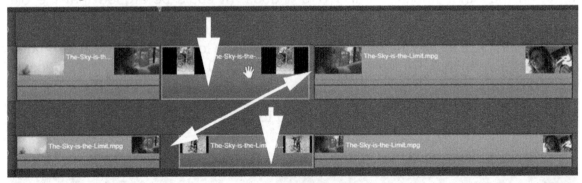

The really cool thing about this operation is that a gap to accommodate both photos is created in both the video clips, so the two photos retain their relationship with each other, as do the video clips. This is important when moving titles or other overlays, and vital if you are dealing with sync audio.

With this new feature you can select a group of clips on a number of tracks and drag them to another part of the project without fear of disrupting the synchronisation of the entire project.

Obviously, if the alteration you are trying to make doesn't require the maintenance of sync, you can override this behaviour by switching to Insert mode, when each insertion is calculated on a track by track basis.

Smart Mode, Drag and Drop and Gaps

When you are in Insert or Overwrite Mode, a gap is treated just as a clip with no content. In Smart mode it is seen as a chance to work some more magic. The first bit of magic happens when you drag an item from the timeline to a gap.

Smart Mode filling a gap with room to spare

Undo the last action and try dragging the photo on track 3 up to the beginning of the project on track 1. As the item is smaller than the gap Smart mode assumes that you don't want to disturb any clips that you have already placed on track 1 so works in Overwrite mode. It's not destructive because there is nothing to overwrite, but you can think of it as overwriting the darkness or silence of the gap.

If the clip is larger than the gap, or you wish to place it so that it overlaps some section of an item, then the behaviour when using clips from elsewhere on the timeline is very Smart - it creates a gap that is just big enough to maintain the sync between all the tracks, and overwrites the rest of the item into the gap.

Partial gap created when dragging a timeline item

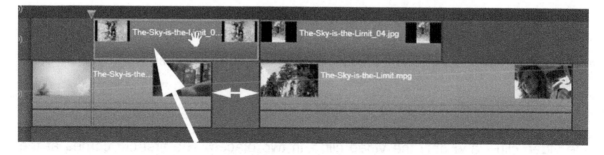

Gaps and dragging from the Library or Source viewer

What would be the most helpful behaviour if you were trying to place an item into gap but is too big for where you are putting it? Smart mode assumes that you want to truncate the photo, video, audio or title to **fit** the gap. What is more, the start of the gap is defined as the place your scrubber is currently hovering.

Let's try that now on the timeline. Restore the project to the two tracks before we added the second photo. Now drag a new photo from the Library (not the timeline!) to the gap at the start of track 1. Because the default duration of a photo is 3 seconds and the gap in this case is more than that, placing the scrubber at the start of the track leaves room for the whole photo - and notice the original photo further down the track is undisturbed.

If you then slowly drag the scrubber right, the Out point of the new photo bumps into the original. Dragging right further neither overwrites the second clip, nor does it push the whole of the second clip right, but the clip I'm currently dragging gets shorter! Smart Mode is automatically adjusting the duration so it fits the space in to which I want to place it.

Dragging into a gap on the timeline from the Source viewer

It is also possible to set an In point of a source clip in the Souce viewer before you drag it into a gap, so that the incoming is at the point you desire, but the Out point is set to achieve the desired duration. I gave an example of this on page 89.

Smart Mode Deletion

In Multi-track situations Smart Mode also has special properties when you delete a clip.

I'm going to modify the sample timeline in order to demonstrate the extra power of Smart. Firstly I've removed the second photo I added, just for clarity. Then I've split the video clip - and only the video clip - in two places. The first cut comes at the junction of the shot of the wheel and the shot of the lake, which is about 5 and a half seconds in. The second split is between the shots of Fred and Daphne at just over 7 seconds. If you want to try this and are having difficulty locating the first split point you might want to temporarily turn off the video monitoring of track 1 by clicking on the eye icon in the track header.

The timeline now consists of three shots on track 2, and a photo superimposed that straddles the first two video shots.

Modified timeline to show the Delete options

Again, I'm going to manually switch to the other editing modes to show you the two "normal" options. First, I switch to the Overwrite mode

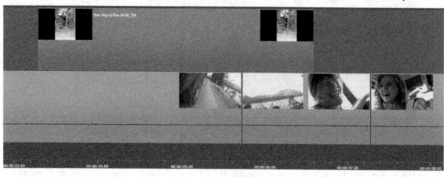

and then select the middle clip of video. Pressing delete has the effect of leaving a gap in the timeline track of the same duration. Nothing else on the timeline moves.

Deleting in Overwrite

Undoing the delete, switching to Insert and deleting the clip shows the third shot moving left to fill the gap left by the removal of the second shot.

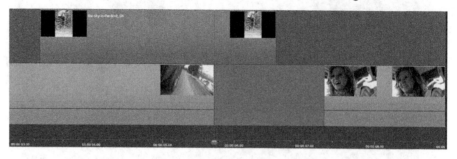

Deleting in Insert

Both of these modes ignore the other track, so that the photo on track 1 is unaltered. Using Insert is probably the more unhelpful of the

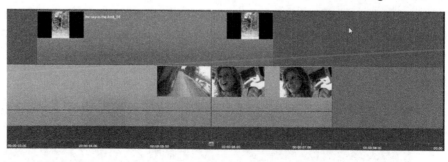

two options, because I didn't want the photo to be superimposed over the shot of people in the van, and now it is.

Smart mode tries to be as helpful as possible without deleting anything - it can't know your exact intentions, but it assumes you don't want any of your timeline to have gaps where there is nothing on any track.

Smart mode removes some of the gap but preserves the whole photo

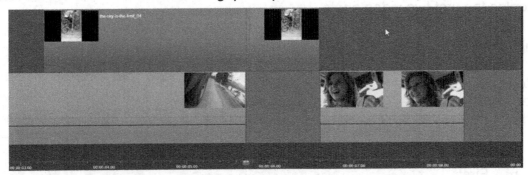

OK, one more example of Delete to show you what happens to content after the deletion point. I've now restored the timeline to before the Smart Delete and dragged two more photos down to tracks 1 and 3.

Before Smart deletion

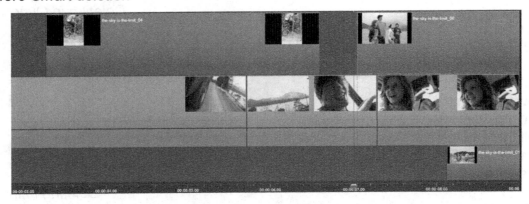

Selecting the middle video clip again and using Delete not only removes the clip and pulls up the gap as much as it can without overlapping, it also pulls up the two photos on the other tracks.

After Smart deletion

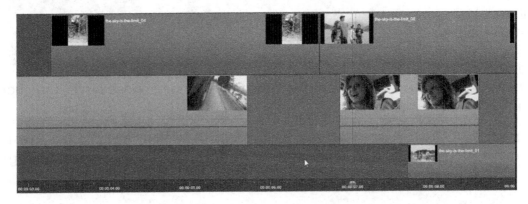

If there were items further down any of the tracks, even ones scrolled off the bottom of the screen, they too would have been moved left unless the track they were on was locked.

By the way, the Alt modifier switches Smart Delete to a simple Overwrite Delete if you are using the Trash icon.

Trimming

There are two types of trimming. The Quick mode use Green trim bars. You hover the mouse near an edit point to generate a trim handle icon, Click, hold, and as you start to drag a green trim bar appears on the edge of the clip you are trimming. The process is described in detail starting on page 48.

Advanced trimming is more powerful. It allows you to trim with frame accuracy and adjust up to two trim points on every track at the same time. Advanced trim bars are yellow. We haven't explored them yet, but are to do so shortly.

If you keep inadvertently generating yellow trim bars, you are a few pages early for Advanced Trimming. There is an option in the Control Panel/Project settings to *Activate trim mode by clicking near cuts*. Uncheck this if you keep creating Advanced trim points in error while trying the following examples.

Smart Mode Quick Trimming

Even in a single track situation, Smart mode has special features when Simple trimming a clip.

However, Quick Trim never affects any other track on the timeline in any way, even in Smart mode.

For the next demonstration we need two video clips with a gap between them on the timeline. You can create your own timeline or follow my example.

Two video clips and a gap with In and Out points labelled

I've split the 9 second clip we are currently using about halfway at the cut between the tilting tree shot and the shot of the van wheel, then dragged the second half 2 seconds to the left.

Just for clarity, I've numbered the screenshot with the points I'll be adjusting. 1 is the first clip Out point. 2 is the Gap In point. 3 is the Gap Out point. 4 is the second clip In point and 5 is the second clip Out point.

Trimming the Out point of the first clip shows Smart mode behaving in Overwrite mode - the duration of the clip and the Out point are being altered with no effect on the positioning of clip 2. If you try dragging the Out point left, the gap gets bigger. If you drag it right, you will eventually start overwriting the incoming video of clip 2.

Quick trimming in Smart Mode on point 1, the Out point of the first clip

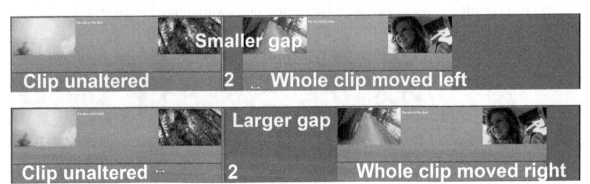

Smart mode flips its behaviour when it is trimming a gap. Undo any actions you have taken on the clip 1 Out point, and now work on trim point 2, the In point of the gap..

When trimming a gap Smart Mode gives Insert behaviour. Making the gap smaller by dragging the In point to the right causes the second video clip to move to the left.

Quick trimming in Smart Mode on 2, the In point of the gap

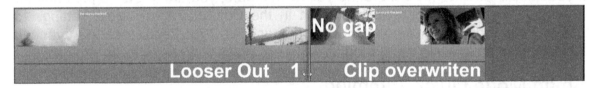

If I drag the Out point right to make the gap bigger, the second clip moves right too.

Because a gap has no content, it would make no difference if we Simple trimmed the Out point - point 3 on the screenshot on the previous page - rather than point 2 as shown above.

I find it easy to forget that I'm sometimes operating on a gap and at other times on a clip because of how natural the Smart mode trimming behaviour feels once you get used to it. To help cement the principle, it is worth studying how Smart mode trims the In and Out points of the second clip.

Quick trimming in Smart mode on 4, the In point of the second clip

Quick trimming in Smart mode on 5, the Out point of the second clip

If you sometimes get confused, just remember the Smart mode treats gaps differently - and don't forget the Alt key as a remedy to any unwanted behaviour.

Overtrimming

This is something that can occur in bother Quick and Advanced trimming. We encountered it in the second chapter on page 97.

Overtrimming can occur with video as well as audio (but not photos). Start an empty project and place the *Sky is the Limit* footage on the main track, then drag it right so that there is a gap between the start of the movie and the start of the clip. Now Quick trim the In point to the left. The program allows you to do this even though there is no video before the start of the clip.

However, there isn't any video. I've overtrimmed the clip so the timeline displays a red "dead meat" area. When this is played back, you will see it consists of a frozen frame of the start of the clip.

An overtrimmed video clip

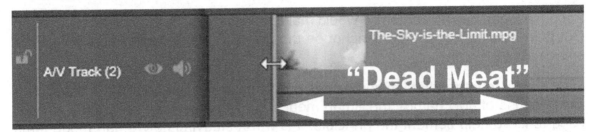

Why would that be useful? In other editors you might be used to the program simply refusing to let you extend the clip. Pinnacle Studio lets you do that to give more flexibility when adjusting multi-track projects. The red colouring is a warning that the video is frozen.

Advanced Trimming

Time to finally generate that yellow trim point. Because the next section will be demonstrated more clearly using video clips with well defined action, I'm going to use some new source material. If you want to use the same clips as me, then Appendix 1 will tell you how to get the video clips I'm going to use. They are called **Car Clips 1, 2** and **3**

I've started with all three 8 second clips positioned on the timeline. The timecode you can see in the screenshots is superimposed on the video clips themselves.

The three clips on the timeline

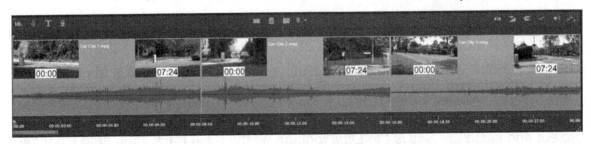

Before we start, you might want to remind yourself of what happens if you trim the first clip's In point with Simple trimming – a green bar shortens the duration of the clip by removing frames from the front of the clip, and all three clips stay in the same position on the timeline.

Undo any trimming you have done. Now let's set an Advanced Trim point on the In Point of clip 1.

Put the Timeline scrubber at the start of the Movie and then press the T key on the keyboard.

Trim Mode activated

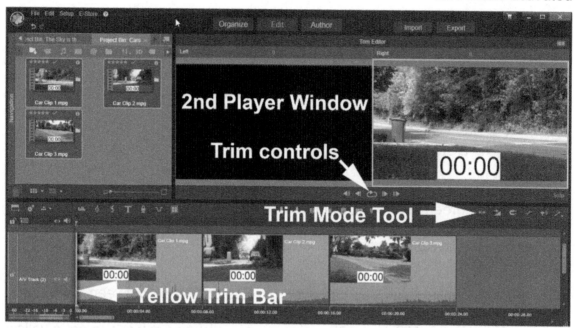

So what happened there then? If you haven't seen it before, you should have been pleasantly surprised at the presence of not one but two player windows top right, with the area label "Trim Editor". The left preview has black level, the right window the first frame of clip 1.

Let's start using trim with the mouse. Hover in the lower half of the first clip near the yellow bar, click, hold and drag right. The first thing you should notice is the whole content of the timeline moves to the left – Smart Mode in Advanced Trim works in **Insert Mode**. You will see the first clip's opening frames thumbnail being updated, and the same frame being displayed in the right-hand preview window.

Trimming the first shot by 1 second

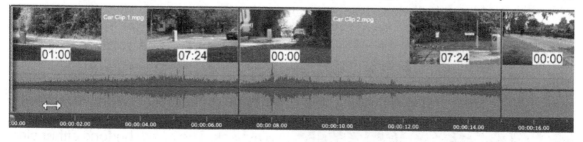

To get rid of the trim bar, I press the T key again. Clicking on the Trim button has the same effect. The T key and the Trim mode button on the timeline toolbar are interchangeable, so if you prefer working with the mouse, then use that control.

Won't it get very confusing if Smart mode in Simple Trim works in Overwrite on clips, but in Advanced Trim it works in Insert? Hopefully not, once you are aware of the feature. That's why the trim bars are different colours, for one thing. Also you will tend to be using the different trimming tasks for different operations. There is a third way of setting an Advanced Trim point which will also help you differentiate, particularly if you use it by default.

Trim mode activation settings

Earlier I advised you to alter a control panel setting if you were generating yellow trim bars instead of green in error. If you turned it off I think it's time to turn that feature on – in the *Control panel, Project Settings, Activate trim mode by clicking near cuts*. Now, when you click and release near an In or Out point, you get the Advanced Trim bar. The Trim tool still works, by the way.

When editing in this mode, you can even use the difference between Simple and Advanced trim to switch between modes. Click, hold and drag to get Overwrite. Instead of adding the ALT key to the mix, you can click and release to get a yellow trim bar, then click and hold again to drag in Insert Mode. If you are a "Mouse only" type, you might well prefer this workflow.

Adjusting Trim points accurately

The biggest advantage of the Advanced trimming is that you can adjust your edits with frame accuracy.

I'm going to put everything back to the beginning now with a quick couple of undos, then turn my attention to the Out point of clip 1 and set a trim point. In the process instead of just dragging, we can use alternative ways to control the yellow Trim point.

The Trim and Loop buttons

Underneath the Trim Editor are five simple controls. The middle one is Loop play, which allows us to examine the edit at normal speed by playing a short section either side of it, continually looping until clicking it again stops the playback. The arrow buttons either side trim the edit – left to right they trim 10 frames back, 1 frame back, I frame forward and 10 frames forward. You should experiment with these controls to appreciate the accuracy.

There are keyboard alternatives as well – the arrow keys (or Z and X) for single frames, or with Shift added for 10 frame jumps. An alternative are the four keys **M** , **.** and **I** (remember you controls may differ if you don't have a US/UK QWERTY keyboard). These mimic the four buttons on the Trim Editor.

Trimming with the Player Windows

Dragging on a Player window to adjust an edit

Although it's not immediately obvious, you can also drag on the Player windows to adjust the In point and Out points of the currently selected trim point.

You should explore both methods of adjustment before we start working through the next few pages. I suggest you experiment by trimming exactly 24 frames off the Out point of clip 1.

Setting, Removing, Changing or Adding trim points

Apart from the added accuracy, Advanced trim offers a number of other advantages. One that opens up a hugely powerful option is that you can have **more than one** trim point at the same time - two on each track, in fact.

With *Activate trim mode by clicking near cuts* set to On, you can use your mouse to set up to two yellow advanced Trim handles for every track that has content.

- To set a single trim point, click and release just to the relevant side of the edit you wish to trim.

- You can use the Trim icon or T key to set the first trim point. It appears at the nearest edit to the cursor.

- To remove a trim point, hover over it, click and release.

- To change a trim point, click and release on the new location.

- To add a second trim point to the same track hold down Ctrl before you click and release.

- To add trim points to another track just click and release as above.

- To remove all the trim points click anywhere other than near an existing or potential trim point. You can also click on the Trim icon or use the T key.

- To make a trim point the one that is active, Ctrl click on it.

Try changing the trim point to the In point of clip 2 and trim that by 3 seconds.

With *Activate trim mode by clicking near cuts* set to OFF there are a number of differences to the above set of rules.

- You can only set your first trim point with the T key or the Trim icon, and if there are items on more than one track, a trim point will be created for each track. To stop this happening you need to hold down the Shift key.

- To get out of trim mode you must use the Trim icon or T key again, clicking is of no use.

- Once in Trim mode, the rules for adding and changing trim points are the same.

For the remainder of this book I'm going to expect you to be using *Activate trim mode by clicking near cuts* set to ON.

Trimming with the Trim Editor

Pinnacle Studio provides two player windows when Advanced trimming. You can return to using just one by clicking the Dual Mode button or using the Ctrl-D keyboard shortcut. The single view trim mode view will always show you the frame at the trim point you last set.

When you are in Trim mode, you can't use any of the normal jogging controls, but you can scrub through the timeline with the scrubber, even though it returns to the trim point when you release it. Space and the JKL keys work, but only in Loop play mode - you can place areas of the movie other than either side of the edit.

The way I've been explaining how to use Advanced trim up until now is relevant with either one or two Player windows. However, because of the way Pinnacle Studio arranges its edit windows there is very little advantage in disabling Dual View even

even if you are using a small display. Switching back to Dual View gives a lot more information and greater control over trimming. The player windows are labelled Left and Right and the content of each window will generally be the respective left and right trim points.

If the window doesn't have a yellow or orange border then it isn't displaying a trim point, but rather the frame to the left or right of the trim point displayed in the other window. To begin with, let's look at using the Trim Editor with just one trim point.

I'm going to start again with the timeline by deleting all the content and dragging clips 1, 2 and 3 to butt up together at the start of track 2.

Trim editor set to work on the In point of clip 2

I click to set a trim point on the In point of clip 2. The Trim Editor appears with a yellow border round the Right preview, which is showing the first frame of clip 2 - the active trim point. Above the window a number is displayed in orange - in my example it is 0, showing that the current trim point is set to an offset of zero into the start of clip as it was originally placed on the timeline. (This figure is reset if you add new clips to the timeline.)

Using the trim player window to edit the incoming video

If I hover my mouse over the Right trim window, I get an In point handle. By clicking and dragging left or right I can trim the clip right there.

A double headed mouse cursor will have appeared during the trim. I have adjusted the In point to 5 seconds, showing a 125 frame offset.

If you have trouble with accuracy, don't forget the trim buttons under the player, or the keyboard shortcuts for single frame or 10 frame adjustments.

If I play the edit in loop mode I see it is a poor edit. I should have been able to predict that by looking at the outgoing frame to the left, because of the very similar looking car that has just entered the right of frame. My brain can't help thinking that the car we cut to on the incoming shot is the same car and the edit is a jump cut.

Adjusting clip 1's Out point

To quickly adjust the Out point of clip 1 I don't even have to move my mouse to the timeline - clicking on the left trim window sets an In point at the displayed frame! This only happens if no trim point is already set in that window, but it is very useful.

I can now drag the Out point of clip 1 left to tighten it by 9 frames, excluding the part of the video where the black car comes onto shot.

So, that's a great way to use the Trim Editor, even if you are adjusting single edit points.

Holding down the Alt key during dragging operations in the Trim Mode windows switches Smart trimming to Overwrite mode, should you wish to do that.

One final feature I need to mention in the Trim Editor is the Solo button bottom right. When it is active (coloured orange), you see the clips at the current trim points in their raw state, without effects added or other tracks overlaid over them - *Solo*. Otherwise, you see the composite view of the current timeline. Until you have content on more than one track, or add an effect to a clip, you won't see any difference whether this button is active or greyed out.

Two Trim Points

Working with more than one trim point is even more powerful. To add a second trim point to a track, hold down down the CTRL key before you click.

The rule is that a single track can only have a maximum of two trim points; one of them must be an Out point, the other an In point. It doesn't matter where they are in relation to each other as long as there is one of each.

I have added trim points to either side of the edit between clips 1 and 2. This arrangement is called "rolling the edit point". Every frame we take off one clip causes a frame to be added to the other clip.

Rolling an edit point in the Trim Editor

Try dragging the clip in either trim mode window. Alternatively, try the trim buttons or keyboard shortcuts.

In my example clips, I can easily use the Trim Editor to roll the edit point and find frames for both the incoming and outgoing, that are clean of other vehicles or items like the bollards that give the game away that we are looking at the same stretch of road. What's more, I'm not affecting the total duration of the two clips combined, nor am I affecting the In point of the outgoing shot or the Out point of the incoming.

Rolling the edit point is a good way of polishing an edit that feels uncomfortable without having to restructure the movie around the edit. It's handy with audio as well.

OK, if you want to play devil's advocate, you can say that this is quite easy to do in Overwrite mode with just one green trim point. You don't get the benefit of two preview windows, though. Neither can you use single frame jogging. If you want to edit more than one track at a time you are going to find Overwrite very destructive, and using different modes for different trim points would cause mayhem.

Incidentally, this is a good time to mention that by default **all** the trim points in Smart mode work in Insert mode, even if they are operating on a gap. The Alt key modifier does work (except if you use the keyboard shortcuts), but it affects all the trim points putting them all into Overwrite mode.

Adjusting the Placement

Let's now look at what happens with the trim points further apart. Adding a trim point on the right edge of clip 1, then holding down Ctrl and clicking on the left edge of clip 3 should set up the timeline as shown in the screenshot.

Trim points set to the outside of clip 2

Trimming the clip left and right shows how this combination moves clip 2, maintaining the chosen In and Out points. Clips 1 and 3 stay where they were, and their video is either hidden or revealed as clip 2 is moved.

We are adjusting the **PLACEMENT** of clip 2 with this trim point selection.

Outside trimming reveals "dead meat" on clip 3

Outside trimming back to the right. Note the content of clip 2 remains unaltered

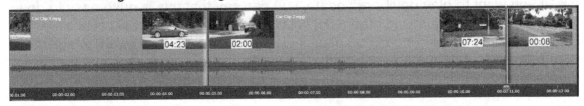

The In and Out points are **OUTSIDE** the clip we are adjusting. Note that if the two trim points bracketed a sequence of clips, all these clips would be moved as one.

Be aware that this operation isn't the same as just dragging the clip in Overwrite mode because no gaps are created on the timeline.

Adjusting the Content

In and Out points now set to the inside edges of clip 2

The next arrangement adjusts the content of clip 2 without altering it's position. I've placed the In point at the start of clip 2 and the Out point at the end.

As I adjust the trim now, the position and duration of the gap into which clip 2 fits doesn't alter, but the video content slides left or right. Moving the content left immediately gives me the problem of there being no more video available on the outgoing of clip 2.

Trimming left moves the content of clip 2, but reveals "dead meat"

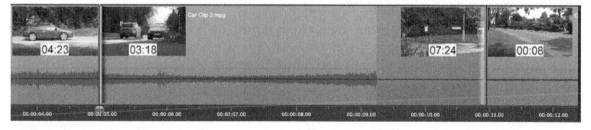

Moving the content right is more rewarding.

Trimming right allows the removal of the empty frames at the end of clip 2

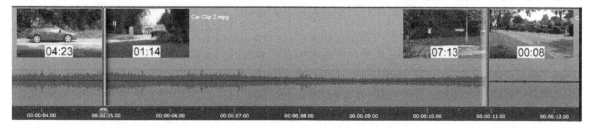

There were empty frames at the end of the shot originally. In this case using the trim function makes it easy to lose those frames while automatically adjusting the In point so that the shot has a fixed duration.

We are adjusting the **CONTENT** of clip 2 with this trim point selection - the In and Out points are **INSIDE** the clip we are adjusting. Again, note that if the two trim points bracketed a sequence of clips, all these clips would be moved as one.

With the dual mode view of the Trim Editor, it's also easy to keep an eye on the incoming frame as well – in some circumstances this might have a bearing on the final choice of content.

So, even before we look at the use of trimming on more than one track, I hope you've seen some useful possibilities.

Setting Trim Mode and Shift

So far, the examples of setting Trim mode only use clips on one track. Trim mode is particularly useful when editing projects using more than one track as you set a trim point for every track it will help keep your projects in sync. However, the default behaviour of the Trim mode tool or T key varies, depending of the project settings.

If you have the "Activate trim mode by clicking near cuts" switched ON then Studio adds a single Trim point. If you want to automatically set a Trim point for every track, you have to hold down the Shift key.

If you have the "Activate trim mode by clicking near cuts" switched OFF then Pinnacle Studio 19 adds a Trim point to a clip on every track. If you want to set a Trim point for just one track, you have to hold down the Shift key.

Pinnacle have made a few attempts to make keeping track in sync easier, and the second type of behaviour was added to persuade people to add multiple trim points by default. As it's no longer the default behaviour and adds other confusions, I'd encourage you to ignore it.

Multi-track trimming

Once you are in Trim mode, the mouse can be used for setting further trim points regardless of the mode selected in the control panel. Once a point has been set for a particular track you will need to use the Ctrl key to set the second point. From then on, each time you click near an edit point, that will become the *current* Out or In trim point, depending on whether you click to the left or right of the edit.

Any track that you don't set a Trim point for will be excluded from the trim operation, as if it had been locked.

So, if you want to make an alteration to a movie and keep all the tracks in sync, you need to put at least one trim point on each track. Where you put that trim point will depend on *how* you want to maintain sync.

There are two relationships between tracks. In the most obvious case one track will be of a video of a person talking, and the other track will be the audio of them talking. If we move one track without the other, the speakers mouth won't open and close in time with the audio. Keeping them in sync will always involve moving the content of both tracks by equal amounts.

The second relationship is the start and end of clips relative to each other and the timeline. The obvious case would be that when we cut to the audio of the person as they begin talking, we also cut to video to see them begin to talk. In this case we would apply trim points to the same place for both tracks.

It is sometimes desirable to begin to hear the person speaking before we cut to them in vision. In this case we would apply trim points to both tracks, but not in the same place.

This is best illustrated with some examples. I'm going use video clips as they make better screenshots!

Timeline set up for multi-track trimming

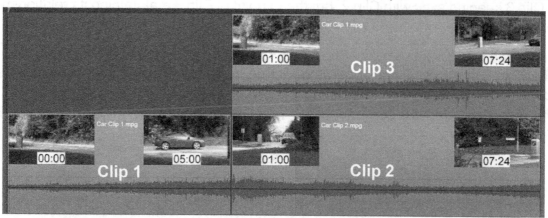

I've set up a new timeline using tracks 1 and 2. Clip 1 is on track 2 with it's Out point set to 5 seconds. Clip 2 follows, with its In point set to 1 second. Clip 3 has been placed above Clip 2 on track 1, with its In point also trimmed to 1 second.

Let's imagine we are going to add a Picture-in-picture effect to track 1 and we always want Clips 1 and 2 to stay in sync relative to each other.

If I want to tighten the incoming of both clips and cut to them at the same point on the timeline, I set a trim point on the In points of both clips.

However, if I want to cut to Clip 2 on track 2 earlier and still see all of the clip, but not start the Picture-in-picture effect on track 1 until 5 seconds into the sequence (it might be lining up with a beat in some music, for example) *and* still keep Clips 2 and 3 in sync I put a trim point on the **outside** of Clip 2 – the Out point of Clip 1 – but a trim point on the **inside** of Clip 3 – the In point of Clip 3.

Maintaining clip 3's In point relative to the timeline

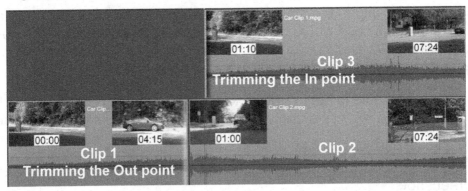

Trimming backwards 10 frames with the Trim Editor shows clip 2 moving, the content of Clip 3 keeping sync with Clip 2, but the In point of Clip 3 maintaining its relationship with the timeline.

If I wanted to cut from Clip 1 to Clip 2 at 5 seconds, tighten the In point of Clip 2, see all of Clip 3 and I don't mind when the Picture in picture effect starts I swap the trim points over – the In point of clip 2 and the Out point of the gap preceding Clip 3.

The reverse of previous operation

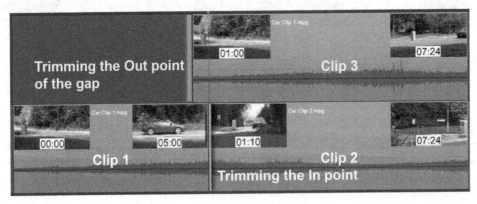

Trimming forward 10 frames shows I have achieved the desired effect.

Overwrite and Advanced Trimming

You can use the Overwrite mode with more than one trim point selected, either by switching to the Overwrite edit mode or using the Alt key in conjunction with the Trim Editor controls or the mouse - but not the keyboard shortcuts. Using overwrite does open up some other possible alternatives when working on more than one trim point at a time.

In the example I gave earlier with trim points set outside a clip, content remains in position but the editing points are moved. Gaps are created **inside** the trim points and if required, "dead meat" is generated on the **previous and following** clips. The later example with the trim point inside the clip boundaries also results in the edit points moving, but gaps are created **outside** the clip you are moving and "dead meat" created **within** the clip itself.

I'll be frank and say it's not a common editing requirement for me, but something you should consider using if it is vital that none of the content is shifted relative to the timeline.

Advanced Trimming and Transitions

Creating a transition

The main narrative of this book hasn't introduced transitions yet, but for reference I'm going to include how to trim clips that have transitions added to them.

A clip on the timeline has a transition added if there is a grey "fold-over" at the beginning or end of the clip that occupies the top half of the track where the thumbnails are displayed. I'll show you how to add and manipulate transitions in detail later in the book, but for now try hovering your mouse at the top of a clip. The fold-over icon will animate when you are in the correct area. Click, hold and drag and you will see the green trim bar indicating Quick trimming, but as you drag you will notice that just the transition grows in length.

With a transition in place, you have two control points at the start or end of a clip and you can manipulate the normal In or Out point with Quick Trim and the transition duration remains constant, or you can operate on the edge of the transition icon and alter the duration of the transition.

In Advanced trim the normal methods set **both** points as a trim point so your transition duration will remain static.

Normally, setting a trim point adds two bars

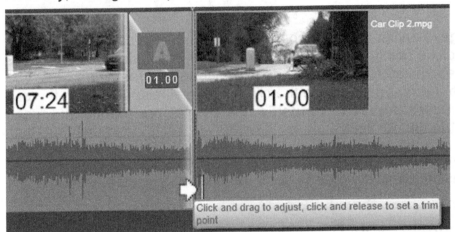

However you can choose to alter just the length of the transition or the In or Out point of the clip. To achieve this we need to split the trim point and we do this with the Alt key and the mouse.

Alt-Click allows you to split the trim points

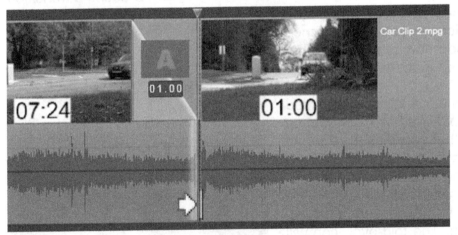

Hold down Alt and click on the upper half of a clip boundary and you will only set a trim point for the transition. Once a trim point is set, if you use Alt when clicking on either the upper or lower part of the boundary, you can toggle trim points off and on individually.

With this feature you can choose to accurately trim both points together or separately, and add one or both to a multi-trim point selection.

If you don't want to alter the duration of a transition, don't split the trim points. If you want the beginning or end of a transition to be trimmed in Insert mode while content underneath the transition works in Overwrite, set the trim point for the transition only. Setting the trim point to the lower half of the track has the opposite effect.

Even if there isn't a transition at an In or Out point, you can use the Alt click method of selection to create a split trim point, which will create a transition once you start to use trimming.

Multi-track Trimming and keeping sync

Sometimes I read of people struggling to keep the clips in a multi-track project in sync. I've written a whole chapter on this subject, starting on page 459. Techniques include the use of split and delete for trimming, and Ctrl-Shift selection to make gaps in the timeline that you subsequently fill using the overwrite mode.

In an ideal world the automatic addition of a trim point per track will allow you to trim your projects and keep them in sync. Studio can do this for you, as discussed on page 266. Although I recommend that you don't put your trust in this tool, but I'm going to examine it here.

Every track that has a trim point set will have its content remain in sync with the other tracks as you trim the movie. However, the trim points chosen by Studio have to cope with many situations, and it is important to check that positional sync is going to be affected in the way you wish before you start to trim.

To understand in which situations you might need to change the chosen trim point, you need to know how Studio chooses where to put them.

Consider a timeline that has a main track of continuous clips, and gaps between clips on other tracks.

If you set a multiple trim In point and the gap on the other track is equal in size or larger on the right, then a trim point is set on the In point of the gap. When you adjust the trim point, everything will stay in sync, both in terms of content and position.

If, however the gap is larger on the left, the trim point is set to the In point of the clip after the gap. When you trim, the content of the clip after the gap will stay in sync, but the position of the In point remains static – so if this is the start of a title, for example, the title will begin later in relation to the clips on the other tracks.

In addition, if the gap extends all the way to the start of the project – there are no clips to the left of the selected trim point on that track – then however far down the track the first clip is, it will have its trim bar set to the In point.

In order to maintain both content and positional sync, the trim point needs to be changed from the In point of the clip to either the In or Out point of the gap.

If you are setting a multi-trim point to the Out point of a clip, then all the above logic is flipped – if the gap is larger to the right then you will lose positional sync unless you alter the trim point of the track with the gap.

This Smart behaviour gives you the most flexibility, but can catch you out if you can't see all the tracks when you use it.

Multi trim set up on a complex project

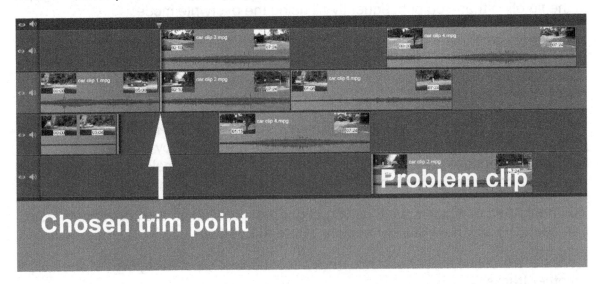

In the example illustrated by the screenshots, the Multi trim point has been set to the In point of the second clip on track 2. The clip above that is in line and has the same point added, so its content will stay in sync, but the In point will stay in line with the track below. This would also be the case if the clip on track 1 started a bit later.

The second clip on track 3 is further from the chosen trim point than the end of the first clip on that track – the gap is greater to the right than the left. The trim point is on the In point of the gap, and as we trim both the content and the relationship of the trim point stays in sync with track 3

Track 4 has nothing on the track before the clip, so even though the gap is larger to the right, the trim point gets set in the same way as it has been for track 1 and 2.

When we trim, although the content stays in sync, the In point remains stationary relative to the other tracks.

When the trim point for track 4 is a clip In point, positional sync is lost

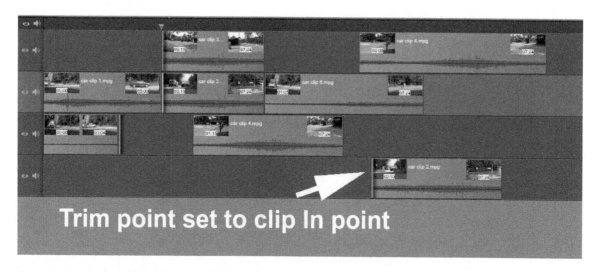

Trim point set to clip In point

One way of stopping the final behaviour from occurring is to move the trim point from the In point of the clip to the Out point of the preceding gap.

If you change it to a gap Out point, sync is completely maintained

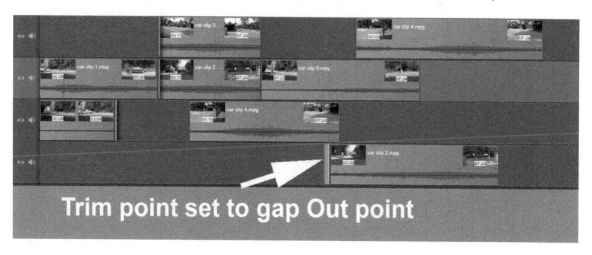

Trim point set to gap Out point

This problem is discussed in conjunction with a project in the *Keeping Movies in Sync* chapter.

By the way, if you can't reproduce the above problems and are using a version later than 19.0.1.245, it may be that Pinnacle have listened to users and found a fix!

Advanced Editing Features

The next five chapters of this book can be used in two ways. I'm going to use sample projects to demonstrate a series of features in Pinnacle Studio, but as well as using each feature for the purposes of the project, I'm going to describe it in greater detail for reference.

So if you just want to work through the projects, you can skip the full details of a feature and jump to the next section, and then return to the skipped section when you want to learn more. You can also learn about how each feature works without actually building the project yourself – for example, if you are familiar with most of the functions but want a detailed description of the Title Editor, then use the Index or sub-headings to skip straight to the section about the titler.

I hope that you do make the projects, because you will get a better view of the features in action. The first project is a holiday movie of a flight in a light aircraft over Mount Snowdon in North Wales. The second project is a slideshow using the BMX photos. Finally, I'll combine the two projects to enable me to show you some further features of Pinnacle Studio and create a disc project from them.

If you have read *Pinnacle Studio 14 or 15 Revealed* you will be familiar with some of the source material, but I'm making a slightly different movie to show off more advanced functions. It does mean that if you have the files associated with the earlier books you won't need to download them.

If you don't have the source files, you should be able to download them if you have a reasonable Internet connection. Check out the appendix, then please visit the website www.dtvpro.co.uk. I realised that my service provider was not providing a fast service to some parts of the world in the past and you will find alternatives links for the bigger files. If all else fails I can send the files to you on a data DVD at what I hope you will find a reasonable cost. The complexities of small scale book publishing means it is very hard to include a disc inside a book.

A Flight over Snowdon

For the first project you need one video file. It is called *Project1mp2.mpg*. Acquire this by one of the above mentioned means and then copy it to a location on your video hard drive – don't try to work on it straight from the data DVD. If you don't have your own workflow for video storage, place it in the My Videos Windows Library. Now create a Project Bin named *Flight Over Snowdon* and use Quick Import to add the file to the Pinnacle Studio Library.

Switch to the Library and preview the video file. It's a bit over 10 minutes long. The first few shots are exterior, with the remaining video being taken from inside the Cessna as it takes a pleasure flight to view Mount Snowdon – the highest peak in England and Wales.

It's a great memory for me. I can watch it and remember the day clearly. The family was on holiday in Wales, and we all had ideas for days out. My wife wanted to climb up Snowdon, my daughter wanted to take a boat trip to see the seals and dolphins, but I really fancied a pleasure flight from Caernarfon Airpark to see Snowdon from the air. I got my wish on the clearest day, although there was a bitingly chilly wind.

While we waited for our flight, I took some shots with my handheld DV camera. I was really just checking the camera, but once aboard the aircraft, decided I had enough battery power and tape to let it run for the whole 30 minutes. Some of it is very wobbly, the camera is set to automatic, and although my camera has a fairly good zoom lens, bouncing around in a light aircraft makes it hard to get decent tight shots. You might also be surprised if I told you that in the past I was a professional broadcast TV cameraman, but my excuse is that I was on holiday to enjoy the day with my family, not to make a documentary!

There is about 30 minutes on the original tape. As I said before, I've trimmed it down to under 11 minutes, and burnt in a timecode top right to help us locate precise parts of the file to the nearest frame. I think we should be able to make a short movie that could hold a detached viewer's interest.

Here is a list of my highlights:

- The take off

- Passing the Nantlle Ridge

- Recognising the peak of Snowdon

- Seeing the construction work at the top of Snowdon

- Following the Mountain Railway back down

- View of Caernarfon and its Castle

- The landing

What about the Audio? The soundtrack is virtually useless. On the ground it's all wind noise and in the air, apart from take-off and landing, it's just a drone. We could record a voice-over, but there isn't much to say that cannot be covered with a few well-placed titles. However, some uplifting music might go down well.

It's a simple story. Plane takes off, flies over some spectacular scenery, and lands (safely!). Let's start work.

Using Scenes

NG Studio has inherited a feature from Classic Studio that lets you divide video files into Scenes. We looked at it briefly in the Import and Library chapters but now I want to show you how to use Scenes in a real project.

I'm going to work in the Main Library while preparing the Scenes. I could do some of the work in the Compact Library but there is no point in struggling for space, and one feature I'm going to use can only work in the Main Library Preview window.

With the *Flight Over Snowdon* bin open in the Main Library, right-click on the *Project1mp2* file and hover over the Detect Scenes context menu option. You should see a choice of three options.

Scene detection options in the Context menu

The option *Content* will divide a file when it detects a sudden change in the video. For analogue tape based cameras this will almost certainly detect when when you have stopped and then restarted recording. On edited material it will normally split the video at each cut point. However, there may be false detection, such as when a photographer's flashgun goes off.

The next option, *Date and Time* is useful for DV and HDV cameras with timecode embedded in the file. The files will be split every time there is a

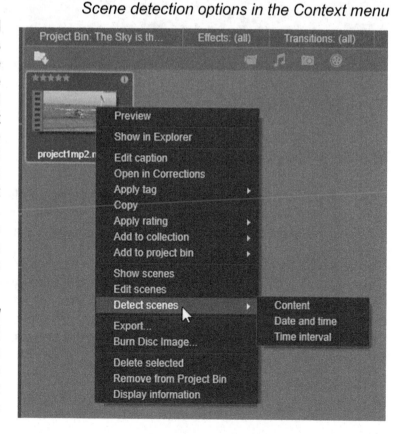

discontinuity in the timecode which will coincide with pausing or stopping and restarting the recording. If you try to use this option on video files that don't have the required timecode, Studio will default to detecting by content.

Time Interval allows you to specify a duration for each scene. You might want to use this setting when working with material that has no significant shot changes to subdivide files into more useable chunks.

It is also possible to perform scene splitting manually, as we will see in a short while.

I'm going to select Content. A Scene detection box opens with a list of the files selected – you can apply this operation to multiple files. It also has a checkbox that forces Studio to open Scene view at the end of the operation, but uncheck that as I want to show you something before looking at the scenes.

Scene Detection Dialogue

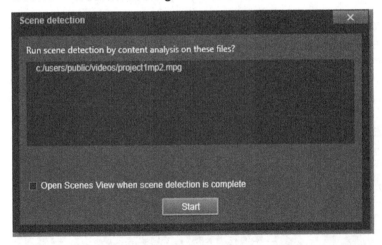

Clicking *Start* begins a process that takes less than a minute on my computer, with a progress bar running across the box to keep me informed. When complete, take a close look at the file thumbnail and you will spot it has obtained multiple borders, indicating the file has been split into scenes. If you use the context menu option *Show in Explorer* you will also find that a new file

has been created in the same location as the video file with the additional suffixes .scn.xml. This is a simple text file that contains the scene detection information. Opening it shows a list of the frame numbers where each scene starts.

Returning to Studio, you can now open the Scenes view in two ways – either the Scenes icon on the toolbar at the bottom of the Library, or the context menu option Show Scenes. Either way, you will see an orange filter bar across the top of the Library browser and 20 thumbnails in place of the original single file, each one showing the start of a scene as detected by the software.

Refining Scene Detection

Having detected scenes automatically, we can now adjust them manually. In my example clip, there have been a number of "false" detections where a big camera bump has caused an unwanted break. There may also be occasions when you want to split scenes based on events that haven't triggered a scene break.

Flight footage split into scenes using Detect by Content

First, let's look at **Combining scenes** You can only re-join two scenes together if they are adjacent in the original file – it isn't possible to add together the first and last scene, for example. If two or more concurrent scenes are highlighted with the orange border, right-clicking on one of them should reveal the Combine Scenes command available from the context menu. If you don't see that option, then the multiple selection you have made contains a scene that isn't part of a continuous run.

To see that on the current example, Click on the first scene to highlight it then CTRL-click on the last scene. You won't find Combine scenes available in the right-click menu.

Combining the last three scenes

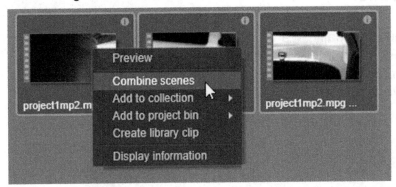

Now, let's do a few useful things with this tool. The last three scenes have been created because of the bump caused on landing. By multi-selecting them the Combine scenes option does become available. Select it, and you will see the three scenes changed into one scene.

There are a few more combinations I want you to do. I'll list them starting from the end:

- Combine clips 16 and 17

- Combine clips 7 and 8

- Combine clips 4 and 5

You should now have 15 thumbnails showing in the browser window. Compare them carefully with the screenshot before proceeding.

15 scenes remain after combining the clips

Splitting clips is something you can only do when working in the main library, because you have to use the library preview window. In Scenes view you can open the Library preview by clicking the roll-over play button on the thumbnail or right-clicking and selecting Preview from the context menu.

You should see the Split button as the third icon from the right on the preview toolbar, as shown in the screenshot.

Let's try this on the project footage. Open clip 13 in the preview window – it's the one with the dark close-up shot of the castle at the beginning. Use the preview controls to investigate the start of the scene and you will see that there are six frames of the castle, then we cut to a wideshot through the window as the plane is banking on to its final landing approach. Why the scene detection did this, I'm not sure, but I want to fix it.

Clip 13 lined up in the Library Preview Window. The Split Clip button is arrowed

I'd like to split this scene into two – the (probably unusable) castle shot, and then the final approach shot. Position the scrubber on the first frame of the final approach (00:09:01:09 on the burnt-in timecode) and then click on the Split button.

Two things should happen. A new scene will appear in the browser window consisting of the 6 frames for the castle, and the current preview will reset so the the first frame is what was frame 7.

Close the preview and examine the two scenes with their roll-over scrubbers and you will find we have achieved our aim. The file is split into 16 scenes. If you now study scenes 14 and 15, you will see that they are in fact a continuous shot, with a scene break triggered because the pilot pulled down the sunshade. Combine these clips so that we have 15 scenes, some of which we will use in the project.

There are some circumstances where the Split button doesn't appear when you might expect it to. If you have used the Edit scenes button to open the preview window and don't see the button, close the preview and, without leaving Scenes View, reopen the scene you want to edit. The split button should now appear.

You can use the manual approach to scene generation for subdividing clips even though you have applied no automatic detection. Some examples where you might consider doing this might be dividing footage into usable and unusable shots, or if you were covering something like a musical performance, where the camera changed shots between the musicians.

One recommendation is that you don't cut your scenes too tight. If there are a few frames on the beginning or end which you think are probably unusable, don't be judgemental. There will be plenty of chances to trim the scene further, but if you realise at a later date that extending a shot past the chosen scene break would be useful you will have to go back to the original clip to retrieve the extra frames. One good example is when using dissolves. A camera shot that starts to go soft as if fades out is not too objectionable – and may even look deliberate!

Having split our file into scenes, we can just go ahead and use the scenes in a project. There are some limitations to this approach, though. You can't rename Scenes or use them in Collections, for example. The solution is hinted at in Scene view itself, where the program recommends that you convert scenes to Library clips. For anything other than a simple editing job, I would agree with that approach.

Creating Library Clips

What is a Library clip? Like Scenes, Library clips only exist in a virtual world. If you see the shortcut icon on a thumbnail it shows that the clip points to another real file. Unlike Scenes, because Library clip data is stored in the Pinnacle Studio Library database rather than a .scn file, you can edit the caption and add metadata.

The context menu for Scenes is somewhat limiting but it does allow us to create Library clips. *Preview* leads to a viewer with a Scene Split button as we have just observed. At the bottom is *Display Information* leading to the usual window, but with data about the start and duration of the scene within the source video files.

Scenes View Clip Context menu

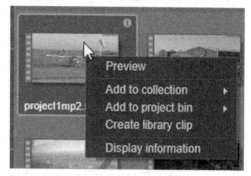

The remaining three options can all be used to create Library clips . *Create library clip* creates a clip that shows up in the same location as the source video when viewed in the Pinnacle Library (assuming you have Library media enabled). Note that you won't see this in Windows, as it's not a real video clip. *Add to collection* and *Add to project bin* uses the normal method of adding something, but they have to create a Library clip in order to do so.

It's also worth noting that you can drag scenes from the library browser to a bin or collection in the Tree view and clips will be created automatically.

One functional difference between these two methods of creating library clips is that the Create library clips method only allows you to create one clip at a time, whereas *Add to Bin* or *Collection* also creates clips from scenes, and you can apply the function to a multiple selection of scenes. Therefore, even if you don't really need to put the clips into a bin or collection, it might be more convenient to do so.

Returning to our project, I'm not going to convert all the scenes we have created into library clips. Being selective will reduce the clutter. In other circumstances you might well add anything that could be even vaguely useful and maybe use ratings to help you filter out the less important shots.

Make sure you are back in Scene view with 15 clips in the browser. Select them all with CTRL-A and then hold down CTRL and click on scenes 2, 7, 9, 11 and 13. This will have the effect of deselecting them, leaving 10 clips with an orange border around them. Right click on one of the clips and select *Add to project bin/Flight over Snowdon* and click OK.

The contents of the Flight over Snowdon bin

Now switch off scene filtering so you return to the *Flight* project bin. You should see 11 clips, the original file and the ten new Library clips shown in the screenshot.

Library clips can be a powerful feature, and I'm hoping that Pinnacle will develop this function in the future to allow the creation of clips from the source viewer.

Customising Library clips

The obvious thing to do with our new clips is to give them decent descriptive names rather than the timecode based ones that they have at the moment. This is easily done with the *Edit caption* right-click context menu command or clicking on the caption of an already highlighted clip.

Rename the clips in the order they appear on screen, using the same names as me so that the screen doesn't re-order itself differently. If for some reason the order of your thumbnails doesn't match mine, the most likely reason is that the Library is sorting your view in some order other than alphabetical by name. Use the Details view to change the sort order as detailed in the Library chapter. Check this before you start to rename the clips

Firstly rename the first thumbnail to **Whole clip** so that it moves to the end of the order. As you rename the remaining clips don't enter the "Clip n" part. The sort order will change but if you stick to the list, all will be well anyway.

Clip 1 – Ext take off 1, *clip 2* – Ext take off 2, *clip 3* – Int take off, *clip 4* – Nantlle Ridge, *clip 5* – Peak 1, *clip 6* – Peak 2, *clip 7* – Mountain Railway, *clip 8* - Caernarfon Castle, *clip 9* - Final approach and *clip 10* – Landing.

The Flight Over Snowdon bin after renaming

You will notice that all the converted scenes have a "shortcut" icon top left of their thumbnails, indicating that they are Library Clips, not real files. Now we have converted the scenes into Library clips, the whole range of metadata is open to us. Sorting by criteria other than *Name* can be achieved. One useful ordering in some circumstances might be by *Duration*.

Corrections

Now the scenes have been converted to Library clips, we can add Corrections. If you skipped here to find out what Corrections are for and how they work, you can try out the following exercises on any suitably dodgy video, audio or photo.

What is important to note is that Corrections can be applied to all Video and Audio clips as well as scenes – you don't have to go through the whole "Scene detection, convert to clips" routine I've just described.

Corrections are designed to be applied to clips before you use them in a project, but that isn't a hard and fast rule. If you apply a correction to a whole clip, it will also be inherited by any scenes you create from the clip, and any library clips you create from those scenes. You can also apply a Correction to a timeline clip without adding it to the source or library clip first by using the Effects Editor (which we will look at later in the chapter). Another thing you can do is add a different Correction to a clip and re-save it as another Library clip so you can have two versions of the same clip.

Just as important to note is that you can remove a Correction by using the *Revert to Original* command. Removing the correction from the source clip doesn't affect the scenes or library clips created when the correction was in place. Removing it from a clip on the timeline doesn't affect the source or library clip.

So, what are Corrections and when would you use them? You can adjust the colour balance, aspect ratios and video properties. Shaky video can be stabilised. You can create still frames from video. Audio can be sweetened, photos cropped, straightened and have red-eye removal added. Basically, they are functions that you recognise might be needed before you even begin making a project.

If you shot a whole tape or card of video material with manual colour balance but had the setting wrong your pictures might be all too blue or yellow. You could re-colour balance all the poor source material by applying a correction to the source video file. If at a later date you wanted to refine the correction, you could modify it on the timeline clips of your choice.

If just one scene were wrong, you could apply the correction to a library clip created from just that scene. Maybe if you placed a video clip, whatever the source, on the timeline and decided it required correction, you could apply the correction to that timeline clip.

It's an important point that when working on the timeline, you can't copy and paste corrections between clips. If you think you are likely to want to do that you need to use Effects - and the all important Image Correction tool is available as both a correction and an effect.

I'm going to apply two corrections to our project footage to show the workflow, before describing the rest of the corrections. One of our shots is burnt out – the one I've re-labelled Mountain Railway. I had switched the camera to manual by accident, and it is a couple of stops overexposed. I'd still like to use it in the project, though.

Use the Right-click context menu on the thumbnail of the Mountain Railway library clip to select *Open in Corrections*. You can also just double click on the clip if you wish. (If you aren't making the project, just choose any reasonably short video clip.)

The Corrections Editor

You should be presented with an editing window that looks similar to the screenshot. In the top left corner you can choose if you are correcting the Video or the Audio. Select *Video* if it isn't already highlighted. On the left of the screen there is a preview of the audio waveform and a box labelled Channel Mixer. In the centre is a preview of the video clip with the familiar player controls and timescale underneath. Switch to Audio and the previews rearrange themselves to bring Audio to the main screen. We will look at that in a moment, so switch back to Video. Along the top there are now 4 tabs. Click on *Enhance*.

Image Correction CPU is the tool provided by Pinnacle Studio 19 for enhancing video and it will appear on the right of the preview window. There aren't any presets, but there are a comprehensive array of settings. The top box is Automatics, and often you won't need to stray any further down the list in your quest to correct video. *White Balance*, when checked, will look at the colour temperature of the video and normalise it. The balance of the Mountain Railway clip is OK, but click this box anyway – you should see little or no change in the preview. Notice the small grey button alongside the checkbox has turned orange. This is an important indication that is prevalent throughout the Corrections and Effects editors in Studio. Orange means On. You can normally turn the setting Off by clicking on the orange button to switch it back to grey. For a checkbox this may seem like duplication, but at least there is a consistent interface.

When you enable the automatic White Balance, a further slider appears below. Again, this is a feature that you will see throughout the Corrections and Effects interface. The slider will be at zero, but if you drag it to the left or right the value alters, and when that value is not zero, the orange button appears to the right. Now, disable the setting by clicking the button to turn it off. OK, that makes sense – it returns to zero. The good bit is if you click the button again – when you turn it on, the setting returns to the previous value.

This is a useful function in many circumstances. While you are previewing a shot, you can check what effect each control is having without destroying the value you have chosen.

If you want to remove the alteration completely - and disable the grey dot - double click on the parameter name.

You may not have even noticed, but there is an overall On/Off button for the entire effect. It is alongside the correction name at the top. You can switch the entire effect on and off from there without affecting any settings – useful for checking what you have done. Also, to the right is a small Minimise icon. This won't seem useful now, but in other situations you may have a whole host of effects stacked up and not enough space to display them all. Using the minimise icon will reduce the box to just show its name and the On/Off button.

A word about White Balance and Colour Temperature. The slider you see will compensate for the usual problems. The human eye and brain adapts to recognise "white" as white. Daylight is blue relative to most artificial light – old style tungsten bulbs give out a much more noticeable yellow light. This variation is measured as a colour temperature – the temperature that an ideal "black body" radiator (such as the Sun) emits light of the same hue as the white light we are measuring. A candle might have a colour temperature of 2000 degrees Kelvin. It's light will look yellow if it isn't the only source of light. Normal daylight is around 6000 degrees K, but can climb much higher.

Colour Balance controls

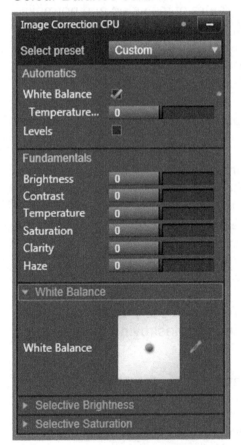

So the slider provided can adjust for these types of variations. If you have lit a whole scene by candlelight, and used automatic colour balance, the picture won't look yellow. You actually might want to bring some of that yellow back into the picture for artistic effect. On the other hand, if you had the camera on a daylight setting, the video will look far too warm and you may want to cool it down by moving the slider to the right and adding blue back into the picture.

While on the subject, cast your eyes down the list of corrections and you will see **another** *White Balance* control. The small arrow icons you should be familiar with from the library can be used to reveal or hide settings. When open, this control takes the form of a joystick. Grabbing the knob in the middle will allow you to adjust what the video thinks of as "white" through a very wide range of variations – outside of the simple envelope defined by colour temperature.

The extremes are cyan, magenta, yellow and green. Magenta is a mixture of blue and red light with no green component, while the two other primary additive colours other than green – red and blue – lie between yellow and magenta and magenta and cyan. If after playing with the control you want to be sure of centring it, double click. An eyedropper tool is available which isn't very useful in extreme circumstances, but if you grab it and click it on something that you know *should* be white, it will correct for that colour balance. The best example in the sample footage we have is the shot of the plane taking off – click on a part of the plane and the pictures should look natural. Now, if the plane wasn't white, you would get a very different result!

We don't need to alter the Mountain Railway white balance, so switch that off. We do need to alter the *Levels*, though. Checking that box in the Automatics section immediately improves the picture in the preview window, as well as bringing up a few more controls. Optimisation has a choice of Full or Contrast. *Full* is the best choice for this example, but *Contrast* will have a more subtle effect by not adjusting the brightness of a clip. Perhaps you have some dark shots in your movie and want to keep a certain degree of the "night" feeling but still improve the contrast.

Setting the Levels

Two more sliders are available to modify the automatic settings. Brightness is fairly obvious in its effect. Although the automatic adjustment has done well, it is still being thrown by the burnt out sky. Once detail is completely lost on video, it can't normally be retrieved unless you record your pictures as RAW (which take up masses of memory). I'm going to lower the brightness even more and just give up on the sky as a bad job. I've set the brightness to -5.

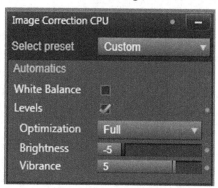

Vibrance is a control that brings the colours to life by increasing the saturation. You need to be careful not to add too much as it can result in "noise", but a setting of +5 seems to look OK on our example. When you click on the OK button at the bottom of the editor, you will be returned to the Library and you will notice the Corrections icon has been added to the thumbnail clip to let you know that a correction has been added.

If you want to do more work, the rest of the controls can be used in conjunction with, or instead of the automatic settings. *Fundamentals* allows control over *Brightness*, *Contrast*, *Saturation* (the amount of colour – turn it right down for black and white pictures) *Clarity* (the sharpness of the picture – turn it up too much and you will get noisy pictures) and *Haze*. This last control is a combination of the first three that allows you to compensate for hazy pictures with just one slider.

We have already discussed *White Balance*, while *Selective Brightness* adjusts the relative brightness of the video at five different points. If you don't want the very dark parts of you picture to be quite so dark, you can adjust the *Blacks. Fill light* lifts the parts of the picture just above black level, and so on up the scale.

Selective Saturation controls the amount of colour in the picture, along the 3 primary and 3 secondary colour axis. If you just want to make Dorothy's shoes a bit brighter red without affecting anything else, increase the Red setting.

Adjusting settings accurately

Dragging Sliders isn't the *only* way of adjusting any of these settings. If your mouse has a wheel, hovering over a slider and rolling the wheel will adjust the value. Double clicking will reset the value to zero. More control is available if you carefully click on the numerical value itself – the slider disappears, the value becomes highlighted, and you can type values in from the keyboard.

Parameter slider highlight

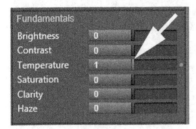

The best way to alter the values accurately is with the keyboard. Click once on any slider and a small orange bar appears at the end of the slider, indicating that the slider is active. Now, pressing the up arrow moves you to the slider above, the down arrow to the slider below.

Better still you can alter the value in large increments with the Page Up and Down keys or in small increments with the left/right keyboard arrow keys. The keyboard controls in particular will be very handy when you come to use effects such as Picture-in-Picture.

OK, you have looked at the footage, and you might think that a manual setting is what you want, but you also want to vary it as the shot progresses. How do you do that? Well, in Corrections, you can't. You will need to use keyframing, and Corrections doesn't have that feature, probably because of the way it is intended to be used. However, not only is keyframing part of the Effects Editor we will meet later, but the very same Image Correction CPU effect is available there.

Editor Toolbar controls

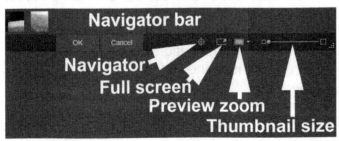

Before I move on to the other corrections, there are additional features of the Corrections and Effects Editor video preview window you need to be aware of. At the bottom right of the toolbar you have a size slider – the same design as used for thumbnails in the Library. In the Editors it allows you to zoom in and out. You can also use the mouse wheel or CTRL + and – on the keypad. Having zoomed in, if you want to move the preview around, click on the video and drag – the pointer turns into a hand. Double clicking re-centres the image within the window.

The button to the left has two drop-down settings. You can select one of two icons – fit to window, or *Set to actual size*. When clicked on, they do just what you would expect!

The third control from the right switches preview to full screen, where you can use the escape key to return. Alongside is a compass, which opens the Navigator along the bottom of the edit window. If you have the Navigator open during the use of corrections, it won't display the usual timeline display – instead you will have a sort of "thumbnail library" of the files in the currently open library tab. The very useful thing about this is that clicking on the thumbnail opens that file in the Corrections Editor, so if you are running through a batch of new clips, you don't need to close and re-open the editor again.

Marking clips is possible in both the Correction and Effects Editors. The button to add them is present with the preview player controls in the same place as in the normal Timeline Preview player. The marker will show up on the clip when it is put on the timeline as a small white triangle. I'm going to put one on our corrected clip now – the Mountain Railway clip. Find the point towards the end just before the camera starts what becomes a messy zoom in. With the scrubber at 08:14:00 on the burnt-in timecode top right, press the M key. This will set a marker at that point, and if you stick with the project, you will see how it looks later when we put the corrected clip on the timeline.

If you open the Marker panel with the drop-down key, you will see it appear neatly below the other small previews on the left. Ah, that's what that space was for! You will notice that the panel isn't fixed, so you can move it around, but it can be docked neatly underneath the other windows. While we are here, it is worth noting that the other small windows can also be dragged around. Although they don't have a close icon like the Marker panel, you can minimise them into a thin strip.

The next tab along from Enhance opens up a small panel for Video properties **Adjustments** on the right of the screen. The drop-down presets allow you to set the current clip to one of a number of 3D formats, while the first two drop-downs have some more mainstream uses.

Adjustment aspect ratio choices

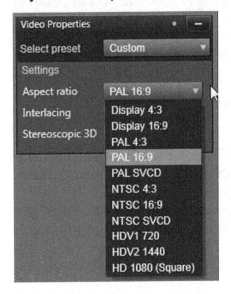

It's sometimes possible that a video is tagged with the wrong information, or that Studio misreads the tags. The most obvious case for me is that video files imported from some DVDs are tagged as 4:3 aspect ratio when they should be 16:9. In the Aspect ratio box you can easily add a correction to override the current format. It's not just a simple choice of 4:3 and 16:9. Various video formats use different "shapes" of pixels. For example HDV video has a horizontal pixel count of 1440, whereas most AVCHD cameras use 1920 pixels, yet both should be displayed as 16:9. NTSC SD video has 480 vertical pixels, PAL 576. There should be an option in the adjustments to suit almost every misunderstanding.

Another cause of issues is the misinterpretation of interlacing, and in particular the order of interlacing. In the next drop-down menu, you can override the detected settings. You really shouldn't mess with these unless you have a problem, but if you have got some footage that isn't actually what it says it is, then with a bit of detective work you should be able to correct the problem here. One problem is that my DSLR shoots progressive video, yet Studio thinks it is Top Field First. This hasn't caused a problem yet, but if it did, this would be where I change the setting. If you are seeing a "combing" effect on moving video when it is rendered to another file, one possibility is that there has been a field reversal. Changing from Top Field First to Bottom Field First may solve the issue.

The final drop-down is to select what sort of 3D video you might be using. I'll talk about 3D nearer the end of the book. If you are seeing something strange on a 2D project, something might have gone wrong here!

The next tab is **Snapshot.** I'm not quite sure why this feature is in Corrections, other than the designers had to put it somewhere. Once you know where it is, that's fine. It's quite a straightforward feature in some respects. You can select an aspect ratio, drag and resize a crop box around the video in the preview window, and when you click on Apply, a snapshot is generated using the current default photo format, given the current project name plus a counter, and saved into the current default snapshot directory. The snapshot settings can be altered in the Control Panel, Import section.

If you are taking a snapshot of a 3D video clip, it will be saved in the JPS format instead.

The final tab in Video Corrections is **Stabilize**. I want to use this one, partly because the video we have used is a bit wobbly, but also it is a feature that can be troublesome if misunderstood.

Using the Stabilizer

Let's set about this straight away, because you will have time to read more while the stabilisation routine is at work. Close the Corrections Editor with the OK button, saving the changes you have made. You will notice that the Corrections icon has been added to the Mountain Railway thumbnail.

Open the *Ext take off 1* library clip in the Corrections Editor, switch to *Stabilize* and check that the Default settings are selected – no borders, Auto Zoom Frames=50 and Max Auto Zoom=120. Click on the Action button Render and Play. You should see a *Rendering...* message, a slowly moving progress bar, and a button that will cause the process to *Render in Background*. You might as well not press that for now, as we will have to wait for quite some time even if you do press it.

The Stabilize effect generating data for the whole clip

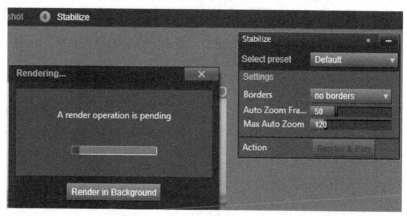

OK, what is going on that takes so long? Studio is scanning the video clip to build up a whole set of data that it is going to use to apply the stabilize effect. The good news is that it will only have to do this once, because if you alter some of the stabilize parameters it can use the same data. The bad news is that it is processing the whole file and not just the section we have selected as a library clip! What's more, it's a fairly slow process. Studio generates a file with the type .bsi and hides it away in the Users folders, but the files are usually no more than a few Megabytes in size as they contain data about the video, not the video itself.

If you are still waiting for the render to end and want to click on the *Render in Background*, you can do so. The render operation will continue in the background, and although you can play the clip or carry on with some other editing task, you won't see the effect of the stabilisation until the render process is over. Be patient. Make a cup of tea – you probably have time.

I can't predict how long the process will take. High definition video on a lower powered computer will take longer to render than the duration of the video. Standard definition will be much quicker.

When the render finally finishes, you can see how stabilisation works with the current settings by playing the clip. The video is reframed to reduce the amount of wobbling. We have selected no borders, so that the filter also has to zoom in a little bit for a small amount of wobbling, more so if the video is very jerky. If the zooming is very fast, the effect might actually look worse than the original video. If you zoom in too far, the video starts to look very grainy. If you select no zoom, the borders of the video show up constantly and it can be very disturbing. If you specify some borders, the amount of zoom is less but the black borders may still be distracting. Your choice of settings will really be determined on how wobbly the video is, how much you are prepared to zoom in, and if you can tolerate borders.

It so happens that the default settings work quite well on the shot we have selected. You can see it is working because the burnt-in timecode disappears out of frame quite often, but if you ignore that the effect looks relatively OK. There are a couple of big bumps that still look bad, but on the whole it's an improvement.

When you exit the Corrections Editor, you may be asked if you want to save the changes (depending on how you exit). Answer yes unless you want to abandon what you have been doing recently.

So, we now have added the two corrections I want to use for the project. If you want to crack on with the project, jump ahead to page 300 and then return here when you want to learn more about corrections.

Correcting Photos

Use the Library to find a photo to experiment with. You can use the stills of our biking heroes in the Public Pictures if you can't find anything else. Double click to open the Corrections Editor and take a look at the different tabs above the preview window. The first one – Enhance – uses the same Image correction as we have just explored with Video.

A neat trick that you can use when adjusting photos is the Before/After View. It is enabled with an icon on the toolbar (shown arrowed in the screenshot) and brings up a line which can be repositioned and rotated with the mouse. The **Before** side of the line displays the unenhanced image, **After** the results of the current corrections. The drop-down menu also offers a side-by-side view and an above-and-below view.

Adjustments offers some different options if you load a photo that has Alpha – which is information regarding which areas of a photo or graphic are supposed to be transparent. This is of most use with titles and other graphics imported from another graphics program. You can choose to keep the transparent information – so that video on tracks below shows through, or ignore it, where it is replaced by white.

Before/After toolbar icon and display

The next three options can be used to prepare pictures for use in your projects. Virtually all digital cameras nowadays have more resolution than Standard Definition video, and quite a lot of cameras shoot more resolution than HD video, so you can **Crop** your pictures quite a bit before they start to look blurred when used in your projects. If in doubt, take a look at the photo dimensions by opening the Information box with the **i** (for information) button on the left of the toolbar – compare this with the project resolution and you will see how much you have to play with.

The Crop tool in action

The **Crop** tool has the name of the photo alongside the information button, and the next two buttons will rotate the picture in 90 degree increments. The floating light grey bar can be moved around the browser so it doesn't mask the part of the photo you are most interested in. It contains a drop-down box to adjust the aspect ratio of the cropping tool –which can be freeform or locked at 16:9 or 4:3. *Preview* removes

Rotation buttons

the bar – it returns when you press escape. *Clear* undoes any changes to the cropping box, *Cancel* takes you out of the crop tool, and *Apply* does the same but the changes you have made are saved as a correction.

The crop tool itself is easy to use – you just drag the nodes to adjust the area it covers. Any part of the photo that is greyed out will not appear in the corrected picture.

Straighten is a similar tool that lets you rotate a photo by + or – 20 degrees. You can select a couple of moveable cursors to line up horizons or the sides of buildings, or just use a simple grid. You don't need to use the slider on the grey bar – you can grab and drag the picture.

Red eye is the effect you get when using flash photography too close to someone looking straight at camera in a fairly dark room – it's actually a reflection coming off the blood vessels around the retina. The tool requires you to draw a marquee around the eyes of the subject who you want to correct. Depending on the photo, the size and position of the box, and the colours involved, sometimes it works well, and in other circumstances not at all. Different programs have different levels of success, so if Studio can't do it, a third-party program might be able to provide a better fix.

Audio Corrections

You will need to load a video or audio clip into corrections to explore these options. They actually start with the *Channel Mixer* box to the left of the preview.

Channel/Mixer and Audio corrections

Beneath the meter is a slider that alters the gain. It obeys the usual rules about adjustments, but take it slowly – the latency means you won't hear a change for half a second or so when you try to make adjustments as the audio is playing. Too many changes and you can cause the playback to freeze. This applies to all the audio functions.

The drop-down box labelled **Stereo** can be very useful. The most common use would be a mono recording on just one channel of your camcorder that needs to be spread out to both left and right channels. The other options will normally be used for correcting some other form of error, such as *Swap channels* when the right and left channels have been cross-plugged.

The **Optimise** icon button to the right of the Stereo drop-down needs to be treated with caution. It should adjust the audio to a good level, but I find it sometimes chooses the wrong setting. This may be caused by selecting the button too early – so I suggest you wait until the waveform has fully drawn itself, and don't have the audio playing before you apply this correction. However, this may be a bug in the program.

To see the rest of the audio corrections you need to switch to the audio tab top left.

The Frequency Spectrum meter and its button

Two new icons grace the toolbar alongside the (superfluous) full screen icon. The wavy line to the left displays the normal waveforms you see on the timeline, but the button that looks like a bargraph switches the display to a frequency meter. Open up a music file and play it, then switch to the frequency meter. The lowest, bass frequency is on the left, and as we move across the screen the highest treble sounds are represented by the bar furthest right. We can use this display to good

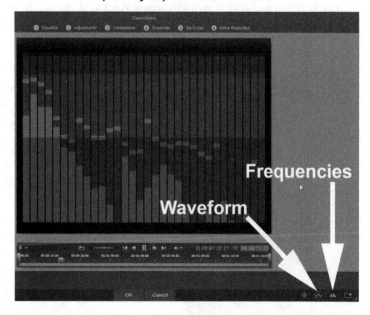

effect, along with our ears, of course, when we turn our attention to the tabs across the top of the Audio corrections window.

Equalize allows you to alter the frequency response to an audio track. Locate the *BMX_Ya-Ha!* music track in *The-Sky-is-the-Limit* project bin and open it in Corrections. Select Equalize from the top tabs and play the music. Try the presets available while listening and watching the frequency meter. The two most obvious examples are Telephone, where the HiCut setting rolls off all the frequencies above

4000Hz and Heavy, which boosts the low frequencies and slightly reduces the higher ones around 2000hz. Note that the sliders obey all the usual keyboard and mouse controls.

You might use Equalize to correct poor audio, or to add an effect. The five top channels can all be tweaked to affect different frequencies. Try adjusting the Gain of the Mid control down to -18, then listen to the effect as you change the Frequency. Turning it down to 125 Hz gives the effect of it bleeding through the earphones of the person sitting next to you on the train. Resetting it to its default of 1000Hz gives the impression that it's coming through the wall from the kids bedroom next door. You can choose how you want to be irritated.

Adjustments only has one setting – enabling or disabling the use of a subwoofer on 5.1 surround sound – the 0.1 part.

A **Compressor** is a tool that helps you stop audio going over a certain limit. It can also boost quiet sections without boosting the loud ones. If you apply this effect quite brutally the result will sound very bad – it is really a **Limiter**. When used carefully it will smooth out the dynamic range of audio to help avoid distortion or inaudibility.

The Compressor Tool

I'm going to resort to an analogy to explain the controls. Imagine you have a very quick person operating the volume control of your Hi-Fi. He is so quick he can react instantly to the incoming level from the CD shown on the audio meter before it gets sent to the speakers. The Threshold is the level at which he begins to take action. If the threshold is -6dB, then if the signal from the CD reaches -5db, he pulls the volume to the speakers down. The amount he does that is determined by the Ratio he has been instructed to use. If that is set to 2:1, if the incoming level is +2, he reduces it to +1. If it is +4, he reduces it to +2. If the ratio is 4:1 and the incoming level is +4, he will reduce it to +1.

The Attack is the speed at which he acts – a slow attack time means that the levels can start to creep up more before he adjusts the volume. The Release is the time he takes to turn the volume back up once the incoming volume has dropped below the threshold. The Gain is a further volume control further down the chain that can increase the whole signal once it has been compressed, so that if it is no longer going over -6 at any time, he can boost it to 0dB without altering the instructions he is obeying regarding Threshold. Knee modifies the compression ratio – a hard Knee will cut in the the full compression immediately the threshold has been reached, a soft Knee will increase the ratio gradually.

Again, a good idea of how to use a limiter can be gained from experimenting with the controls. With the BMX music still loaded, adjust the settings to ratio 4, threshold -16, attack 0.0001, release 1, gain 9 and knee 0. Switch off the whole effect with the button at the top alongside the title, and listen to the music, watching the meter in the Channel Mixer panel.

The levels hit the red maximum on occasions, while at other times almost fall out of the yellow area. Now switch on the compressor while still playing. It will take a moment for the effect to kick in, but when it does, observe the difference – while the meter is staying higher in the yellow area all the time, it isn't ever hitting the red. Of course, the music doesn't sound so good – we have squashed the dynamic range. You might want to try some more radical settings to hear how badly over-compressed music can sound.

You can use compression on audio instead of having to manually adjust the levels. For example, a group of people holding a conversation might get very loud at times when they are talking over each other and getting excited, but there might be very quiet patches as well. A little light compression might save you having to go through the whole audio, manually adjusting the levels.

The **Expander** is the reverse of the Compressor, as the name might imply. Why would you want to do that? If you have a poor quality recording with low level hiss or other background noise, it would be useful to fade the audio out completely when it doesn't have any content that you want to hear. To hear this effect on music – which isn't where you are likely to use it but it gives you some idea – select the Expand 2:1 preset and listen the the BMX track. When it goes quiet – it really goes quiet! The settings are much the reverse of a compressor as well. The *Threshold* is the point below which levels get reduced, *Ratio* is the amount they they get reduced by, while *Attack* and *Release* are the speed at which the operation works, Range compensates for overall level change and Hold is an addition control that delays the application of the attenuation before Release comes into play.

The **De-Esser** is a tool that reduces the sibilance of the human voice generated by pronouncing the end of "S" as well as "T" and "C" and similar sounds. This can be pronounced in some recordings. Because it is at a specific frequency, a De-esser can reduce the effect by compressing just that specific area of the audio spectrum. The precise frequency will vary between people, hence the frequency setting, and too much compression will begin to affect the whole audio, so the Range is adjustable as well.

Noise Reduction is a useful tool, but isn't always as successfully as you might hope. The problem is differentiating between noise (perhaps the distant drone of traffic) and the audio you want (Maybe the voices in the foreground).

Try as I might, it's impossible to use noise reduction on any of my flight clips to make a significant improvement – the software cannot differentiate enough between the frequency spectrum of the wind noise and the aircraft taxiing to have any chance of success. Things work better if the unwanted noise is constant – the drone of a computer in the background perhaps - and the audio you want to save is considerably more varied.

Remember that removing corrections can be done in the Library by using the *Revert to Original* option from the right-click context menu as well as re-opening the clip in the Corrections Editor and switching the correction off. You will also notice that when you put corrected clips on the timeline they have a green stripe running along the top of them. This indicates that a correction has been added. You can right click on the green line to bring up a context menu that also allows you to remove or re-edit the correction.

Storyboarding the Movie

With two of our Library clips having had corrections added, it's time to actually start putting the movie together. For the initial shaping of the story, I'm going to demonstrate the use of the Storyboard. We can leave the Library now by switching to the Movie tab. The Flight bin should still be open in the Compact Library.

Start a New project, switch the timeline settings to Widescreen PAL and **Save as** *Flight Project stage 1*.

We looked at opening and using the Storyboard strip earlier, but to remind you, the third button from the left on the timeline toolbar gives a drop-down choice of Navigator or Storyboard. The small strip icon below the padlock on each track is used to designate which timeline track is shown in the Storyboard view.

With the storyboard open and allocated to track 2, select all the clips except the last one (the Whole file) in the Flight bin and drag them to the storyboard. Yes, they are in the wrong order for our story! Let's put them in the story order I talked about on page 276.

We have two external shots of the take off currently sitting in positions 2 and 3. Use multi selections to highlight them both, then hover, click, wait for the icon to change, then drag left. You will see a nice graphical effect as you move the two clips to the start of the movie.

Multi-clip Drag and drop on the Storyboard

The interior shot of the take off is currently in 5th position. We aren't going to use all of it, but for now move it to a position in between the two exterior shots, currently shots 1 and 2. If you scrub through quickly you will see a huge amount of "double action" as the plane takes off twice, and we will fix that with some major trimming in a moment.

As an aside, you may notice I'm trying to pretend that the shots of the plane taking off have been filmed at the same time, where obviously they were not. This sort of cheating goes on all the time in film making. If you are using this book more like a manual, you might want to pop back to read my description of Continuity editing ion page 55.

What next? Let's put the Final Approach (currently clip 5) and Landing (clip 6) at the end of the movie. The story of the movie now goes:

1, 2 and 3 -Take off

4 - View of the castle

5 - Mountain Railway

6 - Nantlle Ridge

7 and 8 – shots of the Peak

9 - Final Approach

10 – Landing

To fit to the original brief, we still don't have the correct Story order. After the take off, I wanted a shot of the Nantlle Ridge followed by the shots of the Peak. Multi-select clips 6, 7 and 8 and drag them left and drop them after the third take off shot. All we need to do now is swap over the Mountain Railway and Castle shots. Do this by dragging clip 8, the Mountain Railway, to the left so it comes *before* the Castle shot.

Now the shots on the storyboard (and the timeline) should be in the same order as the original list I made and the screenshot.

The final order of shots on the Storyboard

One of the advantages we are seeing here of using the storyboard is that there is no danger of us accidentally splitting a clip – the storyboard thumbnails will only drop into the gaps between other thumbnails. If we were doing this on the timeline care would be needed even with the aid of magnetic snapping. The Storyboard view lends itself to creative and organisational thought processes.

If you have plenty of screen space, you can leave the storyboard open if you wish, but I'm going to close it, and increase the height of track 2 for the next stage, where I'm going to make the edit between the first three shots work

I want to tighten the Out point of clip 1. After the Cessna has finished taxiing past the military plane (it's an Aero L-29 Delfin, in case you are wondering) there is rather a nasty lurch in the shot, despite the stabilize effect having been added. I want you to quick trim this out.

With any reasonably powered computer, you should be able to do this "on the fly". Generate an Out point handle at the end of clip one, hold down the ALT key, click and start to drag left. You should be able to do this smoothly enough to view the video in real or near real time and spot the wobble even when trimming. I think you will agree the shot is fairly smooth until a few frames before the white twin-engined plane starts to appear in the left of frame. Watch the timecode top right of the preview window and home in on 00:00:18:00. You could see this on the burnt-in timecode as well if we hadn't added the stabilize. Once you have found the exact frame, release the mouse button.

The first Quick Trim

That's the sort of skill which should become second nature with a bit of practice – you should be thinking about the edit point and not the process.

TIP – if you can't seem to get the accuracy to find the exact frame, abandon what you are doing, use Undo to repair any damage, then zoom the timeline in. With the scale set to around 30 seconds, you should have the accuracy you need.

We will do the next trim a different way. I'm going to cut from the exterior shot of the plane to the interior shot of the back of my daughter's head, then let the shot pan to the pilot. Using this shot removes any continuity issue with what we should be seeing out of the window.

I've chosen the burnt-in timecode of 00:03:06:06 as not too wobbly to cut to. Find it with the scrubber and press the N key or click on the razor blade. Carry on playing and find a stable frame of the pilot at 03:13:14 and split the clip again. Make another cut at 00:03:38:00 where the plane is about the cross the yellow Hold line. (In reality the plane did stop there and wait for clearance. Real but boring.) The final cut point is just after the plane's wheels have left the ground. You can only really sense this from the interior shot by playing the clip at speed. Play it and hit the space bar to stop the video when you sense the plane has just taken off. I make the burnt-in timecode reading 00:04:09:00. Even if you don't agree, set your scrubber there and split the clip again, please!

This is a good time to open the storyboard again if you closed it. We want to delete the second, fourth and sixth shot. You can do this one at a time (In which case it's a good idea to start with shot 6, then 4 and finally 2) or by multi-selection with the CTRL key and then deleting.

Let's review the work so far. Play the movie from the top – turn the sound down if you like, because it makes the edits jar, and we will be sorting that out later. I'm quite happy with the first three shots now, but it is a shame we haven't used more of the interior shot. Before we fix that, let's sort out the In point of shot 4. Again, I'll do this in an alternative way to demonstrate a point about the storyboard.

Use a quick trim In point on the front of clip 4 but don't hold down ALT. I've chosen a burnt-in timecode of 00:01:05:00 for the point just after take off. We can refine it later. Release the mouse and observe that we have left a gap, both on the timeline and in the storyboard, where it is shown as black space.

A gap in the timeline translating to a gap in the storyboard

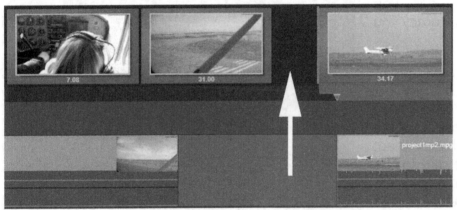

The gap on the storyboard acts as if it were a clip. If you drag the exterior take off clip left to close the gap, it re-appears between clips 4 and 5. I want you to delete it.

The easiest way is to group select all the clips to the right of the gap and slide them left. A useful short cut for this is Ctrl-Shift- click

A lot of the remaining clips are too long. If you are just making a movie for yourself, you might want to preserve all the memories, but to a casual viewer once a scene has been established, then it begins to pall. We also need to tidy up all the wobbly parts. Later I'm going to show you two special techniques for the close shots of the peak and the Castle, but for the other edits I'm just going to list the edit points. If you are a few frames out it's unlikely to be an issue, but by the end of the following process, if you aren't confident that you have matched my edits, you can load *Flight Project stage 1.Movie.axp* from the website or data disc so that we can continue. If you encounter issues with Missing Media when you do this, check out the discussion of the subject on page 152.

Before we go any further, let's check that our projects tally. Move the scrubber to the end of the movie by pressing End, then jog back to the last frame of video. The timecode in the Player window should read 00:06:19:11. If your project differs then you might want to check the steps we have taken so far. If everything is OK, then save the movie before continuing.

Experience has shown me that it's at this point some people get a little lost, mainly because I was giving the reader the chance to use which ever technique they fancied, and there are timecode differences when setting Out points of 1 frame depending on the method.

Because the safest way to be accurate is to use the Split and delete method, that's what I'm going to suggest you do now – we aren't doing anything particularly creative so there aren't judgements to be made that would benefit from using Quick trim. If the following list looks a bit tedious to carry out, you can cheat and load the premade version from the website or data DVD!

In the following list, **MTC** is the Movie timecode you can see top right of the player window, **BITC** the time burnt into the source footage. If you want to be really efficient, you can enter the NTC timecodes into the player window timecode box to move the scrubber to each split point, compare the BITC, and then press N to break the movie at that point.

Split the movie at the following points:

- 00:01:21:10 MTC 00:01:30:01 BITC
- 00:01:43:22 MTC 00:05:30:01 BITC
- 00:02:46:21 MTC 00:06:33:00 BITC
- 00:02:59:22 MTC 00:06:46:01 BITC
- 00:03:33:07 MTC 00:07:35:00 BITC
- 00:03:36:19 MTC 00:07:38:12 BITC
- 00:04:11:07 MTC 00:08:14:00 BITC
- 00:04:28:24 MTC 00:08:36:24 BITC
- 00:04:44:07 MTC 00:08:52:07 BITC
- 00:05:05:20 MTC 00:09:14:01 BITC
- 00:05:46:19 MTC 00:09:55:00 BITC
- 00:06:13:05 MTC 00:10:21:11 BITC

Once you have entered the splits, use the storyboard to multi-select the following clips. I've put the clip duration after each clip number so you can cross reference them with the duration shown under each storyboard thumbnail.

Clip 5 9:16, Clip 7 35:03, Clip 8 27.21, Clip 10 24.07, Clip 11 9.03, Clip 13 3.11,

Clip 15 10.17, Clip 16 7.00, Clip 18 8.21, Clip 20 9.05, Clip 21 31.19, Clip 23 6.07.

Now delete all the clips, then move the scrubber to the end of the timeline with the *End* key. The scrubber timecode should be 3 minutes, 16 seconds and 7 frames.

This is the *Flight Project stage 1.Movie.axp* project you will find on the website and data DVD.

OK, time to review the movie again. Three things really jar for me. The take-off point should be fairly accurate but the plane seems to jump into the air. The shot zooming into the peak is a bit short, and the shot zooming into the castle could be improved. I also mentioned using a bit more of the interior shot as the plane taxied before take off.

I'm going to work through from the top again. Turn off the storyboard as we won't be using it again.

Open the *Int take off* library clip in the preview player. If you haven't been using the Dual display mode, switch to it now with the icon top right of the preview window. The next edit will be a demonstration of 3 point editing. Scrub in preview to a nice clean frame of the military plane (00:02:20:00) and mark an In point with the I key or clicking on the In point tool. The In point calliper should move to the current preview player scrubber position.

Now, let's find a good point to cut from the first clip on the timeline to our new shot. Grab the Timeline preview scrubber and drag it to find an exterior shot of the Cessna taxiing that looks like it will match. Imagine what you would see if you were sat where the camera was. Compare the two frames with the side-by-side previews and think how the cut would work. I've chosen 00:00:13:04, on the Timeline preview timecode counter as the wing of the green plane has just started to enter the left of frame. Use the Razor or N key to split the timeline at that point.

How long do we want to stay on the new shot, or is it better to decide how long we can stay away from the old shot? We don't want to alter the continuity, so both the new shot and the section of the old shot it is going to replace should be the same duration.

Notice that the shot we will be returning to ends fairly soon and we don't want that to be too short. I'm going to plumb for around two seconds each and look for a good point to return. I've chosen 15:20 on the timeline counter because the planes aren't quite in line. Make another split in the timeline.

Now we want to delete the section we are going to replace. Highlight it and press Delete or click on the Trash Can. Oh no, that's wrong, the gap has closed up! We are in Smart mode and that works in Insert mode when deleting in simple cases. Use Undo or CTRL-Z to put the clip back, hold down the ALT key and then click on the Trash can. Right, there is the gap.

Preparing to make a 3-point edit

We haven't set an Out point in the source window, but that doesn't matter, We will use three point editing and allow Studio to automatically fill the gap for us.

Drag the clip from the preview player window into the gap **in the timeline** (not the storyboard - for the sake of the screen shots I have closed it). When it is in the correct place, it should fill that gap and not displace any other clips. Drop the clip by releasing the mouse button and review the edit.

The Source clip is slotted into the gap

If we had dropped the clip into the storyboard, there would have been no smart operation and the whole nearly 3

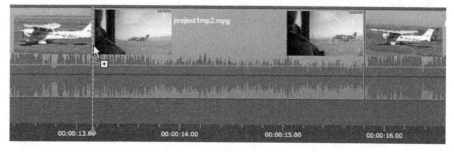

minute clip would have been inserted into the movie – and the gap would still be there!

The next part of the movie I want to adjust is the point of take off. This will be a good demonstration of Advanced trimming and rolling the edit point. Set a yellow advanced trim point on the Out point of the 5th clip. This was covered earlier, but to remind you, place the scrubber just to the left of the Out point and click on the Trim button, or if you work with the setting "Activate trim points by clicking near cuts" turned ON then hover your mouse to get an Out point handle, click and release.

Now set a second trim point on the same track for the In point of clip 6. Because you are already in Trim mode this is achieved by CTRL clicking to the right of the In point.

The preview windows have become the Trim Editor; in the left preview is the last frame of the interior view of the take off and in the right preview is the first shot of the exterior view of the same.

The Trim Editor set up for a Rolling Trim of the take off point

We can now use the trim buttons or the series of keys M , . and / to adjust the cut. Each frame we remove from one side of the cut is added to the other. Therefore the continuity isn't l o s t . Alternatively, you can drag left and right on the preview windows themselves for a very interactive experience, even if it doesn't quite have the accuracy of using the buttons or keyboard.

When I first tried to make this edit work a few years ago, it took me some while to realise why it wasn't working. The human eye thinks the plane is taking off from the tarmac strip in front of the fencing, but the runway is actually further away and masked.

While my estimate of when the plane's wheels leave the ground is perhaps a few frames out, I'm first going to suggest you roll the edit back so that the plane is lower when we cut to it. I have ended up with a -10 offset showing above both trim windows – the burnt in time code reads 00:01:04:14 in the right window.

Use loop play to preview the cut. I think you will agree that the improvement is small but the fence is clearly in front of the plane but behind the tarmac.

We have lost the sense of beginning to take off in the outgoing video, though. Remove the In trim point on clip 6, then adjust the out point trim. I found that by trimming that to -4 frames, the edit seems more natural. You might be able to find a better solution, but I've persuaded myself the edit works much better even with such a small adjustment! Finally, to get out of Trim mode, just click on the trim mode button on the toolbar.

The final choice of edit point

Speed

I think that clip 9, the brief shot that zooms into the peak of Mount Snowdon is too short. That gives us a good opportunity to explore all the features of the Speed effect.

Before I begin to describe the function, it's worth making clear how Studio generates slow and fast motion. It is frame based, so speeding something up is relatively easy. To make something play at twice the speed, Studio removes every other frame. Slow motion involves duplication of frames.   Interlaced video is stretched out to separate fields. The "smooth motion" effect attempts to blend frames and fields, but in my opinion it rarely makes little difference to the smoothness and tends to degrade the pictures.

When you see really smooth slow motion, this is achieved in one of two ways. A special high speed camera can be used that shoots at a frame rate higher than that which will be used for the final product. When this footage is altered to play back at the slower frame rate there is a whole, proper original frame for each playback frame. The other method uses specialist software has been employed to interpolate frames. This only works with carefully shot video, takes ages to render and the software that does it is normally very expensive.

Another feature that Studio lacks is the ability to vary the speed within a clip. If you want to vary the speed of a clip you will need to break it up into sections on the timeline. This also means you can't ramp the speed up or down over a period of time, so that something moving at normal speed *accelerates* to a higher speed.

So bear those limitations in mind when applying the speed effect. It still is very useful, as we will see in one example, before I describe how it operates in general.

If you right click on clip 9 and select the Speed/add options, a box will open as shown in the screenshot. We are going to use the Stretch option first. One thing that won't ever happen when you add a Speed effect is that the current duration of the clip on the timeline will be altered, so often stretch is the best option to use.

The Speed Control box set to Stretch

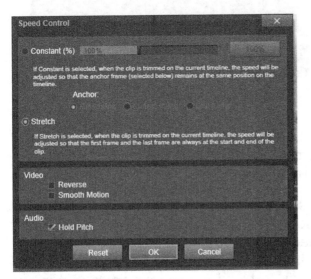

Click on Stretch and make sure all the other boxes are unchecked, then click OK. You are returned to the clips and the only difference you will notice is a yellow striped line along the top of the clip that indicates a speed effect is in operation.

Now use Quick trim in conjunction with the Alt key to increase the duration of the clip by about 3 times its original length. If you look at the In and Out points you will notice that they are still the same frames as before!

Single step through the clip with the jog buttons on the player, the arrow or Z and X keys. Notice the timecode on the player changing every frame, but the burnt-in time code only increments every second or third frame. However, because we are using interlaced video the frame content changes more often than that as each individual field is extracted.

Let's study this in a bit more detail. Right click on the clip and select Adjust duration, and use the boxes to enter a duration of 13 seconds and 24 frames. Now when you study the video clip a frame at a time it should be clear that the video moves every two frames and the burnt-in counter increments every fourth frame.

The Speed effect added to a stretched clip 9

Right click on the clip and use Speed/edit to reopen the Speed control box. You can study the effects of the three check boxes now by checking them one at a time.

Reverse does just that – plays the video backwards. An important point here is that you don't need to change the speed from the original for this to work. The answer to the question "Where is the Reverse Video effect" is "In the Speed control box". Not immediately obvious to a newcomer to the software, but now you know about it!

Smooth motion I mentioned earlier. On our current clip it shows little improvement to the smoothness, but you might find other footage that it has a more useful effect on.

Speed has some interesting uses for audio. Obviously we can add the comic "chipmunk" effect to a voice, or slow audio down to make it more dramatic. One obvious use for speed is making music fit a desired duration, but the natural consequence of this is that the pitch shifts. Slow down the music and it drops into a lower register. Small changes are OK, large ones tend to sound very wrong.

The Hold Pitch checkbox tries to counteract this effect, but has limited usefulness. Odd phasing and digital artefacts creep in, and not always when you specify a large change – sometimes a 1% change can sound worse than a 10% one on certain musical instruments.

If you apply Hold Pitch to the clip and listen back, you will clearly hear why it is sometimes a failure – the digital processing makes an attempt to hold the pitch, but the digital artefacts sound very bad.

When you have finished experimenting with the options, switch off all the checkboxes and return to the clip. I think the speed is too slow for the beginning and too fast at the end to achieve a clear view of the peak at the end of the clip. Right click and select Speed/remove.

Removing the Speed effect

Whoa, what happened there? I said that Speed will never automatically alter the duration of a clip. However, *we* altered the duration when we dragged the clip and when we entered a value in to the duration box. You now have the same clip duration of almost 14 seconds, but with the Speed effect removed, the source material has run out and the pink area indicates "dead meat" – Studio has frozen the last available frame. This is of no use to us! Use Alt and a quick trim to shorten the out point of clip 9 – with the magnet on it will click into place when we reach live video, but we need to go further and restore the Out point to 00:07:38:11 on the burnt in timecode.

You've seen how useful the Stretch mode is. We don't need to do any maths if we want to make a video clip fit a gap or if we want it to run to a particular duration. In most cases you will use simple trimming to make the shot duration suit your purposes, and Studio will work out the speed reduction or increase required.

What I propose to do is divide the clip in to two parts. The first 3 seconds I'll play at half speed, then the remaining 12 frames I will slow down to 10% - 120 frames or just under 5 seconds.

The workflow you might expect me to use is to add a speed effect to the clip and then split it. This won't work, as when you split a clip the speed effect will automatically adjust itself. We need to split the clip first – at 00:07:38:00. Now add a Stretch speed effect to the first half of the clip and increase the duration from 3 seconds to 6 seconds. Play that back and you will see we have achieved the first part of the task.

I'm going to use the Constant effect for the second half of the close up of the peak. Open the Speed control box, select *Constant*. Anchor: *First frame* and enter *10%* as the value, then click OK.

Again, you will see that the duration of the clip hasn't altered. If you bear this in mind as a hard and fast rule – **The Speed effect never alters the duration of a clip of its own accord** – you won't go far wrong. If we had selected a different Anchor then the content of the clip would have been different but the duration would have remained the same. Using *Last frame* would still have resulted in 12 different frames being displayed – ending with what was the Out point of the clip.

Open the Speed control box again. You will notice that a new radio button has appeared – *Keep current anchor*. If we wanted to adjust the clip again this would be useful if we had previously used *Current frame* (the scrubber position).

Back to the clip. It has a slowdown to 10% applied to it, but it isn't in Stretch mode, so however we trim it, the Speed effect remains constant. Alter the duration to 120 frames - 4 seconds 20 frames. When you now preview that section of the movie, you can see we have achieved the desired effect. (At the time of writing a small bug in Studio is resulting in a 1 frame shift in certain Speed operations. This does not effect the project, but may confuse you. Hopefully it will be fixed by the time you read this.)

Snapshot

We saw that you can generate a snapshot of a video or photo in the Corrections Editor. There is also an easier way to do this on the timeline, where you will generate a still frame of what you see in the Timeline player window.

Snapshot has its own tool icon on the toolbar that looks like a stills camera. If it isn't showing, check the custom setting in the far left tool, "Customise toolbar". To tidy up the shot of Caernarfon Castle I'm going to apply a freeze frame at the end of what is now Clip 12. If you have the Storyboard open, it's the third from last clip.

Make sure the the Flight bin is open in the Compact Library, then park the scrubber on the last frame of the clip Click on the Snapshot button or press the S key. A new asset will be created in the open bin. By default it will be a Jpeg with a name using the format *projectname.projecttype_Snapshot(x).jpg.* In the current example, the snapshot will be called *Flight Project stage 1.movie_snapshot.jpg*

The Snapshot tool and a new Snapshot open in Latest Import

Drag this photo down to the storyboard or the timeline at the end of clip 12. If you haven't adjusted the default project setting for durations, a 3 second freeze frame will be added to the end of the clip. (If it is a different duration, adjust it to 3 seconds).

When you play that back, you should see no quality change when the freeze happens. If you do see a slight difference on higher quality source material, try changing the default snapshot format setting to .bmp in the Control Panel/Import section.

You can use Snapshot for many things. I often take a grab from menus of my disc projects and use them as labels to print onto the DVD disc.

Transitions

Studio offers a number of ways of adding transitions, but before I describe the methods, let's just take a look at a few basics.

A transition is where you switch between two clips with both being on screen at the same time. The classic transition is the dissolve, but there are many types of increasing complexity. I'm not a great fan of complex transitions in most circumstances, but I'm not going to go as far as some people do as to condemn them as giving an amateur look to movies – there are plenty of circumstances where, when used consistently, they can bring creativity or a sense of fun.

Why would you want to use a transition instead of a straight cut? Apart from adding variety, a transition can subjectively imply a passage of time. If I have a shot of someone sitting in a chair reading a book and simply cut to a closer shot, the grammar of film implies that the reader is still on the same page. If I dissolve to the closer shot, the viewer will surmise that time is passing – our reader could have read a whole chapter.

It's an important point that when you use transitions between two video clips, if you don't want either the outgoing or incoming video to freeze, or you don't want to see any more of the video than is already on the timeline, you have to overlap the two sources. So, if two 10 second clips are adjacent to each other and you add a 2 second transition between them, the total duration of the two clips drops to 18 seconds.

If you have come from Classic Studio or other entry level editors this process is so automated that you might not even be aware that the overlap is automatically added. In NextGen Studio, however, it is possible to add a transition in such a way that the video clips are extended instead of overlapped. If there is no more video to use, then the last, or first, available frame is frozen and extended.

This makes adding transitions potentially more complex, but like many functions in Studio 19, you can normally let the Smart mode and default behaviour sort things out for you.

Why would we sometimes want to *avoid* overlapping video if the alternative might lead to unwanted video being included? Because NextGen Studio behaves as a true multi-track editor, with no single track having control over the others unless we wish it to, if you were *forced* to overlap video when you added a transition, you wouldn't always be able to keep tracks in sync.

Adding Transitions with the mouse

There are numerous way of adding transitions in Studio. The simplest method involves the use of the mouse on the In or Out point of a clip. Hover your mouse over the top of the first clip on the timeline and you can generate a transition handle as shown in the screenshot.

Creating a Transition handle

Click and drag it to the right and the handle turns into a double headed arrow and a ramp appears to the left indicating a transition has been generated. If you have adjusted the timeline view suitably you will also get the duration box showing up when you drag. Continue to drag right until the duration box indicates

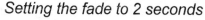

2 seconds or the timecode top right of the preview player shows 2 seconds as the scrubber position and then release the mouse key. You have added a transition to the first clip of our movie.

Setting the fade to 2 seconds

You can easily argue that it isn't a transition, it is a fade-in. I could equally argue that a fade in is a transition between black (the default when there is no video on the timeline) and the incoming clip.

Hover your mouse over the transition and if the view is sufficiently expanded you should see the duration appear in a dark grey box, along with a small icon indicating the transition type. If your mouse is over the grey slope a few moments later a tooltip with the name of the transition will appear – in this case "DefaultFade"

Although it has its uses, there are a number of things that aren't too convenient about this method of adding transitions. Because the style of generating the fade is in effect "freehand", if you want the end of the transition to coincide with a particular frame of video or another event on the timeline (the beginning of a music track, for example) that's very easy, but if you just want your transitions to be a consistent length, it's quite fiddly. You can fix the duration by clicking on the duration box and typing in numbers, but that's still not ideal. Also, you only get the DefaultFade, so if you wanted anything else you would need to replace it.

However, before we look at other ways to add transitions, I want to demonstrate the various modes that can be used with the freehand method as it is easier to see how they affect the timeline. The next transition I want to add is to indicate a passage of time. Move the scrubber down to the cut between the shots of the Nantlle Ridge and the view of Snowdon at around 1'34". Turn on the navigator view, set the timescale to 10 seconds with the context menu option and arrange the tracks for a clear view.

If you experiment with hovering the mouse you will see you can generate a Page Curl indication on either the left or the right of the cut. Use the left hand one to create a transition on the outgoing shot, pulling it out to roughly 2 seconds. As you do so, watch the thumbnail of the incoming shot. It updates as you adjust the transition to show us what the last clear frame before the transition begins will be. If you think this through, this must mean that the incoming video is being pulled to the left to create the overlap.

When you let go of the mouse button, you may spot that the entire project length as shown in the Navigator gets a little shorter. The duration shown above the Timeline preview player will reduce as well. Studio has created the overlap automatically and the first frame of the incoming clip has been moved left to create the first frame of the dissolve.

If you have adjusted the view sufficiently, the duration box should now appear within the area of the transition. If you adjust the transition again the box will stay visible so instead of typing in an exact duration you can set it to precisely 2 seconds using freehand dragging.

So, in Smart Mode, Studio uses Insert to create an overlap when you create a transition on the Out point of a clip, shortening the duration of the project as a result.

If you create a transition on the In point of a clip, the Smart behaviour is Overwrite. Reset the transition you just created with Undo and hover over the right of the cut. Drag the handle right and create a transition of 2 seconds. The project hasn't changed in duration this time and no clips move on the timeline. Instead, additional video is added to the end of the outgoing clip to create the overlap.

Why does Smart mode have inconsistent behaviour when dealing with In and Out points? If you create a transition on an In point using Insert mode, then the resulting transition is identical to one created on an Out point, so by varying the Smart mode behaviour, you have two choices without having to switch out of Smart or use the Alt key.

Insert mode (top) and Overwrite mode (bottom) when creating transitions

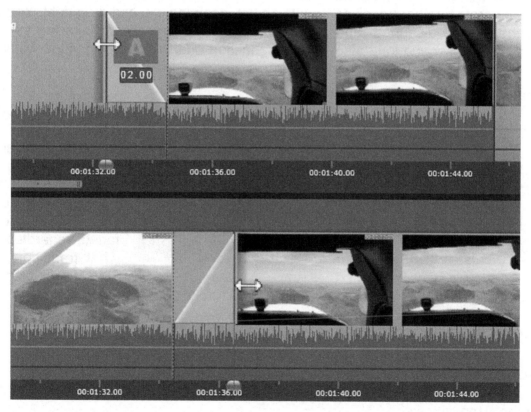

There are many criteria that might affect your placement of transitions. Between these two operations you can create a working transition in most cases. However, in some circumstances you might encounter a problem. Perhaps you don't want to move the clips relative to the timeline because they are synced up with audio on other tracks. However, the default Smart Overwrite option might result in including video that you don't want to see, or may not even exist, resulting in "dead meat". In this case, you can use the ALT key to switch the mode.

Let's say that we want to add a transition in overwrite mode, but if we do so to the In point of the second clip – dragging right - the additional video added from the outgoing clip is unsatisfactory. By holding down ALT and adding a transition to the Out point of the first clip – dragging left - the transition will use frames from the incoming clip to create the overlap. The transition will start and end earlier as a result.

We can also split the transition so it becomes two separate fades – down to black and back up again. In these circumstances, you probably don't want to overlap the video. Reset the video around the edit point so there is no transition. Use ALT drag left to create an overwrite cross fade on the outgoing clip of one second duration, then generate another transition handle on the incoming clip and drag right. You will see the overlap disappear and a **V** shape will have appeared. Make the second transition one second long also. Play the junction and the outgoing video will fade out, followed by the incoming video fading in.

Creating a fade down and fade back up

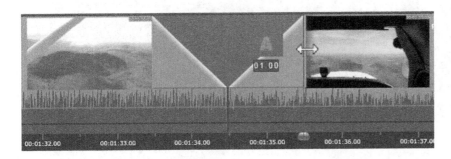

Listen to the audio. It will be clear the sound is also faded in and out. On an overlapped transition the audio will always be cross-faded, regardless of what transition you use. If you want to do anything else, you need to detach the audio tracks as described previously.

Replacing Transitions

There are two ways of replacing the DefaultFade transition with something else. For a full choice of transitions, open a new tab in the compact library and switch it to Content/Transitions.

Here you can browse endlessly for something that takes you fancy. I want to cut to the chase and I've already got an idea for using a "clock" type of wipe because it's one that really tells the viewer time has passed. Rather than browse for a clock wipe, just type the word "clock" in the Compact Library search box and you should see the four that Studio has to offer – I'm going to use the simple Clock wipe in Standard 2D

Transitions. Drag and drop it from the library to exactly on top of the fade out we have created at the end of the Nantlle Ridge clip.

Replacing a transition by dragging a new one from the Library

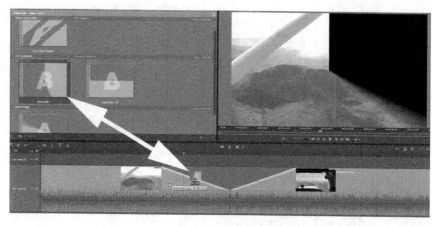

If you preview the result, you will see a classic effect as we transition from the video to the black level underneath. In the titles chapter I'm going to show you how to have another colour other than black as the background by placing a title on the track below, but for now bear in mind that it in actual fact we aren't transitioning to black, but to **transparency** and if there were something below, that would show through.

The vast choice of transitions can be a bit overwhelming, and I mentioned in the Library chapter that you might like to rate some of your favourites with stars to make them easier to filter in the Library. Another technique is to build up collections of transitions. However, Studio recognises that you are likely to normally use a small subset of transitions in most projects and facilitates this with the transition context menu.

Transition Context menu

Right click on the next transition on the timeline – the fade up. Of the two options available, *Find in Library* will be useful if you want to continue to drag and drop the same transition to other parts of the project but have lost track of its location. Hovering over *Transition* opens a submenu, the lowest of which is *Replace by*. Select that and a very helpful box appears. Here you have a choice of the two standard dissolves which are the same effect but achieved by slightly different means, a selection of recently used transitions, and a further list of all the transitions you have given a 5 star rating. All in all a very handy choice. Select Clock wipe from the list of recently used transitions, then preview the result. Between the two transitions we have created a two-stage clock wipe. Maybe it is a bit heavy-handed, but it has allowed me to demonstrate a number of functions!

Using the Transition Context menu to replace a transition

Now I have revealed the Transition Context menu, I need to explain the rest of functions contained in the menu.

Basic Transition editing

Edit allows you to alter a few basic parameters for most transitions. You can alter the duration here, or reverse the direction of some transitions. Some transitions will have an enabled *Edit* button that can access the Hollywood effects or New Blue editors. There is another way to modify some transitions which I will show you later on when we look at transitions in the Effects Editor.

Copy puts the currently selected transition into the copy buffer. You can then paste it to a single highlighted clip or storyboard thumbnail, or to a multi-selection of clips. You can even Copy and Paste between projects.

Whenever you Paste a transition from the paste buffer to the timeline, it is added in Overwrite mode.

Ripple is the traditional Studio way of adding transitions to a group of clips. You need to have selected a group to activate the command. Copy and paste can be used for the same thing now, but Ripple only requires one click.

In NextGen Studio, Ripple adds transitions in Overwrite mode. This can cause issues with overtrimming and you may see frozen frames. In Classic Studio Ripple worked in Insert mode. I'll show you how to add multiple transitions in Insert mode in a moment.

Remove is self-explanatory, and is just one of a number of ways in which you can get rid of transitions. As you cannot multi-select transitions, you might prefer to use the Clip Context menu for this operation – which I will show you next.

Transitions and the Clip context menu

It is worth now looking at the Clip Context menu, where not only is there a further way to add transitions to a project, but where clips that already have a transition have further options.

Open the Clip Context menu for the first peak clip by right-clicking on it and you will see a number of options relevant to Transitions.

In and Out Transition option is available for all clips. Look at the In Transition option and because there already is an In Transition in place you will see you have the ability to *Edit*, *Copy*, *Remove* as well as *Add/Replace by*. These all behave in the same manner as the Transition context menu. The Out Transition option will currently have Edit, Copy and Remove greyed out.

Clip context transition options

If there is no transition, you can *Add* one. Select the *Out Transition Add/Replace* option and you will see the same options as those we

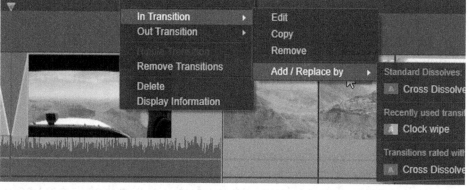

used to replace the DefaultFade with the clock wipe a few pages back. Choose to add a Clock wipe transition and observe the result - with Smart editing selected the transition is added using Insert mode, so that the timeline shortens.

Use Undo to remove the transition. The timeline returns to it's original duration. Let's now select the clip to the left - the shot of the Nantlle Ridge. This doesn't have an In transition. Open the Clip context menu and and add Clock wipe. You will see it has been added in Overwrite.

So, the context menu options for adding In transitions behave in the same manner as other methods of adding. In the Smart mode, adding an In transition - to the right of a cut - works in Overwrite. Adding an Out transition - to the left of a cut - works in Insert.

Leave the new Clock wipe in place. You should now have 4 transitions.

Two further options are available when a transition is part of the selected clip.

Ripple Transition allows you to add multiple copies of the current transition to other clips. It is shown in Clip context menus when there is a transition to ripple, but is greyed out if there aren't further clips highlighted as targets for the ripple effect. If the source clip has both an In and Out transition, you get the choice of which one you ripple. However, Ripple always works in Overwrite mode. I'll show you how it works in a moment.

Remove Transition is also only in evidence when there are transitions to actually remove. As I mentioned before, this will work on multi-selections. Both In and Out transitions are removed.

Transitions and the Storyboard

The **Storyboard** thumbnails also have a right-click context menu that has the same Transition options as the context menu for timeline clips. However, there is no indication of the existence of a transition when you look at the storyboard - you need to glance down to the timeline to see if they exist. Also, it's not possible to alter durations without using the timeline or the Effects Editor (more of which in a moment).

Adding multiple transitions

I've already mentioned two ways of adding transitions to a group of clips. **Ripple** is a convenient way that works well with photos, as it operates in Overwrite mode. If you don't want to shorten the duration of your movie that's very useful, but if you have video clips that don't have any leeway in your movie you can end up with overtrimming and therefore freeze frames.

The Overwrite behaviour also affects the use of **Copy and Paste**. Multi-selecting clips and pasting will work fine with photos, but may give you problems with video.

So, the way to ensure that you aren't in danger of overtrimming any video clip when adding multiple transitions is to use the *Out Transition/Add* clip context menu command. Use the normal window selection tools to highlight all the clips you want to add a transition to the end of, and use the right-click option to select a transition. Your chosen transition needs to be a dissolve, recently used or rated with five stars.

Just to reiterate, if you use the *In Transition/Add* command, you will get Overwrite mode and you might get frozen frames.

Adding transitions from the Library

If you have done any work with transitions in Studio already, you may know that I haven't yet mentioned one of the most obvious ways of adding them to the project. If there isn't a transition at an edit point at all, you can simply drag one from the compact library and drop it on the edit point in the timeline.

With Smart mode on you will get different behaviour depending on which side of the editing point you drop the transition. Drop it on an Out point and you get Insert behaviour – the overlap required by the transition will be created by moving the incoming clip and everything on that track that follows it to the left. Drop it on an In point and you get overwrite behaviour, and the overlap is created by extending the Out point of the outgoing (left-hand) clip, with the attendant risk of adding unwanted material of a frozen frame because there isn't sufficient footage.

Using the ALT key doesn't have quite the same effect as it does when you drag a transition handle. Overwrite mode is forced whichever side of the edit you place the transition. Using ALT and placing the transition on the right of the edit doesn't flip the behaviour back to Insert because you would simple be creating the same transition as if you hadn't used the ALT key and placed it on the left. Smart indeed – because if you want to drag and drop transitions to a project that has assets on other tracks you want to keep in sync, Overwrite is the mode you should use. If you really want to use Insert in these circumstances, refer to the Trimming chapter, page 269 where you will see how to split a trim point for transitions.

Let's explore drag and drop by adding a new transition between the final slow motion close shot of the peak of Snowdon and the Mountain Railway shot. Line that up on the timeline. I'm going to ask you to use a different transition for both variety and to demonstrate another feature later on. Type "peel" into the Compact Library Transition tab search box and Page Peel should be near the top of the list in the 2D-3D category.

Drag it to both the left and then right of the edit point to observe the behaviour. Hold down ALT and continue to drag it around to confirm the Smart behaviour is different as I described. Take particular note of the timeline appearance when the transition is to the left of the cut and you are holding down the ALT key – the "dead meat" coloration appears under the transition slope because there isn't any video available to generate the overlap required, and the program is warning you that you will get a freeze frame instead of moving video. Move the transition to the right of the cut to compare the different appearance.

When you have observed enough, drop the transition on the right of the cut to maximise the amount we see of the slow-motion close-up of the peak. It doesn't matter if you hold down ALT or not. You will have generated a 1 second transition in Overwrite mode. The Page peel allows you to see the burnt-in timecode more clearly to see that the Outgoing video is being extended, and because we used a fixed speed effect then we see extra frames.

What about the duration of the transition? This is normally set to 1 second by default, but you can change the default in Control Panel/Project Setting – if you tend to make gently paced movies a better default choice might be two seconds or more.

Of course you can then go on to alter the duration of a transition using the techniques described in detail earlier – type into the duration box or generate a Transition handle, click and drag. Bear in mind the Insert and Overwrite behaviour when doing the latter.

A word of warning when using this method of adding transitions. If there isn't sufficient space to add a transition of the default duration, Studio will simply refuse to do so, displaying a red cursor. If you have set the default duration quite long, or your movie has lots of short clips, you might think the program has a bug until you realise this. A workround would be to use the next function.

Dynamic Length

You have the ability to add **Dynamic Length transitions** from the compact library by toggling the button on the toolbar. With all the buttons enabled it is the fifth from the right, next to the magnet.

Dynamic Length Transitions Tool

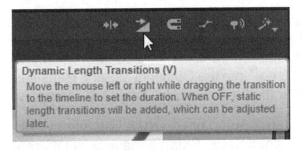

When this mode is active – the button coloured orange – drag and dropping transitions from the Compact Library becomes a freehand style operation. With the timescale set correctly, you can see the duration of the transition you are generating in the small duration box.

Let's add a further transition in this mode. I want to place it on the In point of the shot overlooking Caernarfon Castle. We will use Page Peel again, but this time I want you to enable Dynamic Length transitions. As long as you have the timeline adjusted to a suitable scale it should be very easy to create a 1 second 12 frame transition on the incoming side of the edit (the right).

I find this a useful and efficient way of working when consistent transition duration is less important than lining up transitions with other assets. It is also useful when I'm concerned about what video will be used to create the overlaps. For example, I want the incoming video to be fully visible at a particular frame, but there isn't an inexhaustible amount of video before that point to play with. With a Dynamic Length transition I can add the transition in overwrite, and adjust it so that the duration is as long as I want, without it showing any red shading under the transition slope – all in one operation.

In situations where you want to juggle the timing and positioning of a transition with limitations imposed by the lack of usable footage you can create a transition in one mode and then further adjust it in another.

Have a look at the transition we have just created. Because of the way I've suggested we added the Page Peel - it's effectively extended the Out point we chose so carefully to avoid the zoom - we start to see that zoom in before the transition has completed.

I'd like you to fix this. It is a little tricky and best done with the timeline zoomed in and the magnet off for the greatest accuracy. We are going to now lengthen the transition in Insert mode so we can hide some of the zoom. Generate a transition handle and hold down the ALT key, then lengthen the transition to 3 seconds. When you play back the result, the zoom now starts after the source video has been obliterated by the effect.

Send To Timeline

One method of adding transitions that I haven't demonstrated is that of using the Compact Library Context menu option *Send to Timeline*. I have to admit to not using it much, but if it suits your workflow, it's fairly straightforward to understand. The transition is sent to a position determined by the scrubber - it goes to whichever cut point is nearest. If the scrubber is on a cut point, an In transition is created for the second clip. In Smart mode, Inset or Overwrite behaviour is determined in the same way as if you had dragged the transition there.

The Effects Editor and transitions

It's time to open the Effects Editor. Double click on the Mountain Railway clip, or use the context menu on that clip. You will see a new window that looks quite similar to the Corrections Editor, but with four tabs across the top of the window. By default the clip will open in the Effects tab. Let's not jump ahead yet – switch to the **Transition In** tab to reveal what you can see in the screenshot.

We can now edit the In transition - the Page peel we added earlier.

The controls around the preview are very similar to those we saw in the Corrections Editor. Refer back to that section for an explanation of them if required. The additions you will notice are the names of groups of transitions under the tabs, the Page Peel transition box on the left, a dotted line added below the timescale of the player window, and the Solo button on the toolbar.

The Effects Editor in Transition mode

You can change the type of transition here by selecting one from the groups at the top. Click on *Studio HD Transitions* and a film strip very similar to the Storyboard will appear below the groups. You control this in the same way as well – grab and scroll. Find the Laser transition and click on it and you will see the Page Peel box is replaced with one entitled Laser. This has no options at all, but we will look at other transitions in a moment.

If you look more closely at the dotted line beneath the timescale you will notice a slider on the left. Grab it and slide it right so it is about twice as long as before. We have adjusted the duration of the In Transition.

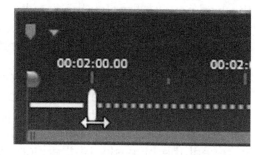

Let's return to the Movie Editor for a moment by clicking OK. Hover over the new transition to check the length, because the slider isn't a very accurate tool. If it isn't exactly 2 seconds and 1 frame (the duration I have), then adjust it exactly using either of the two methods shown before. (As this is an overwritten transition, my 1 frame error won't affect the overall duration of the movie.)

Now return to the Effects Editor by double-clicking the clip and switch to *Transition In* again.

The Navigator in the Effects Editor is very useful. Click on the toolbar to enable it. If the Storyboard is open in the Movie Editor, you will see Thumbnails. Go back and switch off the storyboard, return to the Effects Editor and you won't see the thumbnails we saw in the Corrections Editor, but the same track strips that the Navigator displays in the Movie Editor. You should notice that the current clip is shown as orange. Click on the next clip to the right – and it opens in the Effects Editor, still at the Transition In tab. Very handy, and it will be even more useful if you want to switch between tracks.

Page Peel should be showing as the In Transition. While we have a transition in the editor that has some editable controls, let's use them to refine it. The controls in the box work in exactly the same way as Corrections – you can drag the slider, enter numbers or use the keyboard shortcuts as well as enabling or disabling the various parameters with the small buttons on the right.

The first thing to look for is if any different presets are available in the drop-down box. Page Peel has a number of these but in this instance I'm not going to use any of them. Each transition that is modifiable will have a different range of controls, and I can't itemise every one, but we will use Page Peel as an example. In most cases you should be able to work out what they do from the name, and if in doubt, experiment.

Progress defines how far the transition has occurred when we first see it. Putting a high positive number here will start the transition already in frame. Peel has two parameters that let you change the radius of the curling of the page and it's direction. Edge softness doesn't seem to have much influence on this transition, but in others it is quite effective.

We will alter the Backside parameters – what is on the other side of the Page Peel. By default it is the outgoing video. If you click on the Use Colour checkbox you get a plain colour, but with the 3D highlighting that gives the shiny look to the curl. Check the box now and replay the result. Sometimes I hit a program bug at this point and the whole of the transition isn't modified. If that happens to you, switch to another transition and back to Page Peel and it normally corrects itself.

Black isn't that impressive, really. You can choose another colour by clicking on the Black area beneath the checkbox and using the Colour Selection tool. I will look at how to use that in in detail the chapter that deals with the Title Editor, but for now we can get a nice result by using the Colour Picker tool instead. Progress the transition to reveal the blue sky of the incoming video, click on and hold the Colour Picker (which looks like an eye dropper), drag it a bit of blue sky top left of the viewer, and click. Exit the Effects Editor by clicking OK and test your new transition on the timeline. I think that looks rather neat!

Using the Eyedropper to set the colour of the backside of the transition

Of the Standard Transitions only Barn Doors has any significant options. Some of the others can have their progress and softness altered. 2D-3D and Artistic have some very useful parameters, while Studio HD has none. The final category Add-ons are for third party transitions and the button *Plug-in* will take you to the editing program provided by the third party.

Just to re-iterate – the small editing box that opened when you used the context menu to Edit the transition is no indication that further controls aren't available in the Effects Editor – so if you fancy modifying a transition, you need to look more closely to see what is available.

The Solo button and context menu

Back in the effects editor, **Solo** controls whether we see just the clip we are working on, or any other track at the same point that may have an influence – in the simplest example, an overlaid title. You can also choose to see the transitions on the clip you are editing or not. Some of this is easier to explain with multiple tracks and I will cover the Solo button in further detail when we use it in the Title Editor Chapter.

When the Solo button is engaged, instead of seeing the entire set of layers as shown on the timeline you normally just see the source video. However, when you switch to the In or Out Transition sub-tab, although the Solo button remains engaged you will see the transitions attached to the current clip.

Open the Mountain Railway clip again in the Effects Editor – clicking on the Navigator being the easiest way to do this if the Editor is already open. Switch to In Transition. When the Solo button is on, as you scrub through the clip you will only see the In Transition. Switch it off and and you will also see how the end of the clip is affected by the In Transition of the **next** clip. Look at the dotted line under the timescale and you will see that it actually becomes solid when that transition is in progress. Because that transition belongs to the next clip, we cannot alter the duration here, as we did with the first transition.

Click on Solo again to turn it on and then open the options with the small drop-down arrow – you will see a choice of 4, but the reference to "tracks below" isn't relevant at the moment. With "Shows media only" selected we can have a look at the end to see how much of that bad zoom in is actually being used as overlap for the incoming transition, but isn't really visible because of the type of transition we have used. This is where we marked the clip way back when I was showing you the Corrections editor, and the Marker is still in place.

Switch to "show media and transition" and we will see the incoming transition from the next clip even though Solo is on.

The *Transition In* and *Out* tabs can be selected even if no such transition exists. Open the last clip of the movie in the Effects Editor (you can use the Navigator) and select Transition Out. You will see a slider handle. I want you to add a one second fade to the end of the movie – but instead of trying to drag accurately, try the following. Open the Standard Transitions at the top of the editor, scroll along to Dissolve GPU and click – yet another way to add a transition! The duration is determined by the default value in the Control Panel. Quit the Editor with OK and you will find a fade out on the timeline.

Studio won't normally let you open the Transition Out tab if a clip is being used as overlap material for a transition by the next clip, and the same principle applies to Transition In of a clip that follows another with an Out Transition. I have managed on occasions to enable this situation with odd results, but I can't reproduce the problem consistently.

We have finished adding transitions for now. If you want to check you haven't missed any, your project should have 6 in total (or 7, if you count the Fade in/out as two!) and the project duration should be **00:03:25.08** with the scrubber on the frame after the video.

Save the project now with a new name - Flight Project stage 2. If you want to be sure of complying exactly with my version, you can load that from the data DVD or the website.

Corrections in the Effects Editor

The second sub-tab in the Effects Editor is Corrections. This is how you can access corrections you have already made or add new corrections at the clip level on the timeline. The function behaves in exactly the same way as the main version in the Corrections Editor, but the changes you make are applied only to the clip itself and not the entire source file.

If you open the Mountain Railway clip and switch to Corrections/Enhance you will see the Image corrections parameters that we added earlier. If you want to have a further go as tweaking the clip you can do it here.

If you decide to use Stabilize but have already rendered the stabilize data, doing so from here is quick and easy. Open the required clip by using the navigator, then open the Stabilize sub-tab. Check the small button after the effect name, click Render and Play and you should see the effect straight away. Click on OK to return to the project, and you will see a green corrections indicator has been added to the project.

Effects in the Effects Editor

To open any clip on the timeline in the Effects Editor you can use the right-click context menu. Unless the clip happens to be a Title or a Project, this is also the default action when you double click. If you want to add an effect to a Title you have to use right-click. In all cases, the Editor opens with the Effects sub-tab open, showing that this is the main event and the other tabs are a sideshow.

Open the 6th clip on the timeline – the exterior shot of the take-off – in the Effects Editor. You will see all the familiar controls from the Corrections Editor, but with a different strip of sub-tabs at the top. These divide the available effects into useful subcategories. Open the first one, 2D-3D effects.

In general this category alters the position, shape and size of the video. There are many variations and you can preview the effects by hovering your mouse over the effect thumbnail and see it applied to the main preview window. One of the most useful effects for manipulating video is here, 2D Advanced Editor. Clicking on the thumbnail adds the effect to the video and opens the parameter box to the right of the preview window. Please do that now and you will see the preset 2D Advanced Editor effect added to the clip, squeezing the video into a smaller, tilted box with soft edges positioned to right of the screen.

The 2D Editor Advanced effect added

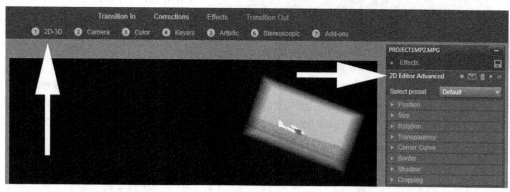

Now reopen the 2D-3D category and move your mouse over to the Flip GPU effect. Notice that the Flip is added to the current effect rather than replacing it. Click on that effect as well and then take a look at the right side of the preview window. Two effects are shown, because it is possible to stack up more than one effect on a clip. At the top we now have Flip, and down at the bottom 2D Advanced. Open the 2D Advanced parameters by clicking and the Flip box closes but the parameters are still being added.

The Flip effect also added

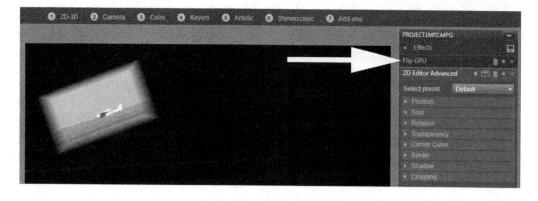

The order in which these effects are applied can be very important in many cases. To change the order, grab the tab on the far right of the 2D effect and drag it up the list so it is above the Flip effect. When you release the strip, the effect order is reversed and the video is flipped *before* it is resized and moved, giving a different result.

Changing the order of the effects alters the result

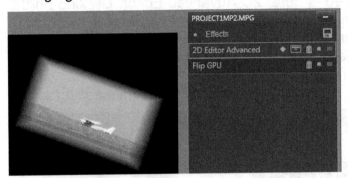

The enable/disable button is next on the left on the effects strip, allowing you to turn off an effect without removing it from the list. One more to the left is a trash can, which you can use to get rid of the effect entirely from the list. Do that now with the Flip effect to remove it.

Now click on the fourth button from the right on the 2D effects strip. This expands all the parameters so you can see everything that can be altered. If you have a large screen they may all fit in the window, but if not you can use the scroll bar on the right.

The icons controlling each effect

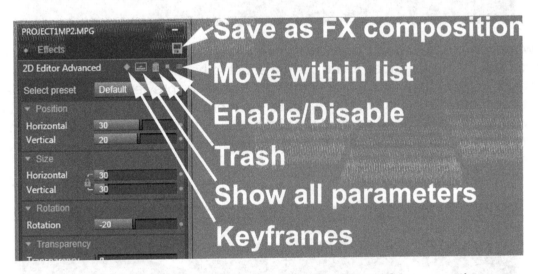

Again, the controls here can be used in the same variety of ways as those we saw in Corrections. Hover over the value 30 in the Size Horizontal slider, click to get an entry field and enter 50. Notice that the removable lock with the Vertical parameter means that it changes to 50 as well, retaining the correct shape. Drag Edge softness down to 0. Click to select the Border width, then use the PageUp and Down keys plus the arrow left and right keys to set it to 1.5. Set the Position to Horizontal 0 by double clicking on the parameter name. That's the variety of ways to control parameters. Also set Vertical to 30 and the Rotation to 0.

Having spent a little time setting up a new set of parameters, it is possible to save them as a new effect. The floppy disc icon at the top of the effects list opens up a box where you can select which of the currently used effects to include and what name you want to call the new FX Composition. Give it the name 2D Top Centre then click on Save.

Casting your eye to the sub-tabs above, you will now see a new category, My FX Compositions. Have a look and you will see it contains the effect you just saved! Now close the Effect Editor to return to the timeline.

The saved custom effect will appear in a new category

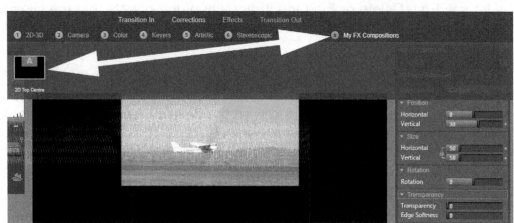

The clip we have just edited now sports a pink bar along its top edge. This shows it has an effect added. Studio provides a separate context menu for effects. If you hover over the pink line – and you need to be quite accurate – an *fx* cursor appears. Right click and bring up the context menu. However, you can also reach the effects menu using the Clip context menu.

The fx cursor

If you are wondering why the only main entry in the *FX* menu is Effect, that is because the same menu caters for Corrections as well, so if a clip had both a Correction and an Effect added, you could choose which you work with. We saw earlier that the options for Corrections are quite limited, but for Effects they are much more powerful.

The FX context menu

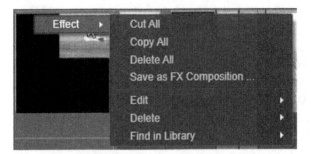

We can **Cut**, **Copy** or **Delete All** the effects on a clip. Cut or Copy obviously leads to the conclusion that we can Paste, and if you put an effect into the paste buffer with either Cut or Copy, opening up a clip Context menu and using Paste will add the effect to the new clip.

Of course, multi-selection of clips will allow you to paste the same effect to a series of clips in the same way as pasting transitions. This is a useful point to remember for the times you might be adding an effect to a number of clips.

You can save the clips effects as a Composition from there as well and the final two options let you Edit, Delete or Find In Library any of the effects that the clips have added to them on an individual basis. Note that you can't find saved compositions using this last command.

Let's just take a break from the Effects Editor for a moment to discuss adding effects from the Compact Library. Open a new tab, select Content and *fx Effects*. From here you can drag and drop any effect to a clip on the timeline, even one of your saved compositions. It's also a much more convenient place to browse for effects because of the Library's organisation tools. Most of the thumbnails give a good idea of what an effect does, and if that effect is animated in some way you can play the effect in the preview window.

Artistic effects are mostly obvious, but there are a few effects that don't otherwise have a home that you will find here. The oddest in my opinion is De-interlace, which is an effect to change video from interlace to progressive. Some of the effects could also be put in **Camera** which also contains some effects that could be in Artistic or even 2D/3D. I suppose what I'm suggesting is that you might want to browse for effects rather than expecting them to be in what you consider to be the most logical place. **Colour** contains technical and artistic effects that alter colour, and includes the powerful Image Correction tool that we have already met in the Corrections section of this chapter. **Keying** contains Chromakey and Lumakey for when you want to Overlay foreground video over another background – most notably used for green screen effects. Slightly oddly, I think, there is also a Transparency effect in this category.

If you have the Ultimate version of Studio, you will also have a whole bunch of New Blue (and Red Giant plug-ins if you have owned earlier versions of Ultimate and transferred them across). Many of these will give you hours of endless fun, others offer very subtle artistic enhancements. Many people get so enthralled by the power they seem to stop making movies at all and just learn to use these effects.

I skipped over Audio effects. Obviously when you try to use these in the Effects Editor, you need to select Audio from the top left tabs. There are a few differences between audio corrections and effects – Equalizer, De-esser are common to both, but you don't have compression and expansion tools as effects. The Channel tool and leveller are the same as those available in the Channel mixer box to the left of the preview window. The remaining tools add effects of a more artistic nature. Stereo Spread and Grungelizer have their own Plug-In buttons to open a separate interface.

Keyframing effects

You will notice that a lot of the preset effects actually move. This is controlled by **Keyframing**, a powerful way of changing the parameters of an effect over time.

Turning on Keyframing

There are many effects that can be very nicely enhanced with the use of keyframing, and there are also many situations where you can use a combination of effects and keyframes to build up something quite spectacular. I'm going to use a very obvious example within the project to show how you use keyframes. Once you know how to manipulate them, great possibilities open up.

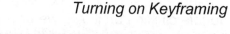

Open up the take-off clip in the Effects Editor again. Put the scrubber at the start of the clip. Currently keyframing is not enabled. To do so, click on the small diamond icon to the right of the effect name.

You will see the addition of 3 small keyframe controls to the left of the markers button, and a line will have appeared below the scrubber with a new

The keyframe controls

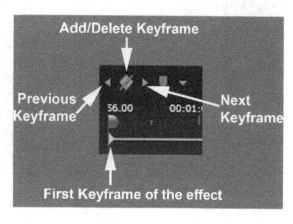

diamond shaped keyframe beneath the line of the scrubber.

Before I talk through the use of the controls, let me tell you the final result I want to achieve. The video will start full frame. After a short pause I'm going to zoom the video to the position it is in now, hold it there for a while, then zoom it back to full frame.

One keyframe isn't any use at all, so let's set another one. If you were going to be efficient, you would set them with precision to begin with, but because I want to show you how to modify them later, I'm just going to put them in approximate positions for now.

Move the scrubber to the 1 minute 04 second mark on the timescale. Clicking on the white diamond button to the left shows you the first way of setting a keyframe. When you do so, the parameters in the box are applied to the video frame at the keyframe.

We still haven't really achieved anything, but bear with me! Move the scrubber to the 1 minute 00 second mark. Now alter a parameter in the box – set Vertical to 0 by double clicking on it. Ah, we now have three keyframes. Touching one of the sliders when we aren't over an existing keyframe adds a new one. While you are here, reset Size to 100 and Border width to 0.

Three keyframes set

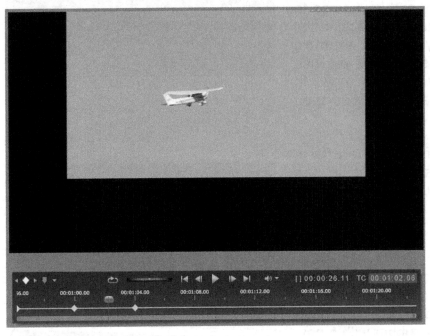

You can move the scrubber between keyframes with the small arrowheads either side of the button we use to add a keyframe. You will see that the first keyframe is still causing the video to be squeezed to the top, which we don't want. There are normally two ways to delete a keyframe - the small context menu you get by right-clicking on a keyframe, or using the keyframe button when it has a line through it, showing you that the scrubber is over a keyframe and it will delete, rather than add.

Unfortunately, you can't delete the keyframe at the start of an effect. We would normally have set this one first, but I'm being inefficient, as I said. Let's manually set its parameters to the same as the second keyframe.

Play the video clip using the controls under the preview window. That's a start. Now we want the video to zoom out again. To do this, let's try copy and paste.

Keyframe context menu 1

Hover exactly over the first or second keyframe (they should have the same values) and right click. *Copy keyframe* should be available, so select it. Now move the mouse to the 1 minute 12 second mark and carefully right click on the white line on which the other keyframes sit. The scrubber should move there and two options will present themselves.

Keyframe context menu 2

We could Create a keyframe (the same action as clicking the diamond button) or Paste the one in the paste buffer. Choose the paste option.

Check the video again. You will see because of my inefficiency, I've yet to cause the video to hold in the zoomed in position. We need another keyframe between 3 and 4 with the same value as keyframe 3. Use copy and paste to do that, placing it at I minute 8 seconds. When your keyframe line looks like the screenshot, exit the Effects Editor with OK and preview the effect on the timeline.

Next, I want to place some video **under** the exterior take-off shot. For this I'm going to use the interior take off-shot. Check that the magnet is on, then use CTRL drag and drop to place a copy of clip 5 immediately below it on track 3. Use Quick trim to extent it right so that the Out point lines up with the end of clip 6 on the track above. For the sake of tidiness, tighten the In point in the same way so it lines up with the start of clip 6. We now have the exterior shot *continuing* on track 3. It is actually in sync as well. If you want to check this, make a temporary trim to the In point of clip

6 on track 2, creating a gap. When you play past the cut point, you won't see a jump. Fix the gap and have another look at the effect.

Clip 5 extended on a track below clip 6

That's quite a nice effect, but I think you will agree the timing could be a bit better. It would be good to cover up the underlying shot a bit earlier, so the pan back to the cockpit doesn't register so much.

To do this accurately, we can go back into the Effects Editor to move some of the keyframes. As you scrub through the clip, you don't see the underlying video if the Solo button has been engaged. Switch it off, and you can see the interior shot as you scrub through.

You can drag the keyframes around, but on older computer using this effect requires so much computer power that I don't get a smooth preview update. Try loosening the last point by dragging it left to see if your computer is any better at this. In some circumstances with some effects this will be the way to alter keyframes, but not in this instance.

Look at the underlying video's burnt in timecode as you scrub through. The pan back to the cockpit starts at 00:04:23:00. Line the scrubber up to that point and drop a marker. Now carefully drag the last keyframe - the fifth from the left - to line up with it. If you want more accuracy, zoom the timescale of the preview window in a bit with the scrollbar below it.

I want you to check how well you have lined things up, because it gives me a chance to show how useful the navigator can be in multitask situations. Open the navigator using the toolbar button. Put the scrubber on the newly moved keyframe, then click on the blue clip below the currently selected orange clip. Select Solo. The preview switches to that track but the scrubber stays in the same place. If you have done the job accurately, the burned in timecode should be the target I set – 4 minutes 23 seconds 00 frames.

Check the effect again. The zoom speeds are a bit mismatched. I moved the second keyframe from the left - the one that controls the start of the zoom out - to the left so it lines up with 00:04:15:00 on the underlying video. The five keyframes need to be at 00:56:05, 01:02:09, 01:04:00, 01,08:00 and 01:10:09 to work with further projects in this book.

Watch the effect full screen, by switching off Solo and using the full screen icon on the Effects Editor toolbar. I think the border looks a bit distracting because if flickers and the solution to this is to make it thicker. Use the techniques I've just shown you to step through all the keyframes, including the very first one, and alter the border value to 5.

One last thing to look at with the Effects Editor open. If you open up all the parameters using the Expand All tool, as you scrub through the video you can see the settings change. This is a good indication of how the values alter. If the setting has a different value between each keyframe, it changes gradually from one value to another over the time between the keyframes. If you want a setting to suddenly jump, this is possible, but you need to put two keyframes just one frame apart.

There is one submenu in the Effects Editor that only appears when the source is a photo – Pan and Zoom. We will look at this in detail in a later chapter where I make an example slideshow.

Fixing the project audio

I'm going to do three things to the audio on the project. Most will be familiar to you if you have completed the first project, so for a more detailed description those of you who skipped that part of the book might want to refer back. I'm going to just describe the steps.

Right click on clip 5 and Detach Audio.

Extend the detached audio track using quick trim to the start of the project and the end of clip 6.

Open the mixer panel and reduce the clip volume for the detached audio on track 2 to -6dB.

Mute the audio on the video section of tracks 2 and 3.

Make sure Magnetic snapping is on and drag a fade up at the start of the detached audio track to match the video fade up. At the end of the audio clip drag a fade down to the left so that it clicks into place with the clip marker we added to the take-off shot in the Effects Editor.

Go to the end of the movie and mark the point that the plane's wheels hit the tarmac (00:10:10:08 BITC) with a marker. Open a Compact Library tab at Sound effects and search for "skid". Drag the effect from the Vehicles category to the detached audio track and line the start of the clip up with the marker you just set.

Using the Surround/Stereo Panner

I'm just going play with the Stereo Panner briefly. If you don't have a way of monitoring stereo on you computer, you might want to use a pair of headphones for this trick. Scrub through video and put another marker at the point where the plane becomes level. The plane obviously touched down firstly on its right wheel, so I'm going to pan the sound effect to enhance that impression.

The first keyframe added to pan the sound effect right

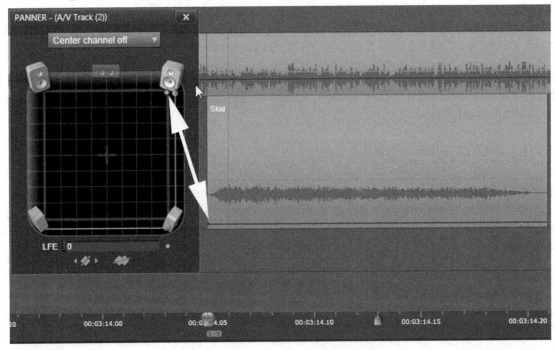

Open the Audio Mixer with the toolbar icon, make the sound effect track active, move the scrubber to the start of the sound effect, and then click on the Surround/Stereo panner. I've dragged the panner to the timeline to make a more compact screenshot. Now move the scrubber to the start of the skid effect and grab the blue dot at the top centre of the panner all the way to the right as shown.

You should be familiar enough with keyframes now to recognise what is happening here. The blue line has moved to the bottom of the track display, indicating that the sound is panned to the right. If you look closely you will see a small blue dot - a keyframe - at the start of the track.

Now progress the scrubber to the marker I just got you to put down. This is where the left wheel will touch the ground, so now crank the blue dot all the way over to the top left. Another keyframe is created and the blue line goes as high up the track display as it can. Now to the end and return the blue dot in the panner window to the centre.

Play the effect and see what you think. It made me laugh the first time I heard it!

If you decide to use the Surround sound features of Studio, you can use the panner to control track positioning The panner has a drop-down menu that controls the Surround options. 5.1 Surround Sound consists of five normal channels and one Low Frequency Effect channel. Four channels give left/right and front/rear positioning. The fifth normal channel is normally behind the cinema screen because that is where the dialogue normally comes from. The LFE channel is used for all those scary effects when the alien spacecraft lands or the shells start landing in the the movies. Because low frequency bass is difficult to locate the position of, it doesn't really matter where the speaker is - and that's why you can put the subwoofer for your theatre audio system anywhere in the room.

We can use the blue dot to position the current track within the left/right/back/front image. The drop-down menus can be used to channel the output of the current track to the centre channel, use it as part of the surround image, or ignore it's presence. The fader at the bottom controls how much of the track audio is sent to the LFE channel.

Finally, some music…

Adjust the timeline view to see all the project and all the tracks. Select the currently empty track 4, put the scrubber at the start of the movie and then Select All (CTRL-A) to highlight the whole project.

Open the Scorefitter window by using the toolbar icon shaped like a treble clef. You may want to browse for something you like, but I suggest *Inspirational/I'm Home at Last/In My Element*. When you have chosen your music or accepted my suggestion, click *Add to Movie.*

When you first play the movie, you may have to wait for the Scorefitter music to render. Preview the movie and see what you think. Ask someone else to view it for a second opinion.

I'm not claiming this to be anywhere near a finished project. There is a lot of work we could do. In the next chapter I'm going to show you how to use the Title Editor to add information, a bit of animation and do a bit more keyframing.

However, if you aren't bored with the footage yet, there is a lot more you can experiment with. Different transitions, perhaps more of them, would be worth looking at. Further corrections to the shots would be worthwhile. There are a lot of shots that don't colour match, particularly when when you look at the peak of Snowdon. If you want to browse through some of the add-ons you could give the entire movie a more filmic look. There are many shots where you could use the stabiliser. The sound could be a lot more elaborate if you used the source audio for more shots before the take-off and adjusted levels with volume keyframing. The list is almost endless and you could spend almost as long finessing the project as you have done creating it.

Save the project in its current form anyway to use in the next chapter. Call it *Flight project stage 3*. You might want to add the titles before you make any more improvements, so you can follow the next chapter exactly.

The Title Editor

Pinnacle Studio 19 boasts an extremely powerful Title Editor. It can produce multi-layered motion titles that can also include assets from the Compact Library.

Before we get carried away with its power, I'm just going to add a very simple title to our Flight project to introduce you to using the editor at its most basic. The aim is to add a plain looking lower third caption at the start of the project telling us what the movie is called.

Prior to opening the editor to create a new title, it's always a good idea to decide what track you want to add the title to. If you don't, then after creating a title and closing the editor, it will be placed on the currently active track at the current scrubber position – which may disrupt your project. Most titles will be overlaid over other video or photo sources, and Studio tries to persuade you not to use Track 1 for video. Unlike Classic Studio, the track order for overlay is top to bottom, so if a track is above another, its content will be overlaid on top of the tracks below. Placing a full frame video on Track 1 will obliterate everything below.

So for most projects, you should leave Track 1 clear for your titles. If you haven't done so, you will need to create an empty track at the top of the pile. The quickest way to do this is using the Track header context menu command *Insert New Track/Above*.

With the *Flight Project Stage 3* loaded, highlight Track I and move the scrubber to 2 seconds in so that it lines up with the end of the fade up on Track 2. (If you haven't made the project, either load it from the website or data DVD, or practice on any other video of your choice).

Now we want to *Create Title*, and there are two paths to this function. You can click on the T icon on the Timeline toolbar, or use the keyboard shortcut CTRL-5. Either way the Title Editor should open.

Hopefully the appearance of the Title Editor (shown overleaf) has a degree of familiarity. It's a cross between a Movie and an Effects Editor. The Compact Library is top left as usual and is identical in function to the one in the Movie Editor. The lower part of the screen has a timeline style area with control icons above and below, many of which will be familiar.

In the centre a preview window has a text box pre-populated with the words "Your Text Here". The background will be the video track underneath. Solo OFF was made the default in Studio 17. For clarity, turn it on - it's bottom right if you haven't seen it yet.

The Title Editor

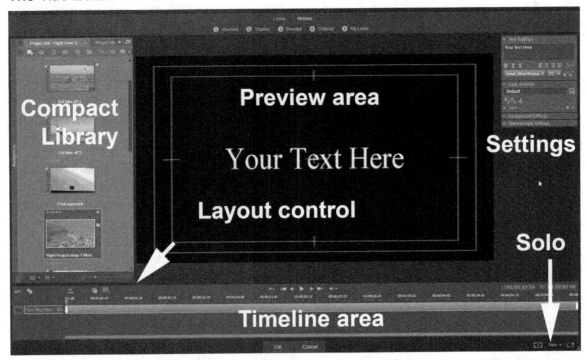

To the right is a *Text Settings* box that resembles an effects or corrections control panel. Above the timeline area and between the Compact Library and Preview Window is an inverted T that controls the sizes of the areas in the same manner as we can resize the Movie Editor.

The first title moved into position

If your first action is to just start typing, the *Your Text Here* text disappears and you are presented with a flashing cursor. If that doesn't work in clearing the box, click on the end of the text and delete it. Type the text **A Flight Over Snowdon** into the box but don't press Enter – hover your mouse over the border of the box and a 4-way arrow will appear. Drag the text box down so that it lines up with the lower inner frame line and release it there.

If you want to accurately align the title box with an object and the mouse isn't giving you enough accuracy, when it is selected (**not** the text within it) the keyboard arrow keys can be used to "inch" the title box around a pixel at a time. You won't use this feature very often, but in some circumstances it will be very useful.

Wrap text on and off

The nodes around the edges can be used to **resize** the text box. How the text behaves is controlled by the Wrap Text tool.

With this control on, the text retains its font size and your control of the text box will be limited – you can change the shape but the area will stay the same, and the text will re-wrap itself to fit in the box. Switch the control off and the text will resize itself to fit the box, even to the extent of altering the height of the text without altering the width or

vice versa, therefore changing the aspect ratio. The corner nodes maintain the aspect ratio of the box, but if you grab the sides the shape will change.

What is more, switching between the two modes allows you to resize the text, then alter the box aspect ratio to change the way the text wraps. It's one of those features that is much clearer with a little experimentation, I suggest you do just that now!

The Title Tools

Above the box in the centre is another node that allows you to **rotate** the box as well. Try these features out, but return the text box to its original size, shape and angle using Undo before proceeding.

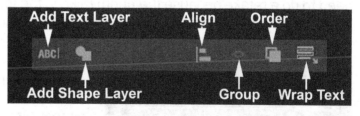

Alternatively, you can simply delete the layer with the Delete key while the frame - not the text - is selected.

To add a new text box once the editor is open, you use the **ABC** tool on the bar above the timeline on the far left. The other tools will be introduced as we need them.

I know there are a dozen things you might want to change, and I'll show you them all soon, but we have already created the simple lower third title. How is it going to look over the underlying video?

Moving the title with the background enabled

Click on Solo again to deactivate it and the video on the other tracks will appear. If you are using the project, you can now see that the title might be in danger of overlapping the plane's wheels. It would benefit from being a bit lower, so drag it down a bit and then click on Solo again to see where it sits relative to the frame lines. By sitting the bottom of the text on the inner line, with the bottom of the "g" overhanging, we should get the best result.

Safe Areas

What are those frame lines for anyway? A long time ago, broadcasters defined what are known as "safe areas". Because early TV sets were set to **overscan**, and some overscanned considerably more than others, two areas were defined. The outer frame is the area that any important action should be contained within. The inner frame is where any text that the viewer is expected to be able to read should be placed. It was even deemed that some objects you *shouldn't* see could be included if they were in the very outer area. I distinctly remember a sit-com director decreeing that we didn't need to do a retake because the boom mike in the top of shot "was well within cut-off". 20 years later when I watched the show on DVD the boom was clearly visible.

Safe Areas

Modern TVs and the habit of watching video on computers mean that the "safe areas" are a bit of an anachronism. Most people see almost, or even completely,to the very edge of the frame. However, artistically you might consider it isn't a good idea to put important information right on the edge of a composition anyway, so they are still a good rule of thumb.

Incidentally, if you have no intention of taking any notice of the safe areas, or if you find that they are cluttering your view, they can be switched on and off with the control to the left of the Solo button on the toolbar at the bottom of the editor window.

Titles on the timeline

Click on OK at the bottom of the Title Editor window and it closes, but deposits the title on the track and at the cursor position we set before we entered the editor. Check out the result by playing the video. The first thing that immediately becomes apparent to me is that the title duration is too short. It has taken on the default duration as defined in Control Panel/Project settings – the default is 3 seconds. A broadcaster's rule of thumb for a title is that it should be on screen for you to be able to read it out loud twice, so it fails this test.

A title behaves on the timeline in almost exactly the same way as any other asset. All the editing functions treat a title in an identical manner to video, photos or audio. The only difference I can find shows in the context menu, more of which in a moment.

To extend our title, just use a simple Quick trim to extend the Out point of the title to line up with the cut at the end of the first video clip. It should now be over 11 seconds long, and neatly disappear at the end of the first shot.

Before we return to the wonders that await us in the Title Editor, it is worth noting that many of its powerful features aren't the only way of treating titles. For example, while we can add **Motions** using the editor, if all you want is a simple fade up or down or alter the timing of a title it is often easier to do it on the timeline.

Let's do that right now. You could use any of the techniques we explored in the previous chapter. I'm going to suggest finding the Dissolve CPU transition in the compact library (don't forget the search box if you haven't rated it with 5 stars) and drag that – with dynamic length transitions switched off – to the start of the title. You could also consider using the right-click context menu to add an In transition – you might find it quicker.

Having added a fade up to the title, I'm going to change my mind. I've decided the title would look better if it fades up at the same time as the video clip. This is where using transitions can be much more convenient than Motions. Quick trim the In point left to line up with the beginning of the project.

If this is the first time you have tried this on a multi-track project, notice that it is possible to push the whole of the project to the right so we could start the title even before the video. Now generate a transition handle at the end of the title fade up and trim it right to line up with the end of the video transition. Transitions need not be limited to using dissolves. I find that the Push transitions can look very effective, for example.

The title on the timeline

Another tool to consider when you want to manipulate titles is the Effects Editor. If you double-click on a title it opens in the Title Editor, but if you right-click the Context menu offers you the Effects Editor as an option. Anything you can do with video, you can do to titles – including keyframing. You can also add some really neat third party effects if you have them in your version of Studio. More about adding effects later.

Even the need to have multi-layered titles with different motions need not always force you into the Title Editor because there is nothing to stop you adding as many timeline tracks above the main video as you require. However, the more complex the title the more likely it will be that the Title Editor is the place to develop it.

Titles and the Library

Studio comes with a vast array of pre-made titles. They are stored in the Library and can be dragged to the timeline just like any other asset. The Title Editor also has the menu options to *Save* or *Save Title as...* so you can save any titles you make yourself in the My Titles Library location – a location which can be defined in Setup/*Control Panel/Storage locations*. You can treat the pre-made titles as templates, because even if they don't quite fit the bill for your current project, it is often easier to get a professional looking title by modifying a pre-existing one than starting from scratch. If you are browsing titles, consider using the Main Library, from where you can double click on a title and go straight to the Title Editor.

Back to the Editor

Having tried to persuade you that you don't need to use the Title Editor for anything too complex, there are still a few functions that you will have to use it for – changing the font, its size and the text appearance, accurate positioning – and adding certain motions that can't be done with effects or transitions. Let's return to the editor and work our way through the essential functions first before we get carried away with the bells and whistles. Open the "A Flight Over Snowdon" title in the editor by double clicking on it. You will need to scrub down the timeline a little, or switch on Solo, to see the title. Now turn your attention to the right of the preview window

Text Settings

At the very top of the text setting box is a text entry field that will contain the currently selected text. If it is showing up as empty, click on the text box in the preview window. Now you know what text you are modifying, sure, but this text entry box has other uses because you can modify or completely change the text with it. This may seem like duplication because you can do that in the preview window, but when a title gets complex, particularly when using the Roller or Crawl motions, this box could come to your rescue. Entering or editing the text here is less resource hungry, so if the Title Editor becomes slow or even unstable consider using this box.

Setting the Font

Our title should be using the font Times New Roman as the default. You will see the font name in the next box down. Open the drop-down menu and you should be able not only to see a list of fonts, but the names will be in the style of the font. The text you wish to change needs to be highlighted, so ensure that the whole title is selected before choosing the Arial font. Yes I know, I'm just swapping one boring font for another, but trust me.

Notice that when you swap fonts, the text size on the screen can vary significantly. You can resize your text on screen, but it is a good idea to get the correct font size so that no significant recalculation is required. Set the Font size to 60. Alongside the font type, you can also select a specific font size from the drop-down box or use "Larger" or "Smaller" buttons to alter the size a step at a time.

Text Flow options

In between the two boxes is a row of text formatting tools. Bold, Italic and Underline should be obvious. Highlight the title text and select Bold to make the text a bit stronger. Note that you don't have to apply these attributes to a whole text box – they just get applied to the section of text that is highlighted. To the right of the attributes are the choices of justification - left, centre, right and justify. When the text neatly fills the box it is in, as is currently the case, you won't see any difference. Once you start to use multi-line titles by using the Enter key, you will appreciate these controls.

The final control on that line alters the text flow. You can produce some fun effects here as well as it being useful for other forms of writing.

Looks

Below the text settings, there is a box of parameters which define the **Look** of the text. This is the colour and appearance of the text, including any edges or shadows. Studio has a very large range of predefined Looks and we access these from the Looks tab at the top of the window, which contains five categories. When you open the categories, you get the same film strip type of interface we have seen in the Effects Editor. Have a browse through what is available – from the subtle to the outright garish. You will be able to preview the effect in the preview window. I'm going for something that will just help the title stand out when it is superimposed over bright parts of the picture, a Look in Standard Effects called **Medium Edge**. When you find it, click to apply. If you deselect the Solo button and scrub through the title, you can see how it helps define the text when the fire engine is in the lower foreground.

Medium Edge

I'm going to suggest a little modification of the Look as a way of explaining how they are built up. The Medium edge setting consists of two components – one **Face** and one **Edge**. It's also possible to have a **Shadow**. As a general principle a Face is in the foreground, an Edge is behind a face but is a little bigger so that a bit of it pokes out around the edge, and a Shadow is behind them both but offset a little so it gives the effect of being a shadow on a "wall" behind. The shadow effect is enhanced if it is slightly transparent. So, in theory a Face doesn't need to have its size or offset changed, but Studio doesn't discriminate and offers the same set of variable parameters to each text layer. In fact, the different types are only there as a starting guide because you can rename them and alter the order of the layers.

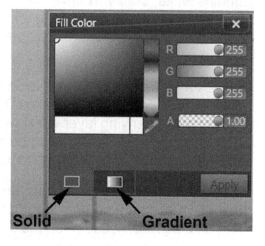

Underneath the name of the current look are three icons that let you add additional text layers. If you click on the left hand icon (with the tooltip *Add Face Detail*) a new layer Face 2 is added to the top of the list. Crank the Offset sliders around and you will see it move, allowing the other layers beneath to show through. Experiment by setting X to 1, Y to -1, Size to 110 and Blur to 25. That's a pretty rubbish looking effect but I'm going to make it look worse before I make it better.

The Colour Selection box

The Colour Selection Box

For the next stage to be obvious, I want to change the colour of Face 2. I mentioned the colour selection box earlier in the book, but now it is time to look at it in detail.

Click on the Fill box of the Face 2 parameter set and the Colour Selection box appears. The selection box is moveable, so left click on the header and hold the button down, then drag it away from the stack and put it up to the top of the preview area.

Solid   Gradient

Any colour that can be displayed on a TV or computer can be created by mixing three primary colours of Red, Green and Blue. The range of values is from 0 to 255 for each primary. These values can be controlled with the top three sliders on the right of the box. The resultant colour is displayed in the rectangle above the button I've labelled as *Solid* in the screenshot. Make sure that is selected for now – gradients will be covered in a moment. Keep an eye open for a scroll bar. If the menus are getting too big, these tabs are at the bottom of this menu.

You can adjust the sliders with the mouse, or type in values. With all three set to zero you get black, and with all three set to 255 you get white. Every other possible shade can be generated by a combination of the three values. If you look at the bottom slider, Studio provides a clue as to what will happen if you lower the value for Blue – the white will start to move towards yellow.

All the controls are interactive. The larger rectangle at the top left of the box has a dot you can drag up and down to affect the **Brightness**, left and right to affect the **Saturation**. Between this and RGB sliders is a **Hue** control. Alter the Hue, Brightness or Saturation and the RGB sliders move as well.

Because of the way the colours are displayed within the controls, you don't really need to work out which value you need to change to achieve your desired colour – one of the settings should be displaying a colour which is in the direction you want to move.

There is no real substitute for just moving the controls around to help you understand how they interact. When you have finished, create a solid pure blue colour and click apply.

The area that shows the applied colour hasn't all turned blue – a patch to the right remains white, so if you have made a mistake you can revert to the original colour just by clicking here. Not that useful if it used to be white, but if you were making subtle changes and decided you preferred the previous choice this makes it easier to undo.

There is a further slider below the RGB controls that controls **Alpha**, which would be better understood if it were called Transparency or Opacity. This determines how much of the underlying layer will show through. 0 is completely transparent, 1 is solid. Set it to 0.5. This value can also be set in the Looks settings when you are dealing with Solid colours, so you need not decide right away how much you might need.

While we are studying the Colour Selection Box it is worth looking at Gradients. With this tool you can define how the colour changes over the area to which it is applied. Click on the gradient button on the bottom right and a new bar appears at the bottom of the box. Two cursors are initially set to the left and right of the bar, and if you click on one and select a new colour you will see the gradient appear. To the right is a direction control, and when you rotate it the angle at which the gradient will appear on the screen changes.

The Gradient Controls

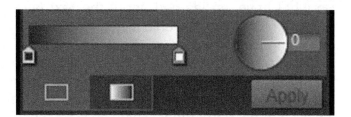

Finally, you can alter the position of the cursors, which changes where the gradient starts and ends. The closer together you place the cursors, the more abrupt the gradient. You can also create more cursors. I'll use the Gradient control later in the chapter.

Moving Blue Shadow

The final tool is the Colour Picker, which looks like an eyedropper tool. We used this in the previous chapter to change the colour of the Page Peel. When you have finished experimenting reset the Face 2 colour to a solid R=0, G=0 B= 255 and A=50, *Apply* the colour and close the Selection box.

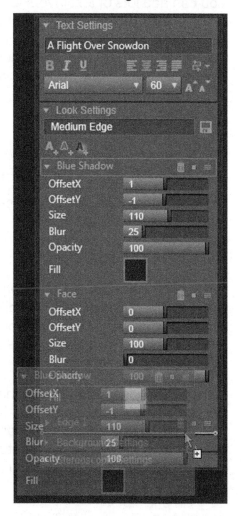

Face, Edge or Shadow?

What I have in effect asked you to do is create a Face 2 but give it the attributes of a Shadow – a bit of offset, transparency and blur. It looks rubbish because it isn't in the right place to be a shadow, though - it is in front of the Face and Edge 1. Let's move it to the background.

Click on the box that holds the name Face 2 and rename it to *Blue Shadow*. Click on Blue Shadow and drag it down the list. In the same way as you can move tracks about on the timeline or effects in an effects list, you will see a thin line appear when you are able to drop the text layer. Drop it at the bottom of the list. The screenshot shows this happening with all the boxes maximised, but you may find it easier to do with them minimised.

Have a look at the title properly – click away from it to get rid of the selection shading. The white face and black edge are in front of the blue shadow and in my opinion the title doesn't look too bad now. Switch off Solo and scrub through the clip – it seems to stand out better even as the camera pans past the fire vehicle.

So what have we learned about the text layers you can add as Face, Edge and Shadow? They are convenient labels and when we add one to a Look they are placed according to their intended effect. Faces get put on top, Shadows at the back and Edges in the middle. However, Studio allows **all** the parameters possible to be applied to **any** layer – and the layers can be re-ordered. This might almost be too much flexibility – why would you want to add an offset to a Look that only had one text layer? Indeed, you probably wouldn't. Studio's consistency of design, however, lets you do so if you *did* have a reason.

You can add lots of text layers to build up a Look, and even if you see a pre-built look that's seems too complex to be done that way, dissect it and you will find that is the case. When you spend time making a Look that you like, you can rename it and save it by using the floppy disc icon under the Look settings header. Any Looks you created can be retrieved from the fifth Looks category *My Looks*.

Motions

I said earlier that you don't always need to add title motions to achieve decent animation, but there are number of distinct advantages when using the Title Editor.

Each title layer can have three separate types of Motion. **Enter** effects bring a title onto the screen, **Emphasis** acts on the title during the time it is on screen. **Exit** takes it off screen. Each layer can have all three, and the relative durations are variable for each effect and each layer.

Many of the motions act on a letter by letter, word by word or line by line basis. To achieve this outside the Title Editor would require a separate title for each element and that would be very cumbersome. Even some of the effects that apply to the whole page layer have some very impressive 3D effects that would take quite a bit of setting up using a normal effect.

To add a motion effect, click on the right-hand tab at the top of the editor, then choose the sort of motion you want – in this case *Enter*. A filmstrip style selection will open up at the top of the screen, and for our first example chose *Type*. Although you should be able to preview the effect automatically when hovering, it can be a real drain on graphics cards, so if your computer struggles just click on the effect and then play it.

You may wonder what is so different with this effect rather than just doing a straight wipe, but the speed at which it is being played isn't doing it justice. I'm going to show you how to extend it.

Browsing the Entry Motions

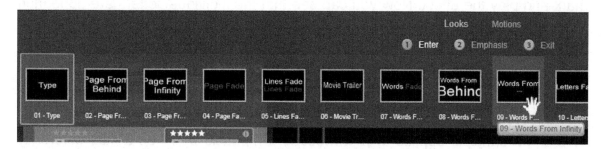

I've not been paying much attention to the Timeline display up until now, but you should notice it has started to get interesting. The first and only layer is a blue strip just under the timescale with the label. These blue strips are called progress bars.

A Flight Over... is shown in the screenshot below. In the progress bar headers there is a tab that indicates what sort of layer it is – in this case ABC means a text layer. Next is a name box that will contain the actual text, but if you enter a new name, it isn't reflected in the title itself – so if all the layers have similar names you could change them to something more helpful. The small Eye Icon lets you hide or show the layer in the same manner as the Movie Editor timeline control does.

When we come to add more layers, more progress bars will be added to the timeline window and you can use the track headers to drag, drop and therefore change the order. The track headers also have right-click context menus which will make more sense when you know what all the functions do – but none of the options in the track header context menu are exclusive to the menu - you can achieve them all in other ways.

Extending the Type motion duration

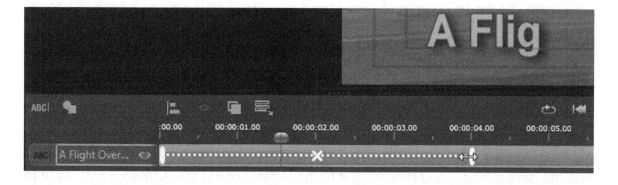

What should have caught your eye is a dotted line with a handle at each end and an "x" in the middle that has been added to the start of the only track currently on the timeline. This shows that an entry motion has been added. The handles control the start and end of the motion. Drag the right hand handle to the right to the 4 second mark and play the effect. Now you can see that the individual letters are appearing one at a time. Imagine the clack of a keyboard on the sound track and you can see the potential of this effect!

If we didn't want the motion to begin at the beginning of the title, we could drag the left hand handle left. When there is more than one layer this will be of more use. If you wished to delete the motion, you can click on the small x in the middle.

This same principle applies to Exit motions. Emphasis behaves a little differently when you add it – if there are no entry or exit effects in place it will occupy the entire timeline. Emphasis also has a few special effects that actually start and end with text off the screen, the Roll and Crawl effects. I'll use these a little later as well.

Alignment grid

The Alignment Grid

Sometimes you want to just place your titles consistently, and there is a tool for this on the toolbar. It's actually hidden under a slightly misleading tool tip and icon, but the *Group Align* button that is third from the left contains a "relative position" grid that works on single layers. Highlight the title and open the button, then try the nine boxes at the bottom of the menu. Each one will align the text with an edge of the Title safe area, apart from the middle box which is the best way of ensuring your title is dead centre for the screen. Use the *Bottom Edge* setting to ensure that the *Flight* title is central, then close the grid, select the text box again and use the arrow keys to inch it back down to sit at the same height as before. Finally, close the Title Editor.

Shapes

In order to show off some more of the Title Editor's features, I'm now going to produce a different style of graphic to go over the taxiing shot that is fifth on the timeline. Put the timeline scrubber at the beginning of this shot, make sure track 1 is selected and then re-open the Title Editor. Create a title "Caernarfon Airport" using an Arial 60 font and the default Look, and then drag it to the bottom of the title screen. I now want to build up a simple graphic to place behind the title using the Shape Tool, second from the left on the tool bar.

The Shape Tool

Open it and select Add Rectangle. A white box will appear in the centre of the screen. Resize and move it with the nodes in the same way as you would a text box so that it fits the top half of the title safe area, then open the Face attribute and change the Fill colour to a Light Cyan – R=128, G=255 and B=255. Set the Alpha to 0.5.

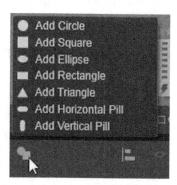

Now create a Horizontal Pill; leave the height at its default but use the nodes to stretch it out to fit the width of the Title safe area. Change the Fill colour to a solid black with an Alpha of 1.

Title, Rectangle and Horizontal Pill

From that short introduction you can see how it is possible to create a few simple geometric shapes. We have also added two extra layers to the timeline. I now want to align the layers. I could do this in a freehand style, but it is unlikely to be accurate. To use the Group Align tool we need to group the objects, and there are two types of grouping. A *temporary* grouping is all we need here, and we can use the normal Windows multi-section process, either in the shapes themselves, or the track headers.

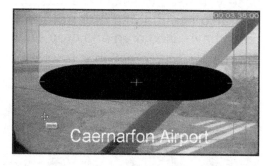

Select all three layers, open the Group Align and select Horizontal Center. Unless you had a very steady hand when you moved the first title, you will see it line up with the other two shapes. Now use Vertical Center and you will see all three object line themselves up. Don't panic that you cannot see the text for now - I'll show you how to reveal it in a moment.

Group Align

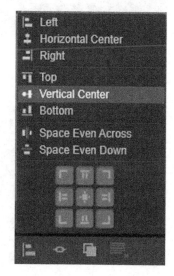

An important point to remember here is that objects line up to the first one that you selected. If the group isn't at the top of the screen, use Undo, select them again making sure the cyan rectangle is selected first, and the group will end up at the top of the safe area.

Just a word about another Alignment tool – Space Evenly Across/Down. This will save you work when making titles with lots of components. You don't need to line stuff up meticulously, just set the Left/Top and Right/Bottom objects in the correct places, multi-select the rest and use Space Evenly. This will come in particularly handy when you make menus, which uses a very similar editor.

Order and Grouping

Just like video on the movie timeline, the top track on the title timeline is in the foreground. We can't see the actual title because it is hidden behind our two shapes. We can try to manage layers and their order with the context menu on the title screen, but it is often hard to select the correct object and I'd recommend you use the track headers to bring up a context menu, and then use the *Order* tool on the toolbar.

However you get to the Order function, the options are self-explanatory, and in this case you need to select the text and use *Bring To Front*. You will then see the title, and also see that the order of the layers in the timeline display has changed. We could have used drag and drop on the tracks here, as I mentioned earlier.

The Order Tool in action

I said we only need to make a *temporary* group to carry out the actions we have just performed. So, what is a *permanent* grouping then? I now want the two geometric shapes to always stay together, regardless of how I move them, or be both affected when I add a Motion effect or a Look.

Select the two shapes and use the the icon that looks like a Chain Link tool

to form a *Group*.

The Group Tool

Where did the text go? Look at the timeline and you will see what has happened. Our new **GroupLayer** has been formed and moved to the foreground. I'm not quite sure why it has been moved to the foreground, but it's no good there!

Beware of using drag and drop on the timeline track headers to bring the text to the front this time – it will probably end up contained in the group.

Using the Context menu to move the Shapes to the back

Select the group and use *Send to Back*. You can also *Ungroup* items, and a very handy option is the *Regroup* tool, which will reform the last grouping you had. If you have to split a group up to change one parameter, this will save you having to remember what was in the group.

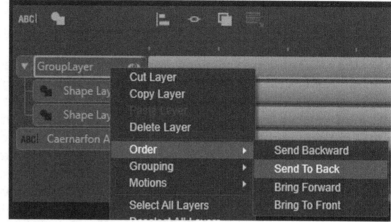

I suggest that you rename the group of two shapes as Title Background and then use the small arrow to hide the component parts. This will make the display clearer, but if you decided to change the colour of just one part you will need to reopen the group.

I never claimed that this title was going to be subtle. Add the Barrel Roll Entry and Exit motions to the background layer, and the Page from/to Infinity Entry and Exit motions to the title layer.

Layers renamed and the Entry and Exit motions added

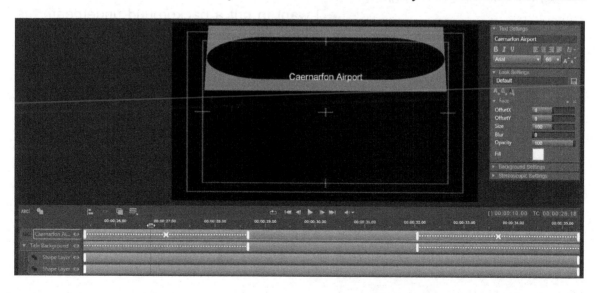

When you create a title within a project, it is automatically stored in the Movie or Disc project file where you create the title. However, before you close the Title Editor, you might want to consider using *Save As...* in case you want to use this title in another project. It will be added to the default location for My Titles in the Library and can be retrieved at any time for use in another project.

When you have seen the title in action, you might not thank me for that suggestion!

Quit the title editor and play the title; I think you will agree it isn't on screen for long enough. What will happen if we alter the duration with regard to the timing of the motions? Let's see – use the duration box to extend the timing to 10 seconds and play the section again. You will see that the various components have all kept the same relative duration, so the motions are three times longer. If you think about it, that is really the best course of action that Studio can take, otherwise if you decided to shorten the title too much, and the motions were reduced, there would be no time when the title was static. Of course, there will be times when you will want to adjust individual timings within a title if you alter the overall duration, so you will have to dive back into the Title Editor timeline and adjust the handles on the progress bars.

Background Settings and using other assets

Beneath Look Settings is another box for *Background Settings*. Here you can define a background for your title – turning the whole title into a solid one that doesn't show anything below - unless you added a semi-transparent background.

Creating a background Gradient

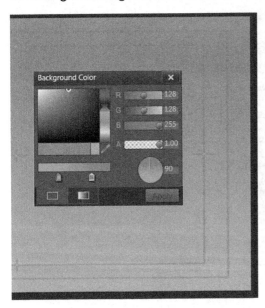

I want to put a background underneath the Clock wipes between shots 7 and 8, so I'm going to make a full frame title now. Move the scrubber to the start of shot 8 and open the Title Editor, then *Delete* the text box that automatically appears. Now open up background setting and click on the Drop Zone box to open the Colour Selection box.

Using the methods outlined earlier, create a gradient with a half saturated blue at the top of the screen (R=128, G=128, B=255) and 75% saturated green at the bottom (R=64, G=255, B=64). Move the gradient sliders to about the 25% and 75% positions as shown in the screenshot. Set the rotation to 270 and *Apply* it to the background.

When you close the Title Editor you will have spotted my deliberate mistake – by putting it on Track 1 the new title obliterates the underlying video. Drag the title down to track 3 and adjust it to cover both transitions. If you want to practice with colour selection a bit more, you could try to make the colours more natural.

Want more complex gradients? Double click on one of the gradient sliders to create a duplicate, which you can then slide to a different spot on the gradient and then change the value of the colours.

That background box can hold other assets - hence the name. If you drag a photo from the Compact Library to it then it will fill the whole background. If the photo is the wrong aspect ratio for the project a small icon to the right lets you choose if the photo is either stretched or cropped to fit.

Using a video asset as a background

That's the first time I mentioned using the Compact Library. Its presence might lead you to wonder what else you could drag to be a background source. You might already be ahead of me… yes, you can use a video source.

Now, I'm not quite sure why you would want to use a video as a background to a title when you could just as easily overlay the title over another Movie Timeline track, but the option is there if you want it. However, this feature is also in the Menu Editor, where it is definitely useful!

One type of asset you can't use in titles is Projects. This would be taking the complexity a bit too far for my brain.

Adding assets as layers

This has opened a whole can of worms, though. You will also discover that you can drag assets from the Compact Library not only to the background, but also to form new layers within the title, and even to be the Fill for text looks. That's right; you can have text which has video playing where the letters should be! This last option can occasionally look pretty good by using big letters and suitable video, but it's unlikely to win you any awards for subtlety. Think opening titles of a 70's cop show and you won't be far out.

Motions can be added to the videos that you have added as shape layers and they can be positioned and sized anywhere on the title page; the limit is your imagination. Again, I'd venture to suggest this might be a job best carried out in the main Movie Editor, but the option is there – particularly if you want to intertwine layers of texts and video. It does show off the power of the Title Editor very well.

Back with more mundane tasks, you can use photos or other graphic files, and those graphics can have transparency. I've successfully imported Photoshop (psd), Portable Network Graphics (png) Truevison (tga) and Tagged Image File Format (tif) files into Studio.

If you want to create your own logo in another software package, please do so. Alternatively I have provided a logo for you to use called FlightGraphic.png which you will find on the Data DVD and website. Load it into the Library and then open the background title we have just created. When you drag the logo to the title window you will see the transparency. Use the resize nodes to make the graphic fill the width of the Title Safe Area and place it in the centre of the screen using the Align tool.

Placing a graphic file with transparency into a title

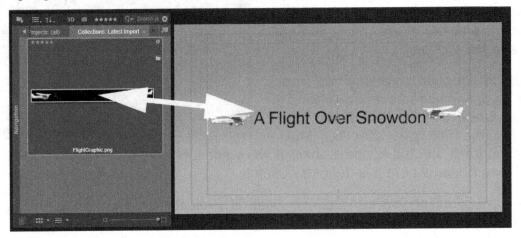

Arrows and Special Characters

One common requirement when using titles is to be able to use a pointer of some sort to indicate something on the underlying video – you might want to highlight an individual player in some sports footage, for example. There are lots of ways to do this, including the use of elaborate effects, but perhaps the quickest way is to add an arrow. You can include an arrow as text in a number of ways. The first involves using the Windows Character Map. This is worth investigating as this is it is also how you can include characters not available from the keyboard such as a copyright symbol.

You will find the Windows Character Map buried in All Programs/ Accessories/System Tools, (in Windows 8 you can find it on the Apps page under Windows Accessories). If you intend to use it often I suggest you create a shortcut to it on your desktop. When you find the downward pointing arrow near the bottom of the list, *Select* it and then use the *Copy* button to put it in the paste buffer. Create a title on track one above the Peak 1 shot, clear the text box and use Paste or CTRL-V to add the arrow from the buffer. If the font size isn't 72, change it to that. Change the Look to Large

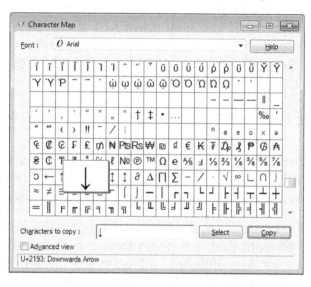

Edge. Now return to the timeline and trim the new title so that it starts once the In transition ends and runs for the whole duration of the shot. Return to the Title Editor, switch off Solo, make sure the scrubber is at the start of the title and then rotate, resize and reposition the arrow to point at the summit of Mount Snowdon as shown in the screenshot. Add another text layer with the title "Mount Snowdon - 1,085 metres" (Arial 48 Large Edge) and place it as shown.

The Mount Snowdon pointer before keyframing

When you scrub through the title with Solo off you will see by the end of the shot the arrow is missing the peak by some way. I'm going to fix this in a minute, but let's round up special characters first.

There is a font that contains a whole array of more sophisticated arrows in the place of letters called WingDings

3 which might offer you some interesting alternatives. Near the bottom of the font list are three that obviously start with W but show as a series of symbols. You might find other characters of some use to you in the other two fonts, WingDings 1 and 2.

If you use a particular symbol a lot – perhaps a Euro currency symbol – and it is missing from your keyboard, it might be worth looking up and even learning the ALT keycode. If you hold down ALT and type a number on your numerical keypad then release the ALT key, the symbol will appear. Some common ones are € - 0128, ↑↓→← - 24 to 27 and © - 0169. A quick trip to Google will bring up dozens of websites that list others.

Effects and Keyframing on Titles

I said many pages ago that you could add video effects to titles. The following exercise shows the basic principle in action, but bear in mind that any effect in the Library could be potentially used – again, the limiting factor is probably your imagination!

I'm hoping to make the arrow point at the peak of Snowdon more consistently. Before I attempt that, I'm going to add a stabilize correction to the shot to make life a bit easier. Hopefully you added this correction to the whole file earlier so you won't have to wait for the render process. If you didn't, prepare to make a cup of tea while you wait. If you did add the correction, all we need to do is enable it for this shot.

Close the Title Editor, then open the Peak 1 shot in the Effects Editor. Select the Corrections/Stabilize tab and ensure that the Default preset is selected. Now click on the Enable button above the Preset Selection drop-down and click on Render and Play. If it plays straight away, great; if it doesn't, put the kettle on. (If you are wondering why it takes so long, read the Corrections section of the previous chapter.)

When the Stabilize is working, we can get to the title in the Effects Editor in one of two ways. You can click on the green strip above the current clip in the Navigator, or close the Effects Editor, right click on the title and select Open Effects Editor from the Context menu. That is how you will get to the Effects Editor in normal circumstances because double-clicking on a title opens the Title Editor.

I'm going to use 2D-3D/2D Editor Advanced effect. Select No Preset, and then switch off the Solo button to see the underlying video. Switch on Keyframing. (I've covered this in detail earlier, so if this is new to you, refer to the previous chapter.)

Set a keyframe at the end of the clip. Now alter the Position parameters to line the arrow up to point at the peak. Don't get it too close otherwise you will need to set more keyframes. You can guide the arrow into the correct place using the keyboard shortcuts Page/Arrow Up and Down if you wish. All the last keyframe needs is a vertical value of 10. Horizontal can stay at 0.

Setting a keyframe for the end of the title

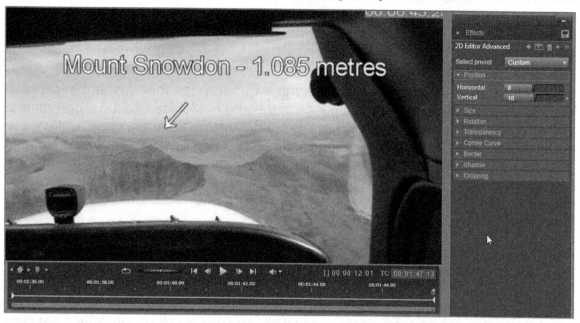

Play the effect back. Actually, that's not bad! The arrow points to the correct peak all the time. Lets try adding one more keyframe. The arrow is at it furthest away from the peak at around half way through the clip – where the Vertical setting is currently reading 5.1 - TC 00:01:41:17. With the scrubber in that position, start altering the Horizontal parameter and a new keyframe will appear. Again, setting the parameters is best achieved with the keyboard shortcuts. I have ended up with the values H = -4, V = 0.

OK, play that through. I'm going to settle there in this project. As I was working on the clip I found that adding a couple more keyframes improved matters, but after a while the title was moving so much it looked worse unless I was absolutely spot on and applied dozens of keyframes. Please add a few more to see how much more of an improvement you can make, but don't spend too long!

What we really need for this effect is a tool called Motion Tracking. Studio doesn't have that yet, but I'm hoping it will be added in a later version.

Incidentally, the next shot that zooms into the peak shows work going on building a new Café which wasn't completed until the following year. If you fancy creating a title to point out the crane it would be a good way of practicing your skills without me holding your hand throughout the process. A text title could span both parts of the shot, and you could add a further title on a new track above to appear as the zoom in starts, with a keyframed arrow fading up to show where the crane is. Just a suggestion!

Crawlers and Rollers

Some of the Emphasis motions have a more general use than just enhancement. We are all familiar with the roller captions at the end of Movies and TV programmes. They normally roll up the screen from the bottom, listing the cast, crew, writers, the name of the transport captain and who provided the portaloos. Crawls are sometimes used for a similar purpose, but you are more likely to see them used to add information that won't all fit on one title card – maybe the latest football scores or stock market prices. Crawls generally go right to left so they can be read. Studio provides Roll Down and Crawl Left as well.

It's normally best to type your text in before adding the motion effect. The speed of the crawl or roll is dictated by the amount of text and the duration of the title, so if the text is whizzing past too fast to read, then you will have to reduce the amount of text or increase the time that the title is on screen. Another point to bear in mind is that moving text is harder to read, so you should choose a strong look, or place them over a background that helps them to stand out.

The following example places some information over the Mountain Railway shot. I'm going to use a crawl effect and build it up in stages, starting with the unreadable and ending up with what I hope is a satisfactory title.

Place the scrubber at the start of the Mountain railway clip, and with track 1 selected, open the Title Editor. Use the Arial font, size 60 and create a text box containing **The Snowdon Mountain Railway carries tourists to the summit between March and October, weather permitting!**.

Adding the Crawl Left Emphasis motion

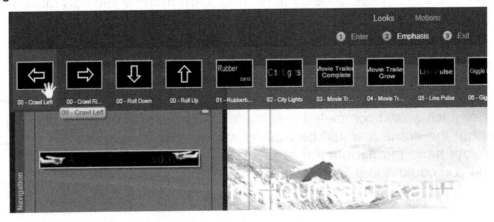

Return to the timeline and readjust the title so it starts at the end of the In transition and lasts the whole length of the clip but doesn't overlap the Out transition. Play it again. OK, the speed isn't too bad, but the title is obliterating the railway we are trying to point out!

Now, back in the Title Editor, add the Emphasis Motion Crawl Left. It may take a few moments to reformat the text. Close the Title Editor with OK, then play the clip. Goes through quite fast, doesn't it?

Open the Title Editor again and using the Align tool to line the text up with the top of the safe area. With Solo turned off, as you scrub through the title you will spot the next problem without returning to the timeline – the sky is nearly white most of the time and therefore the white text is unreadable. So, change the Face Fill colour to black and see if it's any better.

That's seems an improvement, but when you play it back in preview the second half of the crawl gets a bit muddled up with the mountains in the background. Let's try something else instead.

In the Title Editor again create a mid-grey rectangle, use the Order tool to *Send to Back* and adjust it to be the full width of the screen. Line it up with the title and adjust the height so it is slightly bigger than the text. I think the title will look better white, so change it back.

The title against a grey banner background

That's better. It still seems a bit quick to me, though. We can't lengthen the shot, so we can't make the title any longer. We could slowmo the video I suppose, but then again, we could just edit the title text. You'd have to do this if you spotted a typo anyway so it's a function worth exploring. Go back into the Title Editor and change the text. Remember my hint earlier about using the small text box under Text setting if you get into difficulties. On long roller captions this is quite likely.

I've just changed the beginning to **The Mountain Railway runs to the summit** because we know it is Snowdon, and we don't need to specify that it carries tourists – it is hardly a through route!

Finally, I'm going to put a 10 frame fade up and down at the beginning and end of the title.

I'm finished here. You could use a motion to make the background strip appear and disappear if you prefer. You might also want to put a final roller caption on with a credit for yourself, Pinnacle Studio and the words "The End". Don't bother to give the cameraman a credit, though. He was rubbish. When you have made your own improvements, save the project as *Flight Project Stage 4*. We will use it in later chapters.

Creating long credit rollers

If you work with preview rendering turned up high and want to create long credit rollers you will soon find yourself bogged down waiting for the title to preview render - the program appears to become unresponsive and the render process can be very slow. It's best to turn preview render off, but if you are using a complex Look or backgrounds you won't be able to preview the title smoothly - even more so if the background is moving video. So my suggested workflow for a very long title would be:

- Turn off Preview rendering. Put any background or other graphic objects into the title editor and create a few lines in plain text of the correct size and font. Turn it into a roller by adding the Roll Up motion. Use the small text box to complete the text.

- Preview the result without preview optimisation. If preview is jerky, turn off the backgrounds using transparency or the monitoring icons. If there is a video on a track below, disable that as well. Check the credits and correct as required, then set the duration by trimming.

- **Now** add the look you want and re-enable the backgrounds. Preview will now be jerky but you should still get a good idea of how the credits are going to look.

- Turn on preview rendering and make a cup of tea. When you have drunk the tea the credits should be ready to preview. If they aren't, have another cup of tea.

- If you spot something you want to change, turn off preview optimisation before attempting to re-edit the title.

Stereoscopic text effects

One text parameter that you may have spotted and I haven't yet mentioned is Stereoscopic settings. These affect the size and positioning even if you haven't set your project to 3D, although obviously you won't see full the 3D effect even if they move. The only control is the Depth setting, which moves the text closer (negative values) or further away (positive values). Each text layer can have a different value, so with a bit of work you can build up some interesting 3D effects for your Stereoscopic projects. They are most effective when combined with Entry and Exit motions.

Working with Photos

In this chapter I want to explore the use of photos within video projects. One reason for including still pictures within a movie might be as supplementary material. You could have made a video recording of a holiday, perhaps, but some days you just took your stills camera with you. The photos can be included in the holiday video.

Many people like to make projects that consist entirely of photos, producing a slideshow of a series of photographs, sometimes with quite elaborate motions added to the stills. These can be particularly moving when you chart someone's life using a collection of photographs taken over the years. I'm planning to embarrass my daughter enormously if she ever gets married!

There is a whole documentary genre that uses old photographs as source material, and to make these more interesting a style of animation has developed over the years, initially using rostrum camerawork. While you may have heard of it described as the "Ken Burns" effect after the celebrated American documentary maker, the technique came to the fore with the release of the Canadian film *City of Gold* in 1957, directed by Colin Low and Wolf Koenig. The film makes use of some 200 glass-plate negatives of life during the Klondike gold rush, and the resolution of the source material was so high that a rostrum camera could zoom into a one inch wide section of the 10 by 8 plates and still achieve good enough pictures to fill a cinema screen.

This is an important point. If you want to use a photo as part of a video project, the resolution of the photograph needs to match the resolution of the video project, more or less; otherwise the photo will look blurred. Now this isn't normally a problem. Even if you scan a 5 by 4 inch photo using a 300 dots per inch scanner, the resolution will be more than Standard definition unless the photo is particularly grainy. More likely your photos will have been taken with a digital camera, and only the cheapest cameras will have a resolution less than High Definition Video.

We do have to be very careful about resolution, though. Most photos aren't the same aspect ratio as video, so when we crop them to fit the screen, we immediately lose some of the resolution. The photo may have been taken in portrait mode, which limits the resolution even more if we don't want to shoot off the sides.

The main reason for wanting high resolution photos, though, is so that we can reframe them and also so we can animate them – send the software "rostrum camera" around the photo, selecting the view, adding movement, pace and style to a movie. The more resolution you have, the closer you can go.

Now, if we had those 10 by 8 inch glass plates, we would be very happy indeed, but most digital cameras have a horizontal resolution of 3200 to 4500 pixels. For a SD project, you can zoom into about a quarter to a sixth of the picture. HD isn't so good – even with a top of the range DSLR, the resolution is 5600 – so you can only zoom into a third of the picture before the onset of blurriness. If you are thinking of working in 4K, then you will need a very good stills camera to even think of zooming in much at all.

When you take photos that you think you might put into a video project, regardless of the quality of your camera, you can do a few things to help. If the camera has a choice of aspect ratios, select one that matches your video camera – most likely to be 16:9 in this day and age. This will force you to frame the photograph to suit the video project. Never use your camera in portrait mode by tipping it on its side. Finally, if your subjects are people and objects, rather than landscapes, make sure you fill the frame. Either use an optical zoom lens if you have one, or get closer if you can.

In a previous chapter we looked in detail about the corrections you can apply to photos even when they are in the Library, but we can add these corrections to any photo in a project by opening the Effects Editor and switching to the Corrections tab. Therefore we can adjust the exposure and colour balance, and crop, straighten or reduce the red-eye effect. You should use these tools whenever possible and not, for example, decide to use the Rotate Effect that is intended for Video. There are good reasons for this.

Only the tools specific to photos will maximise the resolution available. If you reframe a photo with a video tool, the photo will be down-sized to the project resolution **before** the effect is added. This is a bad thing, because although you might get away with a 10% zoom in, anything more will start to introduce fuzziness. If the effect you want to use is going to reduce the size of photo – you want to shrink it and put on screen using a picture-in-picture effect perhaps - that's Ok, but otherwise steer clear of the video reframing tools.

Adding a photo to a project that you want to remain static is as simple as it is to add a video clip. You drag or send it from the Compact Library to any suitable timeline track. The default durations that are defined in the Control panel, and for photos this is normally set to 3 seconds. The timeline context menu options *Scaling/Fit and Fill* can then be used if you want to simply remove or retain the black bars that are created when a photo isn't the same aspect ratio as your video project. If you want to reframe it more creatively, then you use the Pan and Zoom tool that I'm about to describe in detail.

One important point to remember when you work with photos is that, unlike video or audio, you cannot run out of material – the "dead meat" issue. A photo (and a title) can be any length you want it to be, because unlike video it is a static picture. Studio will extend a photo to any duration you like without complaint. This means adding transitions requires a little less thought, as we will see in a few pages time.

A fast paced Photo Project

For the next short project I'm going to make use of photos and demonstrate some of the techniques you can use to enliven them. I will use the sample music and photos that are provided with Pinnacle Studio, so you don't need to download anything or use the data DVD. You might prefer to substitute your own music and photos if you have something suitable. By the way, if you are more interested in making slow, leisurely slideshows, don't think that the techniques won't be relevant.

I'm going to use a Bin to store the photos, although you could chose to create a Collection.

- Create a Bin called *BMX* and add the eight *The-Sky-is-the-Limit* Jpeg photos that are in the Public Pictures location.

You may have already done this if you tried out the Tags tutorial.

- Also add the audio file BMX_ YA-HA! *wma* file from the Public Music location.

If you can't find them, they are on the website and data DVD. You will also find there a saved version of the project with just the music and markers, and another with all the photos loaded but without animations added, as well as final versions for both PAL and NTSC.

- Start a new project and set the timeline to PAL Widescreen.

Don't despair if you are a NTSC user – we can convert the sequence at the end to NTSC without causing any problems, because it won't contain any video.

- Open your *BMX* Collection in the Compact Library.

- For the sake of clarity delete timeline tracks 1 and 4 and rename track 2 as Photos and track 3 as Music.

- Save the project as *BMX_photo_project*.

Right, first we need some music – and not too much either.

- Put the *bmx_ya-ha!* music file on the Music track.

- I want to use the last 16 bars including a short drum intro. If you aren't musically minded the In point is 00:00:48.13.

- Split the clip at that point and delete the first half

- The remainder should be 34 seconds 10 frames long.

- Trim the end of the clip, or adjust the duration so it is 24 seconds long exactly, then put a 1 second dissolve on as an Out transition.

(If you have an issue here, use my saved project.)

- Use multi-selection on all eight photos and drag the clips to the start of the *Photo* track.

Check that no corrections have already been applied. If you worked through the Flight project chapter very faithfully, you may have applied a *Crop* tool to photo 01. If you have, right click on the green line on the timeline thumbnail and use *Corrections/Revert to Original*.

Eight photos at 3 seconds each on a 24 second piece of music has created a photo project. Play it if you wish. This wasn't my intention when I set about creating the music clip, but it rather conveniently has created a simple sequence that works, even if it isn't going to win any awards. Now let's set to work.

The BMX photo project in its first stage

The intention is that we will use parts of the photos more than once, with increasing complex Pan and Zoom effects, but I'm going to start with a series of very fast cuts that are in time with the drum beats at the beginning of the music. The drum sequence lasts a bit over a second.

- Select all the photo clips and use the right click Context menu to globally change the duration of all the clips to just 4 frames – 00:00:00.04.

Preview the timeline and you should have a very fast intercutting sequence that nearly lasts for the whole of the short drum intro.

- Zoom the timeline in to about two seconds duration and look at how the cut points line up with the audio waveforms.

The first 8 photos forming a fast cutting sequence

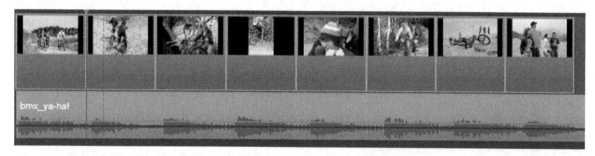

As cuts are a little bit out use quick trim to adjust them.

- Lengthen the first photo just by one frame using ALT to force Smart mode to work in Insert mode. The next six cuts line up quite well.

- Try to alter any of the cut points and you will see the "granularity" caused because the smallest unit of time by which you can make an adjustment is one frame.

Trimming the cuts to match the beats

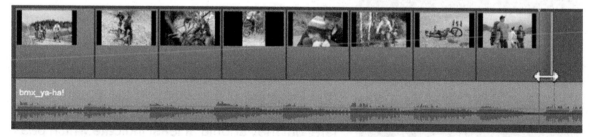

This is sometimes why music editing isn't very successful when using a Video Editing program. Some programs do let you edit music to greater accuracy, but not Studio. However, the human eye is a little less critical than the ear when it comes to timing, and getting within half a frame will be good enough – I've never met anyone who can immediately tell if a video is less than half a frame out of sync with the accompanying audio.

- Extend the last photo by a single frame as well.

Your timeline should look like the screenshot, so play the sequence again. Very pacy, I think you will agree.

Using Markers with Music

I mentioned that after the drum intro there were 16 bars of music. In common with most popular music, the time signature of BMX_Ye-ah! Is 4/4 – that is four crochet beats to each bar, with the music generally composed into blocks of 4, 8 or 16 bars. I'm going to attempt to start each new photo at the beginning of a bar. It can be quite fiddly to find the start of each bar just using the waveforms. In fact, some music has waveforms that are too complex to really see the beat and bar structure anyway.

The bar marker timecodes

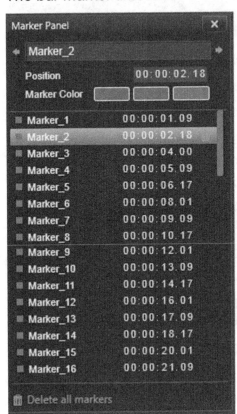

If you have a reasonable sense of timing, one handy trick is to use the **Marker** feature to mark the start of each bar as the music plays.

- Try counting the beats – "**1** 2 3 4, **2** 2 3 4, **3** 2 3 4, **4** 2 3 4" a couple of times along with the music track before you start.

- Hover your finger over the M key, play the music and proceed to hit the M key at the beginning of each bar.

You may struggle to do this, or you may find it very easy. If your marked bars are way off, don't worry, I'll give you the timecodes. Even the most talented musician may not hit the beats exactly, and because of the delay in the program, the markers will almost certainly be a few frames late, but they should at least indicate which peak in the waveform you should be aiming for when you edit.

You might want to drag your markers a little closer to waveform peaks. The screenshot gives a list of the 16 bars I will be using for the rest of this project.

Introducing Pan and Zoom

It's time to start applying the Pan and Zoom effect, but to begin with we will use it simply as a cropping tool.

- Drag the first two pictures (The-Sky-is-the-Limit_01.jpg and 02.jpg) to the end of the current 8 shots on the timeline.

- Quick trim them so that they last two bars each, snapping the ends into position with the timeline markers at 00:00:04.00 and 00:00:06.17.

- Now double click on the shot of all four kids on the timeline – shot 9.

- The Effects Editor will open, but because you are working on a photo, there will be an additional tab at the top of the screen – *Pan and Zoom*.

- Select the tab and ensure that the sub tab *Static* is selected.

What you should be seeing now will be pretty familiar to you if you have worked through the Effects section of the book. The lower toolbar has sizing controls and a navigator On/Off button, which when turned on gives us the Timeline view Navigator so we can switch between photos. Top right a settings box has appeared where we can manually add values or choose a preset. Top left is an important tool – a small preview window. A timescale and set of playback controls are in the usual place below the main preview and the photo has a white frame with resizing nodes around it.

The first three options in the *Select Preset* drop-down menu are relevant to static Pan and Zoom.

- Select *Static Small Zoom* and you will see the white frame shrink to lose the edges of the photo.

- Take a look at the preview window to see how the photo would look if we returned to the timeline.

- Although the framing is technically OK – no black edges, all their heads are in frame – you, like me might want to tilt the frame down a bit to get the bottom of the bike wheels in shot.

- I've also used the top left node to tighten the frame a bit more, so there is less headroom and air on the left of frame.

Photo 01 reframed in the Pan and Zoom static editor

The mouse controls work on the frame in the same way as they do in the Title, but you cannot change the aspect ratio, which is fixed to the same ratio as the project. You should end up with something similar to the screenshot.

- Switch to the next photo using the Navigator bar in the Editing window. If it isn't showing, use the compass-like icon on the toolbar to reveal it.

- Click on the blue strip to the right of the currently selected orange clip.

- The next photo will appear. If you have the Storyboard displayed in the main editor, the timeline strips will be replaced by thumbnails, but the principle is the same.

- Use the *Attributes* settings to reframe this picture. I've entered 30 as the Zoom Value by clicking twice on the number and entering it manually.

- To adjust the vertical setting, highlight the box with one click and then use the Page Up and Down keys and the Left/Right arrows to get the top of the white frame as near the top of the picture as possible.

These keys give you a little more accuracy than the mouse, should you need it.

Reframing photo 02 using Attributes

So, you can see that Static Pan and Zoom is really just an alternative to the Crop tool in Corrections, but the effect is just added to the picture on the timeline. One thing you currently can't do with either of these tools is apply them to a multiple selection of photos, even using copy and paste. Each photo needs to be treated on its own merits. This is another good reason for using your stills camera in the same aspect ratio as your video camera if at all possible.

Pan and Zoom effect indicator

A new feature added to late builds of PS18 and PS19 is that Pan and Zoom effects are indicated by the same pink bar over the timeline clips that are used to show you that other effects have been added. Unfortunately at the time of writing, that is all it does - gives an indication - as there is no context menu associated with the Fx line when Pan and Zoom are all that is applied. So if you have a photo that appears to have an effect added but you can't see a difference between it and the original, you have added a Pan and Zoom at some point and then reset it to the default settings. If you find that right clicking on the pink line does bring up a context menu, then Pinnacle have addressed this deficiency in a later build than the one I'm currently using.

Using animation

- Return to the timeline by clicking on OK.

- Put the next two photos (03 and 04) on the timeline and trim them to two bars each.

- Open timeline clip 11 (photo 03) in the Pan and Zoom Editor and switch to the second sub tab *Animated.*

Two things should become immediately apparent. There are now two frames, one green and the other red. Beneath the timescale a keyframe line has appeared. Hopefully you are familiar with the concept of keyframes from earlier sections of the book, but if you have skipped here, keyframes are used to define a new set of parameters at a particular time, and as the clip plays, the parameters will gradually change from one set to another. We will see in a moment that, for photos, the parameters can behave in a more artistically pleasing way than they do for effects.

Do you see the two keyframes at the beginning and end of the timescale? Is the left one green and the right one red? If they are, then Pinnacle will have fixed a minor bug that was present at the time of writing. If they aren't, grab the end of the timescale bar and slightly shrink and then expand the view. The keyframes should assume the correct colours. These tell you something. The green frame is the beginning of the animated move, the red is the end.

- Use the preview transport controls to play the effect while watching the small preview.

You will get a very good idea of what is going to happen when you return to the main program. Because of the size of the window, this type of preview takes far less computer resources, so you can watch what is currently programmed, smoothly, and without having to wait for the move to be rendered.

According to the manual, the default animated pan and zoom is a slow zoom out. I find that in fact the type of move varies with the picture content, resolution of the picture and so on. I have to be honest and say I'm not really sure how clever the software is being at analysing the photographs, but often the default choice is quite well framed. You can revert to this setting at any time by clicking on the *Automatic* button. Oddly, sometimes I seem to get a slow zoom *in*, not a zoom *out*. It's quite possible that the software has been enhanced since the manual was written.

- Use your freehand mouse skills to set the red frame as a tight two shot of the girls.

- Set the green frame to see as much of the picture as you can see without shooting off the sides.

Notice that each frame has a coloured dot that indicates the centre of frame, and the dots are connected by a white line. This is the path that the animation will take – currently it is a straight line because there are only two keyframes.

The Start and End frames are colour coded Green and Red

• Go back to the timeline by clicking on OK to check your work so far.

The next picture has been shot in portrait mode, so it is going to be a bit more problematic.

• Open it and set the Zoom size to 70.

• Put the green frame as low and the red frame as high as you can without shooting off the edges of the photo.

When you play it back, you should get a tilt up from the bike wheels.

This is a good shot with which to explore another attribute – the *Smooth* checkbox. It's not ideally named in my opinion, because it affects the **timing** of the moves. Other software calls it **Ease In** and **Ease Out**, or **Acceleration** and **Deceleration**. Without the Smooth checkbox enabled, each move will be at a constant speed.

• Enable the Smooth checkbox to add it to the tilting shot we have just created.

Play the movie and you will see the effect - The animation will begin slowly, accelerate to full speed and then slow down as it reaches the target. I think you will agree that it is too slow even though the Smooth effect has enlivened it a bit. We haven't got any more picture and if we zoom in more then the image becomes blurred, so the best option is to shorten the shot.

• Trim the picture from two bars to one bar in duration and play back the result.

Better? I think so.

Low Pass

The *Low Pass* checkbox is designed to eliminate patterning effects on detailed pictures. This can be caused when you re-sample a photo to change it's resolution. When the re-sampling is changing - as when you perform an animated move - you may see a strobe effect or crawling dots appear and disappear during movements. The downside of using Low Pass is that it softens the picture slightly, so only use it when you have to.

Multiple Moves

The keyframe interface doesn't just restrict you to a start and end position. You can add as many intermediate keyframes as you wish.

Put the close two shot of the boys, photo 05 at the end of the timeline

Make it fit into a two bar space between markers 8 and 10 using Quick trim.

Open the Animated Pan and Zoom editor and set the green frame to the full width of the photo and frame as much of both faces as you can.

To enable you to grab the green frame for reframing, hover over the centre dot.

Set the end frame as a close shot of the boy on the right – if you made the first project in the book you will know him as Shaggy.

Drag the scrubber to halfway into the shot – it happens to be at 12 seconds (we are also halfway through the music).

The white lines you can see indicate the framing at that moment during the shot. As soon as we change it, a new keyframe is created.

- Manipulate the frame so that it shows a close shot of the boy on the left – Fred.

- A new keyframe appears.

I'd like you to make the shot size the same as that of Shaggy.

- Move the white box over the green one and adjust the size.

It can start to get a bit difficult to select the correct box when they overlap so much. One way of selecting the correct box is to click on the appropriate keyframe on the timescale below. If you get into a muddle when trying to line the two boxes this may well get you out of trouble.

- When your Pan and Zoom window closely resembles the screenshot, try playing it back on the timeline.

Three keyframes with the white path curve linking the centre points of each frame

Once you have more than two keyframes, the path between them is very unlikely to be a straight line. Pan and Zoom tries to add a natural look by adding curves instead of rapid changes of direction, so if you study the path as it approaches the middle keyframe you will see it overshoots slightly  so it can curve back. This gives the impression of a human eye scanning the photo, rather than a computer program.

Because the first half of the shot has further to travel than the second half, it looks as if the move slows down a little for the second part. We can compensate for this by moving the keyframe. This won't have any effect on your chosen framing, it will just alter the point in time when the animation reaches that framing.

- Try dragging the middle keyframe two divisions to the right (about 10 frames).

- When you play that back, I think you will agree the second half of the shot looks if anything faster than the first part.

Dragging a keyframe alters the timing but not the framing of a move

So, to alter the perceived speed of a move, you can adjust the position of the keyframes. Keep in mind that the speed of a move will depend on both the distance travelled *and* the amount of zoom you are using – Pan **and** Zoom – as well as the amount of time you allow for it to occur. The less time allowed, the more you pan and the more you zoom, the faster the animation will appear to be.

We used Smooth before, and now is a good time to try it out on a multi-keyframed move.

- Check the Smooth box and play the effect.

Because of the deceleration as we reach the close shot of Fred and the acceleration as we move away, we almost pause on Fred's face.

- Add the photo of the two girls cycling – 06 – to the timeline for the next two bars.

- Enter Pan and Zoom/Animated and set the green frame so that is the full width of the photo, with Velma (the blond girl) and her sunglasses just in the top of frame.

- Set the red frame to a close up of Daphne on the right.

- Put a new keyframe at the 15 second mark and frame up a clean single on Velma on the left, not quite as close as the end shot.

- Select Smooth.

That is beginning to look a bit frantic. Have a look at the white path of the move (it's a bit hard to see because of the white top that Velma is wearing); you should see a reasonably smooth curve. What is happening is that the Smooth feature is accentuating the zooming that is going on.

- Turn off Smooth and the effect is actually better because we start to get a sense that the girls are cycling past the camera.

This brings up the point that sometimes *Smooth* can actually not live up to its name at all. When applied to some moves it makes them less smooth. OK, that's a bit tricky, isn't it? We can only have smooth on *or* off for the whole of the animation. I'll show you how to split a Pan and zoom into two separate shots in a moment.

Holding a still frame

You might be beginning to feel a bit seasick. There are many times when you will want to hold a still frame, then move, then hold the end of the shot for a while.

- Put the beach photo with the bike in foreground on the timeline and trim it to fit bars 12 and 13 and to end at the start of bar 14.

- Set up a Pan and Zoom that starts on the four kids and a bit of the bike wheel, then zooms out to include the whole bike.

I'm aware that the start of the shot is a bit blurred, but it is because the camera is focused forward, not because we have zoomed in too much. By including a bit more of the wheel, we take the curse off the shot.

I showed you how to copy and paste keyframes when we looked at Effects. The same thing works with Pan and Zoom.

- Right click on the green keyframe and use Copy Keyframe from the Context menu. (You might need to move the scrubber out of the way to open the context menu.)

- Hover the mouse pointer under the 17 second mark, right click and choose Paste Keyframe.

Copying the green keyframe

When that context menu is open, you will notice an option to *Create keyframe* – an alternative to moving the frame or parameters if you just want to alter some timing without altering the size or position of the frame.

- Repeat the above process to put a copy of the end red frame at the 18 second mark.

What we have now are four instructions – Start at position 1, stay there until the second keyframe, move to position 2, stay there until the fourth keyframe.

Two keyframe copies to generate a pause in the animation

- To see if it works, return to the timeline and play the animation.

Now, if you are seeing a certain amount of wobbling about when you expect the animation to be static, you are almost certainly using an older version of Studio. In 18.5 and later, the animation should not wobble.

I've heard reports that the problem wasn't fixed in the 32-bit build of PS18.5 If you find it happening to you, the way to stop it happening is an undocumented feature; Copy the keyframe you want to stop wobbling, paste it alongside and then drag it right on top of the original. If you alter the duration of any moves with double keyframes, you will need to reset the double keyframes or you may see flickering in the final export. However, I'm very hopeful that this bug has now gone for good in PS19!

By the way, if you want to load the completed projects from the website or data DVD, they still have the double keyframes so that they work in all version of Studio.

Adding transitions to photos

There isn't anything particularly special about how you go about adding transitions to photos. All the methods described in the Flight Project chapter can be applied. As mentioned before, the bonus when using photos is that you never run out of material, so you can set the duration and placement to your exact requirements – very handy when making a slideshow to music.

- Put photo 08 on the timeline after the 15th shot.

- Don't bother to trim it to length yet.

- Add a 1 second Dissolve CPU from the Library as an Out transition to shot 15.

- You will see shot 16 pull itself under shot 15, maintaining the duration of both shots while creating the overlap.

Sadly, the mix is now early relative to the music.

- Quick trim the outgoing shot by clicking and dragging the lower half to the right while holding down ALT.

- By eye you can even up the transition so that it bridges the marker that indicates the start of a bar.

- Now quick trim the Out point of the last shot on the timeline to snap it to the marker at 00:00:20.01.

Final layout of the transition

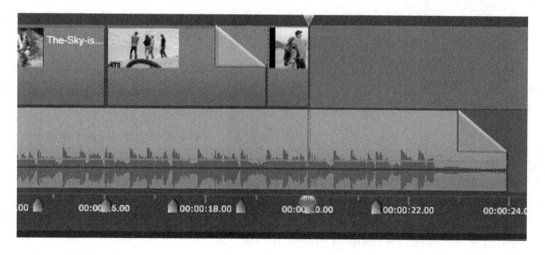

Matching frames

I mentioned earlier that I would show you how to split a Pan and Zoom into two separate shots so that we can apply *Smooth* to one half and not to the other. The way you achieve this is by copying a keyframe from one Pan and Zoom effect to another.

- Add a simple Zoom In to the four-shot of the kids currently at the end of the timeline, starting with all four and zooming into Fred and Velma on the right.

- Add *Smooth*.

- Return to the timeline and test the effect.

It should work quite nicely with the transition.

- Add another copy of the same photo for one bar only at the end of the timeline.

- Return to the first copy in the Pan and Zoom Editor – the one with the zoom added.

- Right click over the red keyframe and copy it.

Copying the keyframe

• Switch to the next copy of the photo using the navigator below.

• Now, we cannot paste the current keyframe in the paste buffer directly over the green keyframe at the start of the timescale.

• Paste it alongside and then drag it on top of the Green keyframe.

• Repeat the paste operation at 00:00:20.10. This will create a short "hold".

• Set the red frame to a two shot of Daphne and Shaggy, copy the keyframe and paste a copy at 00:00:20.20.

- Make sure that *Smooth* isn't checked.

There you are. Two types of move on what appears to be the same animation!

Copying keyframes from one effect to another is a very useful trick. Bear it in mind the next time you find yourself struggling to match shots together.

The last shot

For the final shot, I've returned to the first picture again. I'll let you create something with your new found skills. Don't forget this is the last shot of the sequence so I suggest we put a fade out at the end, matching the one on the music.

My suggestion is start on the wheels of Daphne's bike, and move up to her face before panning across the faces of the other three cyclists. The track forms a smooth (that word again!) curve that is made more fluid by the addition of a keyframe that I've put in to alter the trajectory of the move rather than frame on anyone in particular. I'm sure you can improve on this if you wish.

My version of the final animation. Note the additional keyframe to modify the path

Save this project as *BMX_photo_project_final_version* before you move on. We will use it in later chapters.

Converting project formats

I mentioned at the beginning of this chapter that you could convert this project to NTSC without worries. If that is the format you will use to make DVDs, change the timeline settings to Widescreen NTSC and wait for the timeline to re-render if you need to. Now you can test it - there should be no unseemly flickering in preview, but if you are working with a bugged version of Studio and have had to use double keyframes you may see some, so check if any keyframes have been shifted from a frame boundary.

When you are happy, save the project as *BMX-photo_project_NTSC*. When we use this project later on you have a version that won't need to be converted.

If you want to change this project to HD, it's also not an issue - again, change the timeline settings. If you have a Blu-ray player but no other HD equipment, then here is a chance to see how much better an AVCHD disc is. Make a SD DVD from the project, then change the timeline setting to 1920x1080 and create an AVCHD disc, burned to a standard DVD. Compare the two discs on your Blu-ray player. On smaller TVs viewed at a distance there may be little difference, but on any large screen TV you should be suitably impressed.

More Advanced Tools

This chapter aims to explain the editing features that we haven't yet used so far in the book.

Subprojects

The feature in Pinnacle Studio which I believe gets overlooked and also misunderstood more than any other is Subprojects. While I think there is a little more development to be done in this area, they introduce some really useful options when both editing movies and creating optical discs. They offer a number of benefits:

Simplifying a project vertically. A particular section of a movie may require the use of many tracks, while the rest of the project does not. You might have built up an elaborate opening sequence that means the number of tracks used makes it difficult to display all of the the timeline clearly. Creating a subproject will allow you to reduce the track count.

Protecting a section of a movie. When a group of clips are contained within a subproject, it isn't possible to disrupt the relationship between the clips.

Applying a global effect. Because a subproject is treated as a single clip, you can add an effect to the whole subproject. This is particularly useful for keyframed effects that apply changes over time.

Simplifying a disc project. When you build a disc project, you are unlikely to want to make changes to the details of the movie or movies themselves. Using subprojects rather than rendered copies of the projects both simplifies the timeline and protects the movies from inadvertent changes.

In the past, the alternative to using subprojects would be to render the movie to a new file. This will always bring with it the possibility of reducing the picture quality, even with a very careful choice of settings for the new file. The other disadvantage with rendering out to a new file is that making even a small change within the file requires you to go back to the original movie and carry out the whole render again.

One thing subprojects aren't a substitute for is the troubleshooting process of rendering sections of a project to a new file to overcome problems at the Export stage.

A subproject always starts life as a fully fledged project that you load into your current Movie or Disc project. The Library and Compact Library hold all the projects you have made with the current installation of Pinnacle Studio 19. Any projects that are on your computer that currently don't show up in the Library can be imported just as if they were any other asset. Therefore if you can only find a project using Windows, use the Importer or Quick Import to link it to the Library.

One very important thing to understand about creating and using a subproject is that it is a **non-destructive** process. This means that any changes you make to a subproject aren't made to the original project from which the subproject was generated. If this doesn't quite seem logical, think of the subproject as if it were a video clip – if you trim a clip on the timeline it doesn't change the clip stored on your hard disc, so there is no reason to expect subprojects to behave any differently.

Subprojects and Preview rendering

In the following examples we are begining to push the limits of smooth previewing on all but the most powerful computers, and even if up until this point you have not needed to have the optimisation set to over 50%, you might need to increase that now for smooth playback. See pages 8, 36 and 522 for more details.

In addition, Studio will sometimes override the setting for more complex subprojects, so don't be surprised if you see preview rendering occur on some sections even with the level set to zero.

If you do struggle to get a smooth playback, set the level to 100% and open each subproject by clicking on it on the timeline, wait for the rendering to occur, close the project then reduce the level to that you normally work at.

Adding Subprojects to the timeline

I'm going to explore the use of subprojects by using them to build a short movie that will become the introduction to a Disc project we will make in the next chapter. Start a new movie with the SD widescreen project setting to suit your country – PAL or NTSC. Use the Compact Library to find the *BMX_photo_project_final_version* we made in the Photos chapter, or if you are creating a NTSC project, locate the *NTSC* version.

If you haven't actually made any of the projects we are going to employ you can find suitable versions on the website and data DVD.

Drag the chosen project down to the start of track 2. We will use this music, but I'm going to squeeze the video of the project into a box.

Adding a subproject to the timeline

The subproject Context menu

To open a subproject in the Effects Editor we need to right click and use the context menu, so do that now and select the *2D-3D* effect *Studio PIP* (Picture-in-Picture) and the preset *Top Left Corner*. We have pushed the whole movie into the corner with just one effect, and although we could have done that by copy and pasting the effect to all the individual clips, the next thing we are going to do would not be practical.

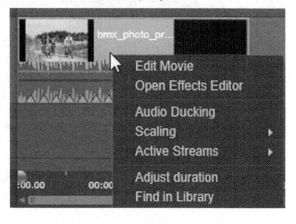

The BMX_photo subproject with the Studio PIP effect

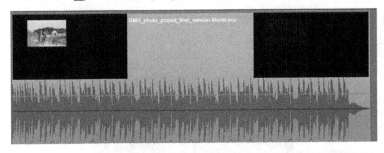

Locate *Project 1_4* - the final version of the Mystery Machine movie we completed at the end of chapter 2. You will have made a version that matches your TV standard, PAL or NTSC. (The project is also available from the DTVPro website.) Drag that down to track 3. Hopefully you have still got the markers in place within the BMX project, so in the PAL version it should be very easy with the magnet turned on to snap the start of *Project 1_4* with the first full bar of music. The subproject on track 3 should now start at 1 second 09 frames PAL. The NTSC version may mess you around a bit because the marker isn't on a frame boundary, so you should check that the project on track 2 starts at 1 second 11 frames.

Two subprojects with effects added on the timeline

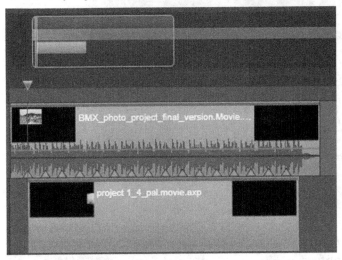

Right click on the new subproject, deselect Audio in *Active Streams* and then open the subproject in the Effects Editor. Add the 2D-3D 3D Editor CPU effect and make sure that the default preset (which is a Travel Left) is selected.

Return to the timeline and check out the progress so far. The keyframed effect on track 3 would have been a nightmare to add to individual clips, matching frames for each cut. We could have rendered the project to a file but it wouldn't have been as easy as the procedure we have just performed.

I should make it clear that I built up this project with a lot of trial and error. I had a concept in mind, but as I started putting the shots together new ideas occurred to me. When you are building up your own movies, much of the fun to be had is by thinking creatively and having new ideas. The next edit was one of these ideas.

The foreground subproject obscures the background quite badly at around 16 seconds in, so I decided to move the BMX PIP. By timing the move carefully, we can tie it in with the underlying video. Open the lower clip in the Effects Editor. With Solo selected, you can see Fred's eyes flick from left to right. Park the scrubber at the frame before his eyes move (16.07 PAL, 16:11 NTSC), and then use the navigator to switch to the upper track. Without moving the scrubber, enable keyframing on the Studio PIP effect (the diamond shaped button to the right of the effect title). The timescale will appear, and a keyframe will automatically be created at the scrubber location.

Return to the lower track and place the scrubber at the cut to the shot of the back of the van, return to the upper track and use the Keyframe diamond tool top left of the timescale to create a new keyframe. In the Parameter box to the right change the horizontal position from -20 to +20, then preview the effect.

Third keyframe added to the PIP effect

I'm trying to create the impression that Fred is watching the PIP effect as it moves across the screen, and I subsequently played around with the positioning of the PIP to try to improve that impression. I settled on the following figures for the start and second keyframe – Position H= -30, V= 30. For the third keyframe I changed the Position Horizontal value from -30 to + 30. Even if you don't fully agree, please change the effect to those values as it has a bearing on what we do later!

Before we carry out the next stage, I'm going to demonstrate how you might create a project to be used as a subproject from within another project. Save the current project as *DVD Intro_1,* and then in the Compact Library locate and double click on the *Flight Project Stage 4* movie so that it opens as a project (and not as a subproject!)

The contents of the Flight Subproject

Select the 10 clips on the top four tracks up until the Nantlle Ridge shot, by drawing a marquee around them. Note that we don't include the Scorefitter music on the bottom track. Use Edit/Copy or

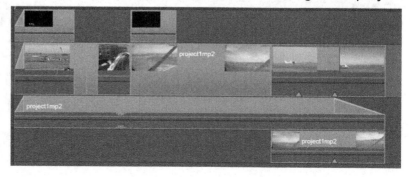

CTRL-C to put those in the paste buffer. Start a new Movie project, change the settings to PAL or NTSC Widescreen depending on what type of project you are making, then Edit/Paste or use CTRL-V to place the clips in the new project. Save it as *Flight Subproject*.

If it was your intention to remove the clips you were putting into the subproject from an original project (to be replaced by the subproject) you could even *Cut* instead of *Copy*. Then when you tried to start a new project you would be offered the chance to save the original project, with the clips removed, when you started the new project. This doesn't allow any margin for error though, because the Undo buffer is cleared when you save a project.

Now that we have created a trimmed down version of the Flight movie, reload the DVD Intro project and place Flight Subproject at the start of track 4 as a subproject.

Subprojects as clips

If you play the movie, you will see it works quite well until we cut away from the first shot of the plane. The new subproject is far too long, though, so let's go about editing it. We can just treat it as a clip to begin with, although there is a significant difference to understand later on.

Let's begin by splitting the subproject in two at the shot change when the title disappears. Line up the scrubber on the cut (00:00:13.04 PAL and NTSC) and use the razor tool or the N key. We now have two subprojects, just as if we had spilt a clip and generated two clips.

Now use Quick trim on the Out point of the first project to shorten it a bit more. Dragging left should mean the Out point snaps into place with the bar markers imbedded into the BMX project and you should be able to trim it to 00:00:08.00 on the TC counter above the Timeline preview window.

Trimming the first half of the split subproject on track 4

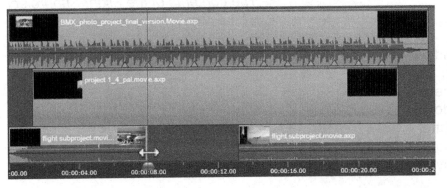

Use the speaker icon on the track header to mute the audio for track 4 and then play back what we have so far. We are using as much of the plane shot as we can before the shot starts to get masked. Perhaps musically we are cutting away from the shot a bar too late, but it seems a reasonable compromise.

Editing Subprojects

I'm just going to jump ahead slightly to make an important point. I'd like you to open the first subproject on track 4 as if you were going to edit it. To do this, you double click on the subproject, or use Edit Movie from the right-click context menu. A whole new window opens on top of the current Movie Editor that is a clone of the Movie Editor. OK, you don't have the Windows drop-down menus or the Mode tabs, but everything else is there for you to edit the subproject just as if it were a movie.

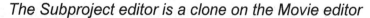

The Subproject editor is a clone on the Movie editor

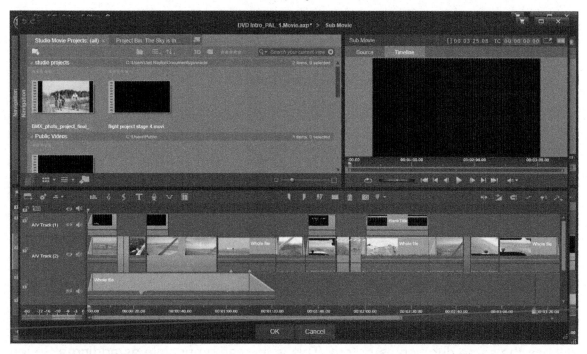

Look at the timeline. Just like me the first time I used subprojects, you might not be seeing what you would expect to see. The timeline is the length of the **whole** subproject and includes clips that can't be seen, even though on the main project timeline the subproject ends after eight seconds. Therefore, if we want to re-trim a subproject, the material is there to do so. Mentally compare this with what happens when you spilt and then re-trim a clip; exactly the same thing occurs.

Let's close the open subproject on track 4. To return to the main project, click on the Close X icon top right of the window. In the same way as if you had opened the Effects Editor, if you have made any changes to the subproject you will be offered the chance to *Save* your changes – not as a file, but just to commit to them - *Don't Save* – return to the main project with the subproject unchanged from before we opened it – or *Cancel* – carry on editing the subproject. Choose *Don't Save* in this instance, because I don't want you to make any changes.

Back in the Main project, we have black video under the other two tracks before the second subproject starts. My intention is to use a bit of the view out of the window before take off, then the take off and the keyframed effect where the interior and exterior shots are both on screen. Hopefully we can see the keyframed movements either side of the point when it is obscured by the Project 1 subproject.

Open up the **second** version of the subproject on track 4 to the right. This one we will re-edit. Completely delete track 1 from the subproject by using the track header context menu, therefore removing the titles. Then delete what is now the second track from the top that contains the detached audio.

Below are two tracks both labelled AV Track (4). Delete the lower one that has no content. Now remove the first four clips on track 2, leaving the project looking like the screenshot.

The edited version of the second subproject

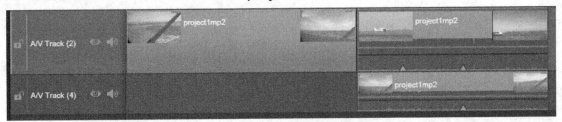

When you return to the main project (responding with *Save* after you click to close the Sub Movie Editor), you might expect the subproject to be shorter, but it isn't – it still has the same duration as before. This is the same principle as adding a Speed effect – the program doesn't change the duration of a clip when you alter it within an editor because of the knock-on effects that it would have on a multi-track project. If you scrub through the timeline, though, you will see that the last 25 or so seconds of the subproject clip are just black. Use quick trim and remove the black level at the end – the trim should snap neatly into place unless you have switched off the magnet.

Refreshing the render files

Something a bit strange happened when I made this movie the second time - although I had edited the subproject, Studio still showed me the video from before the edit. If this happens to you, don't get confused! Delete the render files using the control panel. If this doesn't fix the issue, the next time you trim or move the subproject the problem should right itself. Like all good bugs, when I tried to reproduce it on another system it didn't happen.

A trimmed subproject retains its trims

Assuming you are seeing the correct video, you should notice something else. The In point of the subproject isn't the start of the subproject when we open it up to edit it. When we split the original subproject, we in effect set a later In point. By editing the second subproject we have moved the content, but there is still 13 seconds trimmed from the front. If you Quick trim the In point left you will reveal the whole of the first shot in the subproject. If you do that, use Undo to restore the project.

Refining the second subproject

Scrub through the main project and you will notice there is a point just after 17 seconds when Project 1 almost completely obscures the track below. I want the first half of the keyframed move to have been completed by this point. Drop a marker at 17.20 NTSC 17.16 PAL timecode to help us find this point. Now open the second iteration of the Flight project in the Sub Movie Editor and find the point where the first part of the keyframed effect settles – 00:00:38:12 NTSC 38.10 PAL. Put a marker at this point, quit and save the subproject.

The aim now is to line up the two markers – one on the timeline, the other embedded in the subproject that shows up as a white triangle. Turn off the Audio Stream on the subproject to make the marker stand out more clearly.

Latency and subprojects

Quick trim the front of the second subproject to coincide with the white marker.

We now may have a problem. Unless you have a powerful computer, you are likely to find editing subprojects on the timeline a bit hit or miss. The trimming operation may be jerky and might behave as if the magnet isn't working properly. Ensure the magnet is on. You still may have trouble getting the trim point to snap into place – so zoom the timeline in to help.

What we are seeing here is the program beginning to be overwhelmed by the complexity of the timeline, and the edit controls becoming less responsive. If you have left your preview rending at the default high setting you will be seeing render sections appearing all the time slowing down your work, and if you have turned them off your preview will become laggy. (If you haven't investigated these settings yet, they are covered in the Understanding Studio chapter.) Persevere, though, and you should get the In point of the second project to line up with the internal marker.

The two markers that need to be aligned

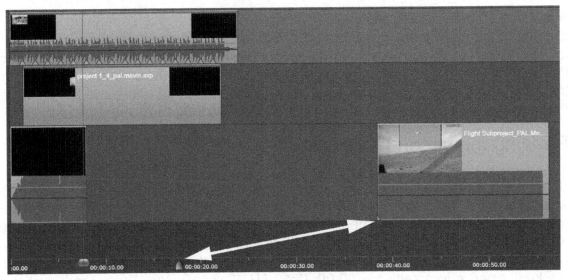

The next operation is going to be even harder, because we are going to overlap the video tracks even more. Drag the newly trimmed subproject left and try to line up the In point with the timeline marker. You may not find this too difficult, but If you were working with AVCHD material you might. Not only is there all this *Latency* going on, but there are a whole bunch of markers on the track above which may be confusing the issue. So get the subproject in roughly the right position and cease dragging.

I'll now show you how to proceed from here with some help from the Trim mode.

Using Trim mode for accuracy

Set an Advanced trim point on the Out point of the gap to the left of the second subproject. Carefully use the trim controls to trim the gap - which effectively moves the following subproject. Slide the clip using the 10 frame, and then the single frame buttons until the markers line up. It should be quite easy with a little patience.

Next, we want to leave the subproject in that position, but loosen the In point so it butts up to the first subproject. Switch the trim point to the right of the edit - the In point of the second subproject. Now use the trim buttons but in conjunction with the ALT key so that the operation happens in Overwrite. If you keep an eye on the left-hand trim window you will see the Outgoing video change to the shot of the plane when the gap has been closed up.

Using Advanced trimming to move the second subproject

Quit trim mode and preview your work so far.

When Subprojects don't work well

I'd quite like to change the timing of the 2D keyframed effect. In the first iteration of this project in the Studio 16 book I led the reader on a bit of a wild goose chase proving that keyframes were redistributed within a subproject when we trimmed the duration. When regenerating the project for this book I found the process rather frustrating. So instead of wasting your time, let me remind you of what happened when we altered the duration of a photo that had an Animated Pan and Zoom applied: The keyframes were redistributed. If you reduced the duration by 50%, the full animation still occurred, but in half the time.

The conclusion I came to was that it was best to abandon trying to adjust the 2D animation of the plane taking off and revert to using the clips within the main project. We could just start again, but it's worth knowing how to turn subprojects back into clips on the timeline.

Extracting clips from Subprojects

In order to alter the 2D editor animated effect to suit the new project, I need to deconstruct the second subproject.

The first shot in the subproject from the interior of the plane is OK. Split the subproject at the point when we cut to the exterior shot of the plane about to lift off.

Open what is now the third subproject on track 4, select clip 2 on the top track and Ctrl-Click on the first clip on the lower track to select them both, and Copy (CTRL-C). Close the subproject. It's worth appreciating that when you copy and paste multi-track clips, Studio needs to retain the track structures and won't copy to a different track from the one where the clip came from. So with our subproject, the clips are going to get pasted to tracks 1 and 2, causing the clips there to be moved out of the way. We don't want that to happen, so move the scrubber up to the end of the timeline in order to prevent disruption. Now Paste (CTRL-V) the clips.

The clips extracted to tracks 1 and 2

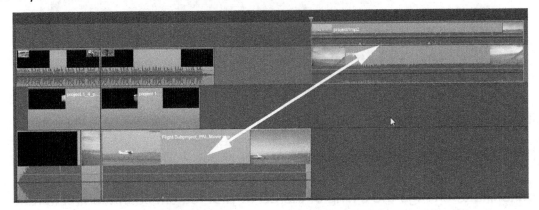

Before we can move the clips to the correct place, we need to create a new track below track 4. Use the track header context menu to create a track 5. Delete the third subproject on track 4, then multi-select the two new clips on tracks 1 and 2 and drag them down to tracks 4 and 5, lining up the first clip with the end of the second subproject on track 4.

Again, latency may be an issue for you here. If you struggle, use the Advanced trim method to position the clips exactly. Quick trim the out points of the new clips to line up with the end of the BMX project on track 2. We are now in much the same situation as before, but it's far easier to make the changes to the keyframes.

The final position of the clips

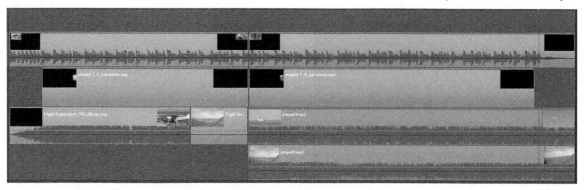

Open the new clip on track 4 in the Effects Editor. You can use your own judgement here regarding the repositioning of the keyframes. I ended up with the following values if you want to copy me exactly:

Second keyframe (start of zoom out): 13:08 PAL, 13:10 NTSC

Third keyframe (end of zoom out): 14:05 PAL, 14:06 NTSC

Fourth keyframe (start of zoom back in): 20:02 PAL, 20:04 NTSC

Fifth Keyframe (end of zoom back in): 21.01 PAL, 21.02 NTSC

It may seem that the above use of subprojects gets very complicated towards the end, and I agree – which is why I abandoned using them for the final stage. Hopefully the steps give you an insight into where they can be used to very good advantage – for simplification, protection and global keyframing – and when you might be better off keeping all of the tracks available on the timeline.

Adding a title

You will need to mute tracks 4 and 5, and I've decided to add a title at the end of this project. I'm just going to describe it and let you create it without me guiding you through.

- Duration 7 seconds.

- A solid background using the Colour Picker to match the sky in the last shot of the plane.

- A central text layer containing the words "Made With", "Pinnacle" "Studio 19" separated with line returns.

- Font *Blade Runner Movie Point*, size 72, Default Look.

- Entry Motion *Lines from Infinity*.

- Make the text box begin later by setting it's In point to 1 second after the start of the title.

Place this on track 1 at the end of the movie, then overlap the last shot by a second and add a 1 second dissolve to the start of the title.

This should make the total project duration 30 seconds. Save it as *DVD Intro_2* for use in the next chapter.

Montage

While the unlimited tracks of Pinnacle Studio Ultimate allow almost any type of composite effect to be created (and the 24 tracks available in the Plus version should be enough in almost any circumstances!), given enough computer resources, skill and patience, the Montage feature is a shortcut to some very complex, elaborate and visually impressive effects that require far less time on the part of the editor. The downside is that you can only customise Montages within certain limits.

If you open the Montage section within Creative Elements in the Library, you will find around 300 items. In addition, there are people who create and distribute Montages for free, and Pinnacle will always be happy to sell you some more.

Most Montages come as themes. There is often an *Opening* for you to start your project with, then a set of *Segues* for you to link together sections, and finally an *Ending*.

Perhaps the most obvious example can be seen in the basic Album Montage. This is an introduction, bridging and closing for a slideshow, and it demonstrates many of the controls.

To examine the Montage Editor, start a new project and Drag Album 1- Opening to the timeline. Switch the project settings to 16:9 and 2D. Double clicking opens the

Montage Editor and we are presented with a tool very similar to the Title Editor. To the left is the Compact Library where we can gather assets to use in the Montage. At the bottom above the Navigator is a blue, single track timeline that acts as a progress bar. Above the timescale and transport controls are four dropzones for adding media, and to the right are the parameter boxes, which vary considerably depending on the Montage.

Typical Montage Theme in the Montage Editor

Load up the Montage with the first three photos of the kids on their bikes in the Public Photos location and put the *Sky* video into dropzone 4. We could put photos or videos in any of the dropzones, but in some dropzones the video will be frozen. Some of the drop zones can also play the audio – they are invariably at the beginning and end of a Montage and have a small speaker icon in the top right corner. Clicking on the icon turns it red and mutes the audio. Click again to re-enable. The slider beneath the video sets the point at which the video begins. To remove an item from a dropzone you can either overwrite it by dropping another item over it, or right click and use the Remove Media command.

One thing to watch out for is the automatic cropping of still photos. If we put the photo of Shaggy that has been shot in portrait mode into a dropzone it is cropped to lose the black edges. Fortunately, it is very easy to pre-crop the photo to the framing you want using Corrections, rather than be stuck with the cropping that the Montage tool selects automatically.

The parameters in the case of *Album 1- Opening* include two text entry boxes to allow you to change the titles. Alongside each is a very small "*I*" icon that leads to a simplified version of the text controls from the Title Editor, complete with Colour Selection box and Colour Picker. The final control turns the background off, or rather, makes it transparent.

Altering the font properties of a Montage text Parameter

Montages can have their durations altered on the Movie or Disc Editor timeline using the normal trim controls, but the internal timing is determined by the blue timeline progress bar within the Montage Editor. The white bars and dotted lines are adjustable by dragging left or right on the handles in the same way as you adjust the motions in the Title Editor.

In the case of the *Album 1 – Opening* Montage, the solid area is the duration of the entire animation, and the dotted portion is how long we hold the full frame of the Video (or photo) in dropzone 4 at the end of the montage. When there is a slider at the beginning of a Montage it affects how long the opening asset is held before the animation begins.

If you alter the duration of a Montage on the Movie Editor timeline, the additional time is added to the end of the effect, invariably extending the duration of the dotted section at the end of the Montage timeline. To slow down the animation, I need to edit the Montage itself by adjusting the Montage timeline slider back to the right. It's also possible to adjust the incoming asset's still duration, so you can re-arrange the three sections to get the desired relationship between the static incoming and outgoing full frames and the linking animation.

The tricky thing when using montages for video is getting in and out of them. If there is a cut in the video somewhere near where you want to begin or end the Montage then it's much easier to line things up. Let's work on a simple example.

In the case of the Montage we have built up, the whole effect lasts 25 seconds. The last shot – the view of the van wheel – only lasts 7 (PAL) frames. If we put another copy of the Sky video on the timeline we can match the cut by counting frames and trim using the In point of the video to the eighth frame.

But, let's say we think the animation is a bit too ponderous. We need to modify the Montage on the Movie Editor timeline first. Using the context menu, use *Adjust Duration* to change the length to 15 seconds, then open it in the Montage Editor. Whoops – we have lost the trim handle. Also we can't type in durations with the Montage Editor so that won't work either.

Exit back to the Movie Editor and use Undo to restore the Montage to 25 seconds. Return to the Montage Editor and adjust the trim handle between the solid and dotted lines to around the 12 second point.

Returning to the movie, you will see we have speeded up the animation nicely, and the outgoing video just plays for longer.

At this point, assuming that the video source you were using was long enough, you could just count the frames and editing on the rest of the Sky video to make the edit seamless. However, it's going to be easier to trim the end of the Montage. Quick trim it to around the point that it cuts to the wheel shot, and then for accuracy, use the Trim mode to generate a yellow handle on the Out point of the Montage. Use the keyboard or Trim mode controls to trim the Out point to the last frame of the trees before the video cuts to the wheels.

Now, when you put a second copy of the Sky video on the timeline, it's easy to trim the In point – it's the first frame of the wheel shot.

Montages behave slightly differently to subprojects when you edit them on the timeline, as we have just seen. The animations don't alter in the same way as keyframed effects within subprojects do. In common with subprojects, though, you cannot add a Speed effect to a Montage.

Using the project timeline context menu for Montages allows you to open them in the Effects Editor. You can even use keyframes effects, so it's possible to spice up the Montages even more – for example, adding an animated 3D Editor effect to one of the Multilayer Mix Animations can make for some spectacularly head-spinning results – I've used the technique to build up an opening title sequence to a discussion programme that would have taken absolutely hours to achieve in other editing programs. Perhaps it was a bit over-elaborate....

The context menu also has the option for you to paste whatever you last cut or pasted from the timeline (but not the Library) into a choice of dropzones, which may be a timesaving feature, particularly if you want to use clips to which you have already added effects - even the speed effect!

The *Paste to Dropzone* function has another use as well. In the Montage Editor you aren't allowed to add Projects or other Montages to dropzones – the program just won't let you. However you can do so by putting the project or second Montage on the timeline, and then using copy and *Paste to Dropzone*. Obviously if you want to use a Montage within a Montage, you need to populate the dropzones of the nested Montage first.

The Montage Context menus showing Paste to Dropzone

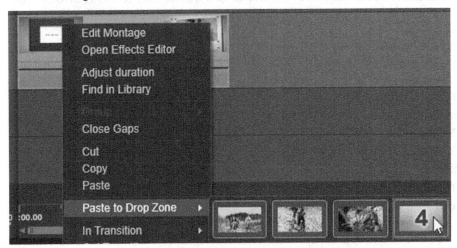

While Montages offer a shortcut to some very neat effects for 2D movie making, if you are making 3D movies they can bring much more. The themes which have stereoscopic qualities are flagged up in the Library – there are over 90 of them. Using 3D Montages for 3D projects will really let you punch home the 3D at the beginning and end of a movie. Also, don't overlook the Video Transitions section of Montages to use in addition to the other transitions available with 3D properties.

SmartMovie

Pinnacle Studio 19 boasts the ability to "automatically" create movies, slideshows or a combination of both. I've put the quotation marks around the word automatic because you do have to do a little work, and you also have a bit of creative control over the end product. The important thing to remember about the Smart Creation functions is that they are only a starting point.

You start making Smart Projects in the Library, but once Studio has done its thing, you can click on the Edit button and the project gets transferred to the Movie Editor where you can correct, refine and embellish the Studio version and put your own spin on things. To investigate the Smart Creation function, switch to the Main Library tab and select the SmartMovie button at the bottom. A flyout window opens at the bottom of the screen.

At its very simplest Studio creates a movie consisting of the photo, video and audio assets in the drop zones, adding transitions at each edit point. The assets default to different durations depending on the settings in the Clip length drop-down menu.

The Library with the SmartMovie window open

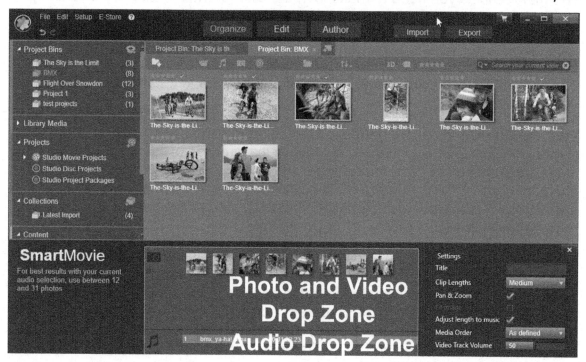

You drag Photos or Video from the Library to the upper Drop Zone. Because we are in the Library, selecting suitable sources is easier because the browser window is larger. The Drop Zone allows you to re-arrange the photos or video clip in any order just by dragging and dropping. Multi-selection works too, so you can CTRL-click a selection and then delete them, or drag them to another position. Double clicking on a photo opens the Photo Corrections Editor, on a video in the Video Corrections editor, where you have access to the full array of tools, in particular the crop tool for reframing the photos. Any corrections added within the SmartMovie don't get echoed back to the Library.

The Audio Drop Zone is below. You can drag music tracks from the Library or add Scorefitter music by clicking on the treble clef icon to open the Scorefitter Editor. You aren't limited to one piece of music and just like the Photo and Video zone, re-arranging the order is possible by drag and drop. Notice that the running total of all the music in the zone is displayed on the left of the list.

The settings list to the right is where you have some control. **Title** allows you to enter a name that is displayed at the start. Studio always puts an Emphasis motion on this title that you may not find is to your taste, so you might decide to put a title on later by omitting any text from the entry box. No text – no title.

The major choice you need to make is in the drop-down box labelled **Clip Length**. Even when using the **Maximum** setting, video clips over a certain length – 1 minute – are never used in their entirety – so a 1 minute 5 second clip will be split and used twice. Photos are set to around 27 seconds.

Short, **Medium** and **Long** result in clips of about 3, 6 and 12 seconds, with photos of a similar duration.

Pan and Zoom adds a little gentle movement to the show. Photos are analysed for content for each P&Z, and there is variation in the direction of the zoom. The direction may be determined by the composition of the photos, but, as with the Automatic Pan and Zoom in the Effects Editor, it is difficult to guess what the actual algorithm is. Pan and Zoom will also eliminate any black borders caused by the photos and project not having matching aspect ratios.

If you don't want to use Pan and Zoom and also don't want to use the Corrections Editor to crop photos the function **Fit Image** will do the cropping for you, but the results may not be very sympathetic to the content of the photos. The comments I made about shooting stills in the Photos chapter apply just as much here – if your camera can shoot in the same aspect ratio as your projects, use that setting, don't shoot in portrait orientation and fill the frame as much as possible.

Adjust length to music is where the feature starts to get very helpful. The duration of the photo and video clips and transitions are adjusted to fit whatever music you have placed in the Audio Drop zone. This is subject to a sensible limit. If the music is short and there are lots of clips, the clip duration isn't lowered below a second, including the associated transition. This means that some clips may be left off the end of the movie. Therefore, the duration of the music *in seconds* needs to be greater than the *number of pictures or video clips.* If you want to make a faster paced photo slideshow you will need to adjust the durations manually in the Movie Editor.

To make the slideshow fit perfectly, the first and last photos will be adjusted to take up any odd number of frames that are left over after Studio does the maths.

Media Order is another useful feature. The Smartmovie will normally follow the pattern you have set in the dropzone – **As defined** - but you can reset this to the time and date of the assets (if available) with the **Chronological** setting. **Random** is just that. When you apply these changes they aren't reflected in the drop zone, so the assets are still displayed in the **As defined** order. You will only see the changes when you preview the movie or switch to the Edit mode.

Defining the Media Order

Video Track Volume controls how much of the original audio is present in the final movie.

Random transitions are added at each edit point, although they are restricted to the relatively simpler types.

Adding music to the Audio Drop Zone shows off the power of Smart Movie more, because the music will define the duration of the final movie.

At the bottom of the settings is an option to define the **Video Settings**. One trick here that will speed up the preview of changes is to build your project in Standard Definition even if your final product is going to be HD. The rendering for the P&Z will be quicker. When you are happy with the final result, change the Timeline setting in the Movie Editor before re-checking the project. The final Settings option - **Clear Project** - empties the drop zones.

At the bottom of the SmartMovie box are three buttons. If you select **Preview** you will invariably get a message bottom left as the movie is generated, then a preview window with the result will open. Notice that preview optimisation will still be working on any animations, unless you have it disabled (which might well lead to jerky playback). Once the Smart Preview window is open, you can make changes to the project, but you will be warned that you need to press play to refresh the preview window.

Edit transfers the project to the Movie Editor for further enhancements. Any changes you make there are non-destructive – they don't get reflected back to the SmartMovie project in the Library, so you can make a variety of movies from the same set of photos even if you decided to delete some of them from the Movie Editor.

Another interesting thing happens when you select Preview or Edit. The current contents of the dropzones are added into a special Collection entitled *Latest Smart Creation*. This is a one-off. The next time you try to preview or edit a different Smart Creation it will be replaced, so there is only ever one of these Collections. So, when you continue working on the Smart Creation that has been transferred to the Movie Editor, you can open the Collection in the Compact Library. If you remove an item from the timeline, it's green checkmark disappears, so you know it is missing.

If you use the Export button, the project is transferred straight to an Export window where you can carry out all the usual operations just as if the project had come from the Movie or Disc Editor.

I find that for Smart Movie to be helpful the video clips need to be chosen with care, possibly even pre-edited as Library shortcuts or scenes. For a wacky "pop video" the tool may have its uses, but to be honest it's not as well developed as the version in Pinnacle Studio 15.

3D editing and monitoring

The principle of 3D video is relatively simple. Humans get a sense of depth perception because they have two eyes, spaced apart. If we can record, edit and play back a separate picture for each eye then all we need to do is feed the viewer's left and right eyes with the separate videos and they will experience the depth perception.

Recording at a basic level is relatively simple. Two cameras placed side by side about the distance of the human eyes will give us the two channels we need. The details of the correct spacing, alignment, synchronisation and recording methods can get very complicated, but that hasn't stopped consumer video camcorder manufacturers, and you can buy 3D cameras relatively cheaply these days, although they are less common than they were a few years back when 3D was added to Pinnacle Studio.

The principle of editing isn't that complex, either. The two video streams must be treated as one stream. That's about it really. The complex bit is how you feed the two eyes individually.

You can use head mounted displays to do that, but it's a pretty expensive and antisocial way of watching a movie. Cross-eyed is a format of two pictures side by side that may allow you to view 3D without any special equipment, if you can do the "cross-eyed" trick. I've never been able to achieve this form of 3D viewing, which requires you to go cross-eyed and stop focusing on the image. All I get is a blinding headache after a few minutes of trying. So this one isn't for everyone!

The first real commercial solution was the use of coloured filters in front of the eyes of each viewer. This is called **anaglyph** filtering. Normally 3D glasses for this method use Red (left eye) and Cyan (right eye) – directly opposite each other in the colour triangle. When you view an image that has been coded as an anaglyph without the glasses you will see odd coloured fringing. Put the glasses on and a 3D image appears. It's not brilliant 3D, even in a darkened room.

There are three other practical methods of displaying 3D on a screen, but they all need complex hardware.

Light can be polarised – so that it vibrates in one plane only – by passing it through a filter. With a screen that transmits two images polarised at 90 degrees and two polarising filters at 90 degrees placed over each eye of the viewer, the eyes can receive two separate images.

Glasses with a shutter system can be used to switch between the left and right eye in synchronisation with a screen that is showing alternative left and right images.

Screens that use masks or lenses to display two images to a viewer whose head is in a certain position are called Autostereoscopic.

Although these three methods all require special hardware, that equipment simply needs to be fed the left and right video streams to work. In the past both streams were combined in a side-by-side view so that only one signal chain was required to connect up the viewing hardware. Formats are now being developed that combine the video signals in a way that is compatible with older equipment.

3D content flag and search icon

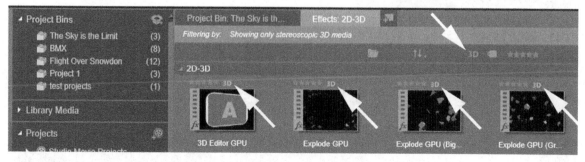

Apart from the requirement to be able to recognise the various 3D video formats and decode and recode them, editing 3D video is no different than 2D. Studio has a wide choice of methods to monitor 3D video, but unless you own a special 3D monitor or are willing to wear Red/Cyan glasses you won't actually see the 3D effect while editing.

3D features in Studio start in the Library. There is a 3D filter available in the Filter bar, and the 3D icon is used to flag any media that Studio recognises as having stereoscopic properties.

The Corrections Editor has a drop-down menu that allows you to define the format – so if it has been incorrectly detected it can be set to the format it should be.

3D Adjustments

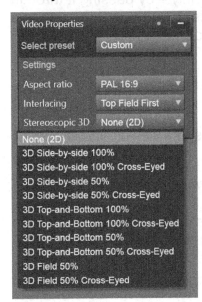

The Effects Editor has three effects within the sub tab *Stereoscopic*. You can use the S3D effect to enhance or even create 3D information – and obviously to use this effectively you will need to be able to view the picture in 3D. For example, if you add a picture-in-picture effect to a photo, you can bring it to the foreground so that appears to "float" in front of the background.

The Eye Selector can be thought of as a similar tool to the audio channel mapping – you can send the left eye information to the right eye and vice versa.

Monitoring 3D images has a default setting in the Control Panel/Export and Preview box. There are 7 options.

Left and Right Eye displays just the channel for the selected eye.

Setting up a Picture in Picture effect to "float" in the foreground

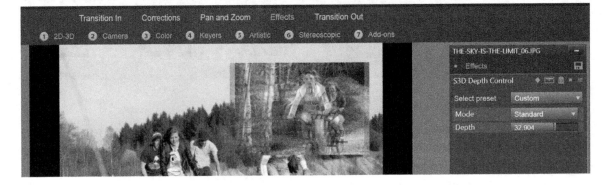

Side by Side shows both channels alongside each other without distortion. Therefore a 16:9 view becomes a 32:9 view!

Differential shows the amount of 3D information by displaying grey where the left and right channels have little or no stereoscopic information,and Red/Cyan when the images diverge considerably

Checkerboard divides the screen area up into rectangles of alternative Left and Right channels.

3D TV (Side by Side) is a signal that can be sent to a suitable 3D capable monitor used for preview. If it is correctly set up, it will display a 3D image. On a non-3D display you see the left and right channels squashed together horizontally to fit into the correct aspect viewing window. This is the format you should use to feed full screen preview on a second monitor.

Anaglyph is the video encoded for viewing with Red/Cyan glasses.

3D monitoring option.

These above choices are not only available in the Control Panel. Any preview window that contains media that has stereoscopic qualities has a new control icon, showing the current display mode. A drop-down menu lets you change the mode for that window. The modes each have their own unique icon, as shown in the screenshot.

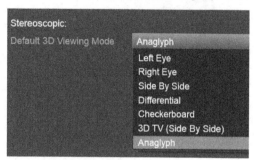

To export 3D movies you need a number of options, due to the various ways you might want to view your images. When you send a 3D project to the exporter and select File or Disc, a further drop-down menu is added to Settings for S3D. If you have a pair of anaglyph glasses and want to view your 3D movie or disc on a 2D screen, then anaglyph is the setting for you. The other settings will be required for more advanced playback methods.

Multistream is an option that is offered with the AVCHD 2 standard, and the file is backwardly compatible with older files, so if you watch a Multistream encoded file on 2D playback equipment, you will just see a 2D picture – no side-by-side images or coloured fringes. You can also make multistream Blu-ray compatible files.

The Voice Over Tool

The Timeline Toolbar contains an icon that looks like a microphone, and when you hover your mouse over it, the tooltip reveals it to be the Voice Over tool. This is how you can record narration to go with video that you have already recorded and edited. You can talk along with the video playback, timing your comments to match the pictures.

The Windows recording selection box

I've always found the hardest part of using this feature in all versions of Studio is getting the microphone to work properly. Many PCs have poor quality microphone input circuits that aren't shielded from interference. In addition, recent PC sound hardware is more sophisticated, but that means that if the microphone isn't already up and working before you launch Studio, it might not be detected.

Listening to the microphone

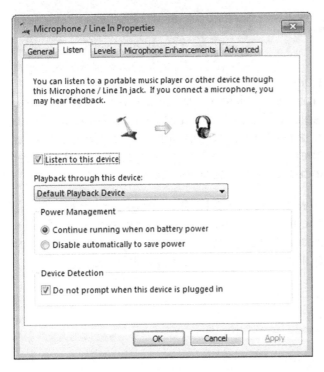

So, get the microphone working in Windows first. The Windows taskbar at the bottom of the screen should contain a small speaker icon. Right clicking on that will allow you to open the Sound panel, and opening the Recording tabs. In Windows 8 and 10 you can go straight to the Recording devices. A correctly connected microphone will be flagged with a green tick, and if you click on the Properties tab you can choose to *Listen* to the microphone and set the levels to test it

In Windows you will probably have to turn your speakers down, but if you can listen on headphones, so much the better as you will be able to set the levels without worrying about the howl-round you get when the speakers feed back into the microphone.

Because the feature is designed to let you watch the screen and also record your commentary, you are going to be near your PC. Make sure the microphone is as close to you as it can be without "popping" (where your breathing causes distortion) and as far from the noise of the PC as possible.

Some microphones will sound low level – even with Studio's fader pushed up to full level. You may be able to address this with Windows settings - look for a Boost setting. If you are going to do a lot of voiceovers I suggest you consider buying a small external audio mixer to feed your microphone into. You can then feed the mixer's output into a line level socket and avoid all the hazards of interference floating around inside your PC case. You can also ride the level of the microphone manually, fading it out if you don't intend speaking for more than a few seconds.

Choosing the correct Audio Device

Once you have achieved a reasonable quality of microphone recording, you can switch off the *Listen* checkbox and rely on Studio to control the microphone. You need to check that Studio has selected the correct source. In the Control Panel under Audio Devices is a button that allows you to change the selected device. Clicking it actually brings up the Windows Sound box we used just a moment ago, so you can select the device. It would be here that you would select the Line Input if you have decided to use an audio mixer.

Returning to the editor and clicking on the Voice Over tool brings up a small dialogue box. The meter and level control seems to work quite poorly on my set-up at the time of writing, so I rely on setting up the levels in Windows. You may notice a short delay as well – more of which in a moment.

You would use the *Mute all* audio checkbox if you didn't have any headphones and you didn't want the audio from the project to bleed back onto the microphone. If you do have headphones and want to hear the project, leave the box unchecked. At the bottom of the Voice Over Tool box you have opened there are also options for you to rename the files and change the location of the file you are about to record.

The countdown in the Voice Over Tool

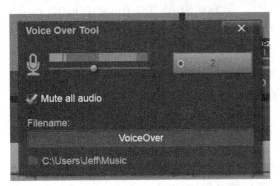

One further change brought about when you open the Voice Over Tool is the addition of a new track at the bottom of the timeline tracks. It will already be labelled *Voice Over Track*, and it boasts a small microphone icon that shows this track has special qualities – all new voice overs will be placed here. You can always move them to another track or retrieve them from the Library.

With the level set and the scrubber placed at the start of the movie, or a little before you want to start your commentary, click on REC to start a 3-2-1 count in. You will hear a click track if you haven't muted the audio as well. Now, you can watch the pictures and make your comments.

When you have finished and pressed Stop, you can decide straight away if you want to make another attempt. If you are happy answer the question "Would you like to keep your recording?" with *Yes* you will find the result on the Voice Over Track. You can now treat it as any other sound – alter levels, edit and even move it along the timeline.

A Voice Over Track created on the timeline by using the Voice Over Tool

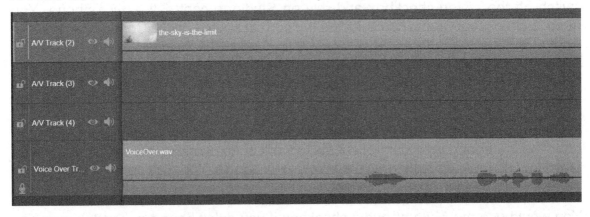

One problem is that on many systems there is a certain amount of what is a called latency – a short delay. For me, any Voice Over recording is about half a second delayed when it is placed on the timeline, relative to the timing when I recorded it. It takes only moments to slide the voice over into the correct place, however, and the delay is totally constant.

Audio Ducking

A new feature added in Studio 19, Audio Ducking allows you to use the audio of one track to lower the audio on some or all of the others. The most likely use for this feature is to lower background music automatically during a voice over.

The best way to demonstrate this is with a sample project. If you want to follow the steps you can download it as a package from the DTVPro website, or load it from the data DVD if you sent off for that. Because it only contains audio it is quite a small file.

Open *Audio ducking demo.movie.axx* and study the timeline. On track 2 is a voice over I have recorded, on track 3 some music. Notice that the voice has been recorded at a lower level than the music – the waveforms are smaller.

There are two routes to get to the Audio Ducking tool. For now use the toolbar icon to the right of the voice over tool which looks like a waveform. A new window opens with a drop down menu and a number of parameters. If your program only shows you two sliders then you have not applied the latest patch – Pinnacle improved the function when the 19.1 patch was released. I also believe that they may change the default values at some stage – so if yours vary, before you embark on this demonstration please change them to those shown in the screenshot.

The Audio Ducking control window

The track that controls the ducking is called the **Master Track**. In this case the default selection, A/V Track (2) should be selected, and that is the track that contains our voice over. If track 2 isn't selected, there are two possible reasons. Either you have changed the track during the current editing session, or you used the clip context menu to reach the Ducking panel. Following this second route will automatically

Audio Ducking

Audio Ducking is a technique that allows a narrator's voice to be heard more clearly and consistently when other audio is happening at the same time, such as background music.

Master Track		A/V Track (2)
Ducking Level		70
Threshold		10

Attack	1.0s	Adjust Start	0.00s
Decay	1.0s	Adjust End	0.00s

● Apply to selected clips   ● Apply to entire Timeline

OK   Cancel

set the master track to same track the clip that you right clicked on was located.

Two check boxes at the bottom of the box allow you to choose which clips or tracks are ducked. When **Apply to selected clips** is checked, only highlighted clips will be affected. As we entered the ducking tool without highlighting any clips you need to check **Apply to entire Timeline** to test Ducking. If you want to exclude whole tracks from being affected the easiest way is to lock the track using the track locks, but if you need to achieve something more complex you might need to use the clip selection method.

Ducking Level affects how much the other tracks are lowered by. If you want to completely mute the tracks, set the Ducking Level to 100. The default of 70 is OK for this example, but if the effect leaves the music too loud in comparison to the voice for your project you can lower this setting.

Threshold is more complex, so let's apply the effect and see what it does before experimenting further. With the value of Threshold set to 10 and *Apply to entire timeline* checked, click on OK. The Ducking window closes and the program adds a series of keyframed volume adjustments to the music track.

Default ducking applied to the demo project

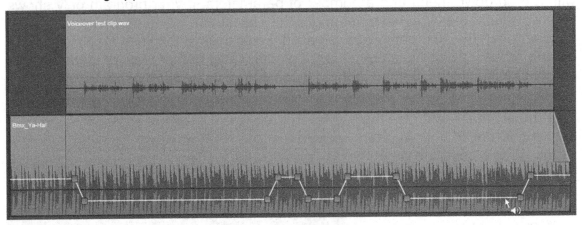

The music ducks down three times. Play the project and I think you will agree that this isn't ideal. The adjustments are being triggered by how loud the voice track is and only the louder sections cause the ducking to occur. My recording level of the voice isn't really high enough and during the second phrase the music comes back up to full level when it really shouldn't.

You might think that all we need to do is increase the level of the voice and re-apply the ducking affect, but that's not how things work – the calculation is made from the waveform, not the level set on the timeline.

Opening Audio Ducking again and adjusting the Threshold to a lower setting – in this case a value of 5 - makes a far better job of things – there is only one ducking event, during a reasonable pause in the voice over. If you set the threshold to zero the ducking would occur for the entire duration of the voice over clip, regardless of levels. If you increased the threshold value then the ducking would only occur for the really loud parts of the voice over.

You can see that the dips in level have slopes, rather than sharp drops and increases. The angle of the slopes, or the gentleness of the changes, are called the **Attack** and **Decay**. These values dictate the speed at which the background music fades up and down. If you are making a fast paced video, you will prefer higher levels of attack and decay, but for a leisurely slideshow you might want the music level changes to be more gradual.

Let's adjust these values. Open the ducking panel again, set the values of both Attack and Decay to 0.2 and then click on OK. What happens may surprise you! Yes, the slopes are steeper as you might expect, but also there are now four dips in level, rather than the original two.

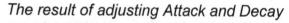

The result of adjusting Attack and Decay

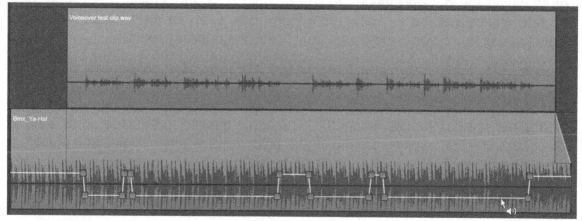

Ducking parameter interaction

At first, it appears that by altering the attack and decay we have also affected the threshold, but this isn't actually the case. The Audio ducking tool is programmed to avoid a situation where the music is faded back up during a pause in the voice over only to be faded back down before it reaches its normal level.

It's possible to demonstrate how this works by changing the values again. Change Attack and Decay to 0.5 and you will see that the first time the music fades back up the keyframes are virtually touching. Now change just one of the parameters to 0.6 and the fade up doesn't happen at all.

However, if you are getting unwanted adjustments but you really do want to use the Attack and Decay setting you have chosen you may well be able to adjust the Threshold value so that a fade up isn't triggered. Try values of Attack and Decay of 0.2 but a threshold of 2 and you can see that the demo project changes to just three ducking events. However, now that the second fade up and down has a sharp attack and decay it is quite acceptable.

Ducking Start and End offsets

When a fade down is triggered, the fade starts *before* the threshold point so that the music is fully ducked before the voice over starts. When the threshold value drops low enough to trigger a fade back up, that begins at the trigger point. With fast Attack and Decay values the default values for Start and End are pretty much what you need. However, for slow fades this may not be the case.

Try changing the ducking values to a threshold of 5 and Attack and Decay of 2 seconds. Notice that there is now not enough time even for the fade up during the longest pause in the voice over – we only have one ducking event.

When you play the result you might agree that it is somewhat ponderous. What if we began the fade down later? As long as the voice over is audible when it begins – and often the first syllable of a voice over will be quite loud – then you can afford to let the fade out overlap the beginning of it. The same applied to the fade up at the end of a voice over – starting it before the trigger point may be subjectively more pleasing.

That's what the Adjust Start and End parameters are for. Try adjusting them to a Start value of 0.5 and an End value of -0.5. Now, not only do the fades work a little better, but there is room for the ducking event during the long pause.

It's worth mentioning that you might want to use shorter Attack times *and* longer Decays. You might also consider using different Start and End offsets. A lot will depend on the nature of the project.

Adjusting the Start and End offsets to slow fades

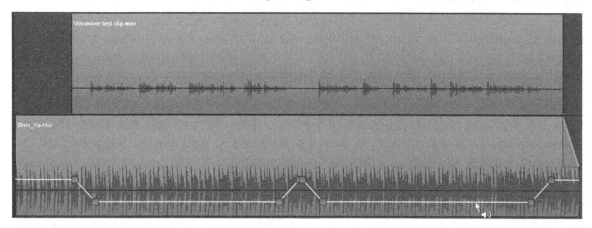

Editing the Ducking

Once the keyframes are added you still might want to move the start and end points or adjust the slopes. If that's the case, you can adjust them manually – see page 77 for details of working with volume keyframing..

Add your Ducking first

If you have already made keyframe adjustments to the music tracks, these will be destroyed when you add the Ducking effect, so don't waste effect on adjustments. You can use a timeline fade though – as I've done in the example project – and this won't be destroyed.

The voice track doesn't get modified, although as I've just said, any volume changes you may have made won't affect the calculation of the Ducking points.

Remove Ducking – Beware!

This tool is available from the context menu, but in version 19.1 it's a bit of a blunt instrument. It will reset **all** the volume keyframes on **all** the unlocked tracks. That includes the Voice track, unfortunately, so you must lock that to preserve any prior adjustments. If I'm unhappy with the result of applying audio ducking, I find it easier just to reapply it or use the undo tool.

Voiceover quality

In my experiments, I've found that the levels of the voiceover you use makes a big impact on how well the ducking took works. It's also important to eliminate extraneous sounds and in particular the breaths of the voice over artist.

If you are going to do a lot of voice overs, one further tip after recording them is to take the file and add a Compression effect. This flattens off the level changes considerably. One advantage is that it's possible to get better triggering of the threshold values, another is that the compressed voice will punch over the music more clearly, so that you don't have to lower the music so much.

If you want to experiment with using a Compressor, note that you must export the file and re-import it as a new file. As the audio Ducking tool works off the waveforms, these need to be recreated.

For my tests I used the Corrections Compressor 2:1 preset and set the Level to +24 dB. I exported the voice over to a new WAV file using the audio export preset. Using that file makes the Voice over much clearer, although I'm sure that I could find better compression settings so that the hiss became less noticeable. I've made a package of the compressed version if you want to hear the difference – *Audio Ducking Demo with Compression.movie.axx*.

Quick Rotate

Rotation is available from the timeline clip context menu. With the increasing use of action cameras - which sometimes have to be mounted upside down - and mobile phones which people use in portrait mode, Pinnacle decided that being able to rotate video as easily as you can rotate photos would be a useful feature.

The Rotate feature in the clip context menu

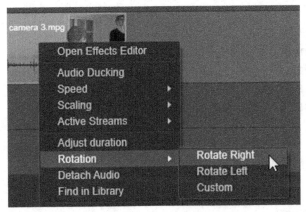

If you select a simple 90 degree rotate, either left or right, the video is spun round and resized. A second application will result in the picture being upside down. The custom setting is a shortcut to opening the clip in the Effects editor.

These rotation effects are simply the application of a 2D Editor preset, so adjusting the parameters once in Custom mode is the same procedure as with all Corrections and Effects. You also get the pink line on clips once the effect is applied.

Apart from the simplicity, another advantage is that if you apply a series of "rotates" they don't add a preset each time. So, rotating the clip left three times result in a clip that has been rotated right, and if you open the clip in the effects editor you will see just one iteration of the 2D editor has been added.

Multi-Camera Editing

If you have been wishing that Pinnacle would add a Multi-Camera Editor to Studio, then with Studio 19 your wish has been granted – and you should have a good idea about the purpose of such a function. If, on the other hand, it's just something you spotted on the new feature list, you might wonder if it's something you can use.

For some projects Multi-Camera editing will be an obvious choice, but even if you are shooting with a single camera it may still have its uses. It allows you to cut or transition between a number of video sources that have been shot "in sync" and in the process create an edited version.

Of course, it's possible to do that without a Multi-Camera Editing function. You can put your various sources on individual tracks and sync them up manually, decide on each edit point and then drag or copy the source you wish to use at any point in the movie up to a higher track. This can be very tiresome after a few edits, though, and it's easy to knock the project out of sync.

Multi-Camera helps in a number of ways. If there is sufficient information it can automatically sync up your sources, or speed up the process if you need to sync them up manually. Once the clips are lined up they can be locked into place. You can view all the sources at the same time in a special display. Cutting between the sources is performed with a single mouse click

Most usefully, you can even do this as the sources are playing in real time, performing the role of a Vision Mixer on a "live" event, but with the bonus that you can go back and improve the cutting points or correct any mistakes you have made.

Once you have completed your Multi-Camera edit, it can then be used in a mainstream project, with the added bonus that you can open it just like a subproject to carry out further changes.

The most obvious example of a project that would benefit would be when you have used a number of cameras to cover an event such as a play, musical performance, sporting event or ceremony of some kind, with most of the cameras running for most of the time. A simpler project might also benefit from the feature – for example a tutorial using a screen capture and a shot of the person giving the tutorial.

Even if you own just one camera there are times when Multi Cam may be useful. Getting your whole family to lip-sync to a song and turning the individual shots into a cut pop video is just one idea that comes to mind!

I'm going to start by describing the workflow and functions of the Multi-Camera Editor, then demonstrate how to use it with a sample project.

Multi-Camera Workflow

There are three stages to producing a movie with the Multi-Camera feature.

The Multi-Camera tool

You enter Multi-Camera mode from the main Edit or Author interface using the toolbar *Multi Camera* icon. It looks like a screen divided into four squares. If you cannot see it, then check your toolbar customisation in case it has been hidden.

Clicking on this tool opens a new window over the main program.

Stage 1 – Source Selection

The main Source Selection window

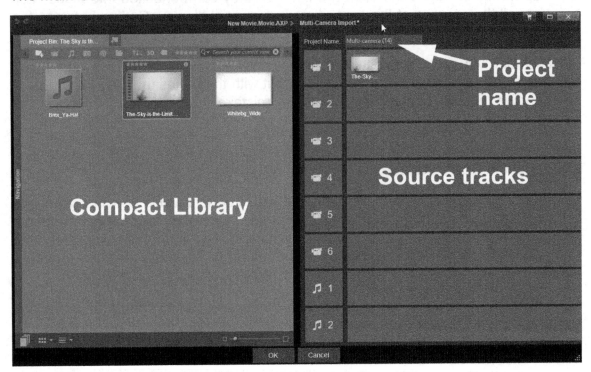

The purpose of this first stage is to select the clips you want to edit. On the left is a version of the Compact Library and on the right are 8 tracks, six for video and 2 for audio (if you have the Plus version, there are only 4 video tracks available). While I've called them tracks, they are in fact storyboard style strips. You drag and drop the sources that you want from the left pane to the camera and sound tracks on the right. You can have multiple clips on each track and drag and drop them between the tracks to change the order if the clips.

Note that while it is irrelevant what you have on the timeline when you enter the Source Selector, it is possible to pre-select items in the Compact Library that will be sent to the first stage of the Multi-Camera interface. If a single video source is highlighted, it will be sent to the Camera 1 track, and if you have multi-selected Library items the subsequent video sources will be sent to the subsequent tracks. The same occurs for audio sources. However, while this approach is quite efficient, it does mean that the sources are placed on tracks in the order that they appear in the Compact Library. You could adjust the sort order, but you can also simply drag and drop the clips between the tracks once they are there.

Stage Two – The Multi-Camera Editor

The main MCE window

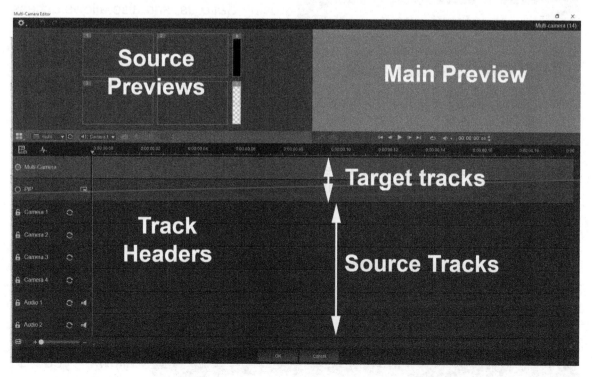

In order to reach this window you need to go via the source selection stage. Let's do that now:

- In the Edit mode of Studio, make sure nothing is selected in the Compact Library.

- Click on the MultiCam tool.

- In the Source selection window there should be nothing on the tracks. Delete any items that are there.

- Click on the OK tab.

The Multi-Camera Editor (or MCE for short) can be displayed as a small window over Studio (949*682 pixels) or Full screen, using the standard Windows Maximise/Restore Down tool top right of the window. The layout of the window is not (currently) adjustable and the source and preview displays maintain a fixed size. If you switch to full screen the editing tracks get larger.

The Save As function in the Settings menu

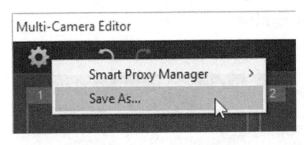

Below the title bar there are a couple of tools on the left. The Setting tool hides an option to save the current project using *Save as*, and also allows access to the Smart Proxy manager. I'll discuss proxies at the end of this chapter. On the right is the current MCE project name. Using the *Save as* option changes this from the default to something more helpful.

The top of the window holds the preview area. On the left are the Camera and Audio sources you have added to the tracks, on the right there will be a larger main preview of the output or selected source. There are also two other potential sources displayed between the Cameras and the Output Preview. *B* is Black Level and inserts black video. *0* is Transparent, which will be of more use when using the PIP track.

The MCE toolbar

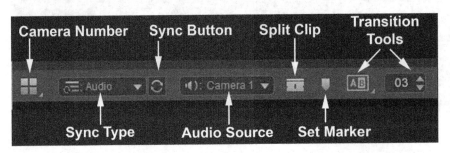

The toolbar immediately below the sources contains 7 items. Furthest left a Multi-Camera icon allows you to switch between four or six cameras. You will only have this choice with the Ultimate version, as Plus is limited to 4 camera sources. Switching to six sources reduces the size of the Camera previews, so I suggest you only use the six camera mode if you are using more than four cameras.

Syncing up the tracks

Sync Selection choices

The next tool offers three strategies for syncing up the camera sources. The drop down box offers the choices and the Sync button to the right moves the sources on the tracks below so that they are lined up correctly.

Audio syncing is the most powerful. The audio waveforms of the sources are analysed and Studio attempts to find a match between them. Assuming that there half decent quality sound on all the cameras you should find this process works well.

Marker syncing is the next best alternative. The user manually places a marker on each track, and when the the sync button is clicked the markers are lined up. If you have shot something with a clapper board or some other type of syncing device this method if reliable. If not you will need to use some sort of visual clue to provide you with a sync point.

Shooting Date/Time will normally only get you in the ball park. Using the file properties relies of the cameras to all be set to the same time of day and stopped at the same time, and even if they are spot on the result isn't going to be frame accurate unless the cameras are all locked together.

You can use a combinations of methods to sync up your sources. Two sources might line up correctly using the audio, so then you can lock those tracks with the track locks. You might be able to use a visual clue to line up another track, then lock that. A track that you line up using the Date/Time might be close enough for you to then manually drag and drop along the timeline. You can do this with frame accuracy if you zoom the view in sufficiently using the slider at the bottom left of the window.

Audio Selection

The next tool to the right allows you to choose your audio source. When you are cutting your video, you might also want to cut between the audio sources as well. For this you would select the Auto option. In most circumstances this is going to sound very odd, but you might want to use this feature to provide a "cut feed" of the audio choices to work on outside of the MCE. If you don't want any audio selected as you make the cuts, you can select None.

MCE Audio selection

The most likely scenario is that the audio on one of the cameras will be the best choice, and you can select which camera you want from the dropdown menu.

When I shoot with more than one camera I like to use a Digital Audio Recorder, either using its internal microphone, a better external one plugged into it, or if I'm recording a staged event, getting a feed from the house PA system. If you do something similar, you will want to place the recording on one of the audio tracks and use that as the source.

The final option is to use the audio from all of the cameras. This isn't quite as odd as it initially sounds because the audio from each camera will be placed on a separate track for further editing in the main program.

The Audio selection controls both the audio of the final movie, but also the audio you hear as you are making your choices.

Editing tools

The remaining three tools are a razor blade for re-editing operations, a marker tool to help with automatically syncing up the tracks, and a transition tool. We will look at these in detail when we make the demo project.

The Main Preview screen

To the right of the camera previews another display previews either the camera sources or the movie as you edit it. Clicking on a clip on a source track puts an orange border around the source window for that clip and also displays it in the larger preview at the current scrubber position. Clicking on either of the two upper track labelled Multi-Camera or PIP displays what is on those tracks.

Most of the controls under the main preview will be familiar to you from all the other preview screens. There is a limited amount of keyboard control of playback, but the most important do work – Space to start/stop and the arrow keys for single frame jogging

Two new icons appear to the left. These aren't undo/redo, but controls to Quick Rotate the source tracks. At this stage in the MCE's development you can't use Corrections or Effects on the sources, but the ability to rotate the video is available with these tools. They only become available when you have a clip selected on one of the source tracks.

The Quick Rotate tools

The Source Manager

In the black area between the previews and the tracks there are two tool icons to the left of the timescale.

The Source Manager and Waveform tools

The first one opens up yet another new window offering a way of modifying the contents of the source tracks once you have entered the MCE. This is a simpler interface where you can adjust the contents of project on a track by track basis using the area on the left to select which source track you are working on.

The Secondary Source Manager

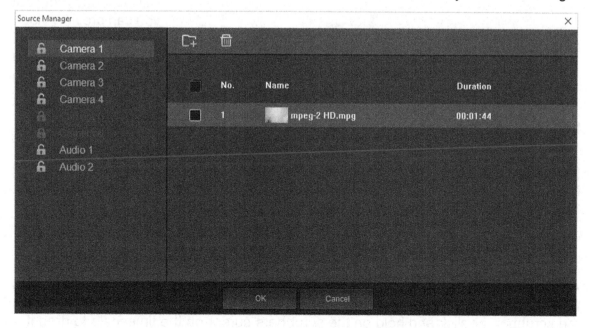

The Corel style Import window

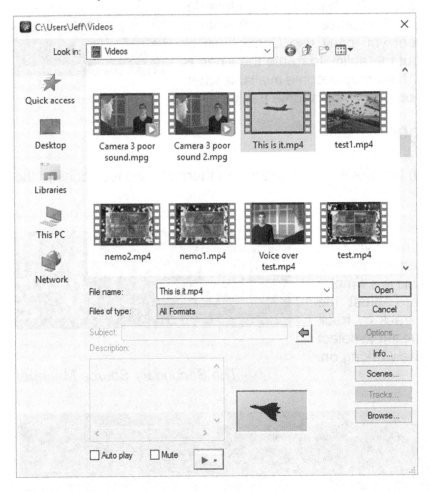

The Folder icon allows you to import new material, the Trash can to remove it, and to change the order of the clips you just drag and drop. Check boxes allow you to create multple selections for deletion.

If you try out the importing tool, you will notice an Import box that is different to the normal Studio tool. It is actually from Corel VideoStudio, and some of the new options such as Scenes and Tracks will be irrelevant, but you can preview video sources in the small thumbnail sized view at the bottom of the window.

Waveform Display

Normally the tracks of the MCE editor show a thumbnail at the start of each clip, but if you want to look at audio waveforms instead you can use the Audio Waveform tool. This may be useful when trying to sync up clips manually.

The Timescale and Timeline views

Above the tracks is the familiar timescale, but again this is of a slightly simple form, with no ruler zooming you can click on the timescale or the target tracks to reposition the scrubber, or click and hold on the scrubbers cursor on the timescale to drag it.

Changing the scale is possible with two controls at the bottom of the Window. The Zoom control works just like any other one in Studio, and there is a handy "Fit to Timeline" tool to the left.

Timeline scaling tools

Zoom to fit timeline

Track Headers

Studio's multi-cam actually has two video outputs. The top track, labelled Multi-Cam, shows the selected source full screen. The track below, labelled PIP (Picture-In-Picture) overlays a shrunken picture over the main source.

Track Header tools

The only control for the Multi-Camera track is a selection button. When the button is red, that's the track you are editing. The PIP track has the selection button and also tool to select one of four positions that the PIP can be placed. It is possible to alter this positioning at a later stage, but for the initial editing you need to stick with one of the present options.

Target Track Selection

○ Multi-Camera

○ PIP

PIP Position

Padlocks

🔒 Camera 1

🔒 Camera 2

🔒 Camera 3

🔒 Camera 4

Sync Locks

The source tracks have two locks. The padlock on the left performs the usual function of disabling the track so that

🔒 Audio 1

🔒 Audio 2

Mute Audio

you can't move or trim the clips on it. The sync button determine if a particular track is included in a syncing operation. Clicking on the sync lock button puts a line through the icon, indicating that the track will be excluded.

The audio tracks also have a mute button so that can be excluded during the edit process.

Importing a source using Right-click

It's hard to describe any more of the workflow without any content in the editor, so I'll show you how to quickly add a clip using the track context menu.

- Right-click on the empty track space for the Camera 1 source track.

- A context menu with just one option appears – *Import source*.

- Click on it and the Corel style Import dialogue opens.

- Navigate to the *C:\Users\Public\Videos* location.

- Highlight *The Sky is the Limit* sample video and click on *Open*.

- The Import dialogue closes and the sample video appears at the start of the Camera 1 track.

This import method always places the clip at the start of the track unless there is already material on the track, in which case it is placed immediately after the current content.

Source Track operations

There are three operations possible on a source clip. You can drag and drop it, delete it and trim the In and Out points.

The MCE Drag and Drop cursor

Despite the drag and drop cursor being a four way arrow you can only move the clip around on its current track. You also can't drop it somewhere that there isn't room for it. There isn't a Delete tool, but you can use the context menu or highlight the clip and use the Delete key.

The MCE Trim Cursor

Trimming involves generating a trim cursor. First, click on the clip to highlight it. Yellow bars will appear at either end. When you hover over the yellow bars trim cursors appear. Click, drag and release to trim the clip. Unlike the main editor, you can't overtrim a clip.

Selecting output

Moving something up to the output tracks is simplicity itself – you simple click on the source window of your choice.

- Make sure that the Multi-Camera track is active with the red button showing.

- Move the timeline scrubber to the shot of Fred getting out of the van at around 24 seconds.

- Click in the Camera 1 source window.

- That's it. At that point in the movie the shot from Camera 1 appears.

- Make the PIP track active.

- Move the scrubber a bit further down the movie.

- Click on the Camera 1 source window again.

Camera 1 added to both Target tracks

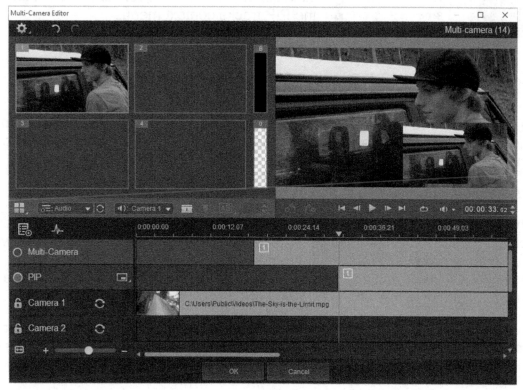

Target track operations

It is not possible to move a clip on the target tracks – after all, you are trying to keep everything in sync. You can delete clips, and trim them to change the point at which they become active. It's therefore possible to adjust to cuts between sources without going to the next stage of the workflow.

The PIP Track context menu

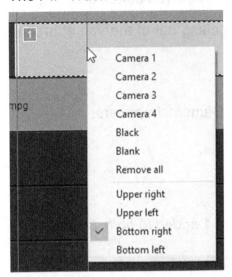

The Razor tool also becomes active when you have a clip on one of the target tracks selected, so that you can use Cut and Delete as an alternative to trimming.

Target track context options

The MultiCam track offers you an alternative way of selecting the first clip you place on the target track with a list of Cameras, Blank (transparent) or Black. You can also delete all the content.

Additionally, you can adjust the PIP position from the PIP tracks context menu.

Stage Three – Multi-Camera in the Main Editor

You exit the MultiCam editor with the OK button. A new MultiCam project will appear in the current Bin and the Latest Import collection. You can tell it is a MultiCam project from the icon top right of its thumbnail.

To use the project, just drop it onto the conventional timeline to play or export it.

At the time of writing Pinnacle were still developing how gaps within the MCE project would be treated in the Main editor. Initially, timeline In and Out point callipers were added marking where the actual content started and ended. In version 19.0.2 this was changed to removing any gaps, including those within the body of the movie, by pulling the content to the left.

If you right click and select Edit movie (or double-click on the project) it opens as a subproject and you will see a number of further differences. All the video sources are present, but locked. The Multi-Camera and PIP tracks, however, are editable so you can add effects and transitions and adjust the cuts as well. One thing you can't do is move the clips, which would destroy the carefully achieved synchronisation!

A Multi-Camera project open as a sub-movie

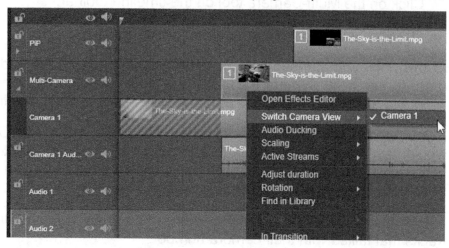

What you get in the way of audio will depend to some extent as to what your audio selection was. Choosing Auto will have enabled the audio stream for all the camera sources on the MultiCamera track. If you chose a specific camera then it its audio will be part of the project as a separate track, and if you selected All Cameras there will be an audio track for each camera. The PIP track never has any audio and the audio tracks will be muted by default, unless you chose one of them as the audio source.

There is a helpful context menu option for the two target tracks – Switch Camera view – so that you can replace the choice that you made with a different camera.

But what if you wanted to use Live switching again? You can enter the Multi-Camera editor with the button bottom right if you wish. Any changes you made within the subproject will be lost – and the program warns you about that. You can also open the project in the Multi-Camera Editor from the Library, either using the context menu or by double clicking.

The Three Camera Demo

I think it's time we used the Multi-Camera feature in anger, as it were. I won't touch on every possibility I've described above because I'm going to keep things fairly simple. To follow the demo you will need four files from the website or data DVD.

- Download or copy the following files: *Guest.mpg, Presenter.mpg, Wide Shot.mpg* and *MultiCam audio.wav.*

- Create a Project Bin named *MultiCam demo* and add the files to it.

- Start a new project and then highlight all four files in the *MultiCam demo* bin using CTRL-A.

- Click on the Multi-Camera tool on the timeline toolbar.

- The first Source Selection window should open.

At this point you can see that the video sources have been added in alphabetical order to the three Camera tracks (unless your bin had been sorted in some other way) and the audio source has automatically been added to the first audio track

If you hadn't used CTRL-A but selected the tracks with CTRL-Click then the clips would have appeared on the tracks in the order that you selected them. This is a better way to start your MCE project if you know what order you want the tracks to be in before you even open the Source selection.

In this case I think it would make sense if the three camera sources were on the tracks that tallied with their camera number.

The Source Selection process

- Drag and drop the Wide Shot clip from the third track to the first

- Drag and drop the Guest clip to the third track

- In the Project Name text box above the tracks, change the project name to Multi-Camera Demo 1

- Click the OK button to move to the next window

- Use the Maximise button for a better view.

Even though the Ultimate version of Studio can handle six cameras, if you specify four or less sources the editing window will open in four camera mode. If you wanted to have the other two tracks available you will need to add more than four in the first place, or use the Camera number tool to switch to six cameras and then use the source manager to reselect your sources.

Syncing up the sources

Switch to Waveform view and study the sync between the sources. Nothing lines up.

The 4 sources showing audio waveforms

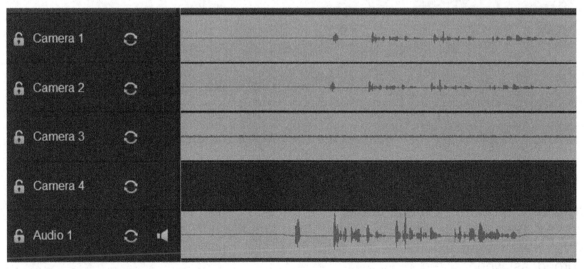

Camera 3 doesn't even appear to have sound – it looks like they forgot to plug up the audio. The separate audio recording has a much healthier looking waveform. Resist the temptation to start putting things on the target track yet – don't click on the source windows. You might want to try playing the individual tracks and watching the previews. Cameras 1 and 2 are slightly out, Camera 3 is early and the audio track is even earlier.

- Switch the Source Sync type to Date and time and press the sync button.

- Some of the tracks move, but there are still issues.

- Switch the Source Sync type to Audio and press the sync button.

- Three tracks line up well, despite the difference in levels, but the camera without dialogue has failed to sync and it has also pushed the other sources down the timeline.

- Click on the Source lock button for Camera 3 to exclude it – a line appears across the symbol.

- Sync the project by audio again.

The three tracks with audio synced up

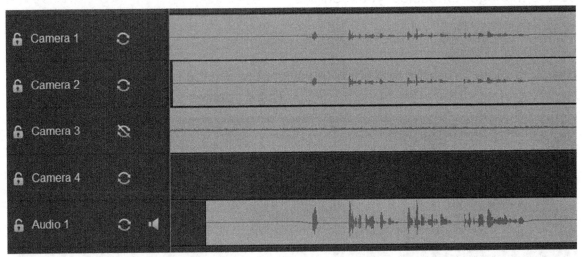

That's a bit better, although we still have to sort out Camera 3. If you zoom the timeline view in a bit you will see that the audio waveforms don't line up perfectly, but they are only up to half a frame out relative to each other. You really won't be able to detect this when the project is put together, and the only solution would be sources that were locked together – not something that generally happens except in the broadcast world.

To sync up Camera 3 I'm going to use the marker method. If we had put a clapper board on the start of the shots, this would have been easy, but in this case I'm going to look for a visual cue.

- Highlight the clip on track 3 so that it appears in the large preview window.

- Jog through the clip to the point where the presenter lifts up the can for the first time. It stops moving at 00:00:10:17.

- With the scrubber at that point, set a marker on the clip using the tool under the source previews.

- Highlight Camera 2 and repeat the process. The sync point is at 00:00:11:08 so place a marker there.

- We don't want any of the tracks already in sync to move, so switch on the track padlocks for Camera 1, 2 and Audio 1.

- Click on the sync button on the Camera 3 track header to switch it back on.

- Select Marker as the sync source and click on the sync button.

All four sources in sync

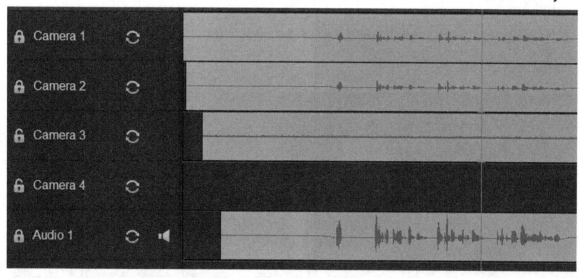

Now all four tracks should be synced up. Select Audio 1 as the Main Audio, highlight a track and play the clips. The three cameras should all be locked to the high quality audio you can hear.

Sending Sources to the output tracks

While the exciting way to do this is with the video playing, it's possible, and often desirable, to do this while just moving the scrubber.

Let's start with the context menu:

- Make sure that the red selection button is lit in the Multi-Camera header.

- Right click on the body of the Multi-Camera track and select Black.

- The whole of the track is set to black level.

- Set the scrubber to a point where camera 1 is settled, but before the dialogue starts – 00:00:03:07.

- Use the Multi-Camera context menu to select Camera 1.

- Ah, that's no good. The whole clip has been replaced. Before you can replace a section of the output track there needs to be some edits defining that section.

- Assuming you haven't moved the scrubber, click on the razor tool to split the target track.

- Now right click on the left hand clip and select Blank.

Changing the first clip to Blank

- Good! We have nothing on the output track until the Wide Shot is acceptable.

Using the previews to select sources

The context menu has limited uses, but as you can see it is a good way to replace a whole shot with another. If you want to switch sources with new In point and without using the Razor tool, you click on the source preview windows themselves.

- Set the scrubber to 2 seconds

- Click on the Black source to the right of the camera previews

- Black level is added from the position of the scrubber up to the next edit – the start of the wide shot.

Black level added at the scrubber position

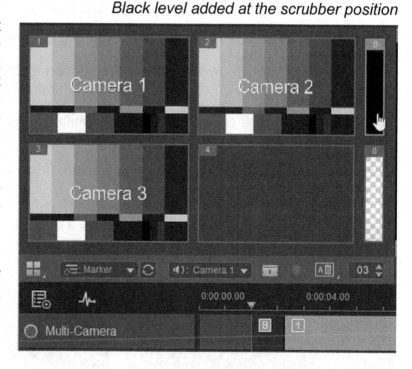

That's an important difference between the two methods of adding sources to the output track – the context menu method replaces the whole clip, clicking on the source preview replaces the clip from the position of the scrubber, whether the scrubber is playing or not.

You can make edits like this for the whole movie if you wish, but you aren't making the most of the editor.

Live Cutting

You should enjoy the next bit – it's like working on live television. I want you to edit the rest of the movie on the fly.

We start on black level, and then cut to the wide shot once it is stable – we have already done that. The first edit comes after the presenter says "Hi" and is motivated by his head turning to his close up camera.

When he says "and cut out the first phrase" use that as a motivation to cut to the guest, who nods. Wait until the Presenter lifts up the drink, then cut back to his close up for the last phrase.

The next cut needs to be sharp – as soon as the presenter starts to lift the can you need to get back to the wide shot.

Finally, as the guest starts to walk in front of the presenter, cut to Black level.

Play the previews and read the above a few times before trying this live:

- Make sure the Multi-Camera track has the red dot showing it is active.

- Set the scrubber to the start of the movie and press play.

- Hover your mouse cursor over the presenter's close up camera in anticipation.

- You will make 5 cuts by clicking on the chosen incoming source at the correct moment, moving the cursor from source to source after making each cut.

- The result will be 5 camera clips on the Multi-Camera track with Black level at either end.

- Review the cut movie to see how well you did. If you aren't happy, try again!

Reviewing the penultimate edit

Adjusting the edits within the Multi-Camera Editor

You may have got the tricky penultimate cut spot on, but if you didn't it's easy to adjust.

- Select the last shot from Camera 2 in the Multi-Camera track.

- Zoom the timescale in to maximum so that you are at the single frame level.

- Generate a trim handle on the Outgoing and drag the edit point left and right.

- As you do so, look at the preview of camera 3. You can see the last usable frame before the camera starts to adjust is a 00:00:14:18.

- Drop the edit at that point and review the movie.

Adding transitions

You can add the default fade at any edit point. With the scrubber within a few frames of the cutting point, the Transition tool highlights to show it is available. Clicking it adds a cross fade of the preset duration determined by the duration box to the right. The transition is normally centred on the cut even if the scrubber was a few frames out:

- Move the scrubber to the last cut between Camera 1 and Black level

- The Transition icon will highlight. It doesn't need to be right on the cut – you have a few frames of latitude

- Click on the icon and a transition A/B icon appears either side of the cut

Playing the movie shows the Wide Shot starts to fade out before the edit point previously set (the Guest walking in front of the Presenter) and end after it. If you examine it in detail the previous edit point is exactly in the middle of the transition.

This behaviour has a bearing on what you might see as the Outgoing shot is faded out as it is unlike the way the main editor works.

- Using the method outlined above add a 3 second default fade between the Black level at the start of the movie and the opening Wide Shot

When you play the result you see the camera still settling as the cross fade occurs. There is also another oddity about the transition because there isn't enough of the outgoing Black level for a full 3 second transition.

Catching a camera moving after adding a transition

In these circumstances the Multi-Camera editor shortens the transition more than it needs so as not to overwrite an entire clip, and it may also apply the transition off centre.

When you are using transitions between live video the algorithm used may well give you the best subjective result. If it doesn't you can adjust the duration or move the edit point. You may even decide to add the transitions manually in the main editor.

Removing transitions in the Multi-Camera editor

It's not immediately obvious how you remove a transition from the Multi-Camera editor target tracks, although once you do know, it's easy!

- Move the scrubber into the region of the first transition so that the transition tool icon becomes highlighted.

- Click on the tool.

- The transition disappears.

Transition duration

We could try a shorter transition at the start of the movie to see if it is better. You can adjust the duration using the duration box, either by clicking on the arrows alongside or double clicking on the value so that it flashes and typing in a new one. However, you can also adjust the duration after the transition is in place:

- Recreate the transition that we just deleted (you can probably just use Undo)

- With the scrubber still over the cutting point click on the buttons to change the values in the duration box

- You will see the Output preview change as the transition is adjusted

- Settle on 1 second and play the result – no, we can still see the camera zooming out

- Remove the transition by clicking on the icon

Opening and ending transitions

Fading up from Transparency

While we could go through a bit of trial and error adjusting the cut with the trim tool to get the opening transition to work properly, because it is at the begining of the movie we can take advantage of the fact that adding a transition between transparency and video results in different behaviour

- Right click on the opening Black level clip and change it to Blank.

- Add a transition The default for that cut will still be set to 1 second.

- Change the duration to 2 seconds and test the Movie.

- In the MCE we don't see a proper fade up from Black, but we will when we put the project into a main Movie.

Putting the project into a normal movie

We have finished making the demo within the special editor now. When you close the window with OK it is saved without you being asked and added to the current bin. You can re-edit it by using the context menu or double clicking.

To export the Multi-Camera project, to use it in a larger project or to use editing tools not available in the Multi-Camera editor you drag it from the Library to a track in the normal edit window.

- Locate the new project in the MultiCam Demo project Bin.

- Drag and drop it to the start of track 2.

A MCE Project on the timeline

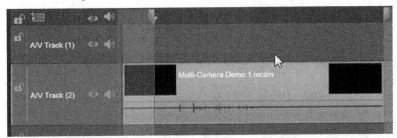

•Notice the In and Out point callipers are set. The In point doesn't coincided with the start of the movie as there is blank material at the beginning..

- Quick trim the In point of the sub-movie so that it clicks into place with the timescale In point calliper.

- Drag the sub-movie to the start of the track.

- Remove the In and Out point callipers with the tool on the timeline toolbar.

Editing as a sub-movie

If you now double-click on the sub-movie (or use the context menu Edit Movie command) you can see the project laid out as I described earlier, ready for further editing. You can also re-enter the Multi-Camera editor using the tab bottom right.

Using Proxy Files

I've deliberately chosen to supply Standard definition MPEG-2 files for the demo above because any computer powerful enough to run Studio properly should be able to handle them within a Multi-Camera project. However, if you want to use HD source material, particularly if it is H.264, then the system may struggle. The preview optimisation tools don't operate within the Multi-Camera editor. Instead, Pinnacle have borrowed the Proxy File feature from Corel's VideoStudio.

I discussed Proxy files in the opening chapter. Briefly, when you add an HD file to a Multi-Camera project a half-resolution, low compression .upx file is created and used for preview within the Multi Camera editor, but when you exit, the Multi-Camera project references the original files which are then used as source material.

The .upx format comes from Ulead, the original creators of VideoStudio, and uses MJPEG compression, similar to DV-AVI. The files have half the resolution of HD but the light compression makes them easy to play back.

The Smart Proxy Manager Menu

The settings for the use of Proxy files are reached from the Settings tool top left of the Multi-Camera editor and clicking on Smart Proxy manager. If

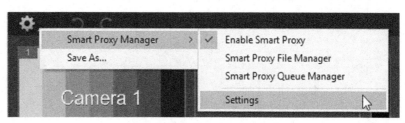

Smart Proxies are enabled then files are created as and when you add them to the Source tracks. If you have already added some content without the feature enable then you will have to add then again once the feature is turned on.

The Proxy file settings

Settings allow you to specify where you want the files to be saved – I'd recommend you change the setting to a location that is easier to find. In the first release of PS19 the location was shared with the default projects folder. If you don't have a lot of free space on your C: drive you might want to use a second hard drive if you have one – proxy files are BIG! I've also seen instanced where the Proxy files system has lost track of its files and if you have put them in a unique folder they will be easier to delete.

The video size parameter seems to behave oddly in the Pinnacle implementation. Sometimes all SD files are ignored, and all HD files are turned into Proxy files, regardless of the setting you choose. I suspect that is the best setting anyway and I suggest you leave well alone.

The Smart Proxy File Manager

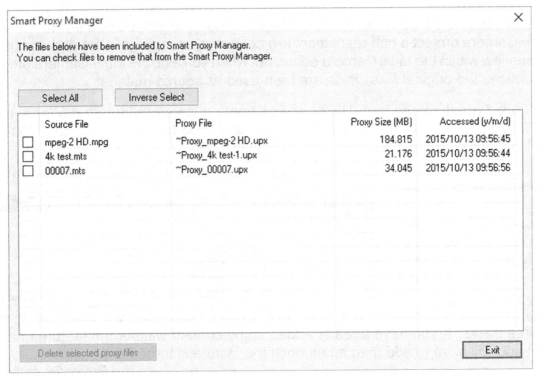

There are two other components to the Smart Proxy Manager. The File manager shows you the files that have been created and offers you the chance to delete them.

The Queue Manager show the files that have still to be created and the progress of the currently running rendering operation.

In the first release of PS19 there are a few issues with the proxy file system. The File manager seems to lose track of the files that have been generated after a program restart. If this happens then you seem to be able to regenerate them by opening the Queue manager. However, this means you are building up a lot of unused files, hence my suggestion that you keep tabs on where the program is putting the proxy files.

The Smart Proxy Queue Manager showing a file being made

I'm hoping that by the time you read this more work has gone into the Mult-Camera editor to solve these issues and the general stability. In time I'd also like to see bigger preview windows. But as a first generation feature I think it's a great addition to the tools in Pinnacle Studio.

Keeping Movies in Sync

Let's be clear about what I mean by "sync" here. I'm not talking about making a video file or burning a disc from a movie project and finding that the lip sync has drifted out in the end product, perhaps by just a little at the beginning but maybe more as the movie progresses. This can occasionally still be experienced, particularly with unusual source file formats, but isn't the issue that it used to be.

I'm talking about you beginning to assemble your movie and place titles, overlays and voice overs carefully in a "first draft" of your movie, then when you decide to modify your creation – which is after all the whole point of using a non-linear editing program – your carefully placed additions keep moving from where they should be relative to the main video.

I've read many discussions about the difficulties that some users have with keeping their projects in sync. Most of the problems are experienced by people who have been using Classic Studio (versions 9 through to 15) and upgraded to NextGen Studio and expected the program to be just as simple to operate. I'm afraid it isn't.

Avid Studio was always intended to be a more powerful program, and with that came complexity. I certainly sympathise with those that feel Classic Studio should have continued to be developed and sold, but also understand the commercial pressures that led to its demise.

If you have come from Studio 15 or earlier, or another relatively simple program that locks everything to a "main" video track, then I'm afraid that there is no "magic bullet" to restore Studio 19 to the same behaviour as you are used to. However, you can still make movies that stay in sync as you edit them by adopting a slightly different approach to your workflow and using the additional tools that are provided in Studio 19.

Smart Drag and Drop

There has been a major improvement in Studio 19 compared to it's predecessors. Dragging and dropping items on the timeline using Smart mode now treats the contents of all the tracks as one object, rather than treating each track separately. This removes one of the main reasons for sync issues, because you can rearrange your movie without having to create gaps and then close them up. However, it's not solved everything.

The Initial Workflow

If you create the rough shape and duration of your whole movie before you add the frills you will save yourself quite a bit of work. It may be convenient to bring a clip onto the timeline, trim it and add a suitable title to that section before moving on, but you can be making the subsequent fine tuning a bit more cumbersome.

If you haven't made the Flight project or at least read the chapters pertaining to it, then I'd urge you to do so. In this chapter I'm going to show you how to make subsequent changes and still keep the titles and audio in sync. However, you can simply load the project from the Data DVD or website should you wish.

However, the workflow I used to create *A Flight Over Snowdon* is a good example of how I like to work so I'll outline the stages I recommend:

- Watch the raw footage and make a rough plan, either mentally or as notes, of the story you wish to tell.

- If you have lots of long takes, use scene detection (or manual splitting) to break them up into a series of useable shots.

- Add corrections, if needed, to shots and photos that you want to use.

- Put everything you might conceivably want to include into a Bin or Collection, perhaps labelling the assets or adding other metadata.

That's a bit of a boring preamble to the actual creative bit, I know, but as you work on the raw footage you can still be having creative ideas!

- Pre-trim your shots in the source viewer before moving them to the timeline. You can always modify your trims later, but the basic decision you make will be remembered should you wish to bring back the same shot from the Library at a later time.

- Put your shots and photos on the timeline in your planned order, then check you are happy with the continuity and storytelling, modifying it as you wish.

- The storyboard makes for a great way of experimenting with the order at this stage, but is virtually useless once you have added material to other tracks.

- Next sort out the sync sound. This will probably involve detaching the audio onto a separate track and dealing with levels.

- You can now start with the embellishments – transitions, effects, music then finally titles.

OK, you might think, that's a great plan, but it's only going to work if I'm sure of what I want to do in the first place and I now have a finished product I can't change my mind without disrupting the sync – possibly even that of the detached audio! Well you can. You've just minimised the amount of further editing you are likely to do.

You might think that the above is a bit prescriptive and will limit your creativity. You could even say (with some justification) that I'm being patronising. If that's the case, just ignore my workflow and concentrate on the next stage.

Reordering your story

We don't always need to tell a story in chronological order – even a holiday video might be more watchable if you swap some of the days around. A drama may have a number of separate strands –the A, B and C stories perhaps – and you might decide to change the way they interleave.

Even at a simple level, you might want to swap over two shots, or perhaps two photos. Let's explore how we can do this using drag and drop.

Load up Flight Project stage 4 from your saved version, the website or the Data DVD and enable the Navigator view so you always have an overview of the entire project.

The Approach shot selected

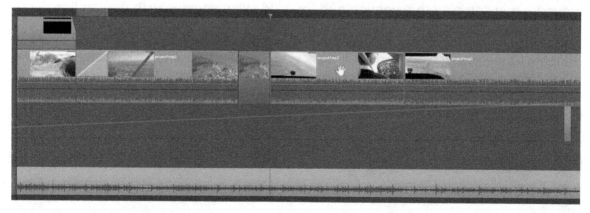

Now look at the last part of the movie. The 12th and 13th shots starting at 2:27.22 are the approach and close up of Caernarfon Castle. The next shot is actually of the plane turning to approach the airfield but the viewer may not know that. What if we wanted to swap those two parts of the movie around?

Study the timeline. There are no assets on any other tracks other than the continuous music on track 4 and we want to leave that in place. So all we need to do is drag and drop shot 14 in front of shots 12 and 13, isn't it? Make sure that the editing mode is switched to Insert mode and then try for yourself.

Click, hold and drag shot 14 to the left. As you do so, the two clips and the transition that are in the way get gradually displaced to the right, taking the place of the shot we are moving. When it clicks into place at the end of the 11th shot at 2:27.21, release the mouse button.

The Approach shot moved

That seemed OK, didn't it? Swapping the clips over was quite painless. More importantly, look at the short audio sound effect on the lower half of track 2. It hasn't moved – you can play that section and the skid still coincides with the landing.

OK, so the answer is Insert mode and drag and drop? Sorry, no. This example is about the only time Insert Mode will work – at the point we are making the swap the other tracks are either empty of have continuous material. To prove my point, try dragging the Final Approach shot further left so it is between the close shot of the Peak (shot 10) and the Mountain Railway shot.

Disrupting the Sync in Insert mode

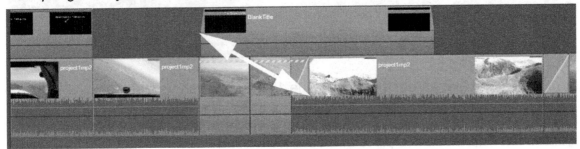

Look what happens to the carefully placed crawling caption we put over the Mountain Railway –it has lost its sync. This is the nightmare scenario that put Classic Studio users off NGStudio prior to the introduction of a new Smart mode in Studio 19.

Now use a series of Undos to restore the project to it's initial state. Select Smart mode from the editing mode drop down and repeat the above exercise.

The example we have here is quite a complex one, and you will see two gaps created. One is left behind where the clip was initially, so that the music remains in sync with the sections of video that you aren't moving.

Two gaps created to maintain as much of the sync with the music as possible

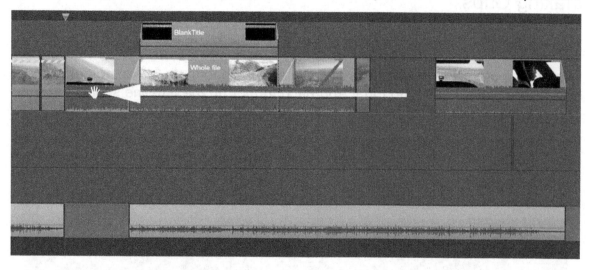

Now the gaps are easly fixed - select the second music clip, and the last two items on the A/V track and pull them left. It would have been even easier if you had not added the music until later. Undo the changes, delete the music and try again - no gaps and the roller title is still in sync with the mountain railway shot!

Better still, you could exclude the music track from the operation by applying a lock to it.

An early bug

Locked tracks are excluded from the gap making process. Until the 19.1 patch was released however, this was not the case. If you lock the music track, and perform the above test a gap should not appear in the music track. If it does, then you need to patch your program.

A solution using Overwrite

Another answer to this problem is probably counterintuitive to many people. We need to use **Overwrite**, not Insert, when moving items around in a multi track project. That mode doesn't shift any other objects in the project other than the ones being dragged, so you can't disturb the sync. But you can't *just* drag items in Overwrite, because they will do just that – overwrite other parts of your movie.

Unless you make a gap.

Making Gaps

That sounds like it might be a bit of a pain, but it's really quick.

Restore the project to its original state. We are going to try to move the penultimate shot as the plane turns onto Final Approach further up the timeline so it is between Shot 10, the close shot of the Peak, and shot 11, the Mountain Railway shot.

First we need a gap. With the current project we could just draw a lasso around all the clips after shot 10, excluding the music. This wouldn't work if you had a long timeline or many tracks though. Instead, use one of Studio's most useful (and probably least used!) shortcuts. Hold down Ctrl and Shift, then click on shot 11.

Creating the gap

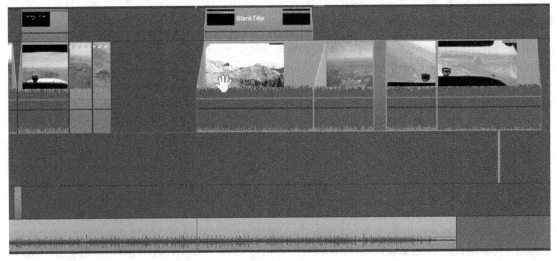

Every item on the timeline, on any track, that starts later than clip 10 will be selected. If an item started exactly in line then that would be selected as well. Now take a look at the clip you are going to be moving into the gap you are about to create, click and hold on shot 11 and drag right to form a gap that is larger than the clip you want to move. Release the mouse button and there is your gap.

Using Overwrite

We should still be in Smart mode, but we don't have to switch the edit mode to Overwrite for the next operation. We can just hold down the Alt key. If you forget, you can even press it after you begin the move and the timeline will correct itself. So select, click, hold and drag shot 14 left into the middle of the gap to see what happens in Insert. Indeed the Mountain Railway shot and its title have been knocked out of sync, as has the skid sound effect. Now press Alt and drag a little further, and everything lines itself back up again! Drag further still to click the shot into place with the end of shot 10.

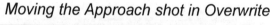

Moving the Approach shot in Overwrite

Closing the gaps

We now have two gaps in the timeline – the residue of the space we made for the shot we moved, and the gap it left behind. The feature to *Close All Gaps* isn't much use here, I'm afraid, but by using the Ctrl-Shift select shortcut it's the work of just a moment.

Select everything to the right of the first gap with the aid of Ctrl-shift and drag it left to close the first gap.

Closing up the first gap

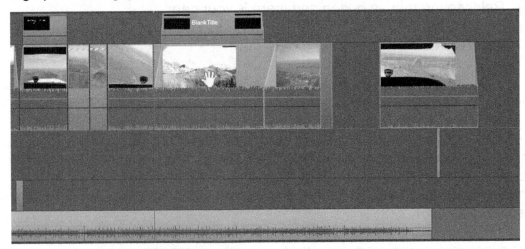

Now repeat the process for the second gap.

Closing up the second gap

Detached Audio and Selection

Earlier in the book we looked at the special properties of Detached Audio tracks and we have an example at the beginning of the project. Below the fifth video clip is a section of audio that is recognised as being sync audio, even though we have started that audio over the earlier shots and extended it over the later one. When you select the video clip, the audio underneath is also selected, because Studio assumes you want to keep these two items in sync. Even if we have slipped the audio relative to the video, as long as it comes from the same piece of video and overlaps, then the audio is loosely grouped with the video. I say loosely, because if you select the audio, the video isn't also selected, and you can break the grouping with Ctrl-click.

The sound effect near the end of the movie is also on the Detached Audio track, but isn't associated with the video clip above.

This behaviour is very important on two counts. If you select a video clip with sync audio, that audio is added to your selection automatically. Additionally if you Ctrl-Shift select Video clip 5, the audio below is also added to the selection, **even though it starts before the video**. That's a very useful behaviour

Grouping

Studio now has a grouping feature (added in 18.5), so you can keep assets together even if they aren't Detached Audio. For example, that Skid sound effect below the landing shot at the end of the movie would be very easy to overlook, particularly if the timeline was fully zoomed out. Grouping it with the video above would prevent you from leaving it behind if you wanted to move the shot. The same goes for titles.

When you use Ctrl-shift for selection, items that are in a group with the chosen clip but start earlier are added to the selection **if they are on a track below**, just like Detached Audio. If they are on a track above though, they won't be added to the selection. So if we grouped the title background on track 3 with the Approaching Snowdon shot above, it would be selected by Ctrl-Shift select of the video. However, if we extended the crawling title above the video so it started before the video and grouped it with the video below, Ctrl-shift select would not add it to the selection when you used it on the video clip.

Deleting

Let's save the current project on the timeline with a new name – we have successfully moved a clip and I want to return to it after demonstrating some features of Smart deletion. Use the filename *Flight recut 1*.

Smart mode behaves very well with regard to sync when deleting. I've yet to find a situation where it has shifted an item that I don't want it to. Sometimes it doesn't always close up the gap, but there are good reasons for that.

First of all, make sure Smart mode is selected and try deleting the shot we have just moved. It's now in position 11 on the video section of track 2. It leaves a gap, and we can certainly close up that gap easily using Ctrl-Shift selection.

Smart Deletion with the music track locked

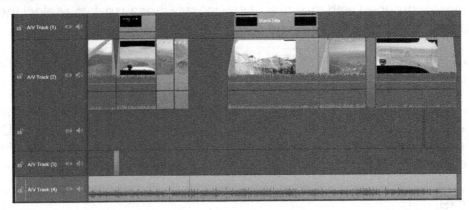

It is worth considering why the gap was not automatically closed up, though. Track 4 contains music and although it starts further left than the deletion point, it does extend past the clips we would like to move up after the delete operation.

Reinstate the shot we just deleted with Undo, then quick trim the Out point of the music so that it lines up with the end of the take-off. Try the deletion again and you will see a more helpful effect – the gap left by the delete operation is closed up correctly.

That's not a practical approach though. You might hope that there is an easier way to exclude the music track from the Smart operation, and indeed, there is.

Protecting tracks by locking when Deleting

Undo everything you have done, or reload the *Flight recut 1* project. Now lock track 4 using the small padlock tool and then delete shot 11. Perfect!

Locking the Music track excludes it from the Smart mode

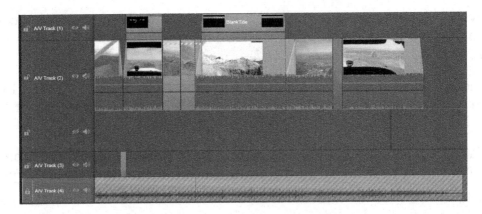

Of course, if there were items further down the music track, they would lose their positional sync with the clips above. You need to be sure that any tracks you do lock don't contain clips that you need to stay in sync. With so many tracks at your disposal, you should be able to avoid getting into such a situation.

Intelligent Deletion

Deletion leaving a small gap for the title background

I'm using the word Intelligent with a pinch of salt here. Please don't think that Studio can read your mind. It will attempt to close the gap as much as possible but doesn't take any liberties. Sometimes it will only partially close the gap if there is something on another track that would be affected. Study clip 7 – the Nantlle Ridge shot just before the double transition, and consider what you want to happen when you delete it.

Now, with track 4 still locked and Smart mode enabled, delete the chosen clip. The gap is closed up, but not completely. The reason for this is that in order to do so, the title background on track 3 would need to be shortened or shifted, and Studio isn't willing to make the decision for you!

Where this Smart behaviour fails to work is shown by what has happened to the overall duration of the video in relation to the music on track 4. The music now continues after the video has faded to black. You may want to adjust the music, or if that is more important – you could be making a music video, after all – you will have to insert some material to return the movie to its original length.

Intelligent Insertion

Studio is very good at bringing new items to the timeline from either the Library or pre-trimmed from the Source viewer. If you drag a clip from either place in Smart mode, everything on every track of the timeline, other than those you have locked, makes way for the new item, so you will never have any issues with losing sync between the existing clips in the movie.

Insertion is even smarter when you bring a new item from the Library or Source viewer into a gap on the timeline. The clip is placed in the gap and no other items move. If the new clip is shorter than the gap then a smaller gap remains. If the new item is longer than the gap it is automatically trimmed to fill the gap exactly – Studio's version of three point editing.

Examples of these behaviours in action are shown earlier in the book, starting at page 249, or you can experiment with the current project.

Trimming a shot to make it shorter

Many people shorten clips by using the razor and then deleting the unwanted part. There is nothing wrong with that; it's accurate and easy to understand. If you use this technique on a multi-track project then Smart mode will help you keep items in sync. You just need to consider the options for deletion and closing up any subsequent gaps outlined above.

However, you may want to consider using a simple quick trim. It's not going to affect any other tracks. Shortening a clip in this manner will create a gap that you can subsequently close by using Ctrl-Shift select and drag, filling with new material or adjusting the adjacent clip.

Restore *Flight recut 1* and adjust the timeline view so you are just looking at the last three shots of the movie. Try reducing the duration of the freeze frame of the Castle (the penultimate shot on track 2) by generating a green trim handle at its Out point and dragging left about a second. If you want to be flash, line the new Out point with the beat in the music at 2:57.19. Ok, we now have a gap. You can choose to close that gap up by Ctrl-Shift selecting the rest of the clips and closing it up, but there may be a problem with this – the movie is going to be shorter overall and not fit the music underneath.

A better choice would be to lengthen the incoming shot of the landing into the gap and this is easy as well – it just snaps into place.

Trimming a shot to make it longer

Obviously, split and delete isn't an option for this kind of operation, so unless you bring in a new, longer version of the clip in from the source viewer or library you need to use trimming.

Restore the *Flight recut 1* project to the state it was in before you trimmed the Castle freeze frame. Now try extending the In point of the next shot – the landing – to the left using a green trim point. It's working in Overwrite, not disturbing any sync, but it is obliterating the outgoing shot of the Castle. That's what we did in two separate operations before, so line up the edit with that beat in the music if you can, release the mouse and study the result.

Shortening the Castle shot by Overwriting it

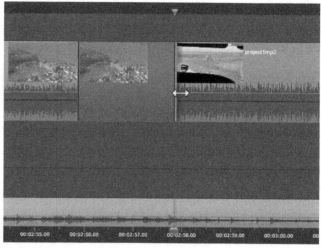

So the thought process here might go something like: "I want to reduce the length of the still shot of the Castle, but I don't want to reduce the overall duration of the movie because I don't want to edit the music. I don't mind making the next shot longer to compensate, so I'll trim that In point rather than the Castle shot's Out point".

What if you didn't mind about the music and wanted to extend the Landing shot's In point without shortening the previous shot? If you force Studio into Insert mode it will work, but on a single track only – hopeless if you have items you want to keep in sync further down the movie.

The elegant answer is to use Advanced trimming with multiple trim points. However, there is a solution that is easier to understand, and because Advanced trimming isn't perfect, if you want to avoid getting to grips with it in the middle of a creative workflow I suggest you go back to the solution we used when moving clips in Overwrite mode

Create a gap!

You should have the hang of this already. Ctrl-shift select the clip who's In point you want to loosen to the right and all the subsequent clips get selected as well. Drag them all right to make a gap a bit bigger than the maximum you think you are likely to want to extend the In point. Now re-trim the In point, and when you are happy close up that gap again using the same technique as you used to make it.

I've talked you through how to extend an In point. If you want to extend an Out point the process is the same, you just make the gap at the end of the clip by moving all the subsequent clips.

Using multiple Trim points

We now get to one of the most powerful, and sometimes the most frustrating, features in Pinnacle Studio 19.

The Studio manual states that you should add a trim point to each track you wish to stay in sync, and this is exactly what you need to do. The choice that you make when positioning these trim points is critical.

Studio can automatically add a trim point to every track, but to be frank, that can be more trouble than it is worth. You might like to look at my dissection of this issue on page 271. I've lobbied Pinnacle to add a more reliable mode, but until they do, I recommend you either add your trim points by hand or check if they have been set in a way that suits the current operation before you proceed. If you have any doubts, resort to creating and then closing gaps.

Advanced trim mode is explained in detail earlier, starting at page 256, but briefly, Studio has two different behaviours when it comes to adding the advanced trim points, controlled by a checkbox in Control panel/Project Settings. I'm going to work with it checked – *Activate Trim mode by clicking near cuts* – because it is a little clearer when setting the first point, and you only get a trim point for each track if you hold down Shift. In the other mode you need to use the trim icon to get into trim mode, and the default is to set a point for each track – Shift disables this and gives you a single point to begin with.

Let's say we want to trim the Out point of shot 11 so that it ends before the camera pans to the pilot. First of all, set a single trim point. Hover your mouse near the Out point to generate an Out point cursor, click and release. A yellow bar appears. If you have difficulty with this operation, zoom your timeline view in to increase the size of the hotspot you are trying to activate.

You can drag the Trim point left or right and see that Studio is now operating in Insert mode as the subsequent clip on the track holds position. This is a fundamental difference between Quick and Advanced trim – the default mode for Simple trim is Overwrite.

As you adjust the clip, you can see that neither the crawling caption above the Mountain Railway shot nor the sound effect for the Landing are moving. We need to add a trim point for each of these tracks. But where?

Click on the Trim mode icon on the toolbar or on the single trim point to exit trim mode, then use undo to repair the changes you made.

Recreate the first trim point at the Out point of clip 11 as before, then consider where we need to place the next one.

Setting the second trim point to the Out point of the title

There are four possible locations where you can put a trim point on track 1 that will keep the crawling title (and anything following it) in positional sync with the shot below.

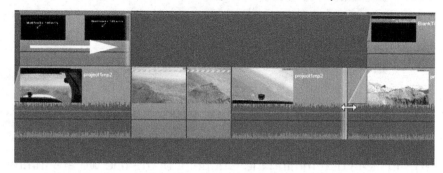

For our first experiment, set the trim point to the Out point of the title to the left of the gap. You will notice that the Preview has switched to the trim point we have just set, so reset that so that we monitor the Out point of shot 11 in Preview.

Use the jogging buttons under the preview window if you need accurate control, but you will need to perform an undo for each jogging operation. As you alter the trim points you see that we haven't made good choice for the second one.

The result of using the above trim points

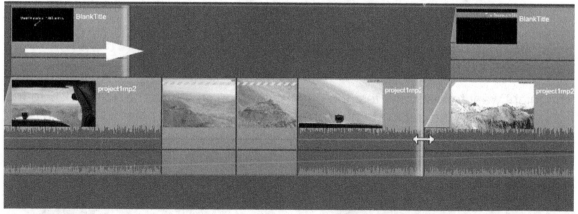
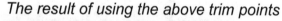

Both the titles are staying in the correct positions relative to the video beneath them, but the Out point of the Mount Snowdon title is being adjusted so that it is shorter and it's Out point no longer lines up with the end of the clip.

Undo all that you have done and try again. Set the first trim point, as before, to the Out point of clip 11. This time, set the second trim point to the **In point of the gap** between the two titles above as shown in the screenshot below.

Setting the second trim point to the In point of the gap

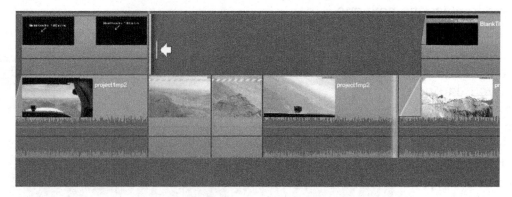

Now instead of trimming the Out point of the title we are trimming the In point of the gap. That's much better – in fact it's exactly what we need!

The result of using the above trim points

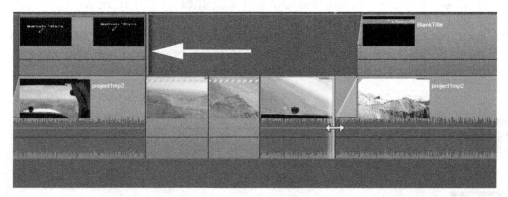

You might want to reset and test the other two potential trim points for track 1 to the right. You can set the track 1 trim point before the track 2 trim point so that you don't need to change the monitored point.

Trimming the In point of the second title

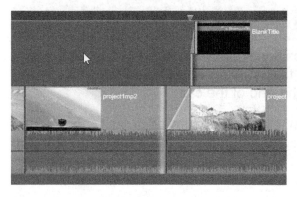 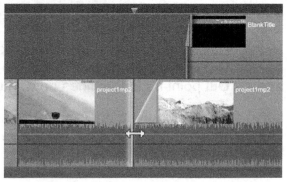

Setting the second trim point to the In point of the crawling title means as you adjust the trimming the title no longer starts in line with the start of the shot below, even though the title is being pulled left.

However, setting the trim point to the Out point of the gap gives us the same result as setting it to the In point of the gap. OK, so we can now work out where to set the trim points, even for the sound effect on the Detached Audio track – that should be set to the In or the Out point of the gap preceding it.

What does Studio's automatic mode do?

Restore the movie back to its original state, hold down the Shift key and generate a Yellow trim point for the Out point of shot 11. You will indeed see a trim point for every track. The one for track 1 is good, but **all** the others are wrong for the operation we need to carry out.

Studio's chosen Trim points

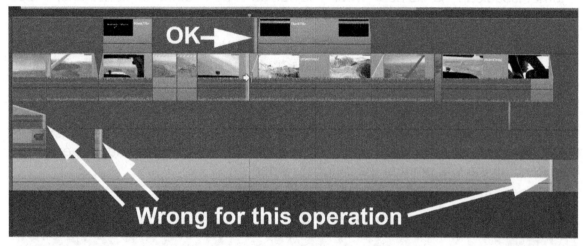

Try adjusting the edit and you will see what I mean - and not only do you lose sync at all the "wrong" trim points, but you are limited to only being able to tighten the edit by 49 frames. This is because of the title background on track 3 would disappear completely otherwise.

Reset the project and hold down the Shift key to generate a Yellow trim point for the Out point of shot 11 again. The other trim points are set as before. Now, let us change them so that we can trim the shot properly. Make the trim point for the Detached Audio the In point of the gap following the first audio clip. We could do the same for the trim points on tracks 3 and 4, but as there is no content to the right you may as well just delete them. Now make the Out point of shot 11 the monitored point.

As you adjust the Out point now, the crawl title on track 1 and the sound effect on the Detached Audio track hold position and stay the same duration. Also, because we aren't trying to adjust the title background on track 3, we aren't blocked from adjusting the edit by more than 49 frames.

Use the jogging buttons to show 00:09:10.03 as the burnt in timecode top right of the left preview window – the pilot's hand is just about to come into shot. Click on the trim tool to return to normal and review the edit. I quite like that!

So from the above you can see that in its current form the automatic Trim selection isn't to be trusted. On occasions it does make the correct choices, but it's only by luck. My advice is to always set the trim points manually.

Transitions

Another issue can rear its head when you decide to add additional transitions. These are discussed in a number of places in the book, in particular starting on page 314.

The important thing to remember is that if you want to add transitions to a multi-track project without disturbing the sync, always try to avoid adding them to the left of an edit point. This means that they are added in Insert mode, the incoming video is pulled up to create an overlap and will shift relative to the other tracks.

So, if at all possible, add the transition to the right of the edit point. The transition is then added in Overwrite mode and nothing shifts. The required overlap is generated by extending the Out point of the outgoing video.

Adding a transition to the left pulls up the incoming video in Smart mode

Adding a transition to the right extends the outgoing in Smart mode

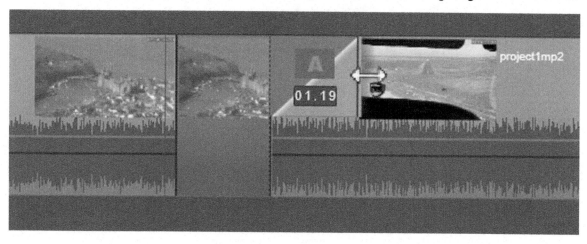

Occasionally there may not be sufficient outgoing video to create the overlap, but this will be indicated by a pink "dead meat" colouration in the area of the transition. You might also sometimes see an unwanted part of the outgoing video.

In these circumstances you can choose to use the "create a gap" method to tighten the Out point of the outgoing video by the duration of the transition, and *then* creating the transition.

Alternatively if you have got to grips with Multi-track advanced trimming, careful use allows you to create the transition in Insert mode as detailed on page 269.

Subprojects

The final tool for protecting sections of your movies from disturbance is to place those sections into subprojects. Complex sequences will certainly benefit from this, and doing so can also simplify the layout of your timeline. Subprojects are described in detail on page 395.

There is no denying that you have to work a bit harder to keep your movies intact when re-editing them in Next Generation Studio. For me, however, it's very satisfying to have complete control of my timeline.

Disc projects and Menus

One of the major ways of archiving and distributing movies is via optical discs, and it's likely to be so for many years to come. Although TV sets are becoming increasingly able to play back files from memory cards or via a network connection, the DVD is still the most convenient way to be sure that people will be able to watch the Movie you send them, and it will stay safe on a shelf for many years.

Blu-ray has become the standard optical disc format for high definition video and is now affordable. The intermediate HD standard is AVCHD discs, which can be created with DVD burners and discs but only played back on Blu-ray players, offering lower costs at the expense of reduced duration and slightly lower quality. The new arrival is AVCHD 2, which actually uses memory devices rather than optical media. It can handle 3D video.

The main reason for an entirely new tab in Studio 19 called Author, rather than Edit, is so that you can add Menus to your projects in the Disc Editor. If you just want to burn a single movie to a disc, then you can do all you need in the Edit tab and Export Window. The subject of making and troubleshooting discs without menus has been covered in detail in the Export chapter. Once a disc project with a menu has been created and tested, the export stage is identical.

In this chapter, I'm going to discuss when you should use the Disc Editor, how to load menus and create them from scratch, how to set up the navigation links and testing your menus.

So when should you use the Author tab? When you want to add a menu to a project, obviously. If you are going to create a project that you are sure will have a menu that is still no reason to *start* it in the Author tab, though. You might at some stage decide that your project could be used as a subproject in another project. If it is a Disc project, you won't be able to do that.

My suggested workflow for all projects is to start them in the Movie Editor (using the Edit tab), and complete them to the best of your ability. When you transfer a project to the Disc Editor it becomes a separate project, and any further work you carry out on the project will not be transferred back to the Movie project that was the source. This is an important point, similar to the one I made regarding subprojects – the changes don't get passed back to the source. If you do make a few changes to a Disc project you can still export it to formats other than disc, and it is also very quick to create a new Movie project from the whole or parts of a disc project. Just always keep in mind that once you open the Disc tab you have started a new project.

It is perfectly possible to have two entirely unlinked projects in the Movie and Disc tabs. You can compile a new disc project by successively opening different movie projects, copying sections, switching tab and pasting those sections into a growing Disc project. I have used this as a workround in order to save me the trouble of closing and opening projects, even when I've not been making a project that won't end up on disc.

Opening the Disc Editor

There are three ways of starting a Disc project. *File/New/Disc* switches to the Disc Editor with an empty project. If there was another unsaved project in the Disc Editor, you will be given the chance to save it before a blank project is created.

If you are in the Movie tab, the File menu option *Create Disc Project from Movie* copies the entire content of the Movie timeline to a new project on the Disc timeline, giving you the chance to save any unsaved Disc project first. At the risk of sounding like a stuck record, let me repeat that you will be creating a new, unlinked Disc project reflecting the state of the current movie. Any change you make in either open project will not be reflected back in the project in the other tab.

Normally, just clicking on the Author tab is enough. If there already is a project there, Studio will assume you want to work on it. If the Disc Editor is empty, Studio will ask if you want to copy the current Movie project onto the Disc timeline.

Let's create a disc project from a movie, then we can have a look at the Disc Editor. Open the *Project_1_4* movie in the Movie tab. If you have a choice, make sure you load the correct video standard for your country - NTSC or PAL. Now use the File menu option to create a new Disc project from it. The first thing to note in the Disc Editor window is the new project name top left of the Timeline preview window. It won't be the same as the movie we have created the Disc project from, and more importantly it will have the suffix Disc.axp. Movie projects have the suffix Movie.axp. If you try to open a Studio project from Windows, Studio will know which tab to open the project in.

The main addition you should notice in the Disc Editor is the **Menu List**. This feature can't exist in the Movie Editor. Where the Navigator or Storyboard is normally displayed there should be a DVD Menu List, occupying the full width of the Edit window. If it isn't showing, you need to switch it on now. The toolbar icon for choosing the display mode, third from the left, should have three choices in its drop-down list – Navigator, Storyboard or DVD Menu. Choose the bottom one and click on the Display icon if it isn't already orange.

The Disc Editor, with the Menu List and Disc Tools labelled

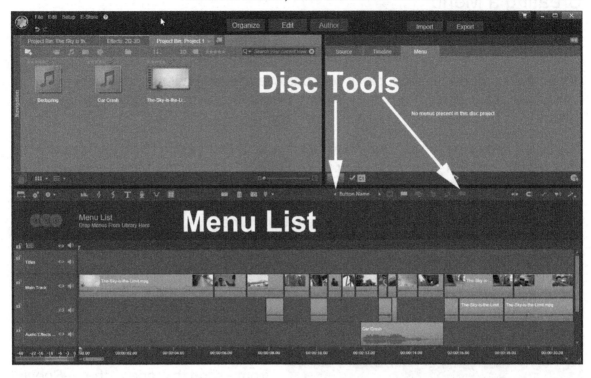

The Menu List has a header on the right that displays three discs. This is just a cosmetic item. The purpose of the List is clearly stated with a message that displays when the list is empty "Drop Menus from Library here", so I guess we can work out how to get started!

Clicking on the List area – even if it is empty – shows up one further difference from the Movie Editor. There are three preview tabs, *Source*, *Timeline* and now additionally *Menu* where the menu will be displayed when we want to preview it. If you switch to the Dual mode preview, Timeline and Menu still have to share a preview window.

Even with the Menu List switched off, the toolbar has 7 new buttons in addition to those that exist in the Movie Editor. They are subject to customisation, so if they aren't showing, check the Toolbar customisation at the far left of the toolbar.

If you open the Disc Editor with a new project, there will only be one timeline track, named Media. This may be all you need if you create disc projects using subprojects created from Movies or have already exported you edited movie to a file.

Creating a Menu

Actually, you can't create a menu from scratch. Sorry. Studio wants you to drag a pre-made one from the Library and there is no direct path to the Menu Editor. What Studio does provide are a couple of very basic templates under the category –*Special* which you are expected to use if you don't want to use one of the many pre-made menus.

There is no point in re-inventing the wheel. If one of the pre-made menus nearly suits your purposes, then you can modify it. You should be confident that even with a bit of mild modification the pre-made menus should work as designed, at least when used in DVDs. I'm not entirely confident that the more advanced menu features always work with AVCHD and Blu-ray discs, at least on some Blu-ray players. Because I like to keep my menus clear and the navigation simple I rarely have issues, but I read of ambitious Blu-ray projects that lead to tears. That's not a cop out – I'm going to describe all the functions – but if you are more interested in the menus than the rest of the disc content then you might find yourself spending some time troubleshooting the end product.

Adding a Menu to a Disc project

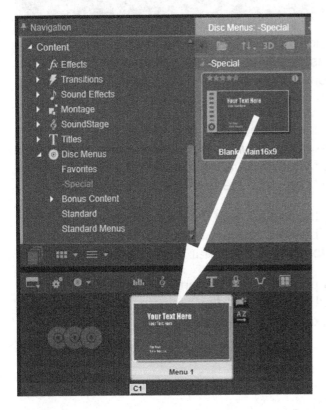

So, because we can't create a menu from scratch, open the –*Special menus* categories in the Compact Library. This is where Studio provides two simple templates for you to create new menus.

The right-click context options for Menus are rather sparse. You can Preview, which shows and plays the menu in the Source preview window (or a small preview window if you access it from the Main Library), add metadata or show information, which is pretty sparse. There isn't a Send to Menu List option. So let's drag the Blank_Main 16x9 menu to the Menu List.

A number of things happen when you drag a menu to the list, most of them because the Chapter Wizard is automatically invoked. Chapter points, Links and Intro Video can appear, depending on the Wizard settings and the content of the menu used. I want to start from the very beginning; I'll talk through the Wizard options when I've explained the basics by building up a menu completely from scratch. I've only come this way because there is no other path to the Menu Editor.

The Menu Editor

Menu Preview and controls

Beneath the Menu Preview window at the far left is a small Edit button. We will explore the other controls soon. Click on the *Edit* button now. What opens up will be very familiar if you have ever edited a title. If you haven't edited a title, I'd suggest you read the Titles chapter before proceeding any further, because I'm going to assume some knowledge of how to use the editing tools.

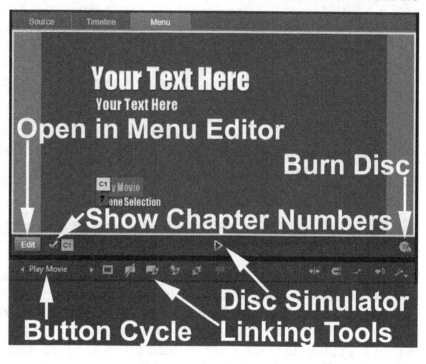

In comparison to the Title Editor the Menu Editor has some additions. A new tab at the top adds *Buttons* to *Looks* and *Motions*. Here you can browse a vast array of *General*, *Navigation* and *Thumbnail* buttons using the sub tabs and drag them down to use in your menus.

The parameter boxes top right have an addition *Button Settings* box, and there is an extra *Button Name* selection control on the toolbar. From this, it is easy to see that a Menu is a Title – but **with Buttons**.

Actually, it can also have audio. Look at the Background Settings parameter – open it up if required – and you will also see an Audio Drop Zone. We will use that sparingly later on.

The Menu Editor

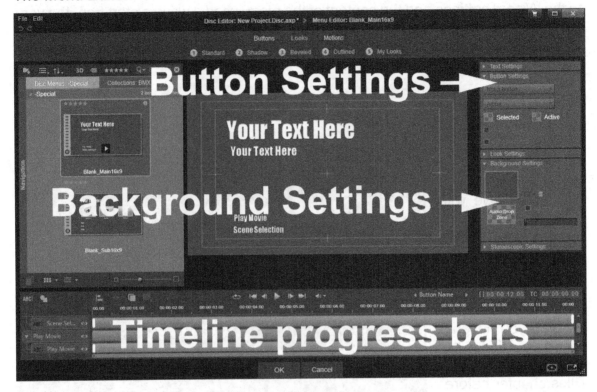

A **button** is a navigation control. When previewing or using the menu on a computer, you will be able to use your mouse to click on a button and the disc will respond to the navigation instruction associated with the button. On a DVD or Blu-ray player you will have to use the up/down/left/right controls on the player or its remote control to highlight a button to make it active, then press an OK/Select/Enter key to activate it. In the Menu Editor, if you select one of the *Your Text Here* boxes with your mouse, you will see the button Settings type is *Not a Button*. Click on the Play Movie text, and the type changes to *Normal Button*. But I'm getting ahead of myself.

Clear everything out of the menu by using CTRL-A and then hitting delete. Use the File menu top left of the edit window and *Save Menu As...* **Completely Blank**. The new menu we have just created will be saved in the default storage location as specified in the Control Panel unless you decide to change the default location.

If you decide to use a different storage location, or move the menus at a later date, new menus can be added to the Library using the Quick Import option. You do need to select All Compatible Media Files or All Files (*.*) as the file type in the Windows style Import Media Files dialogue, however.

Close the Menu Editor, remove the –Special menu from the menu list, find the *Completely Blank* Menu in *My Menus*, then load it into the Menu List. You can also double-click on the Menu in the List to open it in the Menu Editor, so try that now. I know, it's a bit of a palaver. It's almost as if Pinnacle isn't that keen on you making your own menus!

Setting the Menu background colour

Hopefully, you have made the DVD Intro_2 project from the Subproject section. I would like you to set the background of the menu to a sky blue colour using the Background settings box and clicking on the Background Fill box. If you can find the DVD Intro project in the Compact Library (or Import the file of the project from the website or data DVD) then use the thumbnail scrubber to show the last frame before the black level at the end. Now you can use the Colour Picker and set the Background Fill with it. If you don't have either of those assets and want to continue, set the colour to the values shown in the screenshot.

I'm not going to hold your hand through the next creation stage. You may want to use different fonts and colours, but as long as you get a similar general layout, your menus should behave in the same manner as mine. You can see what I have created from the screenshot.

Newly created Main Menu

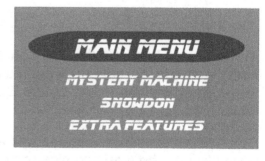

The top half of the menu is a grouping with the text Main Menu (72 pt Blade Runner) and a simple mid grey geometric shape to help it stand out. Below, just within the title safe area are three separate text boxes with the text *Mystery Machine*, *Snowdon* and *Extra Features* in 48pt. I've used *Group Align* to vertically centre the boxes, *Space Evenly Down* and then the *Relative Position* grid to sit them all on the title safe lower line. Note that I haven't made them a group.

Save this menu as *Main Menu before Buttons* because we will use it later. If you want to cheat, the menus are saved at various stages for you to download or import from the Data DVD.

Let's briefly return to the Disc Editor to save the whole project, giving it the name *Disc Project_1*. (Real cheats can pick up the story here by loading the project :-))

Defining Buttons

The Buttons settings box

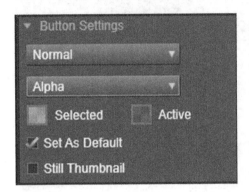

The three text boxes at the bottom of the menu are going to be our buttons – navigation links to play movies, initially, although I will enhance the navigation later on. Open the Menu Editor again and highlight the Mystery Machine text box, then open up the Button Settings parameters at top right of the editor. The first drop-down box defines what sort of navigation behaviour is assigned to the currently highlighted object.

Not a Button is quite obvious. The highlighted object has no navigation properties.

Normal defines the regular navigation – activating the button causes the player to jump to the position in the movie programmed by you. This can be a *Chapter Marker* or a *Menu*. Make the current button a Normal button to explore the next box.

Previous and **Next** are special navigation commands used with *Multi-page Menus* and I will describe those in a few pages time.

Root is another special navigation command. It sends the DVD player back to the first Menu, however many nested menus you have.

The next box down defines how a button is highlighted to show it is *Selected* or *Active*.

Alpha means that only the non-transparent parts of a button are highlighted. This works well with text buttons in particular. Most Thumbnail buttons will look best with this style as well, as only a border around the thumbnail will show the highlighting rather than the thumbnail itself.

Box highlights a square area around a button. This may give better or worse clarity, depending on the type and size of the button and the choice of highlighting colour. This isn't a good option for thumbnail buttons.

Underline is the simplest style of all, just drawing a line underneath the button regardless of its shape. This works best with strong highlight colours.

Beneath the choice of style are two colour selection boxes for the highlighting that occurs. When a button is **Selected** it means that it is the current button, and pressing OK will make the player perform the navigation programmed into the button. When a button is **Active** it means you have selected it, and the DVD player is searching for a place on the disc you have sent it to. On a software emulator or a computer playing a disc image from the hard disc you are unlikely ever to see the Active colour, but it is needed when a disc is in a set top player to let the user know the keypress has been registered.

These colours are set with the usual *Colour Selection* controls. Notice that the preset colours are semi transparent and although solid colours can work quite well for Alpha and Underline styles, they make the previewing of buttons quite difficult when you set the links because Studio uses the Box style by default. For now, I'm going to leave the colours as they are. An important point is that a menu can only have one Selected and Active colour. If you change the colour, it will be applied to all the buttons. Another important point is that the colours tend to look a bit different between the preview and when displayed on DVD players (and even seem to vary between players), so don't get too radical with your choice of colour.

Two checkboxes allow us to set properties for the Buttons. *Set as Default* makes the current button the one that is selected by the player when it first reaches the menu. Normally this will be the first item on the list, but you might want to make it the central button or some other choice. Only one button can have this checkbox set for obvious reasons. The *Still Thumbnail* makes no difference to a text button, but determines if a thumbnail using video plays the video or just displays a frozen frame.

You can only set one button at a time and the order in which you set the buttons is important, so set *Mystery Machine* as a **Normal** button, with **Alpha** highlighting, and **Set as Default**. Now set *Snowdon* as a Normal Alpha Button, then add the same attributes to *Extra Features*. When you have done that, you may notice that extra tracks have been added to the timeline display at the bottom of the editor. More of that later.

Close the Menu Editor by clicking on the OK box at the bottom.

Setting Links

While it is very tempting to use the Chapter Wizard for setting Links, on this first occasion I'm going to add the links manually. Before I do, we need to put more content on the timeline. I'm going to do this by using subprojects for clarity. Drag the *Flight Project Stage 4* to the Main track after the Mystery Machine project and then add the *BMX Photo Project*, using the NTSC version if you are making an NTSC disc.

Chapter markers may show up on a small track below the menu list. The Wizard can be very keen and if you find yourself with Chapter markers and Links already in place, right click on them and select *Delete*.

A selected button and the name tooltip

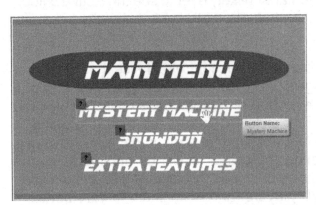

Switch the preview window to Menu. You should see three small red squares with question marks on the left top edge of our three text buttons. If they don't show up, there is a checkbox to the right of the Edit button underneath the preview window and a label with the symbol C1. Check this box to Show the Chapter numbers. The question marks are saying "These buttons don't have any links".

Hover your mouse over the Mystery Machine text button – a tool tip will tell you the name of the button. In the current example, this has been generated automatically. To change a button name for a non-text button, you edit the name in the track headers of the Menu Editor.

The Cycle Tool

We can select the buttons in one of two ways - directly clicking on them in the Menu preview window, or using the toolbar Button Cycle tool. To the left of our new bunch of menu tools is a box containing the button names, with left and right arrow controls that lets you cycle through the buttons.

The tool has another use, though. You can use it to edit the button name. Click on the name and it becomes a text editing and entry box. What if we change the name? Try changing *Extra Features* to *Bonus Features*, then clicking back on the menu. Ah – that's useful! A simple way of editing a text button without having to dive into the Menu Editor. You might not be able to use it all the time – an edit might affect spacing or alignment – but it can be a helpful shortcut.

Highlight the Mystery Machine text button. Hover over it and click and hold down the left mouse button.

Starting to drag a Chapter link

Start to drag the button and once you begin to move the mouse a semi-transparent box will appear with the button name inside it. Drag the box down to the Disc project timeline. Once there, the scrubber becomes active, the Chapter marker strip appears and you find you are dragging about a "C1" chapter flag. Take it all the way to the start of the timeline and release the mouse.

The first Chapter link at the start of the project

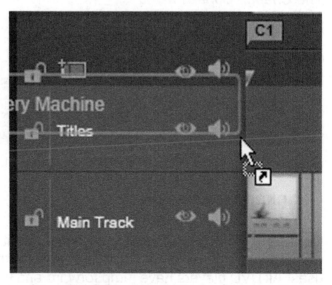

There we are, the first link. You will see that the text button now has a "C1" label in place of the question mark, the Chapter strip has appeared with the C1 marker, but also a M1 marker has appeared at the end of the timeline. This is a return to menu marker which every menu must have at least one of. At its most basic level, it is there so that when the DVD player gets to the end of the video, it knows what menu to return to.

Create a link for the second button to the start of the Flight movie. You should notice that with the magnet turned on, the C2 marker will click into position at edit points and markers. This time you only get a chapter marker, because there is already a return marker.

Creating the third link with Create Link

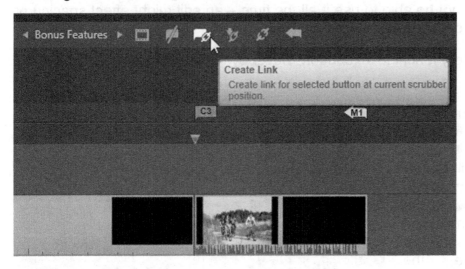

Of course, there are other ways to create chapter links. Click on the last subproject on the timeline – the scrubber will jump to the beginning of the BMX subproject. Use the Button Cycle tool to select the Bonus Features button,

and then click on the Create Link tool – fourth from the left of the DVD tools. There are other methods, too, mentioned later on. If you are adding Chapters manually, though, you have all the tools you need.

If you want to adjust the positioning of the chapters and their links, you can drag them around on the Chapter strip in the same manner as keyframes.

The Chapter Context Menu

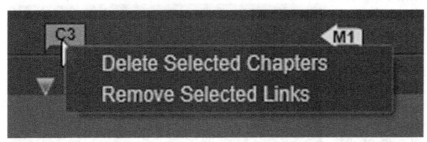

There is also a simple context menu where you can delete chapters, or the links to the chapters. Multi-selection of the chapter markers is possible, so you can delete a whole bunch of them at the same time.

Unlinked Chapters

Deleting a link from a Chapter marker turns it into an unlinked chapter. You may wonder what the use of that is, but chapters without links have a couple of important uses. All DVD players have jump forward and back controls that skip from chapter to chapter. Unlinked chapters are included in this type of navigation, so you can add them to help the viewer move through a long movie.

Unlinked Chapter and tool

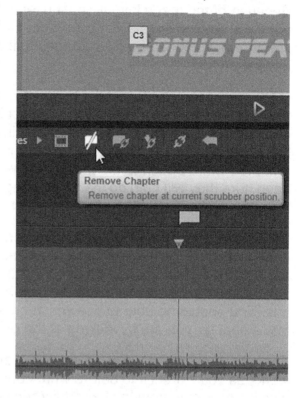

You don't have to add a linked chapter marker and then unlink it. In fact, it's likely that you might want to decide where the chapters should go, an*d then* decide which ones need a link to a button, so there is a toolbar icon just to create unlinked chapters. When the scrubber is over an unlinked chapter this tool allows you to remove it. Double clicking on the Chapter strip also adds an Unlinked chapter point.

For demonstration purposes I want you to add a single unlinked chapter in the middle of the Flight movie. Find the clock wipe at around 2 minutes 25 seconds in, and place an unlinked chapter marker there. We will see the effect when we use the next feature of Studio.

The Disc Simulator

We now have three chapters and a complete menu. Time you checked out the Disc simulator, I think. You enter the Disc Simulator by using the play icon beneath the Menu preview window. The new viewer opens over the top of the Editor. You can click on the buttons to activate them, but first of all, try the control on the bottom right.

The Disc Simulator

It emulates a DVD player remote control, and you should always use this to check that the buttons get selected correctly. If the positioning or box sizes are slightly out, moving around a menu using these controls might not give you the result you expect – you may even be unable to get to one of the buttons. This isn't going to happen with the current project if you use the Up/Down keys (I hope!). What you can explore, though, is what happens if you use the

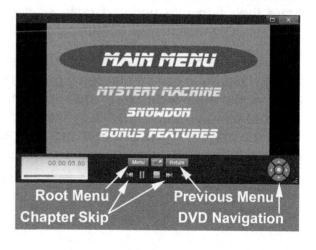

left/right keys. The selected button changes according to the horizontal positioning. Because of the menu layout, most users will try to use the UP/Down Keys anyway, but if you wanted to cater for everyone, then you will need to modify the design. I will create a new menu shortly that does fulfil this criteria, but let's finish setting up the navigation first.

Once you have established the button order and selection is correct, test all the links to check that they go to exactly the correct places. Use the DVD controls for this. You don't have to sit through every chapter – in fact, you also need to test the Return and Menu buttons on the simulator. The Menu button should take you to the root menu and the Return button to the menu from where you came. In the simple example we have here they will both do the same thing, but when things get complicated later on these navigation controls need to be checked to see if they are doing what you expect.

Between the two buttons is a Full Screen tool, and below a simple set of transport controls including buttons that skip between chapters, unlinked or otherwise. To the left a counter tells you the timecode of the disc. At the time of writing the chapter indicator and progress bar seem to have a bug – hopefully fixed by the time you read this. You should be able to see which chapter is playing and get an idea of how far into a chapter you are by looking at the progress bar.

The disc simulator stage is an important step. You can check that all the navigation works as you expect it to before what could be a long render process. To this end, it also is accessible from the Export screen when you have Disc selected as the Export type. There really is no excuse for not checking the links before you render and burn.

By the way, the disc simulator isn't a final judge of what will work on all players. Some differences in the firmware of players might mean you find issues that do not show up when you play the disc on a PC. Differences in DVD and Blu-ray firmware can be one cause of this (along with potential bugs in Studio). Many Blu-ray players can have their firmware updated quite easily, particularly if they can connect to the Internet. It's much harder or impossible on most DVD players.

If you experience issues with a particular player, you may have to modify your projects to suit. One issue can be that some players start a chapter in a slightly different place – the workaround would be to start your chapters with a few seconds of black video, for example. You might need to space menu returns a little apart from Chapter points for some players. If the problem spans a number of players, then the bug needs to be reported to Pinnacle. The more players it affects, the more likely they are to be able to do something about it.

All the menu examples I have created in this chapter have been tested on a Sony BVP S370 Blu-ray player.

Return to Menu markers

You will notice that the Disc Simulator plays all three chapters back to back unless you stop it. This simple menu contains 3 separate movies, so we probably don't want the disc to play on to the next movie. To change this behaviour we need to add some more Return Markers on the timeline.

A Return marker and the Remove tool

The basic principle is that when a DVD player encounters a return marker, it goes to the menu number indicated by the marker. However, to allow you greater flexibility, the player will ignore return markers that try to send it to a different menu than the one that was last displayed. If you have reached the current position of the movie from Menu 1, only a Menu 1 return marker will be obeyed. (If you have graduated from Studio 15, this is a different behaviour than before – all return markers were obeyed).

The tool for adding Return markers is on the timeline, the furthest right of the menu group of tools. Clicking it places a Return marker for the current menu at the current scrubber position. When the scrubber is over a Return marker, the tool changes appearance and can be used to remove the Return flag.

Move the scrubber at the start of the Flight subproject by selecting the Snowdon menu button and then add a return marker. Do the same with the start of the BMX project. You should now have three light blue flags with M1 labels. We'll test the effect in a moment, but I want to add a further enhancement first.

Intro Video

An Intro Video is the (normally short) copyright and other messages you see at the start of a commercial DVD. It's possible for you to do this with your own Disc projects. The video only plays when you first load the disc, then you get taken to the first menu. You may have seen evidence of the Intro Video mechanism when the Chapter Wizard has been at work.

Any clips, audio, titles or subprojects **before** the first chapter point are treated as an Intro Video by Studio. We have already made a video especially for this task, so let's put it on the timeline.

Find the *DVD Intro_2* movie, and drag it as a subproject to the beginning of the main track on the timeline. That's actually all you need to do – we should have added an Intro video. The Chapter timeline will show the C1 marker has been pushed right to stay in line with the movie it was associated with – Mystery Machine. Before that an olive green area with the label Intro Video makes it pretty clear what the movie below is! This doesn't need to be a video, by the way – you could just have a simple title.

Intro video placed before the first chapter

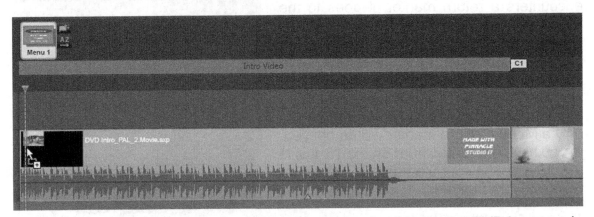

OK, test the modified project and the Disc simulator should play the DVD Intro movie before settling on the main Menu. If you select Mystery Machine, the first movie should play and then you will be returned to the Main menu. The other two Buttons should also just play the named movie.

If you have a blank DVD disc to hand, particularly a re-writable one, you might fancy making a disc of the current project just to test it in your disc player. It would flag up any issues with DVD menu compatibility you may have. This disc project can be saved as *Disc Project 2.*

More Menu creation rules

In this section I'm going to improve the main menu we have just created so that the DVD player buttons behave completely correctly. What I hope to demonstrate is some of the pitfalls of Menu creation. If you work methodically menus will work OK, but if you start to make changes you can end up chasing your tail.

The **positioning** of buttons on the screen can be very critical for consistent selection. The only sure way I have found to make menus that obey the DVD remote control correctly is to make all the buttons the same size, and to ensure that they line up exactly using the Group Align tool. If you want to use text as buttons, then I'd suggest the way to avoid frustration is to group the text with a geometric shape making sure the shapes are the same size.

The **order** of the buttons determines which chapter number they will be associated with, and the order is determined by which layer the button is on. So, when you add your first button, it will be associated with Chapter 1. The next button will be on a higher layer and associated with Chapter 2, and so on.

You might not be aware of which chapter a button is associated when you set the first chapter because Studio will associate the first link with Chapter 1. Only when you set a second link will the natural button order become clear – if the next link is to a button on a lower layer than the first, it will take the Chapter number 1, and renumber the chapter you set earlier as Chapter number 2.

Here is where things get even more complicated. When you change the Order of a button that has already been set, either by using the Order tool, or dragging the timeline tracks to change the order, the underlying button chapter numbering will change.

Confusing, isn't it? You might be beginning to see why Pinnacle don't encourage you to make menus from scratch. If you set the button order too early, it will change if you ever rearrange the layers to help visibility. If you don't have equal sized buttons aligned correctly, the DVD selection becomes unpredictable.

For the next exercise, you need to follow the order I do things in exactly to produce a Menu that behaves as it should. Throughout, the important action is happening on the timeline track below the preview window, so keep your eyes on that. What's more, during the making of this project I sometimes encountered issues where changes I made to old projects didn't always get properly reflected in the new project. Menu behaviour wasn't always what should have been expected. For a completely sane experience you need to start from scratch with the project.

Start a new Disc project, locate the *Main Menu before Buttons* menu I asked you to save earlier in the Menu Editor and put it in the Menu List. If you didn't save it, **don't** use the current menu and remove all the button attributes - remake it or load my version from the data DVD or website.

Open the menu in the Menu Editor. The timeline track headers should look like the screenshot overleaf.

Grouping two layers

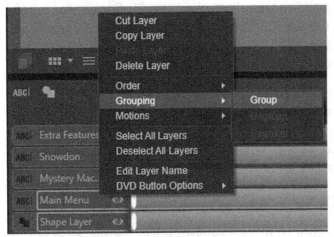

Select the Main Menu track header and Ctrl-click on Shape Layer to multi-select both items. Right click and select Grouping/Group.

Notice that the group gets a new parent timeline track – and is moved to the top of the timeline list. This means it has been brought to the front.

This action is a good indicator of how you can get into a muddle with the Menu Editor. If we group a button with another shape we (inadvertently) apply the Bring to Front tool, thus affecting the button order.

The result of grouping

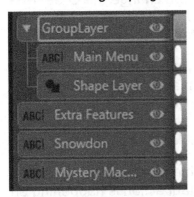

For clarity, rename the new *GroupLayer* to *Main Menu Layer*. Use the small white arrow to collapse that part of the timeline into a green line – we can open it up again with the arrow whenever we wish.

Create a rectangle that is slightly wider and taller than the longest text line, *Mystery Machine*, and change the Look Settings/Face/Fill to a solid blue. Copy the shape and paste it twice so we have three identically sized blue rectangles, moving them apart for clarity.

Three rectangles and the first stage of alignment

Select *Mystery Machine* **and** one of the new *Shape Layers*, and use *Group Align Vertical Centre* and *Horizontal Center*. Now use Grouping/Group on the two items. If the text has disappeared behind the rectangle, use *Order/Bring Forward* on the text only to reverse the positions. Rename the group to *Mystery*.

Repeat the operations in the above paragraph to create groups for *Snowdon* and *Extra Features*. We now want to align them in a neat group, and because we must do this accurately, don't rely on doing it by eye. Get them in rough positions with the *Mystery* button just below the Main Menu, the *Extra* button sitting on the lower Title Safe area and drag the *Snowdon* button somewhere roughly between the two. Multi-select all three and use *Group Align/Horizontal Center* and *Space Evenly Down*. Finally, with all three still a temporary group, use the *Group Align/Relative Position* grid to sit them exactly on the bottom centre of the lower Title Safe line. Your Title Editor should have the same appearance as the screenshot now.

I'm now just going to add one more enhancement. I set the rectangles to a solid blue in order to help us see what we were doing. I want you now to use the Colour Picker to set all three rectangles to the same colour as the background by accessing the Face/Fill box for each rectangle in turn. The rectangles will be present, but become effectively invisible until highlighted.

Save the menu with a new name at this stage - *Main Menu with Rectangles* – in case you want to backtrack. As I said before, there is sometimes a residue behaviour left over if you modify projects with buttons. We can also use it as a template for other menus.

Now, ***in the order you want the buttons to be numbered***, turn the Mystery, Snowdon and Extra groups into Normal buttons with a Box highlight style, setting Mystery as the Default.

Return to the main Disc Editor and recreate the timeline as before, but for clarity I suggest you just load the Project 1_4 video as a subproject. Add all the navigation markers as before and test the project. The DVD player menu navigation buttons should now behave correctly to left/right button presses.

Finally, save the Project as *Disc Project 3*.

More than one menu

Some DVDs will only need one menu, but on longer projects you may wish to add additional menus and create quite complex menu structures. Before you do so, it's a good idea to sketch out the structure you are aiming for, thinking through each menu and what options it should offer.

I'm going to leave the first option – to play the Mystery Machine movie and return to the main menu – as it is.

The second option will lead to a submenu. For the purposes of this exercise I'm going to pretend that the Flight project is much longer, and we need an option to play individual scenes. The sub menu will give us the choice of playing the whole movie and then returning to the sub menu, or going to a scene selection menu. The sub menu should also offer us the chance to return to the main Menu.

The scene selection sub menu will have to be able to offer a large number of scenes so will use the Multi-page menu feature. It will also offer the viewer the option of navigating to other submenus or returning to the main menu.

The third option on the main menu – Extra Features - will let us see the BMX photo project, the DVD Intro project or let us return to the main menu. I'll use this menu to show off Studio's Motion Thumbnail and Backgrounds and the audio options.

Having planned the menu structure, I'm less likely to have to add something as an afterthought. It's a lot less work, and causes a lot fewer anomalies, if the links are all placed at the same time.

Let's make the first sub menu by using the Main Menu as a starting point. Right click on Menu 1 in the list and select Add menu Page. A copy appears as Menu 2. You will notice it uses a different border colour, light yellow. The navigation links for M2 will be this colour. Open the Menu Editor and change the text with care –we don't want to disturb the rectangles, which are now invisible. You could change the background colour as a temporary measure if you wish to be sure of seeing them. I suggest you use the text entry box in Text Setting for your editing, rather than type into the preview window itself.

Menu 2

Change *Main Menu* to *Flight Over Snowdon* and set the font size to 48. Replace *Mystery Machine* with *Play Movie*, *Snowdon* with *Scene Selection*, and *Extra Features* with *Main Menu*. The track header should change as well, but if they don't the menu will still work. Click OK to return to the Disc Editor.

Resist the temptation to add links yet. It will save you a lot of work

and potential confusion later on.

Thumbnail buttons

We now need a menu with thumbnails to use for scene selection. When I was researching this chapter I created one from scratch but the attention to detail to make it work perfectly meant I had written over two pages of rather dull instructions when I realised my menu was very similar to the –Special Thumbnail template. I decided not to ask you to reinvent the wheel on this occasion!

Locate the –Special Blank_Sub16x9 menu in the Compact Library and drag it to the Menu list as Menu 3 – which will be colour coded green. Open it in the Editor and use the Timeline to select the Your Text Here text layer and change it to **Flight Over Snowdon**. Change the font to Blade Runner, 48 point. Change the text boxes for *Prev, Next* and *Main* to Blade Runner as well. As you do so, take a look and the button types allocated to these buttons – they use the Previous, Next and Root buttons described earlier. Finally change the background of the menu to the same blue as the last menu we made – you can use the Colour picker on the thumbnail in the Compact Library.

Have a look around the rest of the menu. The buttons have small text labels that say Chapter #, where the # sign is a special code that will be replaced by the number of the chapter the button is allocated to. If we decided to edit this text at a later date we could alter it to give the scenes a full description, but once we use the menu in multi-page mode, we will be creating a good deal of work for ourselves. I'm also not going to suggest changing the font – to make it readable we will have to make it quite big, which will probably upset the shape of the thumbnail buttons with the attendant issues that may cause to button selection.

Menu 3

There is also a checkbox for Still Thumbnails, which should be checked for the Thumbnail buttons. Motion thumbnails can be quite neat, but I'll save them for the final menu.

As an aside, if you were wondering how you create a thumbnail button from scratch, the answer is you can't (or at least, I haven't discovered a way yet!) There are, however, plenty available for you to use under the Buttons tab.

Return to the Disc Editor. Before setting the links, I'm going to add a small refinement to the timeline. Studio doesn't like setting chapters and returns right on top of each other. For one thing, it can cause navigation confusion because although you can just make out that there is more than one flag (you can see a second border) they are difficult to manipulate. Another problem is that they seem to throw off the navigation in some DVD and Blu-ray Players. Yes, even when Studio refuses to let you create a chapter point on top of another one, you can create one alongside and then drag it on top of the first one. However, it might lead to tears before bedtime.

With the Media track highlighted, place the scrubber at the start of the Flight subproject. Open the Title Editor, delete the text box and change the background to the same colour as the menus, and click on OK. A three second blank title the same colour as the menus will have appeared on the timeline. Copy the title, move the scrubber to the start of the BMX movie and Paste a copy of the title. We now have a blank title at the end of Chapters 1 and 2, giving us room to manoeuvre, and the blue titles will just look like a continuation of the menu. (There is potential here for further embellishment. If we were sure which menus would appear before or after the title, we could add text such as Main Menu to match the menus.)

OK, even though I still have one menu to make, I'm going to set the links for Menus 2 and 3 now.

Remove the unlinked chapter in the middle of the Flight subproject if you have placed one there. If, during the next section the menus don't always preview correctly when you switch to them, open them in the editor to refresh the display. This currently happens on one of my computers.

Linking to Menu 2

Select Menu 1 in the preview window and open the small dropdown arrow alongside the C2 label for the Snowdon button. You will now see a choice of Menu 2 or Menu 3. Choose Menu 2. The red warning flag on Menu 2 disappears, meaning the Menu is no longer unreachable. The Chapter flags and links that pointed to the Flight movie have gone. The Extra Features button now points to the same flag,

but it has been renumbered as C2.

We now need to set links for Menu 2. Click on it to bring it into the preview window. Set the Play Movie button to the end of the title that precedes the Flight movie. Notice the M2 flag that has appeared at the end of the entire project. It has no idea where it should go, so it has taken a guess. Drag it to the end of the flight movie, before the blank title.

Menu 2 links set

Using the drop-downs, set the *Scene Selection* button to point to Menu 3 and the *Main Menu* button to point to Menu 1.

For clarity, I'm going to move the M1 flag for Chapter 1 to the beginning of the first blank title. You can't move a linked marker unless the relevant menu is selected, so zoom the timeline into this region, switch to Menu 1, then drag the M1 flag left to the beginning of the title.

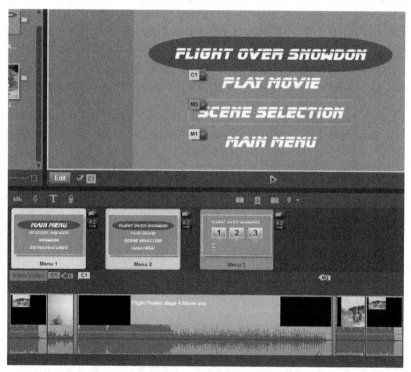

Now click on Menu 3 and look at the buttons in the preview window.

We don't need to set the *Prev, Next* and *Main* buttons as this is done automatically. Set the first thumbnail to the start of the blank title that precedes the Flight movie, and then correct the positioning of the M3 flag to the end of the second blank title by dragging it to the end of the second padding title. (If we had built up the movie and menu structure in a completely linear manner, much of this Return marker repositioning would not have been required, by the way.)

Drag from the middle thumbnail button to about 1 minute 20 seconds into the project. The Chapter marker should conveniently snap to the shot change from the interior shot of the pilot to the view out the window for take off. Use the same technique to set the third thumbnail to the cut between the wide shot of the plane in the sky and the shot of the Nantlle Ridge, around 2 mins 18 secs into the Disc project.

Right, we have run out of thumbnails to add more scene selections to. It's time to use the Multi-menu system to create another copy of Menu 3. Right click on Menu 3 and select Add Menu Page. A new Menu 4 appears, but it is linked to Menu 3 and this is indicated with a connector graphic and also by sharing the same colour – in this case green. This action only happens with menus that have Previous and Next buttons. If they don't, Studio just places a copy of the menu but of a different colour and without the linking indication you can see in the screenshot.

Select Menu 4 (if the preview window doesn't refresh, open the Menu Editor and close it straight away) and set two more links – to the start of the Mount Snowdon shot with the title, and the start of final approach about 3 and a half minutes into the movie. Ignore the final thumbnail for now as I want to use it for a later demonstration.

Notice the Menu 4 hasn't generated its own M4 markers. Multipage menus all obey the first marker in the series, so it will respond to the M3 marker.

After all that work, you deserve a break and a chance to test the Disc project so far.

Menu 3 should have 3 thumbnail links and a Next button but no Previous button. Menu 4 should have only 2 thumbnails and no Next button. If we had added enough chapters to require three multi-page menus, the middle one would have contained both Next and Previous buttons – like buttons, if they don't have something to link to, they don't get displayed.

Setting a different thumbnail

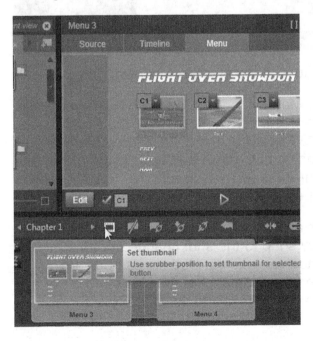

Even if everything has worked as I planned, there is a problem with the first thumbnail of Menu 3. It actually shows the blank title – because that is where the link is set. My deliberate mistake is included so you can correct this issue with the Set Thumbnail tool.

Return to Menu 3 and select the first thumbnail with the faulty picture. Chapter 1 should show in the Button Cycle tool. Now jog along the timeline until preview shows the plane and the full opening title. Click on the Set Thumbnail tool to the right of Button Cycle.

The Chapter flag hasn't moved, but the thumbnail shows something much more useful even than the black video frame we would have got had we set the Chapter marker to the start of the movie. The *Set Thumbnail* button can be used to set to display a still or a moving picture from anywhere on the timeline – even from parts that aren't part of any of the chapters. For example, you can create special little video files, placed at the very end of the project past the last return to menu flag, and set them as the thumbnails for any menu.

I have also deliberately left out a sixth chapter to demonstrate a menu tool that causes some confusion. In many circumstances the Insert Link tool seems to do exactly the same thing as the Create Link tool. I've set up a situation here where you can see the difference between the two functions.

The Scene Selection point I'm going to add is between Chapters 4 and 5 – the start of the Castle shot. We don't want this link at the end because we want the scenes to remain in story order – we don't expect to see the plane land and then view the castle from the air, do we?

If I were to use Create Link on the Chapter 5 thumbnail button it would destroy the link I've already set up for the final approach. What we want is a tool that will insert a new link but ripple down any subsequent links. Chapter 5 will become Chapter 6, and if there were more links, Chapter 6 would become Chapter 7 and so on. With Chapter 5 in the Button Cycle tool display, find the start of the Castle shot with the scrubber and use the Insert Link Tool. You should see exactly what I described happen and we end up with a new link for Chapter 5 and the old link renumbered as chapter 6.

Using the Insert Link tool

At this point you might be wondering what happens if you decide to add even more scenes. I think it's worth doing, because Insert Link is a

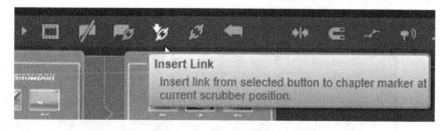

great aid to creating not just new scenes, but new multipage menus.

Let's add a new scene for the moment just before take off. It needs to go before where Chapter 3 is at the moment, so select Menu 3 and click in the third thumbnail to bring it up in the Button Cycle box.

Set the timeline scrubber up on the cut to the exterior take off shot and *Insert Link*. Yes – we get a new Menu 5! It's only got one chapter, so let's add two more. Select Menu 4, Chapter 6 and insert a new link for the start of the Mountain Railway shot. For the last scene select Menu 5 and the final thumbnail – Chapter # - will show in the Button Cycle box. Set it to just before the touchdown at 4 minutes 2 seconds. For this last action we could use Create Link as there are no chapters beyond this point that need to be rippled down.

Incidentally, if you use Play Movie to watch the Flight movie, the chapters we have just set will become unlinked chapters – using the DVD player's skip buttons will take to the next or previous scene. I've saved a version of the project with the title *Disc Project 4* for your convenience.

Motion menus

Right click on Menu 2 and select Add Menu Page. A copy of Menu 2 appears as Menu 3 and all the other menus are rippled down the list. Drag it to the far right of the list and it becomes Menu 6 – a nice salmon colour. Open it in the Menu Editor and delete both the Play Movie and Scene Selection layers. Change the Flight Over Snowdon text to Extra Features, and resize it to 60pt.

I want to add two thumbnail buttons. Use the Buttons tab and open up the Thumbnails sub tab. The first one in the list should be 50's Modern, and it will suit our purposes just fine. Click on it to add it to the menu. Make a second copy and arrange them equally inside the title safe area between the Extra Features text and the Main Menu button. Check that they don't have the Still Thumbnail checkbox set and make the left hand one the default.

The Extra Features Menu

We are going to add moving video clips to this menu, so we need to think about the duration. A lot of the menus supplied with Studio have motion backgrounds which appear to loop seamlessly, but all the menus have a fixed duration that matches the video – designed so that the last and first frame of the motion background video appear not to jump when the menu loops. This effect is spoilt on a lot of DVD players because they take a differing amount of time to loop the video.

Any looping menu that is too busy gets irritating after a while in my opinion, but increasing the duration from the 12 second default will help. You alter the duration by typing numbers into the duration box above the timeline – it is indicated with the two square brackets - [ ] – alongside.

Enter 20 seconds. If we had longer clips, I would suggest even longer.

Adjusting the Menu Duration

Before we set the thumbnails, I also want to add a motion background. Unfortunately you cannot use a subproject for this task, so we will use the unedited *The-Sky-is-the-Limit* video. Locate it in the

Compact Library and then drag it across to the background box. The slider that appears underneath the box can be used to set the In point, so adjust it so that the video starts on the close shot of the red bike frame – the BMX pictures are more dynamic.

Adjusting the In point for the Motion background

I don't want the video to be too bright, so I'm going to use a layer in front of the motion background. Create a rectangle that fills the screen, send it to the back layer, and change its colour to black, but at 50% opacity.

We can now exit the Menu Editor. Previewing the menu at this point will confuse Studio – we should set some links first. In Menu 1, set the Extra Features button to link to Menu 6. In Menu 6, link the Main Menu button to link to Menu 1. Now you should be

able to preview the menu to check out what the motion background does. You may have to wait for the preview optimisation to finish to preview smoothly. The same will be the case when you add motion thumbnails.

Hmm, what about some audio? It will be a bit annoying, but here goes....

Return to the Menu Editor and find the BMX music in the Compact Library, then drag it to the Audio dropbox underneath the background box. Fortunately we can set a fade out on the music by checking the Fade box and setting the parameter box underneath. Set it to 1 second. If you happen to choose music that is too loud, you can adjust the volume by adding an audio correction to the level with the aid of the Channel Mixer before adding it to the menu.

Return to the timeline and put another copy of the DVD Intro project at the end of the project. Now set the first thumbnail button to the beginning of the BMX movie and the second one to the DVD Intro. Put a M6 return marker at the end of the BMX movie.

Try the menu in the disc simulator. It's a bit odd that the two thumbnails are in sync with each other. Find a point about four seconds into the DVD Intro project where there is a change of photo – remember they almost always change on the start of a bar – and set that as the thumbnail. The video will now play from that point.

We now have completed the menu structure. This is the final version - *Disc Project 5.*

If you have made all the projects and completed the DVD menus, I suggest you make a DVD by way of celebration. I successfully rendered this project first time, using the DVD best quality setting.

However, because of the complexity and layering of projects, I suggest you check the *Always re-encode entire movie* box in advanced settings. In my first rendered disc I encountered a few flash frames, caused I think by inaccuracies when Studio smart rendered some of the MPEG-2 files. These would have shown up if I had followed my own advice and previewed the Disc Image before going straight to the burning stage.

Automatic Chapters and Links

The Chapter wizard can help you with simple tasks. For me, if I push it to try anything more complex it sometimes makes errors that are not only difficult to track down, but also seems to corrupt a project in such a way that even removing all the changes made by the Wizard still seems to leave some corruption behind. So I suggest you save your project before using it.

The Chapter Wizard

You access it via the top tab to the right of each menu, and it will only create chapter and links for the menu you select it from.

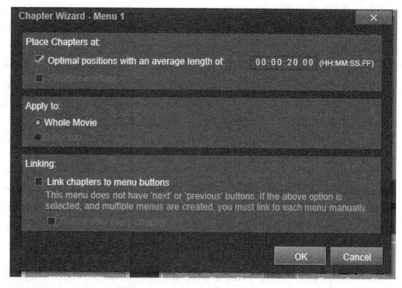

Place Chapters at: gives a choice of *Optimal positions* where you can set the approximate length. Studio tries if possible to place chapter markers on edit points. This still produces quite random results, but if you just want to pepper some unlinked chapters on a movie so you can use the skip function, it is useful. *Timeline Markers* means you have to place the markers. If you have been placing them as you have built up the project this too can be useful, particularly if you want a return to menu after each chapter, but if you are going to have to place the markers manually, you may as well place the linked chapters manually and be sure of the correct result.

Apply to: will create chapters over the whole of the timeline, or just the sections you have highlighted.

Linking: will not only create the chapters, but also add links to the menus. If the menu doesn't have Previous and Next buttons and you try to make too many chapters, although multiple menus will be created you will have to do the linking yourself. At the bottom of the Wizard you can chose if menu returns are added for each chapter.

The other tab below the Wizard allows you to *Sort* chapters. If you have been editing the timeline, adding and altering links, and perhaps even changing the button order while editing, this command will put the Chapter buttons back into timeline order. It's the alternative to you working through methodically and using the Insert Link command when adding more scene selections.

AVCHD and Blu-ray discs

You can make the above Disc project as an AVCHD or Blu-ray disc (if you have enabled Blu-ray) and all the features will work – or at least, all the features work on my Blu-ray player! There doesn't seem to be the compatibility issues that occurred in the past, certainly with the major brands. However, one current issue I have is that return markers aren't obeyed instantly and the Intro Video overruns into Chapter 1 by a few frames. Where I haven't put title spaces in the timeline, I sometimes see a few frames of the next chapter. The pragmatic solution is to include more padding or adjust the markers a little, but unfortunately you may have wasted a disc by then. This may be a case of different player firmware giving different results, but I hope to see it fixed by the time you read this.

As I made two versions of this project - one PAL and one NTSC, I also noticed that the PAL version was more stable and behaved more predictably. However, let's hope that Pinnacle take a closer look at the code so by the time you read this the menus will be perfect!

In summary, when you want to add menus to any project, plan ahead, work methodically and save your project at different points along the way. Most important of all, remember to use the Disc Simulator, and then if you can, use a re-writable disc for the first burn.

Understanding Studio

The aim of this chapter is to explain the installation, set up and inner working of Pinnacle Studio 19. You may be having particular issues, you may be wondering what the best settings for preview optimisation are or you could just want a better understanding of the Control Panel options. Some of these subjects will have been touched on in earlier parts of the book, but I will assume you haven't read those.

Hardware requirements

The current requirements should be included in the pre-sales information as well as being printed on the box. If your computer doesn't meet the minimum requirements, Pinnacle support staff won't be able to offer any help if you can't get Studio running correctly. That's not to say I haven't been able to run the program on lower spec computers, but you need to be very patient. Even if you have a computer that meets the minimum, you will have a smoother ride if you can match or exceed the *recommended* requirements.

I do have one qualification about the requirements - they can be a bit vague, even dated, when it comes to graphics. There is much talk of needing a separate card with a minimum amount of dedicated memory, but the new Intel chips that have built in HD graphics should have no performance issues. So if you have a second generation i5 or i7 or later, don't worry about the specs.

There is a major hike in requirements if you want to edit AVCHD video, and that includes H.264 encoded files that may be inside a MOV, AVI or MP4 wrapper. Just because a computer can smoothly play back a particular file in Windows Media Player or Quicktime doesn't mean that Studio is faulty. Player software doesn't edit video, so it can treat audio and video as separate streams, it only needs to partially decode video in some circumstances, it need not be accurate to the frame and can build up a large buffer before it starts to play.

Because of advances in the second, third and fourth generation of i5 and i7 CPUs, (Sandy and Ivy Bridge and Haswell) the clock speeds required with these chips are much lower.

People often wonder what the most important components of a system for video editing are.

Single and dual core Microprocessors (**CPUs**) will be stressed to their full capacity for most render operations. Some parts of Studio aren't optimised for more than two cores, particularly most standard definition processing and older effects. When working on H.264 and similar video, four or more cores can be brought fully into play. If you look at the Performance tab in the Task manager, you will see that on MPEG-2 rendering, for example, quad core CPUs don't use the full capacity, but load share. Adding more cores will just spread the load even more, so clock speed is important. Use the same computer to render H.264 video and you will see it pinned to 100% use.

Graphics chips (**GPU**s) play a part in the real time playback of many effects and transitions, and are used for pre-rendering these sections of a project. Studio also uses the Intel Quicksync and starting from version 17 the Cuda systems, which can bring the GPU into play for other video related tasks. However adding a very fast GPU will have a less noticeable effect on overall system performance than speeding up the CPU. Avoid less popular workstation cards and those that share main memory. Earlier versions of Studio wouldn't work well with shared graphics memory because they would steal it from the memory needed to run the program, but most modern systems have enough memory to go round.

Don't expect that increasing the amount of the main memory (**RAM**) is going to give a noticeable gain in performance. Starting at version 18 Studio has been available as a full 64-bit program, so if you are running a 64-bit system and have installed the 64-bit build of Studio could theoretically use as much memory as you have free. Remember that Editing programs don't actually hold large chunks of video data in memory though. I am now running Studio on a system with 16Gb of memory and I've never seen it use more than a couple of gigs, unless it is heading for a crash.

While you can't have enough **Hard Disc** space when you edit video, the transfer speeds of all modern HDDs is above that required to play back consumer video smoothly. This wasn't the case in the past, though, when data rates were significantly lower. Unfortunately many of the practices from those days are still quoted as essential to fast video performance. If your hard disk is operating correctly, even a "slow" 5400rpm disc won't be a problem.

There are two issues with HDDs. I've talked about dropping frames and jerky playback in the Import and Export chapters. Very heavy fragmentation, other programs using the disc or a hardware clash between an external drive and capture device can be a problem, but not the true underlying speed of the HDD.

The other issue is render bottlenecks. There is only one set of circumstances where I've seen a benefit from using elaborate multi-disc setups and faster HDDs – when Studio is able to use direct stream copy (Smart Render). This is the only time that the CPU is waiting for the HDD. In every other case it is the other way round. This is discussed in both the Basic Principles and the the Export chapter.

Don't take any of the above to mean that a faster hard drive won't improve the overall system performance when used as a system drive. A Solid State Drive has a remarkable effect on the speed at which Pinnacle Studio loads and swaps windows. It won't, however, improve the render times of non-Smart render tasks or the preview smoothness of AVCHD video.

The **Operating System** has to be Windows Vista, 7, 8 or 10.

The only variations that will affect the performance of Studio are 64-bit or 32-bit. Studio can automatically choose which to install by detecting the OS. If you have any legacy hardware, particularly the PCI card based capture devices, check carefully before choosing a 64-bit OS. The Movieboard and PCI boards don't work on 64-bit systems with 2Gb or more of RAM.

Installing Studio

I doubt if anyone reading this hasn't already gone ahead and installed Studio, but you may well want to re-install it after a hard disc crash or the move to a new computer.

There are two ways to acquire Pinnacle Studio. If you by the physical product – a disc in a box – then as long as you don't lose the disc or damage it, then you have what you need to re-install at any time – the latest patch can be downloaded from Pinnacle's website. The disc isn't copy protected, by the way, so I'd recommend you burn a safety copy or store a disc image somewhere safe.

Downloading Studio is becoming more common. It's important to realise that you don't get unlimited time to download your files, so it is vital that you keep a backup. Even buying an extended download period from the distributor only gives you a two year window. You don't have to buy a backup disc – you can just archive the files you receive.

When you buy a download, the first step is to download a small program called *Pinnacle-installer.exe* from the supplier. This will be saved in your Downloads location for you to run, which will start the process of downloading the rest of the files.

Your serial number

This is the one piece of data that is proof that you have paid for Studio – the files are nothing without it. It consists of 25 letters (there are no numbers). It will be included on the *Thank you* page when the purchase is complete and in the Order confirmation email you will be sent. Keep it safe! You can get Pinnacle to send you a list of all your serial numbers by logging into your support account, but you have to register first to get an account, and remember the account details! One serial number you can't retrieve this way is the iZotope audio cleaner.

The serial number dictates which version of Studio you own, although it is common for both 32 and 64 bit versions. The only reason for download and installing the 32-bit version is if you have a 32-bit OS or legacy hardware or plug-ins that you might need to run. The Installer checks your system and offers to download the correct version, but you can override that and download both if you wish.

Re-downloading the 64 bit version to a custom location

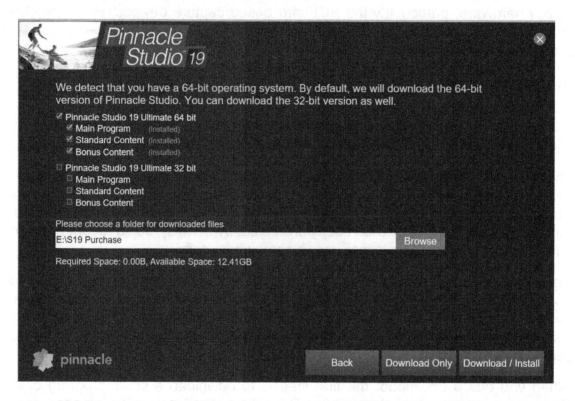

When you perform the download you will be getting the latest version, so if you are still in the window to re-download you may get a newer version rather than having to install a patch. The files will be saved to a location that you specify, and you can choose to download them, or to install the program as well. If you don't choose to install at the time of download, you can trigger that process by opening the *32bit* or *64bit* folder that was downloaded and running the Welcome.exe program. This would be how you could re-install Studio from a backup of your downloaded files

The Install Manager

It's at this point that the Disc and Download versions coincide

The easiest route is to chose the Standard Installation, but for more control you may want to use the Customized option.

The Install manager at the Custom Install screen

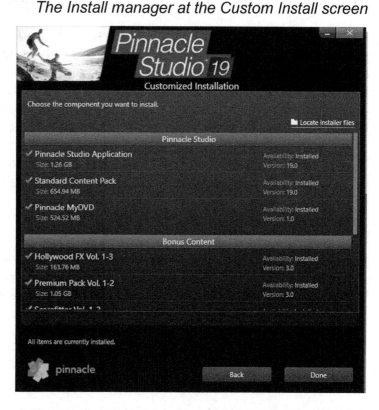

I would normally recommend just installing everything on the list, even if you are using a custom install for troubleshooting reasons. However, if you aren't ever likely to use the Premium packs and you are a bit short of space on your boot disc (perhaps you have a Solid State Drive), the Custom install shows that these components take up a lot of space. In addition, they take a while to unpack, probably because of the amount of video they contain.

Re-installing – what are the risks?

You probably want (or have been advised) to re-install because you don't think Studio is working correctly. However, you might be worried that you will lose video you have imported, projects and the Library settings. If you just use Windows to uninstall the programs and then re-install using the original disc or download then there is **no danger** of that happening.

I would suggest you go to the Pinnacle support website to read the latest FAQ on re-installing Studio as it may change over time, but a basic workflow is to use the Windows Control Panel to uninstall all the components. Sort the list by publisher to make sure you don't miss any, and if you have the Ultimate version, look out for the New Blue and possibly the Red Giant packages as well. Now run the Install program again. When the process is complete you will find your Library and settings intact, because they aren't stored as part of the program, but in the User area of your operating system – one Library and setting file for each user.

Registering

If Studio has been installed before on the computer and the folder containing this information - the Pixie folder – is intact, you won't need to enter a serial number.

Registering Studio is essential to get the full use from it. When re-registering you should use the same email address to the one used before; if you don't you may compromise your serial number. When you register the software a number of the codecs needed to work with video are automatically unlocked, including the all-important MPEG-2 codec. There is a small royalty that needs to be paid by Pinnacle for using the codec, as is the case with a number of the other codecs. However, these other codecs won't be activated until you try to use the particular type of video or audio. H.264 (for AVCHD) may require a further automatic activation, but Blu-ray authoring requires you to pay for a licence - see page 235 for more details

Troubleshooting installations

If a conventional re-install doesn't solve your problems, there could be issues with the settings file, the project that the program is automatically trying to load, or the Library. I also mentioned problems that could be caused by Watchfolders and incompatible files in the Import chapter.

The first trick for troubleshooting a corrupt installation after a conventional re-install is to log into Windows as another user (creating a new one is a good idea) and running Studio from there.

If Studio seems to be functioning correctly when logged on as someone else you know the problem lies somewhere in a project, the settings file or the Library. If the problem still exists, then you most likely have a hardware or software compatibly issue.

The Reset function

You can find this in the Control Panel as the final entry on the left. When you click on the Reset button, the settings.xml file will be deleted along with the effects database. You then need to restart Studio, when the settings file will be recreated with default settings, and the computer re-scanned for content. You won't lose any

Bins, Collections or Metadata, but you will lose any Favourites you added and any changes you made in the Control Panel.

Complete Manual Reset

The Reset and the Library Refresh features (see page 155) will cover most eventualities but if you think there might be something in the Library causing issues you will need to resort to manually tampering with the contents of Studio's Windows folders. That way can delete the Studio setting for the current user and trigger the program to start up in its "freshly installed" state. You will force it to display the opening splash screen as well. You will lose your Library, so you might want to back it up as shown on page 155.

Here's how to reset Studio completely:

- Shut down Studio

- Navigate to your boot drive

- Navigate to *Users/Your profile name/*

- If you cannot see an *AppData* folder, you need to force Windows to show hidden files. Refer to page 156 if you aren't sure how to do this.

- Continue to navigate to *Appdata/Local/*

- Rename the folder *Pinnacle_Studio_19* to *Pinnacle_Studio_19_OLD*

Now when you restart Studio, it will start up as if it were the first time, creating a new data folder. If you don't solve the problem and want to revert to your old user data delete the *Pinnacle_Studio_19* folder Studio has created and rename *Pinnacle_Studio_19_OLD to Pinnacle_Studio_19.*

Another issue could be that you are suffering from corrupt or incorrect thumbnails. This is most likely to occur when trying to Import camera files and is covered in detail in the Import chapter on page 169 . If you are having other issues with thumbnails use the procedure outlined there.

All of the above data will eventually be regenerated by Studio if it has been deleted, so although I'd always suggest using renaming rather than deletion where possible, it highly unlikely that you will do any serious damage, and if the worse comes to the worst you can always re-install the program from scratch, deleting the whole of the *Pinnacle_Studio_19* folder first.

After any sort of reset it takes a while for Studio to recreate it's settings, particularly if you have deleted the thumbnails. Be patient, and if the program appears to be sluggish check the CPU usage in the Task Manager. If you see high usage from tasks such as Com Surrogate, BGRender or NGStudio, then the rebuild may still be in progress.

Graphic card issues

If you have any problems with displaying video or effects, or rendering effects during export, the first thing to check is the drivers for your graphics card. Go to the graphics card manufacturer or the graphic chip manufacturer's websites for the latest drivers. If there is a newer version, update. If you do and the problem gets worse, roll them back, because just occasionally new drivers haven't been fully tested.

Don't assume that any inbuilt update software will automatically keep your machine up to date, and don't assume that because you have just unpacked a brand new computer or installed a brand new card it will have the latest drivers.

If you have a new Intel computer with a 2nd, generation or above i3/5/7 CPU it will probably have HD graphics built in, and Studio may try to use this system for decoding H.264 video. Even if your computer has a separate, more powerful graphics card, you need to check the drivers for the Intel graphics as well.

My i7 laptop allows me to choose which graphics processor to use to run the program when I right click on the Desktop icon. If you have this feature you may be able to use it for troubleshooting.

One other fix that may help is turning off complex Windows themes such as Aero.

Studio 19 allows you a choice of how your graphics card is used for hardware acceleration. You may be able to choose a different mode to avoid problems, and I'll give you details on page 525 .

Registration and activation

There are a number of options in the *? (Help)* menu that deal with activation and registration issues.

Activate & Register Product will open up a dialogue box where you can enter a new name, serial number and email address if you so wish. In the current version of Studio the wording in the dialogue box might make you think that you haven't registered your software, when in fact you have. I'm hoping this will be changed in the future.

Help options

Your **Passport** is as important as your serial number, and it differs from computer to computer. If you decide to move your copy of Studio to a new computer, you can install it with the same serial number, use the same name and email address but your Passport will change. Because the Passport has changed, the activation keys you used before will no longer be valid and will need to be regenerated. Using this menu option will reveal your serial number and Passport if you need to provide the information to Support.

Regenerating activation keys

This option is now reached via the Corel Support website. The menu option *?/Online Support/Technical support* opens a browser window with a number of options. When you reach the site, use the option *Self Help/Install/activate your product* where a website form awaits you.

Studio 19 itself no longer requires activation keys, although you might need them for items you bought in the past.

Restore Purchase

If you bought a Blu-ray licence and reinstalled your software you may find the option missing. To reactive the licence there is a Restore Purchase option in the Control Panel. You need to enter the email address you used for the purchase.

I suspect this will be the way that Pinnacle activates other additional content and features in the future.

The Control Panel

All the significant choices you need to make in Studio are contained in the Control Panel, accessed via the Setup Menu or by using the key combination CTRL-ALT-C. Once the panel is open you select the various sections from the panel on the left.

Watchfolders

These are discussed in detail in the Import and Library chapters. They automatically add assets to the Library. In Studio 19 they are disabled by default. You can make changes to which folders are constantly monitored for the addition of new assets in this section of the control panel. You can specify if the folders you add are monitored for Photos, Video, Audio or all types of asset. Watchfolders can sometime be the cause of stability issues in Studio, particularly if you use unusual file types. Refer to the Import chapter for more details.

Audio devices

This section allows you to select the Windows device used for audio recording. It is discussed in the Voice Over Tool section on page 420.

Event Log

Sometimes things happen in Studio that haven't caused a crash but are important enough for you to want further information about. During a complex operation there may have been messages that you didn't register fully. You will find a record of these events here, where you can use them for troubleshooting, or to refresh your memory as to what didn't go quite right!

The Export and Preview Panel

The settings on this page of the Control panel will never affect the final quality of your movies and discs, although in certain circumstances they have an impact on how long those projects take to render to the final product.

The first four parameters purely affect the Preview you see on your computer.

Quality defines the maximum resolution that Studio attempts to display when playing back anything in its preview windows. *Best Quality* will match the resolution of the project settings. *Fastest Playback* will have half the vertical and horizontal resolution, hence a quarter of the number of pixels. The *Balanced* setting chooses one or the other, depending on the projects settings, so on my system it gives Fastest Playback for a Full HD project and Best Quality for a SD project.

The Export and Preview settings

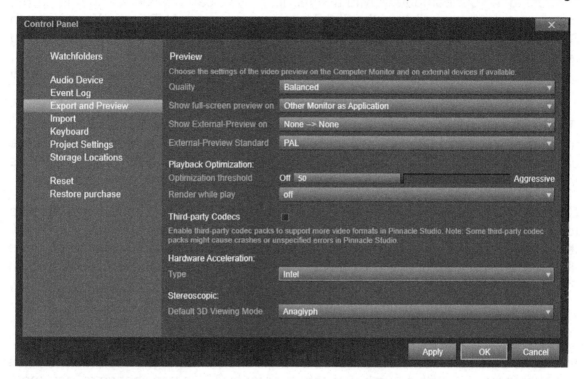

When your system is trying to display video without the help of Playback Optimisation, this setting can impinge on smooth playback, particularly of effects and transitions. If the graphics card only has to work on 25% of the pixels, it can get the job done much quicker, and therefore is less likely to stall and start dropping frames. If you aren't using Full Screen preview then the maximum size of your preview is unlikely to be much more than 60% of your screen size, so if your computer monitor resolution isn't 1920x1080 or higher you won't really see the benefit from the Best Quality setting for Full HD projects.

For Full screen preview and SD projects you should try to work with the Best Quality setting unless you get significantly smoother playback when set to Fastest. Switching between the Quality settings requires you to restart Studio to see the difference, however, so it's quite inconvenient to change them. I suggest you always use Best Quality when using Pan & Zoom on photos, where I often switch to Full Screen preview to check if I've zoomed too far into a photo and therefore getting a blurred result.

The setting you use here also has an affect on Preview Optimisation (AKA background rendering), more of which in a moment.

Show full-screen preview on is only of relevance if you have more than one monitor connected to your computer. With two monitors, you can choose which one shows the preview when you click on the Full Screen icon or press ALT-Enter. You can span Studio over two monitors, which works quite well if you have monitors of matching resolution, but switching to Full Screen still works. If you have a redundant monitor of a lower resolution it's still worth connecting it up if you have the desk space for it and seeing if you find it helps your editing.

For the **External Preview** settings to be relevant you will not only need a TV set or monitor with a composite or S-Video input, but also you need a compatible Pinnacle capture device that has video output as well as input. There are currently no devices that can output a HD preview, so you are restricted to SD.

One advantage of using an external preview hardware device is that you may be able to detect issues with interlacing without having to render a disc and play it on a TV. It can potentially allow you to use two computer monitors to span Studio across, and still have a full screen preview. However, if you are editing HD and don't already own the correct hardware it's probably not worth the investment.

Preview Optimisation

In Classic Studio this feature was called Background Rendering. In NGStudio it works in a similar manner, with a number of enhancements. The name change reflects more accurately what it is designed to do.

Pinnacle Studio can work with compatible video files in their raw state. It doesn't insist on converting them to a format that suits its purposes before you can put them on the timeline - the Proxy files we discussed at the beginning of the book. The advantages include the ability to edit a file as soon as you have imported it, and a reduction in the amount of conforming required to make the final product.

However, even with a simple Standard Definition DV-AVI file, if you add enough layers of effects, overlaid video, transitions and titles to a Studio project, there will come a time where the most powerful computer will be unable to play back the movie smoothly.

The point at which real-time playback becomes unusable varies with the complexity of the timeline, the video format and the computing power available. Some editing programs, when faced with a certain level of complexity, will just stop and tell you that you need to render the section of the timeline that it has decided it can't cope with. Studio doesn't normally do that (Stabilisation is one exception). Instead, you can set the level at which Preview Optimisation begins to take effect. When a section of the timeline has reached a certain level of complexity, that area is re-encoded into a single video file that uses a relatively simple codec – MPEG-2. Once that section has been rendered, Studio should encounter no difficulty in achieving smooth playback.

The level at which Preview Optimisation starts is determined by the slider named **Optimisation Threshold**. At one end – 100% - it is indeed aggressive – I've not found any circumstances where rendering doesn't begin. At the other end - 0% setting it is normally completely off although sometimes rendering occurs if subprojects are involved.

Although Studio defaults to the 100% setting, I don't think that this is a particularly good choice for anyone with a decent computer, particularly if you are making SD projects. If you can lower the setting and still get smooth playback, then you won't be distracted by the rendering, even though it should not interfere with your editing. Apart from the distraction, after a while you start to build up a huge number of render files, taking up space and opening up the potential for errors.

There is a scale, and not just an on/off checkbox, so I would encourage you to experiment to find a setting that doesn't cause the rendering to kick in at the slightest change. Personally, I start working with it at the 50% mark.

Rendering takes place in the background – you don't have to halt work on the project while it occurs. It will slow your computer down though, another reason not to generate unnecessary render files. Its draw on computer resources may interfere with smooth playback, so Studio allows you control over when it is active. The **Render while play** setting has three options, On, Off and Automatic, which halts playback when it deems your system can't cope. I tend to work with it switched off.

Render progress can be monitored by looking at the bars at the top of the timeline. When a section of the movie requires optimisation (as determined by the level of optimisation set) it will be coloured in what I can only describe as a light brown. While rendering of that section is in progress, it will turn green, from left to right. If no rendering is required, the area will be grey.

The files that are rendered from the timeline are stored in a location that you can define – the Auxiliary files location (specified in a section of the Storage Locations settings). If you take a look in the Auxiliary files folder once an area has been rendered, a file with the type EVMS will exist for the rendered area.

You may never have heard of an EVMS file and it would be a good bet to assume that it is a proprietary video format especially created for render files by Corel.

However, if you rename the file suffix to M2V then you can play the file - it's an MPEG-2 file without audio. Studio 16.0 and all earlier versions used exactly those types of files, and as far as I can tell nothing has changed except the file suffix.

The filename will be a meaningless jumble to you and me, but each file has a unique name. The number of files will soon build up. In order to prevent duplicated renders, old files are not deleted automatically. This is really useful, because if you make a change to the program and then decide to undo that change, Studio reverts to the previous set of render files rather than having to make them all over again. A good example might be if you decide to hide a video track with the eye icon, just to check what is happening underneath an overlay track. Yes, a new preview optimisation file is generated, but if you un-hide the overlay track, Studio doesn't need to regenerate the old file.

Another feature of Studio 19 is that it not only renders selectively along the timeline, it can choose to render only certain tracks. It may then go on to render further layers, but that will depend on the threshold you have set. This explains why on a multi-layered project you may sometimes see a section of the movie change colour a number of times before finally going grey. The latest hardware can process multiple streams of H.264 video more efficiently, and Studio is taking advantage of this.

Now, if you have preview optimisation working for you, it seems a shame that the process has to be repeated when you finally export your project. There are certain circumstances where Studio can actually re-use the files that it made for preview optimisation in the final Export. However, they aren't as frequent as you might at first think.

Firstly, if you have the Preview Quality set to Fastest Playback, (or it's set to Balanced and Studio is deciding to lower the resolution) then the files in the Auxiliary location are of no use – they have a quarter of the number of pixels than are needed to match the project resolution.

Next, if the project settings don't match the output format, the files are unlikely to be of use either. You might be making a DVD from HD material, in which case the render files will have too high a resolution to be used. If you are making Blu-ray or AVCHD discs from H.264 video, Studio shouldn't use the MPEG-2 render files either. If it appears to be doing so and you are worried that it might compromise quality, then you can ensure that they aren't used.

The most likely time that the preview optimisation files are used is when making DVD discs. Even then, the time saving may be counter-productive. The great majority of rendering errors at the disc or file stage can be attributed to the use of incorrect render files, and the cure is to delete them and get Studio to rebuild them from scratch.

If you don't need to generate render files for preview, then you may want to make Studio wait until it gets to the Export stage before doing the work. If you can get away with a lower threshold, do so. Also, if you aren't previewing at full quality, remember that background rendered files have no relevance to export.

Studio appears to use preview files when exporting H.264 to a MTS file, and also AVCHD or Blu-ray discs and images. However, it will only use files that were generated for effects, transitions, titles or any other process that triggers preview rendering at less than 100% optimisation.

Preprocessing for Export

Now that I have described the role of Preview Optimisation AKA Background Rendering, one of the tasks of the Advanced Export option Preprocessing should be a bit clearer. By selecting the option *Render Completely before Export,* then if there are usable preview optimisation files then these will be used, and any files that have not yet been generated will be built up before the final export render is generated. You will see the message "Preparing for Export". *No Preprocessing* means that if the preview render files don't exist they will **not** be generated. And all the files are generated from scratch. If you are experiencing odd problems in your exports I recommend that you switch off Preview optimisation, delete the render files, switch preprocessing off and **then** make your file or disc.

Third party Codecs

Another new Studio 19 feature allows you to enable the use of codecs from other suppliers. See page 193 for more details.

Hardware Acceleration

In earlier versions of Studio this option was just a check box - On or Off. Now you can choose between None (off), Intel or Cuda. If you have an Intel CPU with HD graphics, then Intel would be the best choice, although the Intel software emulation is pretty good also. If you have a powerful, Cuda enabled Graphics card, then Cuda will probably give you the best results. If you are experiencing issues with either setting, try None.

Setting Hardware Acceleration

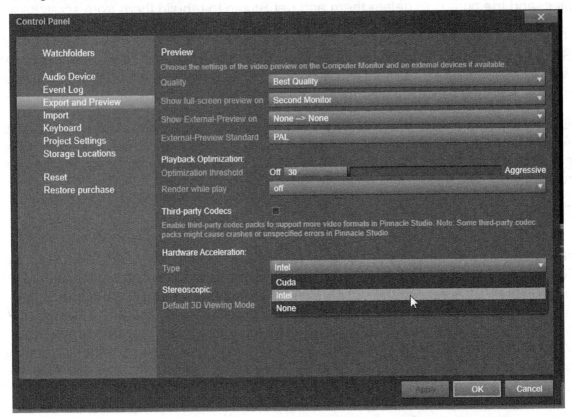

What actually gets speeded up with hardware acceleration? Most of the effects and transitions are GPU based so preview rendering and export of those sections of a movie will benefit. The other big gain is when working with H.264 video. If you export a lot of movies it is definitely worth timing a few test projects to see which settings give the fastest results. However, don't forget to check the quality of the renders as well. I've know some movies made with Quicksync - the Intel application - show some very noticeable rendering artefacts in the past.

Import

All of Studio's Import Option defaults can be set In the next tab of the Control Panel, including where Snapshots are stored. The Import chapter covers what the options are in detail, and why you might choose to store assets, particularly video, on a separate hard drive.

Keyboard

Customising the Keyboard shortcuts

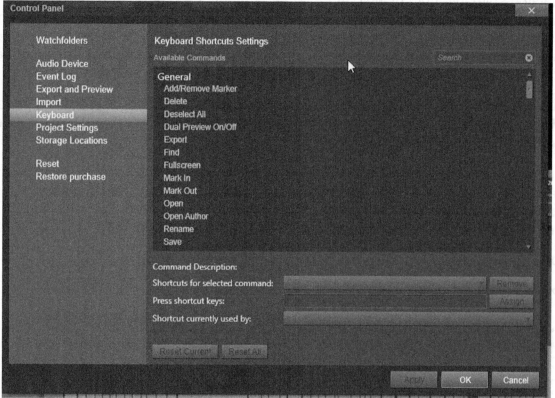

One very nice feature of Studio is the ability to customise the keyboard shortcuts. If you are used to another editor or have a particular operation you use so often you would like to assign it a keyboard shortcut, then you can do it here.

The main window lists all the actions that Studio performs that can have a shortcut assigned to it. Shortcuts can vary between sections of the program – for example the M key adds or removes a marker on the timeline, but when the Trim Mode is activated, it trims the current trim point(s) 10 frames left.

Let's see how we might modify a control. Switching the Dual View on and off may be something you do frequently, and want to assign it to a keyboard shortcut. Enter Dual into the Search box and you can see that CTRL-D is already allocated. That might be all you need to know, and you can use it from now on.

Let's say you use it so often that you want it to be assigned to a single key press. Highlight the *Press shortcut keys:* box and press the D key. In the box below you will see (with the aid of the drop-down arrow) that D is assigned to not just one, but two, functions already, both of which I have never mentioned because I always use the arrow keys. You can assign the D key, but you better remove the other assignment - Go to Previous Edit - because you don't want the scrubber to be moving around just because you have turned on Dual preview. Go to that shortcut and use the Remove button. You will still have Page Up and CTRL-Left available.

When you use OK, the keyboard shortcut should become active. The settings panel allows you to reset either an individual or every shortcut to the default defined by the program and listed in the manual.

There is currently no way within the program of saving and loading customised keyboard set ups, so if more than one person uses the program they will either have to use different Windows user accounts or manually backup and restore the Settings Folder in the same manner as backing up the Library (see page 155).

Project settings

Project settings

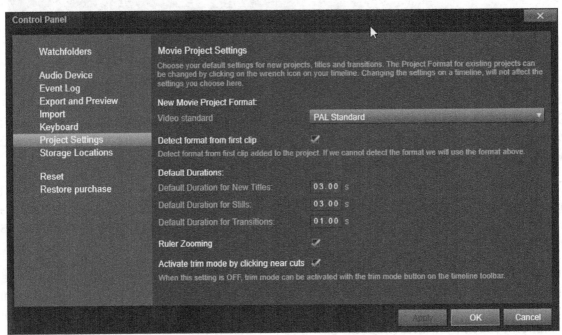

The project defaults are controlled here. By default a Standard Definition 4:3 project is created, but you can select any valid format from the drop-down box. There is also a checkbox that, when enabled, allows Studio to set the project setting from the first clip that you drag to the timeline.

Because the project settings can be changed after you have started work, this setting isn't as critical as it was in earlier versions of Pinnacle Studio. As I invariably work in 16:9, I leave the settings at their default, so if I find myself working on a 4:3 project I know there has been an issue detecting the format of the first clip.

The Default durations allow you to change the length of titles, transitions and photos when you first add them to the timeline.

Personally, I think all the defaults are a bit short, but that's just me. Your choice will depend on what sort of project you are making at the time.

The checkbox for **Ruler Zooming** enables or disables the ability to rescale the timeline by dragging the timescale at the bottom of the Movie and Disc Editor. If you would prefer to have more control over the scrubber you can disable this feature, so that when you click on the timescale the scrubber jumps to that point. There are plenty of other ways to control the scaling – right click for a context menu and select a view or zoom in and out, as well as the keyboard shortcuts.

The checkbox labelled **Activate trim mode by clicking near cuts** is set to ON by default

If you find yourself irritated by being in the Trim Editor when you didn't want to be, then you can switch this OFF. One important point is that the use of Shift to add a point for each track is swapped over between the modes - With clicking near cuts ON you need to hold down Shift to get multiple points, with the mode OFF, Shift forces you to only get one trim point.

Storage Locations

If you have more than one hard drive, or even have a single drive divided up into portions, it really helps housekeeping if you keep your video assets in a different place to your operating system boot drive. It will often help system performance as well, as discussed in the Import chapter. The storage locations defined in this part of the control panel deal with other assets.

The first four items on the list - Movie and Disc projects, menus and titles - will never take up a great deal of disc space, but for organisational reasons you might prefer to keep them somewhere else other than the default locations buried inside the users libraries. One reason might be that you work on an external or removable drive that you move between computers – working on a laptop when away, or a desktop when at home, for example. Another reason would be that you want more than one user on the same computer to share projects, titles and menus. Or you might be obsessively tidy!

If you do decide to change any of these locations, you will be warned that you need to reboot Studio to enable the changes to take place. It is also important to remember that any projects, menus or titles you have saved in the old locations **will not** be moved to the new one.

In the past, disciplined use of the above customisable locations made moving projects a lot easier, but Pinnacle Studio 19 has a Project Package feature that allows you to bundle up a whole project into an archive file. I'll discuss that in just a moment. The Restore Project location is where the project files and the assets required are placed when you extract the package. You may need a lot of space available in whatever location you decide to restore a project, which may make the default location inside the user area an unattractive choice.

The final location is an important one. The files in the render files location can grow to an appreciable size. In Pinnacle Studio 15 and earlier these were called the Auxiliary files. I do suggest you consider placing these in a different location if you have more than one drive – or if you want to keep an eye on the size of your render files.

The most common use you will make of this section is at the bottom of the box – **Delete render files**. It's almost an automatic first step if you encounter preview or render problems in Studio. Some people quite sensibly always delete the render files before performing an export operation. If you aren't in a hurry, it's a sensible route to take, and if you skipped the section on Preview Optimisation above, I urge you to read it as you may be surprised how rarely the render files will be used for export.

It's important to realise that the Render folder doesn't hold **all** the temporary files that Studio generates. It's also known that sometimes junk accumulates in other folders so there will be times that you may want to manually clean out your system. In particular, you may be harbouring many disc images which you have forgotten about. These can take up huge amounts of disc space. There are a number of downloadable free utilities that let you view the contents of your hard drives sorted by how much disc space they are occupying. I use one called TreeSize Free when I want to clean up a hard drive.

Project management and project packages

The Library structure means that it's very easy to work on projects and add assets scattered all over your hard drive. If you import your video and picture files in folders labelled by shooting time and date as I have suggested that will certainly be a possible outcome.

While you can still use folder structures to collect together assets for each project, its far better to use Collections, and the final liberation from hard disc folder tyranny is the new feature that creates and restores project packages. These packages will contain **every asset** used in the project – no more missing media nightmares.

Unpacking a .axx package file

Since version 17, Studio has had a specific File menu command for saving a package - *File/Save Movie as Package* if you are in the Edit tab, or *File/Save Disc as Package* if you are in the Author tab. Project packages have a file type of .axx

Where you save the package is up to you – if you are making an archive or intending to move it to another computer then it makes sense to save it to an external drive or other form of removable media. Be warned that the packages can be very large. If you have only used 5 seconds of a 10 minute video file, the whole of the video file will be bundled into the package. This allows you to carry on editing the project and perhaps increase the amount of content from that particular file, but it does mean that a project only couple of minutes long might require gigabytes of storage space when saved as a package.

Restoring the package requires the unpacking of the assets as well as the project files. If you try to open a restored project via the File menu, you need to select the project type again from the drop-down menu before .axx files show up on the Open project dialogue. When you open a package this way, it is automatically unpacked. If you import a project package via the importer you will need to use the context menu option to unpack the project and assets.

After unpacking you will find a new project file, of type .axp, placed in the Restored projects default location as defined in the control panel. But what about the assets and in particular the large video files?

Studio is clever in these circumstances, recognising if the asset already exists in the correct location. If you have the same file in the same place, the new project is automatically linked to that file. No duplicate copying takes place.

If the asset isn't present on the system where you are unpacking the project then the asset is unpacked into a folder location within the restored projects location – and what is more, a complete folder structure within the parent folder is created to house the asset. There will be a folder with the name of the project and the date and time it was saved, then a folder representing the hard disc the asset was originally stored on, containing all the folders and sub-folders required to form a path to the asset. The new project will be linked to that location.

What's more, if Studio finds some of the files it requires are present and others aren't, it will only restore the files and folder paths that it needs to.

The project package feature isn't perfect, though. It doesn't import the assets metadata, so Library clips, collections, tags and ratings will need to be reproduced. I must also warn you that in some circumstances when testing project packages I have encountered unpacking errors. Admittedly I've been trying to restore projects in deliberately complex circumstances, but still my advice is to check you are definitely able to unpack an archived project on another computer before deleting the original project. I've never had an issue when moving the archive to a new computer, but I don't want to be the cause of your wrath!

A few Frequently Asked Questions

There is no way I can double guess every issue you might have with Studio, but I will list a few of the ones that I have personal experience of. If you don't find an answer here, then please go to some of the support references listed in the appendix, where the most up to date information will be at hand.

Where's the patch?

When this edition was published the current version of Studio was 19.0.1.245. The program should inform you when a major update is available, but if you are having issues, don't rely on that as the only source. When Avid owned Pinnacle, major patches were few and far between for the later products, but there were minor patches, termed hot fixes, that many people overlooked. I've also known of circumstances where the server that informed you of a new patch was switched off.

Corel seem less prone to hotfixes, but it's still worth bearing them in mind, so, manually search the Pinnacle website for a major patch, and then search the knowledge base for hot fixes, describing the symptoms in the terms of your search. For example, if you can't successfully import from DVD disc, try searching just for "DVD Import" and sift through the results.

If that fails try searching the public forums and if you are still stuck, ask a question there. The less vague your question, the more likely you are to get an answer, and the more information you can give about your computer system and software, the fewer supplementary questions you will be asked in return. At the time of writing, few Pinnacle support staff frequent the forum but there is an active user base.

If you are wondering why *everyone* isn't encouraged to apply *all* the hotfixes, it's normally because they haven't undergone a complete test cycle – they fix the current problem but if you don't have the issue they may cause unpredictable results.

Remember that Pinnacle can only fix issues that they know about and can reproduce. Reporting your problems, using an accurate description of the circumstances in which it occurs can result in a bug fix, particularly on a relatively new product.

Studio doesn't run unless you reboot

This is an irritating problem that can occur after a crash. What happens is that the Studio process isn't unloaded from memory, but instead of getting a message saying that a another instance is still running, you just encounter dumb insolence in response to your mouse clicks. To avoid a reboot, open the task manager (CTRL-SHIFT-ESC), switch to the Processes tab and search for NGStudio.exe. End it manually by highlighting it and using the End process button at the bottom of the window. Studio should now start.

Wacky render issues

There is a rarer case of bad behaviour that can cause you untold problems with rendering. If your project crashed, or an export failed, and then subsequently the program seems very cranky, look in the processes list and see if you can find 2 copies of either BGRnd.exe or RM.exe. If you do, then a reboot is required. You could try ending one of the processes, but it's a 50/50 guess!

One error message that you may see when the computer needs a reboot says that an export was only partially completed. I suspect that there is some interaction between preview optimisation and preparing for export that causes this issue - it sometimes causes the preview optimisation bars to turn red.

Why are the Render bars red?

If, instead of brown or green bars appearing over timeline items that need rendering you see dark red bars, the program has failed to render the area. The most obvious cause of this will be that the media is missing, but if that is the case the clips will be yellow and have exclamation marks.

Another possibility is a simple render malfunction. Deleting the auxiliary files normally works in these situations, but the area may have failed to render because the source video isn't completely compatible with Studio - you may need to convert the video to something else.

One more thing that may solve a stubborn render issue is to switch to the advanced export option *No Preprocessing*.

Running out of memory

If you get error messages saying that Studio is running out of memory requesting a restart, then don't rush out and add some more memory to your system. This is a memory leak and will occur regardless of the amount of memory you have – more memory just delays the inevitable. I don't want you to waste money. The cause could be one of many, so search the resources for a fix.

Converting and transcoding video files

There are two sets of circumstances where you might consider converting files. If you are trying to edit AVCHD video on a low powered computer you can convert the files to another format for a smoother operation. The best choice, avoiding significant quality loss, is probably MPEG-2, which can be done by Studio if you have enough patience.

Video files that aren't completely compatible will require a 3rd party program for conversion. I normally use a free utility called Mediacoder for this. If the problem is incompatible audio then in some circumstances you can direct stream copy the video portion of the file so there is no quality loss. Using the program requires a bit of understanding and it is outside the scope of this book, but I do cover its use on the support section of the Pinnacle Studio Info website.

Where can I get support for Pinnacle Studio?

While the obvious answer is to use the Pinnacle website, there are a number of other places that may be able to help. These may change over time, but I will maintain a list on the DTVPro.co.uk website.

Studio 19.5?

Corel have adopted a policy of adding some relatively minor features halfway through the lifecycle of a release. The physical product is repackaged, presumably in an attempt to encourage people who didn't buy the .0 release to do so. However, the upgrade to a .5 version is free via a patch. If you receive a special offer for 19.5 and already have 19.0, then there is no need to upgrade. It also means that version 20 may not be that far away!

Appendix 1 - The files you need

All the files are available to download from the website. However, I realise that not everyone has a reasonable download speed available to them so you can purchase the files you need on a DVD disc directly from the website **WWW.DTVPro.co.uk**. I've set the cost so that I'm not quite out of pocket by sending you a disc!

If you can't even get access to my website, please write to the address at the front of the book and I will send you an order form.

Files you need for this book that should be installed with your copy of Studio:

The video file "**The-Sky-is-the-Limit.mpg**" (in the Video Library under Public Videos)

Eight Jpeg picture files "**The-Sky-is-the-Limit_01** to **08**" (in the Pictures Library under Public Pictures.

(If you can't find these files they are included on the website and disc.)

Files that will make Chapter 6 easier to follow, available from the website and on disc:

Car Clip 1.mpg, Car Clip 2.mpg, Car Clip 3.mpg. These are only 6Mbs in size.

One file that is required for Chapters 7, 8 10 and 11:

Project1mp2.mpg (482 Mb). This file was distributed on the disc for Pinnacle Studio 14 and 15 Revealed and is downloadable from a cloud service via the website. The website also has more compressed versions that may work for you. It is also available by post on the DVD Data Disc.

There is also a **FlightGraphic.png** file (46Kb) to enhance Chapter 8.

For the Audio Ducking demo there are two packaged projects.

Audio ducking demo.movie.axx, and **Audio Ducking Demo with Compression.movie.axx**

Three files for the MultiCam Demo in Chapter 11:

Wide Shot.mpg, **Presenter 2.mpg** and **Guest 3.mpg**. 38Mb in total.

Every project in the book is saved at a number of stages and the **project files** for each stage can be found on the website and the disc. You can use these to cheat. Final versions of the projects can also be seen on YouTube, linked to via the website.

Appendix 2 - Studio versions

Pinnacle Studio 19 is descended from Avid Studio, rather than Pinnacle Studio 15. A number of the assets and effects are common to both previous programs however.

There have been a great many enhancements added during the development of Pinnacle Studio through versions 16 to the current version 19. 3D video is the most obvious, but the Dual view trim mode, Project package feature and the ability to save your own effects compositions will be more useful to many people. Improved performance has been one of the aims of the developers, and therefore S18 was rewritten as a 64-bit program.

There are currently three versions of Pinnacle Studio 19.

The basic version is very limited. Library features such as collections, tags, list view, and sorting by date are missing. Edit functions including the use of the ALT key and the advanced trimming mode are disabled. Most forms of copy and paste don't work and there is no keyframing. You can't use Multiple menus.

This is just a list of the most obvious things. You are also limited to three tracks and it comes with just the Standard Content Pack.

The Plus version has all the functional features described in this book but is limited to 24 tracks. Additional content includes Hollywood Effects Volumes 1-3, Premium Pack Volumes 1 and 2, Scorefitter Volumes 1 and 2, Creative Pack Volume 1 and Title Extreme.

The Ultimate version has unlimited tracks and adds New Blue Film Effects, Stabiliser and Essentials packs II, II and IV, plus 274 New Blue Transitions

Index

1

180 Degree Rule..56

3

3 Point Editing...306
3D...234, 416, 479
    Anaglyph...419
    Autostereoscopic...417
    Cross-eyed..416
    Editing..416
    Filter...418
    Format..418
    Format Adjustment..291
    Glasses...417
    Monitoring..418
    Multistream...419
    Project...38
3GP..210

A

Activate Trim Mode by Clicking near Cuts...........................266, 529
Activating Blu-ray
    Queue Manager..519
Add Exported File to Library...197
Advanced Trim Mode.................................48, 256, 308
    Activating..257
    Control Panel Options...49
    Deactivating...258
    Overwrite..269
    Transitions...269
    When Clicking near Cuts..48
Aligning cursor with clip boundaries...................................31
Alignment Grid..358
Alpha...354
Analogue Capture...179
    Settings..183

Analogue Video.. 179
Archiving Projects.. 531
Arranging Timeline Tracks... 46
Aspect Ratio... 184
    Adjustments.. 292
Asset Tree Window... 126
    Grouping.. 128
Audio
    Calibration.. 73
    Channel Management... 297
    Compressor.. 298
    De-Esser.. 299
    Detaching Tracks.. 82
    Equalize.. 298
    Expander.. 299
    Frequency meter... 297
    Mixing Panel... 75
    Mute.. 33
    Noise Reduction.. 300
    Positioning... 76
    Scrubbing.. 78
    Stereo Panner... 77, 340
    Surround Sound... 77, 341
    System Volume... 33
    Track Monitoring... 84
    Track Volume... 75
Audio Devices.. 520
Audio Ducking.. 423
AVCHD
    Discs... 233, 479, 508
AVCHD 2.. 479
    Cards.. 234

B

Background Programs.. 177, 186
Background Rendering... 36, 522
Bad Media... 225
Before/After View.. 294
Bit Rate.. 228
Bit Setting... 227

Blu-Ray..212
Blu-Ray Discs...235
Book Type..227
Box
    Export to..238
Browser View...139
BUP...222
Burn Disc Image...21
Burn Image...223

C

CBR...205
Channel Mixer..287, 296
Cineform..193
Clip Selection
    CTRL-SHIFT..51
Clips
    Copying on Timeline..86
    Inserting from the Album...105
    Inserting from the Player..105
    Multiple Selection...102, 103
    Overtrimming...97
Close Gap..51
Codec..198
Collections...138, 146
    Drag and Drop..148
    Latest Import..151
    Latest Smart Creation...151
    New..147
    Rearranging..150
    Special..151
Colour Picker...328
Colour Selection...353
    Colour Picker..355
    Gradients...354
Colour Temperature...288
Compact Library..23, 27, 94
    Navigation Bar...94, 152
    Navigation bar..152
Container...210

Continuity Editing..54, 55
Control Panel..21, 520
    Import Settings...192
Converting and transcoding video files.............................534
Copy and Paste...60
Correcting Photos...294
Corrections...138, 285
    Adjustments...291
    Applying to Library Clips..285
    Applying to Timeline Clips..285
    Audio Channels...297
    Audio Compressor...298
    Audio Equalise...297
    Audio Expander...299
    Audio Gain...296
    Audio Noise Reduction..300
    Audio Optimise..297
    Audio Stereo..297
    Before/After View...294
    Cropping Photos..295
    De-Esser..299
    Enhance...287
    Exiting the Editor...294
    Image Correction CPU..287
    Inability to Copy..286
    Inability to Keyframe..290
    Open in..286
    Photos...294
    Red-eye reduction in Photos..296
    Rotate Photos..295
    Snapshot..292
    Stabilize...293
    Straightening Photos..296
    Timeline Indication..300
Crawlers..368
Create Image..217
Create Title...345
Creating Library Clips...282
Crossing the Line...56
CTRL-Shift Clip Selection..103
Cursor

Aligning to clip boundary.. 31
Cut-off... 348

D

Data Compression.. 7
Dazzle.. 182
Dead Meat... 98, 255
Delete.. 142
Delete Render Files.. 530
Deleting the Settings File.. 517
Destructive Editing.. 2
Detached Audio Tracks... 82
Details View... 139
Direct Stream Copy... 208
Disc Editor
    Button Cycle Tool.. 488
    Chapter Markers.. 488
    Chapter Return Marker.. 489, 493
    Chapter Strip... 489
    Chapter Wizard.. 482, 506
    Insert Link... 503
    Intro Video.. 493
    Linking to Menus... 500
    Menu List.. 480
    Multiple Menus.. 497
    Opening... 480
    Other Uses.. 480
    Setting Links... 487
    Unlinked Chapters... 490
Disc Image (ISO).. 223
Disc Projects.. 479
    Create... 480
    Tab... 479
    Workflow... 479
Disc Simulator.. 491
    Menu Button.. 492
    Return Button.. 492
Display Icon.. 24
DivX... 210
Drag and Drop.. 58

Dropped Frames... 176, 185
Dual Mode.. 260
Duration
    Manual Adjustment.. 64
DV.. 201
DV Device... 174
DV Pass-through.. 182
DV-AVI... 196
DVD
    Format.. 212
    Region Encoding... 214
DVD Labels... 233
DVD Player Issues.. 226
DVD RAM.. 213
DVD+R.. 213
DVD-R... 213
DVD-ROM.. 212, 227
Dynamic Length transitions.. 324

E

Edit
    3 Point.. 306
    Adding Transitions.. 314
    Adjusting Clip Content... 265
    Adjusting Clip Placement... 264
    Copy and Paste.. 61
    Cut and Paste.. 60
    Deleting Clips.. 41
    Deleting with Multiple Tracks.. 99
    In Point Handle.. 48
    Insert Mode... 241
    Magnetic Snapping... 44
    Multiple Tracks.. 73
    Multiple Trim Points.. 263
    Out Point Handle.. 48
    Overwrite Mode.. 243
    Quick Trimming.. 48
    Rolling the Edit.. 263
    Scenes... 277
    Smart Mode... 241

    Speed Effect..310
    Splitting Clips..40
    Titles...349
Edit Caption...144
Edit Menu..21
Editing Options tool...241
Effects
    Context Menu...333
    Keyframing..335
    Saving...333
    Timeline Indication..333
Effects and Corrections
    Adjusting Values..290, 332
    Marking Clips...291
    On/Off Button..287
    Toolbar..290
Effects Editor
    Controls...332
    Corrections...330
    Effects...330
    Expand All...339
    Navigator..327, 339
    Opening..325, 330
    Parameters...333
    Re-ordering..332
    Solo..326
    Stacking effects..331
    Transitions...325
Equalize...297
Estimated File Size..199
E-store Menu..22
Event Log..520
Export...21, 112
    Advanced Settings..196, 197
    AVCHD 2 cards...234
    AVCHD Discs..233
    Blu-Ray Discs..235
    Destination...199
    Disc Settings..215
    Formats...209
    Partial..198

To Cloud... 236

To Device.. 238

To Disc... 212

To File.. 196

Export Window... 195

Eyeline... 56

F

Fast Motion... 309

Favourites.. 145

File Menu.. 19, 20

New Movie... 20

Recent... 45

Save Movie as... 38

Filter Bar.. 130

Find in Timeline.. 66, 144

Flash Video.. 210

FLV.. 210

Fragmentation.. 177

Frequently Asked Questions... 532

Frozen Frames when using Ripple.................................. 320

Full Screen Preview.. 33

Double Clicking.. 33

Keyboard Shortcut... 33

G

Gaps

Automatically Filling... 89

Closing... 107, 465

Creating... 464

Trimming.. 98

Graphic Card Issues... 518

Group Align.. 358

Grouping.. 467

Grouping clips.. 106

H

H 264

    Encoding Options..206
Hard Disc Speeds...176
Hardware acceleration...207
Hardware Requirements...511
Help Menu (?)..22, 518
Hi-Fi VCRs..184

I

IFO...222
Image Correction CPU..287
    Fundamentals...289
    Levels...289
    Optimisation...289
    Vibrance...289
    White Balance..288
Image Sequence..210
ImgBurn..227, 231
Import..21, 161
    Blu-Ray..172
    by Browsing...159
    Copying..161, 166
    Digitising..161
    Disc Image...173
    Duplicates..162
    DV and HDV...173
    DVD..172
    Filenames..167
    From...161
    Incorrect Thumbnails Showing...169
    Ingesting..161
    Linking..160, 161
    Locations...167
    Mode..162
    My computer...169
    Quick..122
    Scan for Assets..171
    Start...164
    Subfolders..167
    To...166, 175
Import Option Defaults..526

Importing old projects.. 21
In Point Handle.. 48
Incoming Video.. 52
Information Icon... 28, 138
Insert Mode.. 42, 241
    Deleting... 243
    Drag and Drop.. 242
    Trimming... 242
Install Manager.. 515
Installing Studio... 513
Intel Quicksync... 206
Interlacing
    Adjustments... 292
Intraframe... 201
ISO... 223

J

Jogging.. 31, 32, 67

K

Ken Burns Effect.. 373
Keyboard Custom Shortcuts...................................... 527
Keyframes
    Copying.. 337
    Creating... 337
    Deleting.. 336
    Enabling... 335
    Moving.. 338
    Navigating.. 336
    Pasting... 337
    Setting.. 336
Keyframing... 335
    Volume... 77
Known Bugs... 463, 475

L

Latest Import... 151
LFE... 341

Library
    Areas.. 124
    Asset Tree Window.. 126
    Backup.. 155
    Browser Functions.. 141
    Browser Window.. 125
    Checkmarks... 138
    Collections... 124
    Compact.. 117, 152
    Creative Elements... 124
    Deleting Items... 66, 143
    Details View.. 125
    Details View Options... 139
    Display Options... 138
    Filter Bar... 130
    Importing from older versions....................................... 157
    Item Selection... 141
    Main... 117
    Projects... 124
    Refreshing... 155
    Scenes View.. 137
    Search Box... 135
    Send to Timeline... 66
    Sorting by Ratings... 133
    Sorting the View.. 140
    Strategies.. 153
    Tags.. 130
    Thumbnail Size... 139
    Thumbnail View.. 138
    Thumbnails View... 125
    Toolbar... 125, 136
LIbrary
    Auto Hide mode... 94, 152
Library Clips.. 282
    Creating... 282
    Creation by Dragging Scenes....................................... 283
    Customising... 284
    Renaming.. 284
Library Media... 120
    Quick Importing... 123
Lip Sync... 73

Looks.. 352
    Saving.. 356

M

Magnetic Snapping... 35, 44
    Keyboard Shortcut.. 45
Main Control Bar.. 19
Markers... 59
    Delete All.. 60
    Deleting... 60
    Dragging... 60
    Keyboard Shortcut.. 60
    Using with Music.. 378
MCE, *See* Multi-Camera Editing
Menu Editor
    Add Menu Page.. 502
    Audio Drop Zone.. 483
    Audio Dropbox.. 506
    Button Settings... 483
    Buttons.. 483
    Create Link... 490
    Defining Buttons.. 486
    Motion Background... 505
    Opening.. 483
    Prev, Next and Main buttons.. 501
    Save Menu As... 484
    Set Thumbnail.. 502
    Still Thumbnails... 499
    Thumbnail Buttons... 499
Menus.. 479
    –Special.. 482
    Adding to Library... 484
    Adjusting Background Audio Level... 506
    Button Order... 497
    Creation Rules... 494
    Multi-page.. 498
    Preview... 482
Metadata... 167
Missing Media.. 152
MJPEG... 188, 201

Montage.. 408
   Adding Projects... 412
   Dropzones... 409
   Durations.. 410
   Editor.. 408
   Editor Layout... 409
   Opening... 408
   Paste to Dropzone... 412
   Text Editing... 410
Motion Menus... 504
   Duration.. 505
Motions.. 356
   Adjusting Duration... 358
   Emphasis... 356
   Enter... 356
   Exit... 356
   Progress Bars.. 357
MOV... 206, 210
Movie Editor Window... 20, 24
   Timeline... 24, 34
   Using the Player.. 29
Moviebox... 181
MP4.. 206
MPEG-2.. 202
   and Windows 8/10 playback... 203
MPEG-2 TS... 206
Multi-Camera Editing.. 431
   Adding transitions... 451
   Editing Tools... 436
   in the Main Editor.. 442
   Live Cutting.. 449
   Proxies... 8
   Proxy File Manager.. 456
   Proxy Files.. 455
   Proxy Queue Manager.. 457
   Secondary Source selection.. 437
   Selecting output... 441
   Syncing tracks.. 435
   Waveform Display.. 438
   Workflow... 432
Multiple Trim Points

Adding with CTRL Key..263
Multi-track
    Clip Splitting..96
    Deletion...99
Multi-track Trim Points...266
Multi-track Trimming and Keeping Sync..........................271
MyDVD...221, 239

N

Name...138
Navigator...101
NTSC...28, 214

O

Optimisation Threshold..523
Optimise Audio...297
Out Point Handle..48
Outgoing Video...52
Overscan..348
Overtrimming..97, 255
Overwrite Mode...42, 243
    Deleting..245
    Drag and Drop...244
    Trimming..244

P

Padlocks...99
PAL..28, 214
Pan and Zoom
    Adjusting Keyframes...386
    Animated..382
    Attributes...380
    Automatic...382
    Copy and Pasting Keyframes..................................387
    Curves..385
    Ease In...383
    Ease Out...383
    for Photos..379

    Green Keyframe.. 382
    Holding a Still Frame... 386
    Low Pass.. 384
    Matching Frames... 389
    Multiple Moves.. 384
    New Keyframes... 384
    Path... 383
    Red Keyframe.. 382
    Select Preset... 379
    Smooth.. 383
    Static... 379
Persistence of Vision... 180
Photos... 373
    Resolution... 373
Pinnacle Studio Basic HD Version.. ii
Playback
    Space Bar.. 30
Player Window.. 23
    Controlling... 29
    Dual Mode... 25
    Go to End.. 31
    Go to Start... 31
    Include Audio Icon.. 29
    J, K and L keys... 31
    Jog/Shuttle Wheel.. 31
    Jump Forward and Back.. 31
    Menu Tab... 481
    Play Control... 30
    Ruler Zooming.. 32
    Scrubber.. 32
    Single Frame Jogging.. 30
    Source Tab.. 29
    Switch Tabs Shortcut... 29
    Timeline Scrollbar.. 32
    Timeline Tab.. 29
Preprocessing for Export... 525
Pre-rendering to File.. 220
Preview.. 66
Preview Optimisation... 36, 522
    Render while play... 523
    Threshold.. 523

Preview Quality.. 520
    Balanced.. 521
    Best Quality... 520
    Fastest Playback.. 521
Preview Rendering... 8
Project
    Setting Up... 37
    Settings... 37
    Trim Settings.. 266
Project Bins.. 119
    Add to.. 95
    Avoiding.. 122
    Copy and Paste... 95
    Creation.. 26
    Importing to... 26
    Managing.. 121
    Media Filters... 128
    Quick Importing... 122
    Remove from.. 145
    Using... 121
Project Management.. 531
Project Packages... 142, 531
    Unpacking.. 144
Project Settings... 528
Proxy Editing... 8, 16
Proxy files.. 8

Q

Quick Rotate... 428
Quick Trimming.. 48
QuickTime... 210

R

Ratings.. 133, 138
Razor Blade.. 40
Red Giant Plugins.. 515
Red Thumbnails... 153
Redo.. 21
Registering... 516

Re-installing... 515
Rendering
    Speeding Up.. 201
    Timeline... 38
Rendering Speed.. 200
Reordering your story... 461
Replacing a Clip... 91
Reset function.. 516
Resetting Studio defaults.. 517
Reversing Video.. 311
Ripple Causing Frozen Frames.. 320
Rollers... 368
Rolling the Edit Point... 263, 308
Ruler Zooming.. 529
Running out of memory... 534

S

Safe Areas... 348
Scart... 183
Scenes... 277
    Add to Collection.. 283
    Combining.. 279
    Create by Pressing Space Bar.. 175
    Detect by Content... 277
    Detect by Date and Time... 277
    Detect by Time Interval... 278
    Detection during Import... 175
    Refining Detection.. 279
    Splitting Manually... 281
    View... 278
Scorefitter.. 109
Screen Capture.. 188
Scrubbing Audio.. 78
Search Box.. 135
Send To Timeline... 145
Setup Menu... 21
Shapes... 358
Shortcut... 139
Show in Explorer... 66, 144
Sibilance.. 299

Simple Trimming... 253
Slow Motion... 309
Smart Drag and Drop... 459
Smart Editing.. 42
Smart Mode.. 241
    ALT Key Modifier... 43
    Deleting.. 250
    Drag and Drop.. 86, 104, 245
    Gaps... 249
    Multi-track Deletion.. 99
    Selecting... 42
Smart Rendering.. 208
SmartMovie... 137, 412
    Adjust length to music.. 414
    Media Order... 415
    Pan and Zoom.. 414
    Short, Medium and Long.. 414
SmartSounds.. 112
Snapshot
    in Corrections... 292
    on Timeline... 313
Solo.. 326, 328
Sony XAVC S®... 211
Sound Effects.. 109
Source Preview.. 66
    Clear In and Out Points.. 68
    In and Out points.. 67
    Send Selection to Timeline... 67
Speed.. 309
    Affect on Duration.. 312
    Constant.. 312
    Hold Pitch.. 311
    Reverse... 311
    Stretch... 310
Split Button.. 281
Split Clips.. 39
    Highlighting Behaviour... 42
    Keyboard Shortcut... 40
    on Multiple Tracks... 96
Splitting Video and Audio Tracks.. 82
Stabilize... 293

Building Data..293
Default Settings..294
Render in Background...293
Stereo
    Positioning..76
Stereoscopic...138
Stopmotion...188
Storage Locations..529
Storyboard..24, 61, 300
    Clip Context Menu..322
    Gaps...304
    Viewing..62
Studio doesn't run unless you reboot....................................533
Subcollections...148
Subprojects..395
    Adding Effects..397
    As Clips..400
    Creating...399
    Durations...402
    Editing..401
    Expanding onto Timeline..406
    Using Markers...403
Surround/Stereo Panner..340
Switching between Storyboard and Navigator...........................24

T

Tags...130, 138
    Match..132
    Partial...132
Third party Codecs..525
Thumbnail Cache
    Deleting...169
Thumbnail Scrubber...142
Thumbnail Size..139
Thumbnail View..27
Thumbnails
    Incorrect when Importing from a Camera.............................169
Timeline
    Adding Transitions...314
    Adjust Clip Duration...64, 65

Copying Clips.. 86
Cut and Paste.. 60
Drag and Drop.. 58
Filling a Gap.. 90
Insert Mode.. 241
Multiple Clip Selection.. 51
Overwrite Mode.. 243
Replacing Clips.. 91
Scrubber.. 35
Smart Mode... 241
Timescale.. 34
Toolbar.. 38
Yellow clips with Exclamation Marks.................................. 153
Timeline Export callipers... 199
Timeline Settings... 38
Timeline Toolbar
Trim Button.. 258
Timeline Tracks
Adjusting with the Mouse... 47
All Track Sizes... 47
Delete... 47
Edit Name... 47
Locking.. 100
Track Size.. 47
View Waveforms.. 47
Title Editor.. 345
Adding Text.. 346
Alignment Grid.. 358
Arrows and Special Characters... 364
Background Settings.. 362
Colour Selection.. 353
Crawling Captions.. 368
Create... 345
Edge... 355
Face... 355
Group Align... 358, 359
Layers.. 357, 363
Layout.. 346
Looks... 352
Motions... 349
Opening... 345

Order.. 360
Positioning.. 347
Rotating.. 347
Safe Areas.. 348
Shadow.. 355
Shapes... 359
Stereoscopic Text Effects.. 371
Temporary Grouping... 359
Text Flow.. 352
Text Settings... 351
Titles... 349
and the Library... 350
Default Duration.. 349
Effects and Keyframing... 366
Roller captions.. 368
Toolbar
Customizing... 38
Magnet Icon.. 45
Split Clips... 39
Volume Keyframing... 49
Track Locks... 100
Track Monitoring.. 92
Track Volume... 75
Tracks
Active Streams... 85
Transitions.. 314
Adding to Photos.. 388
Audio.. 318
Context menu... 320
Dragging from the Compact Library........................... 323
Duration.. 324
Dynamic Length.. 324
Editing.. 320, 327
Handle.. 315
in Smart Mode... 316
Overlapping... 315
Progress.. 327
Replacing.. 319
Ripple... 320
Send to Timeline.. 325
Transparency... 319

Trash Can..41
Trim Editor..257
    Controls..258
    Frame Offset..261
    Keyboard Control...259
    Loop Play...258
    Single Frame Jogging...259
    Solo...262
Trim Mode
    ALT Modifier...270
    Shift Modifier..266
    Transitions..270
Troubleshooting Installations...516

U

Undo...21
USB...181
Used Media...138
Using Scenes...277

V

VBR...205
Video
    Disabling with Active Streams..85
    Track Monitoring...84
Viewing underlying Video..328
VOB files...222
Voice Over Tool...420
    Latency...422
Volume
    Adjusting while Playing...81
    Current clip..76
    Disabling Keyframe Snapping...81
    Keyframe Snapping..81
    Keyframing...77
    Master Volume...74
Volume Keyframing...49

W

Watchfolders.. 119, 520

Where can I get support for Pinnacle Studio?..................................... 535

Where's the patch?... 532

White Balance... 287

    Joystick.. 288

Why are the Render bars red?.. 534

Windows Character Map.. 364

Windows Media... 211

Windows Shortcuts

    Clip Selection.. 41

Wrap Text.. 347

Wrapper.. 17, 206, 210, 511

Y

Yellow clips... 153

CPSIA information can be obtained
at www.ICGtesting.com
Printed in the USA
LVOW03s1600070616

491590LV00007B/304/P